D1174948

See 1014 17

BT
198
·M389
1989

JESUS

THE

SAVIOUR

STUDIES IN NEW TESTAMENT THEOLOGY

I. HOWARD MARSHALL

Nyack College
Eastman Library

INTERVARSITY PRESS
DOWNERS GROVE, ILLINOIS 60515

©1990 by I. Howard Marshall

Published in the United States of America by InterVarsity Press, Downers Grove, Illinois, with permission from SPCK, London, England.

All rights reserved. No part of this book may be reproduced in any form without written permission from InterVarsity Press, P.O. Box 1400, Downers Grove, Illinois 60515.

InterVarsity Press is the book-publishing division of InterVarsity Christian Fellowship, a student movement active on campus at hundreds of universities, colleges and schools of nursing. For information about local and regional activities, write Public Relations Dept., InterVarsity Christian Fellowship, 6400 Schroeder Rd., P.O. Box 7895, Madison, WI 53707-7895.

Distributed in Canada through InterVarsity Press, 860 Denison St., Unit 3, Markham, Ontario L3R 4H1, Canada.

ISBN 0-8308-1273-3

Printed in the United States of America

Library of Congress Cataloging-in-Publication Data
Marshall, I. Howard.
    Jesus the Saviour: studies in New Testament theology/I. Howard
Marshall.
        p.   cm.
    Includes bibliographical references.
    ISBN 0-8308-1273-3
    1. Jesus Christ—History of doctrines—Early church, ca. 30-600.
2. Bible.   N.T.—Theology.   I. Title.
BT198.M389   1989
232—dc20   89-29055
                                                                        CIP

| 16 | 15 | 14 | 13 | 12 | 11 | 10 | 9 | 8 | 7 | 6 | 5 | 4 | 3 | 2 | 1 |
| 99 | 98 | 97 | 96 | 95 | 94 | 93 | 92 | 91 | 90 | | | | | | |

To Margaret and Arthur

Preface   9

Acknowledgments   11

Abbreviations   12

Part I: The Aims and Methods of New Testament Theology

1   New Testament Theology   15

2   Jesus, Paul and John   35

3   Is Apocalyptic the Mother of Christian Theology?   57

Part II: The Person of Jesus

4   The Synoptic Son of Man Sayings in Recent Discussion   73

5   The Son of Man in Contemporary Debate   100

6   Son of God or Servant of Yahweh?—A Reconsideration
     of Mark 1.11   121

7   The Divine Sonship of Jesus   134

8   The Development of Christology in the Early Church   150

9   Incarnational Christology in the New Testament   165

10   God Incarnate: Myth or What?   181

11   Jesus as Lord: The Development of the Concept   197

Part III: The Work of Jesus

12   The Hope of a New Age: The Kingdom of God in the
     New Testament   213

13   The Development of the Concept of Redemption
     in the New Testament   239

14   The Meaning of 'Reconciliation'   258

15   Some Observations on the Covenant in the New Testament   275

16   Predestination in the New Testament   290

17   The Problem of Apostasy in New Testament Theology   306

Select Index of Biblical Texts   325

Author Index   327

Preface

During the past twenty-five years or so a good deal of my interest in New Testament study has been directed towards exegetical and theological problems, more especially those concerned with the person and the work of Jesus. Most of my work in this area has appeared in the form of essays which have been published in a variety of journals and in *Festschriften*. Some of these sources are less accessible than others, and it seemed good to gather together a number of these essays which have a general unity of theme in a more convenient form. I am therefore particularly grateful to Mr Philip Law of SPCK and to Mr James Hoover of IVP for their willingness to undertake publication, and to the editors and publishers of the original journals and books for their kind permission to republish the essays in this format.

The material falls into three areas.

First, in Part I, there is some general discussion of the nature of New Testament theology. Here I have included a survey of recent work on the subject, with some indications as to the 'shape' that a theology of the New Testament might take. Then I have considered the question as to whether there is sufficient unity between three of the major voices in the New Testament to make the construction of a theology a viable task. A third essay deals with the roots of New Testament theology in apocalyptic or elsewhere.

Part II of the book is concerned with the person of Jesus. The debate over the last twenty-five years has been largely conducted in terms of the titles used to designate Jesus in the New Testament, and my discussions have inevitably been conditioned by that fact; more recently, there has been a growing recognition that there is much more to Christology than the study of titles. Two essays deal with what is perhaps the most contentious issue in the area, the use of the term 'Son of man'; three are concerned with the use of 'Son', both in the Gospels and in the early Church. These provide some background for two discussions of the place and significance of the incarnation in the New Testament. Finally, there is a discussion of the use of the word 'Lord'.

Part III of the book deals with various aspects of the work of Jesus and its effects. I have included a discussion of the Kingdom of God and studies of redemption, reconciliation and covenant. Finally, there are two essays on the problems relating to predestination, election and perseverance in the Christian life.

The discussion of many of these issues has not stood still, and some of the essays are now over twenty years old. In one or two cases, therefore, in addition to minor corrections in the text, I have done some updating of references and indicated some of the more important subsequent discussions. But (with the exception of the last essay, where I have rewritten a couple of passages) I have not attempted any thorough-going revision of the material, since I have not been persuaded that any drastic change of mind is called for at any point.

I. Howard Marshall

Acknowledgments

Permission to reprint the following essays, which originally appeared in the sources indicated, is gratefully acknowledged:

'New Testament Theology' (*The Theological Educator*, 9, 2, spring 1979, pp. 47-64).

'Jesus, Paul and John' (*Aberdeen University Review*, 51, 1, spring 1985, pp. 18-36).

'Is Apocalyptic the Mother of Christian Theology?' (G. F. Hawthorne and O. Betz [eds], *Tradition and Interpretation in the New Testament: Essays in Honor of E. Earle Ellis* [Grand Rapids, Eerdmans, 1987], pp. 33-42).

'The Synoptic Son of Man Sayings in Recent Discussion' (*New Testament Studies*, 12, 1965-6, pp. 327-51).

'The Son of Man in Contemporary Debate' (*The Evangelical Quarterly*, 42, 2, 1970, pp. 67-87).

'Son of God or Servant of Yahweh?—A Reconsideration of Mark 1.11' (*New Testament Studies*, 15, 1968-9, pp. 326-36).

'The Divine Sonship of Jesus' (*Interpretation*, 21, 1967, pp. 87-103).

'The Development of Christology in the Early Church' (*Tyndale Bulletin*, 18, 1967, pp. 77-93).

'Incarnational Christology in the New Testament' (H. H. Rowdon [ed.], *Christ the Lord: Studies in Christology presented to Donald Guthrie* [Leicester, Inter-Varsity Press, 1982], pp. 1-16).

'Jesus as Lord: The Development of the Concept' (W. H. Gloer [ed.], *Eschatology and the New Testament* [*Festschrift* for G. R. Beasley-Murray] [Peabody, Mass., Hendrickson, 1988], pp. 129-45). Used by permission of Hendrickson Press.

'The Hope of a New Age: The Kingdom of God in the New Testament' (A. R. G. Deasley and R. L. Shelton (eds), *The Spirit and the New Age* [Warner Press, 1987], pp. 319-55).

'The Development of the Concept of Redemption in the New Testament' (R. J. Banks [ed.], *Reconciliation and Hope: Presented to L. L. Morris* [Exeter, Paternoster Press, 1975], pp. 153-69).

'The Meaning of "Reconciliation" ' (R. A. Guelich [ed.], *Unity and Diversity in New Testament Theology: Essays in Honor of George E. Ladd* [Grand Rapids, Eerdmans, 1978], pp. 117-32).

'Some observations on the covenant in the New Testament' (P. W. Bøckman and R. E. Kristiansen, *Context: Essays in Honour of Peder Johan Borgen* [Trondheim, Tapir, 1987], pp. 121-36).

'Predestination in the New Testament' (C. Pinnock [ed.], *Grace Unlimited* [Minneapolis, Bethany Fellowship, 1975], pp. 127-43).

'The Problem of Apostasy in New Testament Theology' (R. L. Perkins [ed.], *Perspectives on Scripture and Tradition: Essays in Honor of Dale Moody* [Macon, Mercer University Press, 1987], pp. 65-80), is reprinted by permission of Mercer University Press.

Abbreviations

ASTI	Annual of the Swedish Theological Institute	NIDNTT	New International Dictionary of New Testament Theology
BAG	A Greek-English Lexicon of the New Testament (W. Bauer, W. F. Arndt and F. W. Gingrich)	NIGTC	New International Greek Testament Commentary
		NIV	New International Version
BASOR	Bulletin of the American Schools of Oriental Research	Nov.T	Novum Testamentum
		NTS	New Testament Studies
BDB	Hebrew and English Lexicon of the Old Testament (F. Brown, S. R. Driver and C. A. Briggs)	PTR	Princeton Theological Review
		RB	Revue biblique
		RGG	Religion in Geschichte und Gegenwart
BJRL	Bulletin of the John Rylands University Library of Manchester	SB	Kommentar zum Neuen Testament aus Talmud und Midrasch ([H. Strack and] P. Billerbeck)
BZ	Biblische Zeitschrift		
CBQ	Catholic Biblical Quarterly		
EBT	Encyclopaedia of Biblical Theology (J. B. Bauer)	SJT	Scottish Journal of Theology
		Stud.Theol.	Studia theologica
EQ	Evangelical Quarterly	TBNT	Theologisches Begriffslexicon zum Neuen Testament
Ev.Theol.	Evangelische Theologie		
Exp.T	Expository Times	TDNT	Theological Dictionary of the New Testament
HDAC	Hastings' Dictionary of the Apostolic Church	THAT	Theologisches Handwörterbuch zum Alten Testament
HTR	Harvard Theological Review		
IDB	Interpreter's Dictionary of the Bible	Th.LZ	Theologische Literaturzeitung
		Th.Z	Theologische Zeitschrift
JBL	Journal of Biblical Literature	TQ	Theologische Quartalschrift
JR	Journal of Religion	TU	Texte und Untersuchungen
JSNT	Journal for the Study of the New Testament	TWAT	Theologisches Wörterbuch zum Alten Testament
JTC	Journal for Theology and the Church	TWNT	Theologisches Wörterbuch zum Neuen Testament
JTS	Journal of Theological Studies	THAT	Theologisches Handwörterbuch zum Alten Testament
LTK	Lexicon für Theologie und Kirche	WTJ	Westminster Theological Journal
MH	Grammar of New Testament Greek (J. H. Moulton, W. F. Howard and N. Turner)	ZNW	Zeitschrift für die neutestamentliche Wissenschaft
NEB	New English Bible		

Part I
The Aims and Methods
of New Testament Theology

1
New Testament Theology

THERE ARE MANY SIGNS THAT WE LIVE IN AN ERA OF INTEN-
sive study of New Testament theology. First, contemporary series of commentaries are explicitly theological in their interest. As far back as 1947 A. M.
Hunter could write: 'The day of the aridly critical commentary is past.
Nowadays the demand is for a "theological" commentary which, while satisfying all the requirements of scientific scholarship, lays the chief emphasis
on the religious and theological meaning of the sacred text. It is a salutary
change of emphasis.'[1] It is symptomatic that one of the most up-to-date and
detailed series today is headed *Herders theologischer Kommentar zum Neuen
Testament.*[2]

Second, we live in an age of theological lexicography, whose fruits may
be seen in the great ten-volume work edited by G. Kittel and G. Friedrich
and also in the less detailed—and hence perhaps more generally useful—
three-volume work edited and translated from the *Theologisches Begriffslexicon
zum Neuen Testament* by C. Brown.[3]

Third, there are innumerable studies of individual New Testament writers
and topics in which the theological interest is dominant. We may let
H. Ridderbos's excellent *Paul: An Outline of his Theology*[4] stand as a representative of this area.

Fourth, we come to works written with the explicit purpose of expounding
the theology of the New Testament as a whole. One can think of at least
twenty books of this kind published during the last thirty years or so. The

scope of the present article will be restricted to a survey of works of this kind, but even so it will necessarily be selective in its treatment.

But before beginning our survey, we must also observe a fifth sign of the contemporary interest in New Testament theology, a proliferation of discussions of the task of doing New Testament theology. Not only do we write New Testament theologies; we also write books and articles about the writing of New Testament theology.[5] A recent German symposium, which gathers together several essays of historical importance, contains a bibliography of about 500 items up to 1974, and the flow has not ceased.[6]

I

In his introductory essay in the symposium just mentioned, G. Strecker observes that when biblical theology emerged as a distinctive discipline in the seventeenth century it had three presuppositions: the unity of the Old and New Testaments; the integrity of the biblical canon; and the identity between scriptural teaching and systematic theology.[7] The modern development of the subject can be seen in terms of the discussion of these presuppositions. First of all, the unity of the Testaments was questioned, and it was recognised that there was a development in understanding from the Old to the New, so that it is not possible to work out a basic kernel of theological ideas which would find expression throughout the various books of the Bible, still less to produce an all-encompassing system of ideas in which there would be an appropriate place for every idea expressed by each biblical writer. Attempts to write biblical theologies, as opposed to Old or New Testament theologies, have virtually ceased, although this is not to say that the task ought not to be attempted in some new way.

Second, if the two Testaments do not form a unity in the flat, do the contents of a single Testament form a unity? This question has various facets. (1) If it makes sense to formulate 'The theology of Paul' by drawing material from his various writings, does it make sense to formulate 'The theology of the New Testament' in the same way by drawing material from its various writings? This would be to assume that there is a common outlook shared by the New Testament writers, but is this really the case? Are there not differences and, some would say even contradictions, between what the several writers say, and is there not some kind of development between the earlier and the later writings? (2) It may be that even within Paul's writings there is development and change, and that it is futile to look for a theological *system* lying behind his writings and coming to expression in them. Did the New Testament writers have a formulated theology, whether individually or collectively? And, in any case, when we take note of the fragmentary and occasional character of their theological utterances, is it possible for us to synthesize a system of thinking, whether as regards their theology as a whole or as regards individual aspects of it? (3) If the nature of the New Testament books is such that they contain differences among themselves and must be seen as stages in a historical development, does it make sense to consider the New Testament as a closed collection of writings (the canon) and not rather include these books in a broader group of early Christian writings? Is not 'New Testament theology' a rather artificial concept?

Third, when these first two presuppositions are challenged, what has in effect happened is that the nature of the New Testament as the authoritative source of Christian doctrine has been challenged, and it is no longer self-evident that Christian dogmatics or systematic theology is simply the systematic expression and application of what the New Testament teaches. New Testament theology loses its normative character, and the question arises whether it can be regarded any longer as a discipline concerned with discovering theological truth and is not rather simply a descriptive historical discipline.

The full fruit of these questionings is to be seen in the work of W. Wrede, who articulated the view that New Testament theology in the traditional sense is impossible, and what has passed under this name should be replaced by a historical study. The task is 'to lay out the history of early Christian religion and theology', or to find out *'what was believed, thought, taught, hoped, required and striven for* in the earliest period of Christianity; not what certain writings say about faith, doctrine, hope, etc.'[8] By putting the matter in this way, Wrede was claiming that the discipline is purely descriptive and not normative: it tells us merely what was believed and said in the first century, and not what the New Testament has to say to us today. He insisted that the discipline was a historical enquiry which would work out the history of early Christian thinking. He was denying that its aim is to set out systematically what the New Testament teaches and claiming that the purpose is to reconstruct the history of the thinking of which the New Testament (along with other early Christian writings) gives us some fragmentary evidence. At the same time, he was pleading that the New Testament must not be studied in isolation but in light of the intellectual environment in which it was written.

The history of New Testament theology in the twentieth century can be summed up as the attempt to follow through the programme that Wrede never lived to complete and as the reaction to the position which he represented. The direct line from Wrede can be traced in W. Bousset who did not write a New Testament theology but rather a study of Christology in the early Church.[9] In his survey of the period, L. Goppelt rightly observes that, although this approach was meant to be purely descriptive and historical, in point of fact it assumed a definite world-view which was at odds with that of the New Testament writers and which led to a distorted view of the history itself.[10]

Over against this approach, K. Barth insisted that the exegete could not be content merely to tell us what Paul said to the people of his own age, but must come to grips with what Paul has to say to us.[11] The point was not exactly new; what was significant was that it was accepted by scholars who adopted a critical position like that of Wrede, but recognized that they must go further. In particular, R. Bultmann attempted to solve the problem by identifying the message of the New Testament as an existential challenge; the heart of the New Testament is the kerygma, the address of God to man which presents him with the challenge to decision and faith. The exegete must ask what understanding of human existence is present in the text. Bultmann claimed that the New Testament authors did not always express their understanding clearly, and that their works must be criticized in the light of what they were 'really' trying to do. He also insisted that much of the message was presented in mythological form and needed to be 'demythologized' in order to be significant for the modern reader. Much of the history of New Testament scholarship in the last twenty years has been centred on discussion of Bultmann's programme.

At the same time we may distinguish other lines of thought alongside this one. Goppelt distinguishes, not altogether clearly, between a historical-positive approach and a salvation-historical approach. The former is represented by a group of writers who come to more conservative conclusions about the historicity of the New Testament material than Wrede and Bultmann, although they are equally committed to the historical-critical method.[12] The other group, associated with A. Schlatter, claims that the New Testament is fully understood only when, after historical analysis has been carried out, it is understood as the fulfilment of the Old Testament. This means that the biblical accounts are understood as witnesses to a self-revelation of God in history. Goppelt insists that the historical analysis of the Bible and its self-witness must be brought into dialogue in order to gain a critical and factually comprehensible picture of New Testament theology.[13]

What emerges from this brief survey? First, it has come to be recognized by virtually all scholars that the proper approach to New Testament theology is a historical one. The New Testament is the fruit of a historical process of development. Its statements cannot be placed alongside one another 'on the flat' but must be seen in the context of a historical development of thinking and doctrine. New Testament theology is not a case of fitting together the scattered pieces of a jigsaw on a plane surface; it is more like creating a three-dimensional structure, some of the components representing earlier and less developed ideas, while others represent more mature and refined concepts.

Second, the question arises whether we can find a unity in New Testament theology by this type of approach. Can we trace a harmonious development from earlier formulations, true in their historical context, to later ones, also true in their context? Or is it the case that earlier ideas may be incomplete and misleading, while later ones may be degenerate, and that different sets of ideas may be downright contradictory? A strong tendency in current thinking is to emphasize the elements of diversity in the New Testament and even to play down the possibility of unity.[14] The attempt to construct a survey of New Testament theology which synthesizes the material on any given topic (E. Stauffer) has not been well received. The general tendency is to examine the thinking of different periods or thinkers (such as the earliest Church, Paul, John, Hebrews) and thus to do justice to their individual nuancing of the Christian faith. It is only rarely that practitioners of the second approach make any attempt to work out a synthesis on the basis of their analysis of the different areas of New Testament thought, and to date the results have been disappointingly meagre. Nevertheless, I believe that there is a real historical unity in the New Testament writings, and that it needs further exploration.[15]

Third, the question arises whether we are reconstructing the history of early Christian thinking or expounding what the New Testament teaches. Perhaps the two approaches should not be sharply separated; the latter cannot be done in isolation from the former. It seems to me, however, that, when all is said and done, the student is inevitably concerned with what the early Christians put down in writing. Granted that we cannot work out the theological 'system' of some of the New Testament writers in any detail, it is still possible to work out their general approach and to deduce the main features of the common faith which they held.

Fourth, we cannot avoid the question whether New Testament theology is merely historical and descriptive. The efforts of scholars like Wrede and Schlatter to establish its autonomy over against dogmatic theology were justified, and it is right that we must begin by asking 'What the New Testament said'. But somebody must ask 'What the New Testament says' and the New Testament scholar cannot contract out of that enquiry. The question is to be answered by exegesis.[16] The reason that Bultmann's answer to it is wrong is simply that it falls down at the exegetical level as an inadequate account of what the New Testament writers said. In my opinion, the salvation-historical approach of Goppelt does better justice to the character of the New Testament. But even if one decides that Goppelt is expressing more accurately what the New Testament said and says, this still leaves the question of whether I believe the message. The New Testament theologian cannot compel belief. He now becomes a preacher, and the preacher's task is to present a message; it is the Spirit who creates belief in the hearts of those who hear it.

In this way we can take up a position regarding the three presuppositions discussed at the outset and perhaps reframe them in a more acceptable manner. We may maintain the unity of the Testaments in terms of their witness to an on-going salvation-history, a witness that is inspired by the Spirit. We may maintain the integrity of the New Testament, granted that we see its integrity in terms of a historical development. And we may affirm the normativeness of the New Testament in the sense that New Testament theology presents the message that is at the heart of New Testament religion and which must fashion any systematic theology that claims to be an expression of an on-going New Testament religion.

We must now consider briefly the content and structure of an account of New Testament theology. First, our concern is with the New Testament writings and the theology that they express and imply. It is the New Testament which is normative for Christian theology, and not a reconstruction of the religion of the early Church. Second, the New Testament writings must be studied historically. This means that the individual writers must be considered analytically so that they may be seen in their historical contexts and so that their rich variety of expression may be appreciated; to fail to do so is to ignore the diversity which is a given characteristic of the New Testament. Third, the stress on an analytic approach has led to a virtual ignoring of the unity of the New Testament, and I would argue that an analytical study of the New Testament writings ought to be followed by a discussion of whether a synthesis is possible which will depict the basic contours of a common New Testament theology. Fourth, it has to be recognized that a detailed and precise expression of the theology of the individual writers is not possible, with the possible exceptions of Paul and John, simply because of the lack of evidence. The theologian has to be content to express the themes with which they are explicitly concerned, and, where possible, to deduce the pattern of thinking that may underlie their explicit statements.

Something must be said, however briefly, about the place of Jesus and the Gospels. The development of redaction criticism has made it clear that the four Evangelists (and not just John) are theologians with individual outlooks, and that discussions of their presentations of Jesus are an essential part of a New Testament theology. Since Conzelmann this has become generally recognized. But what about Jesus? It is obvious that the theology of Paul and the theology of the Pauline writings are virtually identical. The same thing cannot be assumed for Jesus and the Gospels, or for the early Church and Acts. From a historical point of view, the ministry of the historical Jesus and the existence of traditions about him in the early Church form part of the historical context in which theology was done, and similarly the proclamation and life of the early Church form the historical context in which thinkers like Paul operated. To this extent, Bultmann was right to number both the message of Jesus and the early kerygma among the presuppositions of New Testament theology. Nevertheless, it is legitimate to speak of the theology of Jesus, since his message was based upon and expressed a theology, and the same is true of the early Church. It is right and necessary to reconstruct the message and mission of Jesus historically and to see how the kerygma and theology of the Church are related to them. In other words, a historical study of New Testament theology must begin with a historical study of the presuppositions. If, however, we were right in claiming that New Testament theology is the theology of the New Testament writings, then what is the place of the historical Jesus or the historical early Church in New Testament theology? It will be remembered that M. Kähler insisted that our concern is not with the historical Jesus but with the biblical Jesus.[17] It is, therefore, the Jesus of the Gospels who is the normative figure in New Testament theology rather than a putative historical reconstruction. We need in effect to look at Jesus twice, or perhaps three times, in a historical study: first, we must look at the historical events preceding the resurrection and the impetus which they gave to the creation of the Church; second, we must look at the nature of the Jesus-tradition and its influence in the Church; and, third, we must look at the normative expression of that tradition in the actual Gospels. This may seem unduly complicated, but in the interest of clear thinking these three factors must be distinguished. If we accept that the synoptic Gospels give a relatively faithful picture of the teaching and mission of Jesus, it will be clear that the historical reconstruction of the message of Jesus can be taken over as part of New Testament theology with comparatively little difficulty, and it will remain only to bring out the individual characteristics of the three Evangelists. If, however, a more sceptical view regarding the historical basis of the Gospels is adopted, then a different procedure will be required. (It should be added that in the case of the early Church, it will be necessary historically to offer a reconstruction of its message and life as a presupposition for the study of the New Testament writers;

the understanding of the early Church as expressed in Acts will form part
of a consideration of the theology of Luke-Acts.)

II

Against the background of this general discussion of principles we shall now
attempt to characterize briefly some of the main contributions which have
been made during the last thirty years.

E. Stauffer

The first of the 'modern' theologies of the New Testament was published
in Germany during the early part of the Second World War. E. Stauffer's *New
Testament Theology* is almost totally different from other works on the subject.[18] It falls into three parts, the first and last of which are an introduction
and epilogue to the central and longest part of the book. Part I is a kind of
historical introduction in which it is claimed that the background to the New
Testament is the world of apocalyptic, and the term 'old biblical tradition'
is coined to refer to the vast apocalyptic literature based on, and including
parts of, the Old Testament. In a brief treatment of 'the way of the Lord',
which is devoted to the place of Jesus, Stauffer notes three aspects under
which the sayings about the Son of man can be considered: doxological (the
relation between Christ and God seen in terms of glorifying God); antag-
onistic (the relation between Christ and the devil seen in terms of victory
over evil); and soteriological (the relation between Christ and the world seen
in terms of saving the lost).

Then follows Part II, in which New Testament theology is seen against
its apocalyptic background and in terms of these three aspects. It is a survey
of salvation-history which begins with God and his work in creation, moves
on to the fall, and then looks at law and promise in the Old Testament from
a New Testament vantage point. There follows a major section on the coming of Christ which deals with Christology, the saving events, and the nature
of salvation. Then Stauffer moves on to the Church and the world, and
something of the background of the book may be reflected in the discussion
of the martyr-church in the Roman world. Finally, the author discusses eschatology, paying particular attention to the last events in the traditional sense
of the term. With this section the book reaches its climax, but there now
comes Part III, which is a discussion of the beginnings of credal formulations.

Such is the main outline of the book. It contains many good things by the
way, such as discussions of the theology of martyrdom and the criteria for
recognizing credal formulae in the New Testament, and the footnotes pack

in much useful information and pointers for further study. The book has its faults. It draws its evidence from a wide variety of sources, and non-biblical material can be used alongside biblical in order to illustrate and document various points. Some of the author's conclusions are doubtful: his treatment of 'Son of man' is dated, and his belief in universalism ('all will be finally saved') is exegetically indefensible.

Nevertheless, it is a work of great power and suggestiveness. I do not know of any other book which brings out the broad sweep of New Testament teaching and its unity in such a compelling, compact, and vigorous manner. Summarizing always carries the risk of distortion, but the risk is worth running on occasion. This is a book written with enthusiasm, enlivened by illustration from ancient art (unfortunately not easily accessible, and not always relevant), and expressed in powerful phraseology. The problems that it raises are whether a salvation-historical survey, drawing its materials from all parts of the New Testament indiscriminately, can do justice to the insights of the various writers and their individual outlooks, and also whether it is possible to leave aside the problems of historical development.

R. Bultmann

The diametrically opposite pattern was followed by R. Bultmann in his *Theology of the New Testament*.[19] The book concludes with a discussion of the history and task of New Testament theology, where the author makes it clear that he writes under the presupposition that the New Testament writings have something to say to the present, and then argues that the task of a presentation of New Testament theology is to make clear the self-understanding expressed in the New Testament writings in its reference to the kerygma. The New Testament imparts to modern man both the kerygma and also the possibility of that self-understanding which is the proper response to the kerygma.

The structure of the book follows from this. Part I is concerned with the presuppositions and motifs of New Testament theology. It handles the message of Jesus (30 pages), the kerygma of the earliest Church (30 pages), and the kerygma of the Hellenistic church aside from Paul (121 pages). This division is determined by the fact that Bultmann believes that between the earliest Church and Paul there stands what he calls Hellenistic Christianity, a stage that was marked by the Hellenization and Gnosticization of early Christianity. All this is, more or less, kerygma. Theology proper begins with response to the kerygma, although obviously the elements of proclamation and response are closely tied together throughout the New Testament.

So with Part II we come to the theology of Paul (166 pages), and in accordance with Bultmann's belief that self-understanding is at the heart of theology this section is structured into 'Man prior to the revelation of faith' and 'Man under faith'. The former section is a theological anthropology with discussion of human nature, sin, and the law. The second section begins, in good Lutheran fashion, with the righteousness of God, and moves on to grace, faith, and freedom.

Part III deals with the other New Testament theologian, John (90 pages), and again the structure is anthropologically determined as 'Johannine dualism', 'the "krisis" of the world', and 'faith'. In Part IV Bultmann takes up the development from New Testament theology to the ancient Church, and discusses at considerable length (141 pages) the development of church order, doctrine (that is, the idea of doctrine as such), Christology and soteriology, and ethics; in this section the author deals with both the New Testament and the earliest post-New Testament writings.

Bultmann's presentation has been the most influential of all modern studies, whether it is seen positively as a stimulus to new insights or negatively as a goad to provoke creative reactions. It is a historical treatment of the subject, but at the same time it is also an attempt to interpret the New Testament for modern man by applying to it the insights of an existentialist approach. The student ignores Bultmann at his peril, and he will find that many of the points developed by subsequent writers are already there in Bultmann's work. The author has a global grasp of the subject and he tries to deal with the post-Pauline material in a comprehensive and still unrivalled manner.

Nevertheless, Bultmann's work displays characteristics which in the end make it highly unsatisfactory. First, the history is wrong. T. W. Manson rightly accused Bultmann of 'the building of Hellenistic castles in the air' and of producing 'an imaginary picture of the beliefs and practices of a hypothetical Hellenistic community'.[20] Bultmann's third chapter is based on a distinction within the early Church which cannot be drawn as sharply as he attempted, and his assumption that the Hellenistic Church was heavily indebted to Gnosticism remains unproved. It follows that the succeeding sections, built on this foundation, are somewhat wobbly.

Second, Bultmann assumes that the message of Jesus is a presupposition for New Testament theology rather than a part of it because theology could arise only in response to the kerygma. But—even on Bultmann's minimalist historical conclusions—Jesus did proclaim a message to which people responded, and we may well ask whether that message did not stand in some relationship to the kerygma. We need also to ask whether the early Church did not derive some of its theological inspiration from the teaching of Jesus—to say nothing of his deeds. Bultmann's failure to take Jesus seriously is criminal.

It is associated, third, with his almost total ignoring of the Gospels as theological documents. Bultmann completely failed to see that the Gospels were written for a theological purpose, and so he left them out of his theology. Even on his own presuppositions this was culpable, for he regarded them as church documents and not as historical reports about Jesus: why, then, did the Church produce these documents, and what kind of theological outlook led to the writing up of the traditions about Jesus as a form of kerygma?

Fourth, Bultmann interpreted Paul and John from his existentialist point of view as basically witnesses to the self-understanding of faith. Subsequent writers seem to be agreed that this is a wrong emphasis, as a result of which important elements in the two writers are overlooked and others are distorted. The person of Jesus receives scanty treatment; the Spirit is misunderstood; prayer is virtually neglected; future hope is played down.

Finally, Bultmann tends to measure other writers by the standard of Paul and John, as can be seen in his generally negative attitude to the post-Pauline writers. Bultmann picks and chooses what he likes in the New Testament and dismisses the rest.

These are serious faults. Perhaps they are the faults of greatness: better to attempt a great venture and make a mess of it than to make a successful venture at a mediocre goal. Bultmann has done the former, and his work cannot be dismissed as unimportant or unhelpful.

A. M. Hunter

There have been many attempts to sum up the theological message of the New Testament in brief compass, and we cannot discuss these here, but space must be found to include at least one, *Introducing New Testament Theology* by A. M. Hunter.[21] The author sees the New Testament as a presentation of the fact of Christ and the interpretation of that fact. So he begins with a quick survey of the ministry and teaching of Jesus, using the Kingdom of God as his *leitmotiv*, and then he includes a chapter on the fact of the resurrection of Jesus as the foundation of Christian preaching. 'Is the message of the Resurrection history's most influential error or its most tremendous fact?' he asks, and he is not in doubt about the answer. Then comes a chapter on 'the first preachers of the fact' which utilizes the insights of C. H. Dodd into the character of the primitive kerygma. From there Hunter passes directly to expound the four main interpreters of the fact, Paul, Peter, the author of Hebrews, and John, and gives a succinct summary of each of them. Here is a historical treatment which brings out the basic lines of thought in the main New Testament witnesses, and it can be highly recommended as a simple lead-in to the subject.

A. Richardson

Pursuing our chronological survey of writers on our theme, we come next to what is in some ways the most difficult of them to evaluate, A. Richardson, and his *An Introduction to the Theology of the New Testament*.[22] The author writes to defend the hypothesis 'that Jesus himself is the author of the brilliant reinterpretation of the Old Testament scheme of salvation . . . which is found in the New Testament, and that the events of the life, "signs", passion and resurrection of Jesus, as attested by the apostolic witness, can account for the "data" of the New Testament better than any other hypothesis current today'. In other words, it is adoption of the historic Christian faith which provides the most satisfying explanation of the data. This is why Richardson starts with a chapter on faith and one on knowledge before proceeding to a discussion of the central facts of salvation. He deals in turn with the mission of Jesus, the Holy Spirit, Jesus' own reinterpretation of messiahship, the Church's Christology, and then the life, death, resurrection, and ascension of Jesus. This leads on to a discussion of atonement, and the experience of salvation. Finally, the author considers the Church, its ministries, and the sacraments. There is a wealth of material contained in this substantial book of nearly 400 pages, and the various word-studies can be particularly commended. The general pattern of the book is similar to that of Stauffer, and it is open to the same criticism that it fails to tackle the subject historically and to deal adequately with the variety of presentation among the different New Testament writers. The order of treatment adopted by Richardson is also odd, and it means that such a topic as the parousia never gets discussed in its own right, but always incidentally to something else. The author is not free from idiosyncrasy. His own distinctive Anglican position is sometimes read into the material (especially in his discussion of the sacraments), and his undisciplined use of the term 'eschatology' is hair-raising.

C. C. Ryrie

Very different is the work of the American conservative evangelical C. C. Ryrie: *Biblical Theology of the New Testament*.[23] This is not meant to be a profound study of the subject, but is rather a transcript of lectures to students. But the author has grasped the heart of the matter and points out that biblical theology pays careful attention to the historic conditioning of revelation and sees the various biblical writings in their historical contexts.

Again, its task is not to organize the teaching of the biblical writers according to the categories developed in systematic theology, but to develop the subject 'according to the outstanding areas of the thinking of the writer involved or according to the particular distinctiveness of revelation to and through that man or during that period'. Ryrie starts with the synoptic theology, organized under the headings of Christology and eschatology, and then moves to the theology of Acts. While he recognizes the contributions of the authors to these books, presumably they come first because essentially they present the theology of the historical Jesus and the historical early Church. James comes next, followed by Paul, Hebrews, Peter, Jude, and John. The treatment is comparatively brief and simple, and the author deals with certain issues that arise in a dispensationalist frame of reference, but might not occur to other readers. Although this is not a 'high flyer', it is a book that reveals some instinct for the right way to tackle the subject.

H. Conzelmann

If a work of nearly 400 pages can be called an introduction to New Testament theology, presumably it is equally legitimate to refer to a book of the same length as an outline of the subject. Such is the case with H. Conzelmann's *An Outline of the Theology of the New Testament*.[24] This book stands confessedly in the line of Bultmann's approach to the New Testament, but seeks to bring the material up-to-date, to avoid certain misunderstandings which can arise among readers of Bultmann, and to correct some mistakes or doubtful judgements made by Bultmann himself. What has resulted is intended as a textbook for students, and one of the virtues of the book is its useful bibliographical information for each section together with summaries of the current positions on many topics. Conzelmann, however, works largely within the circle of German scholarship and does little to summarize English discussions of the topic. His style too is often difficult (both in German and in translation), and the book is not designed for easy continuous reading. It also presumes a certain amount of knowledge on the part of its readers, and the beginner in the subject will find it tough, but rewarding.

Conzelmann begins by discussing the environment of early Christianity and then moves straight into a depiction of the kerygma of the early Church and the Hellenistic church. Although he insists that these two types of Christianity must be distinguished, he admits that the boundary is a fluid one, and in fact he treats the two of them together. He discusses the experience of the Church before considering its preaching and Christology.

In a second main section he looks at the synoptic kerygma, on the assumption that the kerygma did contain some account of the ministry of Jesus. He discusses what was contained in the basic tradition—the concept of God, the Kingdom of God, the demand of God, and the question of Jesus' self-consciousness—and then looks at the distinctive emphases of the three synoptic writers. Conzelmann's work is important as being the first real attempt to harvest the fruits of redaction criticism of the Gospels.

The third and longest section deals of course with Paul. After discussing general problems and Paul's concepts (here he tucks in Paul's anthropology), he deals in turn with the saving event, which is thus put in its proper place as the centre of Pauline thought, justification by faith (again the Lutheran emphasis!), and then the present character of revelation (the Word, the Church, and the message). One may wonder if this scheme is the most appropriate.

In his fourth section, Conzelmann treats the development after Paul, choosing this title in order to avoid any advance judgement on the material; the topics discussed here are very similar to those tackled in the corresponding section of Bultmann.

Finally, the fifth major section deals with John, but the treatment is not as full as might have been expected. Conzelmann's book is a good introduction to the problems of New Testament theology, but, as in the case of Bultmann, the author makes many categorical statements and judgements which readers will need to test carefully; this almost brusque style is no doubt due to limitations of space, and it is a pity that Conzelmann has not been able to give fuller justification for many of his conclusions. His work is obviously not the last word, but on the whole it is a more sensitive treatment of the New Testament than Bultmann's.

W. G. Kümmel

If Conzelmann provides the student's handbook, equipped with adequate documentation, W. G. Kümmel operates at a more popular level, so far as presentation is concerned, in his *The Theology of the New Testament According to its Major Witnesses: Jesus—Paul—John*.[25] This work appeared as an additional volume in a series of New Testament commentaries which deliberately avoid technicality but nevertheless reflect top-level scholarship. Kümmel, therefore, provides no footnote discussions or documentation, and only a very general bibliography. The book is an exposition of New Testament theology in an easy, running style. Kümmel points out the difficulty of reading the New Testament as critic and believer at one and the same time. He therefore claims that the task of the New Testament theologian is to make as clear as possible what the original writers were saying—and then let the modern reader make his response to them. He also claims that there is so much difference between the various writers that it is wrong to try and construct a 'harmony' out of them; rather, we must examine individual writers and let their message come out clearly alongside the others before we ask whether they show a unity or merely irreconcilable differences. Further, he argues that the chronological order of the writings is so uncertain that the presentation of a New Testament theology in some kind of order is possible only after each various form of the New Testament proclamation has been examined on its own.

Kümmel avoids some of these problems by confining his attention to three main witnesses to the New Testament message. He has no hesitation in beginning with the proclamation of Jesus according to the synoptic Gospels, and claiming that from the Gospels we can learn what he proclaimed; readers of Kümmel's other works will know that he achieves this by a rigorously critical method. He finds it necessary to discuss briefly the faith of the early Church before turning to the other main witnesses; he operates with two stages in the early Church (Palestinian and Hellenistic), but is far removed from Bultmann's fantasies on the matter. The treatment of Paul begins with the experience of salvation and the Christ-event before looking at human sin and then, in more detail, at salvation and the Christian life; in a final section the relation of Paul to Jesus is discussed. The third witness is John, whose theology is treated essentially in terms of his pictures of Jesus and of salvation. In a closing section he concludes that, despite their differences, the three witnesses agree in two points: that God has let his salvation promised for the end of the world begin in Jesus, and that God has met us in the Christ-event and wants to meet us as the Father who wishes to deliver us from our imprisonment in the world and set us free for active love.

Kümmel's treatment is confessedly an incomplete one, and the student will miss the documentation for his conclusions. Nevertheless, this is a profound study, and it is especially significant for the place it gives to Jesus as the proclaimer of God's message alongside the New Testament writers. As always, Kümmel is extremely cautious in the positive conclusions which he affirms; he is content to be the historian, leaving it to the reader to decide whether to believe, and not saying over-much about whether he himself believes, but the discerning reader will not be in any doubt as to where he stands, for example, on the historicity of the resurrection.

J. Jeremias

The work of Kümmel is the decisive turning point in the task of putting the historical Jesus back into New Testament theology. The job was finally completed by J. Jeremias in the first volume of a planned two-part *New Testament Theology*. This important book, subtitled *The Proclamation of Jesus*,[26] contains over 300 pages of exposition of the message and work of Jesus, the fruit of a lifetime of meticulous research into the Gospels and their background, and giving the reader the evidence for the author's conclusions (or references to the author's earlier works on the matter). Although not all of the author's conclusions will necessarily carry general consent, this is beyond all doubt the most important technical study of the ministry of Jesus to appear in this century. However, it is difficult to evaluate Jeremias's work as a New Testament theology, since we have only this one volume and no firm indication of how the author envisages the work as a whole. It would seem probable that Jeremias understands the proclamation of Jesus as the divine call which summons the Church into existence, and the New Testament writings constitute the varied answers that the Church gives to this call.

E. Lohse

The year 1974 saw the appearance of two works on our subject. In Germany there appeared a *Grundriss der neutestamentlichen Theologie* by E. Lohse, a former student of Jeremias.[27] Lohse sees his task as the unfolding of the theological ideas of the New Testament by means of careful questioning of the individual documents to determine how the proclamation of the crucified and risen Christ in the message that founded the Church is developed. He begins by claiming that New Testament theology must show how the kerygma is inextricably bound up with the historical Jesus; in other words, it must show the identity between the historical Jesus and the Christ of faith. Thereafter, Lohse handles in turn the kerygma of the early Church, the theology of Paul, the theology of the synoptic Gospels, Johannine theology, and the apostolic teaching of the Church. This book is meant to be a students' textbook written at a general level, and Lohse provides a clear exposition of these points in 160 pages. He concludes that there is a unity in the New Testament witness to Jesus as the crucified and risen Saviour, but that there are differences and even contradictions between the witnesses. Lohse's book is well adapted to be an introductory textbook, but the author does not have space to refer to opinions other than his own, and his critical views on the historical Jesus in particular are over-sceptical.

G. E. Ladd

By contrast, the work of G. E. Ladd, *A Theology of the New Testament*,[28] is written from a conservative standpoint, and this author could be accused of not defending his view of the historical Jesus over against historical criticism.

Ladd writes as an advocate of a salvation-historical approach to the subject. Hence New Testament theology is not a compilation of teachings but a recital of what God has done in Jesus; the New Testament contains the revelation in word which accompanied and explained the revelation in re-demptive history. One could, therefore, write a synthetic account of the New Testament witness in the manner of Stauffer, but Ladd claims that this is to sacrifice the richness of the variety in the New Testament. On this basis, Ladd treats in turn the synoptic Gospels, the Fourth Gospel, the primitive Church, Paul, the General Epistles (separately) and the Apocalypse. The weakness of this general scheme is that it fails to treat the Evangelists as theologians in their own right, although Ladd is not unaware of the prob-lem. One is bound to wonder, however, whether the Evangelists are placed in their historical position. Similarly, the section on the primitive Church deals with Acts, neither drawing material from other sources (for example, pre-Pauline fragments in Paul's letters) nor reckoning with the possibility that Luke's own viewpoint at a later stage may be reflected in his presentation of the early Church. Within the individual sections the discussion is clear and competent, and adequate documentation is provided. Like other writers, Ladd fails to draw together the various parts of the New Testament and show the sum of their united teaching.

L. Goppelt
In 1975-76 there appeared the two volumes of the last of the major discus-sions of our subject to date, L. Goppelt's *Theologie des Neuen Testaments*.[29] Something has already been said about Goppelt's approach in terms of the history of scholarship. It remains to be seen how he worked it out in detail. The whole of his first volume is devoted, after introductory matter, to the work of Jesus in its theological significance. At least in terms of aim, this goes beyond the approach of Jeremias who was concerned with the procla-mation of Jesus and stands closer to Kümmel. Goppelt recognizes that the resurrection of Jesus was the decisive event that gave rise to the creation of the Church and the continued working of Jesus, but he claims that the Jesus who continued to work in the Church was the Jesus who offered himself to his disciples during his earthly life, and therefore it is necessary to discover what we can about the historical Jesus. What follows is thus an account of the ministry and teaching of Jesus which is similar to those accounts in Jeremias and Kümmel. Although it lacks the originality of Jeremias, this is possibly the best general account of Jesus that we have, and is the best suited to be a workbook for students.

The second volume is entitled *Variety and Unity in the Apostolic Witness to*

Christ. It deals first with the early Church (that is, the Palestinian Church). Unlike other authors, Goppelt treats 'Paul and Hellenistic Christianity' together; he discusses usefully the general character of Pauline theology before taking up in turn Christology, the continuing work of Christ (the message, the Spirit, and faith), salvation, and the Church. It is at this point that we realize the unfortunate fact that Goppelt was unable to complete his work, and consequently there are some gaps in the material; justification, for example, is treated very summarily. The same fact applies all the more to the section dealing with the post-Pauline writings. There are excellent chapters which characterize the theological approach of such works as 1 Peter, Revelation, James, Matthew, Hebrews, and Luke. But the section on John is a mere fragment, and the author produced nothing on Mark and the Pastoral Epistles, largely, we are told by the editor, because, in the current state of scholarship, he did not feel able to give them a definitive evaluation. It is a tragedy that this work will accordingly remain incomplete, since it might well have become the major work in the field. Goppelt's general approach certainly does fuller justice to the material than many of the other works available.

S. Neill

One further work remains to be mentioned. The veteran English scholar S. Neill has written *Jesus through Many Eyes*,[30] a simple but effective survey of our subject which attempts to be something more than a summary of Pauline and Johannine theology with a few other things thrown in. After looking at the life of the earliest Christians before they had any literature of their own, Neill looks at the various major areas of response to the gospel—the Pauline corpus (with discussion centred on three terms, resurrection, Spirit, and reconciliation); the beginning of the gospel (Mark; 1 Pet.); the tradition of Israel (Matt.; Jas.; Heb.; Rev.); in the Gentile world (Luke; Acts); new questions and strange answers (John; 1—3 John); response to response (2 Pet.; Jude; Pastorals). Finally, he asks 'What lies behind it all?' and examines the historical origins of Christianity in the ministry of Jesus. This is a distinctive way of structuring the material; distinctive too is the author's lively style which makes this much more than a solemn and formal study.

The last word has not been written on our subject. But there is much of immense value in the books that we have surveyed, each of which has something to offer to the reader. It is our hope that with this survey we shall have provided some guidance which will enable students to turn more easily to the sources of information which will help them most in their approach to this topic, the crown of New Testament study.[31]

Notes

[1]A. M. Hunter, *The Gospel according to Saint Mark* (London, 1949), p. 11.

[2]This is not of course to suggest that earlier commentaries were all uninterested in theology.

[3]G. Kittel and G. Friedrich (eds.), *Theological Dictionary of the New Testament* (Grand Rapids, 1964-76); C. Brown (ed.), *The New International Dictionary of New Testament Theology* (Exeter, 1975-78).

[4]H. Ridderbos, *Paul: An Outline of his Theology* (London, 1977).

[5]In addition to the discussions in textbooks of New Testament theology, see W. G. Kümmel, *The New Testament: The History of the Investigation of Its Problems* (London, 1973); ibid., *Das Neue Testament im 20. Jahrhundert: Ein Forschungsbericht* (Stuttgart, 1970), pp. 123-46; R. Schnackenburg, *La theologie du Nouveau Testament: Etat de la question* (Bruges, 1961); K. Stendahl, 'Biblical Theology, Contemporary', and O. Betz, 'Biblical Theology, History Of', in *IDB* I, 1962, pp. 418-32, 432-7; G. E. Ladd, 'The Search for Perspective', *Interpretation*, 25, 1971, pp. 41-62; R. Morgan, *The Nature of New Testament Theology* (London, 1973); ibid., 'A Straussian Question to New Testament Theology', *NTS*, 23, 1976-77, pp. 243-65; E. Käsemann, 'The Problem of a New Testament Theology', *NTS*, 19, 1972-73, pp. 235-45; J. Barr, 'Biblical Theology', in *IDB* supplementary volume, 1976, pp. 104-11; H. Boers, *What Is New Testament Theology?* (Philadelphia, 1977).

[6]G. Strecker (ed.), *Das Problem der Theologie des Neuen Testaments* (Darmstadt, 1975).

[7]Ibid., p. 2.

[8]W. Wrede, 'The task and methods of "New Testament Theology" ', in Morgan, *The Nature of New Testament Theology*, pp. 84ff.

[9]W. Bousset, *Kyrios Christos* (Nashville, 1970).

[10]L. Goppelt, *Theologie des Neuen Testaments* (Göttingen, 1975), I, p. 31.

[11]K. Barth, *The Epistle to the Romans* (Oxford, 1933), pp. 1-15.

[12]Goppelt assigns A. Neander, B. Weiss, W. Beyschlag, P. Feine, E. Stauffer, C. Colpe, W. G. Kümmel and J. Jeremias to this group (op. cit., I, pp. 41-5).

[13]Goppelt assigns J. C. K. von Hofmann, A. Schlatter, G. Kittel, T. Zahn, E. C. Hoskyns and F. N. Davey, O. Cullmann, J. Schniewind and G. von Rad, to this group, and regards himself as standing in line with them (op. cit., I, pp. 45-51). The boundary between this group and the previous one is a fluid one; it is not easy, for example, to see why E. Stauffer is not assigned to the second group in view of his emphasis on salvation-history.

[14]For a survey of the problem, see J. D. G. Dunn, *Unity and Diversity in the New Testament* (London, 1977).

[15]Although W. G. Kümmel and E. Lohse make some attempt to deal with the problem, one has to go back to P. Feine, *Theologie des Neuen Testaments* (Berlin, 1953), ch. VI, for an attempt to gather together 'The main concepts in New Testament theology' after a discussion of the individual writers. See the excellent basic study by A. M. Hunter, *The Unity of the New Testament* (London, 1943).

[16]See Stendahl, op. cit., pp. 419ff. for the distinction between 'What it meant' and 'What it means'. It is perhaps clearer to distinguish between the 'meaning' and 'significance' of the text, with E. D. Hirsch, *Validity in Interpretation* (New Haven, 1967).

[17]M. Kähler, *The So-called Historical Jesus and the Historic, Biblical Christ* (Philadelphia, 1964).

[18]E. Stauffer, *New Testament Theology* (London, 1955); the original work was completed in 1938 but not published in Germany until 1941. See the discussion of it by C. K. Barrett, the first of a series on 'Recent biblical theologies', in *Exp.T*, 72, 1960-61, pp. 356-60.

[19]R. Bultmann, *Theology of the New Testament* (London, 1952, 1955); the original work was published in fascicles, 1948-53.

[20]T. W. Manson, review in *JTS*, 50, 1949, pp. 202-6; citation from 203.

[21]A. M. Hunter, *Introducing New Testament Theology* (London, 1957).

[22]A. Richardson, *An Introduction to the Theology of the New Testament* (London, 1958). See the

review articles by K. Grayston, _Exp. T,_ 73, 1961-62, pp. 45-50, and L. E. Keck, 'Problems of New Testament Theology', _Nov.T,_ 7, 1964-65, pp. 217-41 (highly critical).

[23]C. C. Ryrie, _Biblical Theology of the New Testament_ (Chicago, 1959).

[24]H. Conzelmann, _An Outline of the Theology of the New Testament_ (London, 1969); the original work appeared in 1967.

[25]W. G. Kümmel, _The Theology of the New Testament According to its Main Witnesses: Jesus—Paul—John_ (London, 1974); the original work appeared in 1969.

[26]J. Jeremias, _New Testament Theology: Volume One: The Proclamation of Jesus_ (London, 1971); the translation appeared in the same year as the original work.

[27]E. Lohse, _Grundriss der neutestamentlichen Theologie_ (Stuttgart, 1974).

[28]G. E. Ladd, _A Theology of the New Testament_ (London, 1975); the American edition appeared in the previous year.

[29]Goppelt died in 1973 leaving his work incomplete, and it was edited for publication by J. Roloff (Göttingen, 1975-76); it has since appeared in English translation as _Theology of the New Testament_ (Grand Rapids, vol. I, 1981; vol. II, 1982).

[30]S. Neill, _Jesus through Many Eyes_ (Philadelphia, 1976).

[31]It has not been possible to deal with all the relevant works published during this period, but space must be found for at least one Roman Catholic work, K. H. Schelkle's, _Theology of the New Testament_ (Minnesota, 1971 onwards). This work in four volumes adopts an unusual approach in that the author takes up a number of weighty New Testament concepts and offers a historical treatment of each one of them.

[1989] During the past ten years, two English contributions to the subject have appeared. Donald Guthrie published a very weighty _New Testament Theology_ (Leicester, 1981, 1064 pp.). The approach adopted is different from that of its contemporaries. The author has chosen to take up what he regards as the ten main themes of the New Testament—God, man and his world, Christology, the mission of Christ, the Holy Spirit, the Christian life, the Church, the future, the New Testament approach to ethics, and Scripture. Under each of these topics—often with subdivisions—he then summarizes the teaching of the several parts of the New Testament. The advantage of this method is that it gives the student a ready reference guide to what the New Testament actually says on any specific topic. This is particularly helpful for the preacher who wants a systematic survey of the biblical teaching. Needless to say, the discussion is exegetical and there is constant reference to the appropriate scholarly literature. Whether the advantages of the method outweigh its disadvantages is debatable. It is arguable that the historical development of biblical teaching is in danger of being lost, although the author does discuss the material in each section in a chronological order. More important is the fact that the interrelationships between different aspects of the thought of any given author cannot be effectively brought out by this method. Moreover, the structure tends to be systematic-theological and does not represent adequately the actual structure of New Testament thinking.

The other work in this period is a much shorter one by L. Morris, _New Testament Theology_ (Grand Rapids, 1986, 368 pp.), which represents the same basic conservative theological outlook as Guthrie but is differently constructed. Instead of looking at the New Testament thematically, Morris considers the contributions of each of the various writers before coming to a brief conclusion in which he notes their individuality and variety as well as their common witness to basic truths. His concern is with the finished New Testament writings, and he does not attempt to reconstruct the historical development of Christian doctrine. The aim is not to write a technical work, but one that will provide a general overview for the student.

A new series of short works, entitled _Biblical Foundations in Theology,_ has been inaugurated with a book on _New Testament Theology in Dialogue_ by the general editors, James D. G. Dunn and James P. Mackey (London, 1987). The introductory chapter (by Dunn) discusses 'The Task of New Testament Theology', and emphasizes the need for dialogue between different approaches (such as descriptive and prescriptive) that arise out of the nature of the subject-matter itself.

2
Jesus, Paul and John

THE NEW OCCUPANT OF THE CHAIR OF NEW TESTAMENT EX-
egesis in this university is conscious of entering into a goodly heritage which
must challenge and perhaps unnerve him as he faces the demands of biblical
scholarship and teaching in the closing years of the twentieth century. This
heritage is not confined to the work of holders of this particular Chair,
whether under its old title of Biblical Criticism or under its present one,[1]
for the contribution of the two streams of biblical study in this city, the
university faculty and the Free Church College, spans the work of several
departments and distinguished teachers.

The most famous New Testament scholar to work in the university was
Sir William Ramsay, whose most significant writings on the historical background of the early Church and on Luke as a historian were produced during
his tenure of the Chair of Humanity from 1886 to 1911.[2] His successor,
Alexander Souter, also gained renown outside the subject that he professed;
his importance as a scholar stems above all from his outstanding contributions to the study of the Latin fathers and of later Latin, but he also did
significant work on the text and vocabulary of the Greek New Testament.
Students can still use with profit his pocket lexicon of New Testament Greek,
which, as he says, was intended for 'students and ministers, who whether at
home or on a train, may be glad to have a handy volume to turn to in a
difficulty'—a comment which gains in local colour when one notes that
Souter wrote the preface to his *Pocket Lexicon* at Torphins and presumably
travelled in to Aberdeen on the Deeside Railway.[3]

Among the holders of the Chair of Biblical Criticism three especially deserve mention. First, William Milligan, professor from 1860 to 1893, was a moderator of the Church of Scotland and a member of the committee which produced the Revised Version of the New Testament. Next, I must name Archibald M. Hunter, my own teacher, who was professor from 1945 to 1971, and who wrote a whole series of books and commentaries intended especially to help students in understanding and interpreting the theology of the New Testament. And, finally, I must pay my tribute to Robin A. S. Barbour, the most recent holder of the Chair, who is outstanding for the way in which he has brought the insights of biblical scholarship to bear on the on-going life and mission of the Church.[4]

This brief listing of distinguished men and their achievements constitutes a catalogue of some of the main areas of New Testament scholarship—the study of text and canon, research into the Greek language and translation of the Scriptures into English, the assessment of the writings against their historical background, the exposition of the theological message of the New Testament, and at all times an emphasis on mediating the fruits of scholarship to students and to the Church at large.

There is on-going work to be done in all these fields which I have mentioned, and much of it can be carried on all the more efficiently today with the aid of recent discoveries and the development of new methods of research. One might have thought, for example, that the lexicography of New Testament Greek had been thoroughly explored by scholars at the turn of the century, but new inscriptions and papyrus documents continue to shed fresh light on the Greek language, so much so that there are plans afoot to rewrite the famous compendium *The Vocabulary of the Greek New Testament Illustrated from the Papyri* edited by William Milligan's more famous son George Milligan in collaboration with the Methodist scholar J. H. Moulton.[5] The Jewish and Greek background of the New Testament is undergoing ever closer examination as the result of continuing discoveries of new texts and fresh manuscripts and editions of old ones. The task of exegesis is issuing in the production of increasingly long and detailed commentaries which lay emphasis on the theological message of the New Testament.

I The problem of New Testament theology
Unity, diversity and historical development
The particular problem to which I wish to draw your attention on this occasion is that of the theology of the New Testament.[6] Is it possible to synthesize the teaching of the various documents in the New Testament in such a way as to produce what may rightly be called a theology of the Testament, a systematic and unified presentation of its thought? Or do the

writers speak with such different voices that there is really no such thing as a unified New Testament theology but only a collection of fragmentary and diverse teachings? It was tempting for past scholars to assume that the New Testament writers all speak with one voice and that a synthesis of their thought can be made simply by more or less adding together their teaching and presenting it in some kind of system. Indeed, people still do write theologies of the New Testament in this sort of way. Those who are conscious of the diversity of teaching in the individual New Testament writings have the tendency simply to study them in their assumed historical order and to summarize their teachings without trying to bring them into any kind of constructive synthesis. If the former approach stresses unity, the latter stresses variety, and it is not too easy to see how justice may be done to both approaches.

The problem with the first approach is that it assumes that each of the New Testament writers thought and expressed himself in the same kind of way, and that statements from any part of the New Testament can be put together side by side to give a comprehensive account of biblical teaching on any given topic. This, however, is precisely what needs to be demonstrated. Of course, many students do take the fact of this basic unity for granted. If the New Testament writers were inspired by the Spirit of God, and if the Spirit cannot contradict himself, then, it is argued, surely the various parts of the New Testament must be in full agreement, so that one is justified in drawing the raw materials of Christian doctrine from any part of it. By no means all biblical scholars would share this belief, and many would say that the problem is one of picking and choosing between competing sources. But even for those who do hold this view of biblical inspiration, the problems are still present, for the *kind* of theological unity offered by the New Testament writings is still a matter for discussion.

At the most simple level, words are not used in the same way by all writers. For example, the use of the word 'faith' by Paul, the writer to the Hebrews and James is very varied. There are differences in vocabulary and in concepts, and the problem is whether there is an underlying agreement in thought beneath these differences, and, if so, how it is to be brought to expression.

The differences go beyond vocabulary. The writers address different situations, and their formulations and instruction may be shaped to answer different questions. Even within the writings of Paul two rather different attitudes to marriage have been discovered, one in 1 Corinthians 7 and another in his later writings, and the peculiarities of the former may be traced in large measure to the fact that Paul is answering questions and thus dealing only with one side of the matter.

A further factor is that the writers stand within different historical and geographical contexts, so that, quite apart from the effects of specific situations, they are influenced by their place in the larger setting of the growth of the early Church and its thought. It has no doubt always been recognized in principle that any text must by understood in the light of the history which gave rise to it, although there has often been a tendency to examine the teaching of the New Testament documents without taking the history properly into account. But, however much place we allow for what may be called direct revelations from God to Christian apostles and prophets, such as Paul specifically claims to have received, for the most part Christian thinking developed as the result of normal historical influences. Paul's thinking on divorce, for example, was influenced by what had been handed down to him as the teaching of Jesus on this topic, and he went beyond it in personally applying and adapting it to the situation of Christians at Corinth in the 50s. The New Testament thus witnesses to the different, overlapping stages in the historical development of Christian thinking.

Finally, we must observe that the overt concerns of the biblical writers may have been different from those of modern theological scholars. Two prominent recent writers on New Testament theology may illustrate the point. The one pays virtually no attention to the place and significance of prayer in the writings of Paul: does this perhaps reflect a modern situation in which prayer is not so central as it was for Paul?[7] The other writer ignores the Pauline concepts of apostleship and the gospel, although it is quite clear that these topics were of crucial importance in Paul's theological understanding of himself and his mission: does this reflect an over-concern with the topics beloved of traditional systematic theology?[8]

The effect of these considerations is to suggest that in studying New Testament theology the first stage must be to examine the individual writers and their writings in their historical contexts. We must not rush into a synthesis without first examining and analysing each of the components as individual wholes.[9] The full range of, say, Paul's thought must be taken into account on its own terms and in respect of its own structure. It can of course be argued that beneath the concerns that emerge at the surface in Paul's theology, and represent his application of his thinking to concrete situations, there is an underlying theological system which can be stated systematically and used as part of a New Testament theology, but an approach that glided over the overt teaching of Paul would be mistaken, since it is the surface concerns that show what was of real importance in his thinking. It would be foolish to argue that, since all Church of Scotland ministers declare their acceptance of the Westminster Confession (admittedly with some freedom in matters not belonging to the substance of the faith), therefore a reading of the Confession will tell you the kind of things that will figure in their sermons and which really matter in their theology; the truth will be somewhat different, for there can be great differences in emphasis and in consequent perspective and understanding of the whole. It may be suggested, therefore, that in analysing the thought of, say, Paul, one may helpfully distinguish three things. First, there is the general framework of accepted thought within which a writer operates. Second, there is the question of the general thrust of this thinking. And, third, there are the individual emphases which emerge in the working out of this central message in detail. It is by consideration of these three aspects that one may be able to determine whether there is a basic 'system' to his thought which finds varied expression in his writings and which can then be compared with the thought of other writers.

Only then will it be possible to go on to the second stage in constructing a New Testament theology by a comparison of the different writers. At this stage it will be necessary to explore whether there is in fact a basic theological understanding common to the New Testament writers, and then, if this proves to be the case, to attempt to express it. In this sort of way it should be possible to bring both the unity and the variety of New Testament thought to expression. J. C. Beker has attempted to carry out this kind of exercise simply within the writings of Paul by distinguishing between coherence and contingence.[10] There is a coherence which gives unity to Paul's thinking, and for Beker this lies in the apocalyptic concept of the triumph of God, but Paul was able to correlate this theme to the contingent particularities of the human situation, to such an extent indeed that the apocalyptic centre becomes decidedly obscure in Galatians and Romans. This very obscurity in such cardinal documents indicates to my mind that Beker has not correctly identified the centre of coherence, but his basic approach remains a sound one. It may be that in the New Testament as a whole we can distinguish a coherence and a contingent manifestation of it in the different writers. The basic problem that emerges for our present purpose is whether there is such a coherence between the New Testament writers as to make a New Testament theology a realistic enterprise.

The place of Jesus in New Testament theology
Before we address ourselves more closely to this problem, there is another specific problem that must be brought into the picture. It is the question of what to do with Jesus and his teaching. Jesus wrote no book, and therefore he is not a contributor to New Testament theology in the same way as the

actual writers. He is the theme of New Testament theology rather than the author of it, and yet he taught a great deal, and his teaching must surely have some relation to the theology of the Church. On the one hand, his teaching coupled with the account of his life must have formed part of the historical context which shaped the theology of the early Christians, and therefore it must be studied as one of the formative factors in New Testament theology. On the other hand, the teaching of Jesus is a central theme of the Gospel writers, and we cannot avoid regarding his teaching, as it is portrayed by them, as forming a contribution in its own right to New Testament theology. Unfortunately, at both these levels we run into further problems.

The first is that the Gospels were composed after the Epistles and were written by authors with their own theological purposes and their own individual interpretations of Jesus. So we may have to draw a distinction between the teaching of Jesus and that of the Evangelists. Even if this distinction is largely one of emphasis, it must still be carefully explored. We cannot simply compare the Gospels with Paul if we are trying to compare Jesus and Paul.

Second, the process of interpretation that produced the Gospels with their characteristic differences from one another may also have been operative at an earlier point; so that we may need to distinguish the historical Jesus from the various pictures of him current in the early church traditions about him.

Third, we have to recognize that the account of Jesus in the Gospel of John differs markedly from the basically similar presentations that we find in the other three Gospels, so much so that many scholars would question whether we can reconstruct much, if anything, of the historical mission and teaching of Jesus from the Fourth Gospel.

From all this it emerges that the teaching of Jesus cannot be ignored in the construction of New Testament theology, and that it raises a host of problems. These problems may come to a focus if we ask two questions which will also serve to guide us in the rest of our investigation The first question is the relation of Jesus to Paul. It is plain even to the most superficial reading that there are profound differences in subject-matter, emphasis and character between a typical example of the teaching of Jesus, as reported in any of the first three Gospels, and a typical passage from the Pauline Epistle. The teaching of Jesus, it is sometimes said, is non-theological and non-dogmatic, simple and straightforward, but that of Paul is the exact opposite. As a result, some people make a straight choice between the one or the other. Some prefer the simple teaching of Jesus and accuse Paul of being the great corruptor of Christianity. Others take their stand with Paul and relegate the historical Jesus to a decidedly secondary place. How are Paul and Jesus related? Are they in basic agreement in their teaching or not? The second question is the parallel one of the relation between Jesus and John. If the Gospel of John is so very different from the other Gospels, how is it related to Jesus? Of these two questions, the former one has been fairly extensively studied, and there is perhaps something approaching a consensus on how to approach it and even on how to answer it.[11] The second question has received far less attention in precisely this form, but what I want to suggest is that an analogous process of enquiry may prove fruitful. By asking these two questions we may be able to make some progress in considering whether a New Testament theology is a real possibility. Our area of enquiry, therefore is Jesus, Paul and John, and our method will be to look in turn at Jesus and Paul and Jesus and John, making use of the method of analysing the teaching of each that we outlined earlier.

II Jesus and Paul

How is the theology of Paul related to the teaching of Jesus as regards its content?[12] In order to answer this question, we must attempt to set the two bodies of teaching side by side in such a way as to facilitate comparison while preserving the distinctive structure and emphases of each. We shall attempt to do this by outlining each in terms of its basic presuppositional framework, its central theme and its specific, characteristic elements, just as was suggested earlier.

The teaching of Jesus

A   The framework

We can assume that there would have been a common framework of thought shared by Jesus and his hearers, since otherwise there would have been no common ground on which communication could have been based, even if the purpose of Jesus was to make his hearers question their presuppositions. In fact, Jesus accepted the current Jewish beliefs about the existence of God, the revelation of his will in the Scriptures, and his choice of Israel as his people. He accepted the anthropology of Judaism with its belief in the reality of a spiritual dimension to life and in the activity of spiritual agencies, both good and evil. He also accepted the concept of two eras in human history, this present age and the coming age which would be the era of God's perfect rule over his people. Jesus did not have to teach people these things; he could take them for granted.

B   The central theme

Jesus' basic message was that the rule of God, that is, God's sovereign, gracious power operating in the world to create a sphere of blessing for mankind and to destroy evil, would be fully manifested in the near future and could already be experienced through his own activity. There may be some dispute about the details of this statement, but the general proposition is one that would be widely accepted by New Testament scholars.[13]

C   *Specific elements*

The specific elements in the teaching of Jesus can be discussed only very briefly in the present context.

1. Jesus presupposed that his audiences consisted of 'lost' and 'sinful' people. He brought a message of hope for those who felt themselves to be lost', and he attempted to bring 'sinners' to a consciousness of their real condition in the sight of God. In particular, he criticized the official religion of his time for having gone astray in its insistence on observance of the minutiae of the law, its concentration on outward observance regardless of the attitude of the heart, and its lack of compassion for those who failed to live up to its requirements.

2. Jesus announced the sovereign power of God at work to overcome the power of Satan and evil, bringing good news to the poor and needy, and demonstrating the power of God in mighty works of healing and compassion. He emphasized the fatherly love of God for his people and taught them to pray to him as Father.

3. Jesus saw his own role as like that of a prophet and teacher, but the way in which his ministry incorporated the sovereign activity of God and the authority with which he spoke both raised the question whether he fitted into the framework of Jewish expectations for the end-time about the coming of the Messiah. He spoke about the coming and activity of the Son of man, a phrase which was certainly understood messianically by his followers after his death and almost certainly so by himself. He was conscious of a unique filial relationship to God.

4. Jesus closely identified himself with his cause, so that response to his message was expressed in terms of commitment to himself in discipleship. Although he did not organize a new society of his followers, he did call some people to share closely in his work and in effect to be leaders in it.

5. Jesus saw his task as the renewal of the people of Israel who had fallen away from the true relationship to God. Although he restricted his activity almost exclusively to the Jews, he showed a particular concern for the poor and the outcasts of society, which suggests that in principle he was open to the inclusion of Samaritans and Gentiles under God's Kingdom.

6. Jesus taught an ethic of unrestricted love, including love for one's enemies, and practised it himself. This confirms the view that he saw the Kingdom of God as open in principle to all kinds of people.

7. Jesus carried his principles to the utmost limit by being willing to die

for them. However, he saw this suffering not as something accidental, but as something that was part of his destined vocation, and he regarded his impending sufferings and death as being in some way on behalf of other people and sacrificial or redemptive in effect.

8. Finally, Jesus looked forward to the imminent consummation of God's rule, when mankind would be upheld or judged at God's bar in accordance with its response to himself.

To sum up, we may observe that the message of Jesus was expressed in Jewish categories. Its main stress was on the rule of God with its upsetting effects on the Jewish religious ideas and practice of his time. This rule of God was mediated through his own mission, so that, however little Jesus may have spoken about his own role, in fact he acted as the agent through whom God's rule became a reality; to become a follower of Jesus was the same as to accept the rule of God. Thus Jesus was implicitly the agent of divine redemption, and it is highly probable that he was conscious of this and that it came to some expression in his teaching.

The teaching of Paul

Alongside this sketch of the teaching of Jesus we may now place an outline of the teaching of Paul.

A   The framework

We pass quickly over the framework of Paul's thought, since in essentials it was the same as that of Judaism as we have already described it. What we shall find is that when writing to Christians Paul can assume that some of the thinking of Jesus and the early Church has become common ground between him and his readers. For example, where Jesus proclaimed the Fatherhood of God as something new (at least in part), Paul can take this experience of God as Father more or less for granted.

B   The central theme

Paul proclaimed the message that Christ died and rose again; through this gracious act of God people who believe can enter into a new life as his people, the Church. This is the gospel, reduced to its absolute essentials.[14] It fits in with what we have already seen to be the place that Paul accorded to the historical Jesus, crucified and risen.

C   Specific elements

1. Paul has a more developed anthropology than Jesus, characteristic of which is his understanding of man in terms of such categories as 'body' and 'flesh', the latter expressing weak, human nature controlled by sin. People who are dominated by the flesh may try to put themselves right with God by observing the Jewish law, but are doomed to failure.

2. Paul regarded himself as an apostle or missionary sent out by God or by Jesus to proclaim the good news of salvation. His activity, therefore, was essentially proclamation of the gospel, and the centre of the gospel was the undeserved favour of grace shown to sinners by God in Jesus.

3. The gospel is thus the gospel of God, the good news of what God the Father has done, but the main actor in the story is Jesus. Paul saw Jesus as the Son of God who is equal in dignity and power to his Father (although ultimately subordinate to him), but who became fully a man in order that he might stand alongside humanity in its sinfulness; by his death on the cross, understood in sacrificial and redemptive terms, Jesus has opened up to mankind the possibility of deliverance from sin and its consequences. The resurrection of Jesus is the first stage in the mighty act of God which brings new life to the world.

4. Human experience of the results of Christ's death and resurrection is expressed in a variety of ways. It can be seen as justification, the placing of a guilty person in a right relationship with God, or as redemption, deliverance from the power of sin and death, or as reconciliation, the restoration of peace between God and his enemies, or as salvation, deliverance from the wrath of God against sin, or as adoption into God's family. It can also be understood as a sort of identification with Jesus in his death and resurrection, so that the 'flesh' is crucified and the 'body' is raised to a new life in anticipation of the resurrection which takes place at the consummation. Paul sums it up by saying that the life of the believer is 'in Christ', a phrase that means that his life is controlled by the fact of Christ crucified and risen.

5. Paul can also speak of this new life as life 'in the Spirit'. He regards the Spirit of God as a new power which enters the life of believers both individually and corporately, enabling them to conquer the power of the flesh' and bestowing on them various spiritual gifts by means of which they can serve one another. The Spirit enables believers to anticipate the life of the new age.

6. Salvation is entirely dependent upon the gracious action of God and is received entirely by faith. At this point, Paul's teaching is decisively shaped by controversy with Judaism which insisted on the need for observance of the Jewish law as essential for salvation. Paul insists that salvation is not dependent upon keeping the Jewish law but upon faith alone. This means that salvation is open to Gentiles equally with Jews.

7. Believers are incorporated in the Church as the new Israel, composed of Jews and Gentiles. It has a corporate life expressed in terms of its being the body of Christ and thus being in some way a spiritual entity. Its members meet together in fellowship to share in mutual service and encouragement,

to hear the word of God from prophets and teachers, and to join in prayer and praise. Baptism is the rite of initiation, and the Lord's Supper is the ongoing festival that celebrates the death of Jesus, and there are various leaders endowed with the gifts of the Spirit. The members of the Church are expected to show faith and hope towards God and love to one another and to all people.

8. Finally, Paul looks forward to a consummation which will be marked by the coming of Jesus in power and glory, the raising of the dead, and the bodily transformation of the living to share in life with Christ.

Jesus and Paul compared

Such is a sketch of Paul's teaching. Inevitably, it has skated dogmatically over a number of controversial issues, but I hope that it is sufficiently accurate to enable us now to compare the teaching of Paul with that of Jesus.

1. We can see at once that Paul and Jesus share the same basic Jewish frame of reference regarding the nature of God, the revelation of God in the Scriptures, and the nature of man, although Paul develops the last point more fully.

2. The major difference arises out of the central thrust of their teaching. While Jesus preached about the rule of God, Paul preached basically about Christ crucified and risen and his continuing activity as Lord. Implicit in Paul's emphasis is the recognition that Jesus is 'the Kingdom itself'. For, although Jesus spoke of the Kingdom of *God*, analysis suggests that there is little actual emphasis on God in the phrase and that Jesus closely associated his own work with the coming of the Kingdom. It was, therefore, a natural development for the early Christians to recognize that God's rule was essentially manifested in Jesus. Consequently, they did not continue to preach in the same terms as Jesus had done, but to preach Jesus. One may contrast the way in which the followers of John Wesley did not preach about John Wesley, but repeated what he himself had preached. This change has sometimes been expressed by saying the Proclaimer became the Proclaimed, but this way of putting it has been rightly criticized by J. W. Fraser.[15] The point is that Jesus was not merely the proclaimer of the kingdom but the One through whom it came into existence. It is, therefore, more accurate to say that the Bringer of the kingdom became the object of proclamation, or that the Messiah became the Proclaimed One: the Messiah brought the kingdom; his followers proclaimed him precisely as the Messiah.

Closely linked with this shift is that from regarding Jesus as primarily a preacher and worker of miracles to regarding him as the crucified Messiah. This shift was not made by Paul himself, but (like the shift just mentioned) is part of what he inherited from early Christianity. It must be granted that this stress on his death and resurrection was not central in Jesus' own message. Apart from hints of approaching martyrdom, we hear virtually nothing about it until the account of the Last Supper, so much so that it is something of a problem to relate the teaching of Jesus about the Kingdom of God to that about his own destiny.[16] But this development could come only after the death of Jesus, and the important question is really how the followers of Jesus came to regard him as a crucified Saviour rather than as a martyred prophet. The probable answer is that the hints which he gave, especially at the Last Supper, paved the way for a new dimension of understanding.

A further important shift lay in the recognition that Jesus is still alive and active. There is, however, hardly anything in the teaching of Jesus in the synoptic Gospels to trigger off this belief. The source must lie in the Christian interpretation of the resurrection through which the experience of discipleship was transmuted into a spiritual relationship with Jesus. This means that we can recognize some kind of continuity between discipleship before Easter and spiritual experience after Easter.

With this shift in emphasis, a fuller understanding of the person of Jesus was inevitable. Messiahship and prophethood were increasingly regarded as inadequate, and the hints of Jesus about his filial relation to God and the interpretation of his resurrection in the light of the Old Testament led to fuller recognition of his position as the Son of God and Lord.

Thus there took place a profound shift from the content of the teaching of Jesus to the developed theology of Paul, or rather to the theology of the early Church, for the main lines of Paul's thinking were shared with earlier Christians, and it has become increasingly evident that the problem is not so much Jesus and Paul as rather Jesus and the early Church. The events of the crucifixion and resurrection of Jesus and the experience of a spiritual relationship with him must be held to be primarily responsible for this shift in focus.

3. A second major difference is concerned with the place of the Spirit. The references to the work of the Spirit in the synoptic Gospels are remarkably sparse, and it is clear that Christian experience has not been read back into them. Only Christian experience from Pentecost onwards can explain the remarkable stress on the Spirit in Paul's teaching, which goes far beyond anything in the teaching of Jesus. We thus find confirmation that New Testament Christianity is not built simply on the teaching of Jesus, but on his work in bringing the Kingdom of God, his death and resurrection, and the Christian experience of the Spirit. To talk of, or to expect, a simple development from the *teaching* of Jesus to the *theology* of the early Church

or of Paul, is thus wrongheaded. The two cannot be regarded simplistically as essentially the same, or the latter as a direct development from the former. The common element is rather the recognition that in the person and work of Jesus, God was powerfully active to bring salvation to mankind. Only after Easter could it be seen that God was active not only in the ministry of Jesus but also, and above all, in his crucifixion and exaltation.

4. Other aspects of Paul's teaching are related to these major shifts. A significant development is his denial of the Jewish law as the means of salvation and his opening up of salvation to the Gentiles. Jesus' attack on Jewish legalism had a somewhat different thrust, although it too emphasized the importance of the attitude of the heart to God, and thus implicitly stressed the importance of faith over against external observance of the law. Similarly, Jesus' openness to the poor and the outcasts, when carried to its logical conclusion, issues in an openness to the Gentiles.

5. There is nothing in the teaching of Jesus corresponding to the teaching about the Church in Paul. Even though we can find the beginnings of the Church in Jesus' gathering of disciples, the development of the forms of life in the Church and the doctrine of the Church as the body of Christ go far beyond the teaching of Jesus. Jesus saw no need to organize his followers, but it is not surprising if his followers found it necessary to organize to deal with the growth of the Church. One is tempted to ask whether, if Jesus' mission had lasted longer and extended further, he would not have been forced to develop some kind of organization for his followers.

6. At one point there is a striking agreement, and that is in the ethic of love. Although Paul develops it in his own way and applies it to fresh circumstances, there is fundamental unity with Jesus on the simple command to love one's neighbour and even one's enemy as the basis of Christian morality.

From all this we can see that in the teaching of Paul, as compared with that of Jesus, there are certain common factors and certain fairly natural developments such as we would expect with the passage of time and the growth of the Church, but, above all, there is a decisively new appreciation of the person and work of Jesus which recognizes what was implicit in his own teaching and work, namely that he was the Messiah, the agent of God's rule, and not merely the proclaimer of the love and power of God. But before we consider further what this may imply for the nature of New Testament theology, we must bring the question of Jesus and John into the picture.

III Jesus and John

Having already sketched the teaching of Jesus, as recorded in the Church's tradition, let us now place alongside it the distinctively Johannine theology.[17]

The teaching of John

A   The framework

The basic framework of John's thinking is again Jewish. A new feature, however, is that the idea of the two ages is less prominent and is eclipsed by a dualism between God and the world, righteousness and sin, light and darkness, love and hate, and the children of God and the children of the devil. It is not surprising that John has been thought to share the world-view of Gnosticism with its developed dualism. The important feature, however, is that the framework of John's thought is a situation in which man needs redemption; he is in a state from which he needs to be delivered.

B   The central theme

John's own statement of his purpose is to show that Jesus is the Christ, the Son of God, so that through belief in him people may have eternal life.

C   Significant elements

1. The Gospel is concerned with a message, the centre of which is a revelation given in Jesus which brings eternal life.

2. Jesus is presented as the Word incarnate or as the Son of God who came into the world from being with God the Father, and who shares the Father's functions of judging and giving life. His humanity is assumed rather than stressed in the Gospel. Primarily, he is the agent of revelation, although some scholars have found it difficult to define exactly what he does reveal.

While the greatest space is devoted in the Gospel to the last day of his earthly life, so that the accent falls on his death and resurrection, nevertheless his teaching also receives much emphasis, and his deeds or 'signs' become the occasions for lengthy discourses and dialogues. His death is interpreted as his glorification, but it is also seen as a death for others by means of which sin is taken away. This means that the traditional teaching on the atoning character of his death is present, but there is a sense in which the accent falls more on the revelation brought by Jesus than on the redemption wrought by his death, and accordingly it may be correct to speak of a shift from the work of Jesus to his person.

3. The fundamental category of salvation is eternal life offered to those who are 'dead' in their sins, and it is given to all who believe. Receiving eternal life takes place in a new birth brought about by the Spirit of God. Those who are born again in this way become children of God and have a relationship with the Father very similar to that which exists between Jesus and God. Eternal life also brings about a close relationship to Jesus which is expressed in terms of mutual indwelling. There is a communion between

believers and Jesus similar to that between the Son and the Father. A whole range of imagery is used to show that the experience of eternal life is similar to the satisfaction of basic human needs, as, for example, when Jesus offers himself as bread to the hungry. The gift of the Spirit is also promised to believers, and the Spirit is conceived as functioning as a kind of *alter ego* to Jesus after his departure from the world.

4. The Gospel lays great stress on the importance of mutual love among the disciples; love for non-disciples is implicit rather than explicit, and there is no detailed teaching on the outworking of the basic attitude of love.

5. Although the word 'church' is not used, the concept of believers forming an organic unity with Christ is present. But there is no interest in church organization in the Gospel, and the kind of language used elsewhere in the New Testament in connection with the sacraments has become to some extent detached from them; John can describe the last meal of Jesus with his disciples without referring to the institution of the Lord's Supper at it, and he uses Eucharistic language in a totally different context. Implicitly, the Church is related to Israel, but its scope is wider, and the possibility of belief is opened up to the Samaritans and the others. Although the Old Testament Scriptures offer life, the Jews have failed to be led by them to Jesus.

6. Hope of the future coming to Jesus and warnings about future judgement are not absent, but the stress is much more on eternal life as a present experience, and one might argue that believers tend to form a conventicle somewhat separated from the world, although John does distinguish between being taken out of the world and being in it without being influenced by its sinful attitudes.

Jesus and John compared

A comparison of the teaching of John with that of Jesus shows that we have a development not unlike that which we found in the case of Paul.

The basic Jewish framework of thought is again evident, but with two differences. First, the understanding of man is developed in a dualistic fashion which brings out more strongly his alienation from God. Second, the thought of the age to come as a future state has been put in the shadow by a stress on the present experience of the new age. This may suggest either that there has been a decay in the vitality of Christian hope or else that there has been a powerful experience of present salvation.

The motif of divine revelation is very prominent. If Jesus is a prophet and teacher in the other Gospels, here he is much more the revealer of God, although the familiar concept of his role is retained. He remains the Jewish Messiah, and his role as Messiah is the subject of considerable discussion, but his fundamental roles as the Word, the Son of God and the Son of man form the context in which messiahship undergoes new definition. In a sense, John is more concerned with the person of Jesus than with his deeds, and yet the coming of Jesus is a revelatory *event* and his deeds are a mode of revelation. One is tempted to say that in John reconciliation has been replaced by revelation, but this is a misleading contrast.

The content of salvation is defined as eternal life and is presented in a set of images which are drawn from basic human needs. This life is closely equated with Jesus himself; communion with him on a spiritual level is life.

Jesus is depicted as attacking organized Jewish religion, as in the other Gospels, but his attack is more of a total one, and it is the Jews in general who are accused of spiritual blindness without specific criticisms of details of their legalism.

Finally, John has a developed doctrine of the Spirit in relation to the believer and to the world. This goes beyond anything in the synoptic Gospels. On the other hand, he is not interested in the twelve disciples as a group nor in the details of church organization.

These comments show that the teaching of John goes beyond that of Jesus in significant ways and that it adopts a somewhat different idiom. While many of the same motifs appear, and while much of the language is very simple, yet there is a different mood in the Fourth Gospel which in many ways is like that of Paul, but yet is significantly different. Clearly, our next and final step must be to compare Jesus, Paul and John.

IV Jesus, Paul and John
1. All three teachers may be understood as basically presenting a religion of redemption. The key motifs of human need, a divine saving act and the possibility of new life are common to them all. Thus all three portray the needy situation of mankind as lost and sinful. Jesus perhaps lays most stress on those who are lost and victimized, especially by the religious society of his time, while Paul and John think more in terms of rebellion, sin and the resulting state of divine condemnation. Again, all portray the action of God to save the lost. Jesus speaks of the dynamic rule of God which inaugurates a new age now and will be consummated in the future. Paul thinks primarily of his mighty act of reconciliation in the death and resurrection of Jesus. John presents the revelation of God in Jesus which brings light and life. And all three insist on the need for a human response which consists of a total commitment to God and acceptance of what he has done. Jesus himself spoke in terms of repentance and discipleship, and thus made response to himself the way into the Kingdom of God. Paul emphasized faith over against trust

in the works of the law, and John too insisted on faith in Jesus which is associated with the crisis of new birth.

2. In all three cases God is presented as occupying the role of Father towards those who respond to the gospel. He is the author of salvation who acts in grace and love towards mankind.

3. Similarly, in all three cases Jesus is the divine agent of salvation. In the Gospels he is pre-eminently God's messenger, the promised Messiah and the agent through whom his rule comes into effect. In Paul he is the Son of God on whom has been conferred a lordship that sets him alongside the Father. In John he is the Son of God and the Word, closely associated with God so that to see Jesus is to see the Father. Both Paul and John attach immense importance to his death and resurrection as the key events that bring salvation. This emphasis is not present in the teaching of Jesus, although it is not totally ignored, and the synoptic Evangelists recognize it by the relative amounts of space that they devote to the last week in the life of Jesus. It is clear that the New Testament writers are concerned with all that Jesus said and did and not merely with his teaching.

4. Only in Paul and John does the Spirit play an integral role in Christian experience. This motif is particularly developed in Paul, but it is also present in John, especially in his concept of the new birth. This stands in strong contrast to the paucity of mention in the synoptic Gospels, where the Spirit's role is principally to help believers in time of persecution. Again it is clear that the religion of Paul and John is built on the actualities of Christian experience which went beyond what was happening during the lifetime of Jesus. Similarly, in Paul and John there is considerable emphasis on the fact of an on-going relationship between the believer and the risen Lord. In this case, however, the corresponding factor in the lifetime of Jesus is discipleship, so that a basic continuity can be traced.

5. Perhaps the clearest constant motif in all three cases is the ethic of love, which is the central feature of all New Testament teaching about personal relations. The individual differences in how this motif is worked out need not concern us here.

6. In all three bodies of teaching the motif of a redeemed community is found. This community stands in continuity with Israel as the people of God with whom he entered into covenant at the time of the Exodus, but it also stands over against the Jews of the time in so far as they refuse to recognize Jesus as the agent of God. However, Jesus himself was not concerned with organizing a community of his followers, although there are hints in that direction. Paul especially, and John to a lesser extent, reflect the existence of an organized community, but they go their own individual ways in their

attitudes towards its leadership and structure. What binds all three teachers together at this point is their common conception of leadership as expressing itself in humble service or ministry to others.

7. Finally, in all three cases the motif of the overlap of the ages is present. For Jesus, Paul and John the era of salvation is already present, but all look for a future consummation when the present evil age will come to an end and the sovereignty of God will be fully established. If this motif is not especially prominent in John, it is by no means absent.

As a result of this survey we can say that there is a significant number of common features between Jesus, Paul and John, sufficient to show that we are dealing with a basically unified set of teachings. We have seen that all operate against a basically Jewish background. Further, we have seen that, although the central themes are expressed in different ways, in all three cases we are dealing with a religion of redemption, the central features of which are essentially similar. The basic differences are due to the fact that Paul and John present an assessment of the total career of Jesus and of the continuing experience of his followers which goes beyond the scope of the teaching of the early Jesus, circumscribed as it was by its particular circumstances. The experiences of being witnesses of his crucifixion and resurrection and of sharing in Spirit-baptism led to a second stage in the salvation-historical programme of which the first stage was the ministry of Jesus; this is a period of fuller experience, but one that is still incomplete by comparison with the expected third stage of the full consummation of salvation.

Hence we can conclude: First, there is a common basis in the teaching of Paul and John which shows that they stand in continuity with the teaching of Jesus and draw their inspiration from his teaching and the events of his life, including his resurrection.

Second, this common basis goes beyond the very minimal statement of the unity of the New Testament teaching offered by J. D. G. Dunn, who finds that the common thread is basically the continuity between the Christ of Christian experience and the Jesus of history.[18] We have been able to establish a much broader band of basic agreement which comprehends the general character of the Christian faith as a religion of divine redemption, the central place of Jesus Christ as the Son of God and his agent in redemption through his incarnation, crucifixion and resurrection, the nature of the gift of salvation experienced through faith, the establishment of a saved community whose ethic is one of love, and the consciousness that the age to come has already dawned but has yet to reach consummation. This basis could be enlarged by observing, for example, that for all three teachers the salvation events are regarded as the fulfilment of Old Testament prophecy and that the area of fulfilment is the people of Israel now open in its membership, at least in principle, to all who accept Jesus as Lord.

The survey has been confined to the three principal figures in the New Testament, but allowing for the limited and fragmentary nature of their writings it would not be difficult to fit the other writers into the picture and show that essentially the same pattern is presupposed and expressed in their writings. Thus we come to my third conclusion, which is that, after individual analysis of the given writers, we have been able to find a unity of content in their teachings such that the possibility of writing a theology of the New Testament becomes a viable option. Such a theology will follow the type of approach which I have attempted to sketch; it will begin by attempting to portray the teaching of each individual *in its own terms* and will then go on to attempt a synthesis of the total teaching of the whole corpus of teachings. Such an approach will bring out the basic unity of the New Testament writings, but it will do so by understanding the writings each in its own historical context, by placing their teachings in a proper sequence of development, and by highlighting the individual nuances and thrusts of the different teachers.

I am thus encouraged to believe that the enterprise of writing a theology of the New Testament is one that can be entered upon with a reasonable degree of optimism, and, whether or not I ever attempt to enlarge upon this sketch, I hope that I have shown that a framework exists within which the New Testament writings can be properly evaluated both for their diversity and for their unity.[19]

Notes

[1]Inaugural lecture to the Chair of New Testament Exegesis in the University of Aberdeen, delivered on 9 November 1983. The Chair of Biblical Criticism was founded in 1860 and renamed as the Chair of New Testament Exegesis in 1965.

[2]See W. W. Gasque, *Sir William M. Ramsay: Archaeologist and New Testament Scholar* (Grand Rapids, 1966).

[3]A. Souter, *A Pocket Lexicon to the Greek New Testament* (Oxford, 1916). See R. J. Getty's memoir in *Aberdeen University Review*, xxxiii, 1949-50, pp. 117-24.

[4]Other holders of the Chair of Biblical Criticism in the University were David Johnston (appointed in 1893), Thomas Nicol (appointed in 1899), Andrew C. Baird (appointed in 1919) and James A. Robertson (appointed in 1938). Professor Robertson previously taught in the Free Church College (from 1920) where his predecessors were George Smeaton (appointed in 1854), David Brown (appointed in 1857, and co-editor of the well-known *Critical, Experimental and Practical Commentary on the Old and New Testaments* with R. Jamieson and A. R. Fausset [1871]), Robert Johnstone (appointed in 1900), and James Iverach (appointed to teach New Testament in 1907). Before 1854, teaching of New Testament was presumably carried on by the professors of Divinity, Alexander Black, James MacLagan and Patrick M. Fairbairn. Although Fairbairn taught only briefly in Aberdeen before going to Glasgow, he was probably the most distinguished of the nineteenth-century Aberdeen teachers of New Testament; his book, *The Typology of Scripture*, was reprinted as recently as 1953. See *The Church College in Aberdeen* (Preface by William J. Mason) (Aberdeen, 1936).

[5]Published in fascicles, London, 1914-29; one-volume edition, 1930. See C. J. Hemer, 'Towards a New Moulton and Milligan', *Nov. T* 24, 1982, pp. 98-123.

[6]See I. H. Marshall, 'New Testament Theology', *The Theological Educator* 9, 2, 1979, pp. 47-64 (reprinted in this volume, pp. 15-34) G. Strecker (ed.), *Das Problem der Theologie des Neuen Testaments* (Darmstadt. 1975).

[7]R. Bultmann, *Theology of the New Testament* (London, 1952, 1955).

[8]D. Guthrie, *New Testament Theology* (Leicester, 1981).

[9]For the principle of holistic comparisons, see E. P. Sanders, *Paul and Palestinian Judaism: A Comparison of Patterns of Religion* (London, 1977).

[10]J. C. Beker, *Paul the Apostle: The Triumph of God in Life and Thought* (Edinburgh, 1980).

[11]See J. W. Fraser, *Jesus and Paul: Paul as Interpreter of Jesus from Harnack to Kümmel* (Abingdon. 1974).

[12]The general problem of the relation between Jesus and Paul was broken down into a set of three questions by R. Bultmann ('Die Bedeutung des geschichtlichen Jesus für die Theologie des Paulus', in *Glauben und Verstehen* (1933), I, 188. See W. G. Kümmel, 'Jesus und Paulus', in *Heilsgeschehen und Geschichte* (Marburg. 1965), pp. 81-106; cf. pp. 169-91, 439-56. His questions were: 1. Was Paul influenced by the historical Jesus in his thinking? 2. Is the theology of Paul related in content to the preaching of Jesus? 3. What significance had the historical Jesus for the theology of Paul? These questions were formulated in an attempt to state the relationship between the historical Jesus and Paul rather than simply to compare their teaching, but nevertheless they may help us in our quest. It will be clear that the first question is a historical question relating to the possible historical continuity between Jesus and Paul, and the second and third questions are concerned more with the possible theological continuity between Jesus and Paul.

We can deal with the first question fairly briefly. Since Paul had never known the historical Jesus, there was of course no direct influence between the two of them. Even though Paul claims to have had visions of the risen Lord, there is no evidence that there was any kind of lengthy verbal communication in which he told Paul the kind of things that he had said to his followers during his earthly life. If, then, Paul was influenced by the earthly Jesus, it can have been only indirectly through the mediation of other Christians. This means that the question of the relation between Jesus and Paul can be replaced by the question of the relation between the traditions about the earthly Jesus current in the early Church and Paul. In a sense this considerably simplifies our task, since it means that we are not required to delve into the problem of the historical Jesus but can content ourselves with looking at the Jesus-tradition in the early Church. To be sure, we are left with the question of the relation between the historical Jesus and the Jesus-traditions of the early Church, and in the present context I can only record the position, for which I have argued elsewhere, that the Jesus-traditions appear to me to give a reliable picture of the earthly Jesus and his teaching (I. H. Marshall, *I Believe in the Historical Jesus* [London, 1977]).

Undoubtedly there was a relationship between Paul and the Jesus-traditions. It is a matter of historical fact that Paul knew Peter, or Cephas as he calls him, James and John, and it can surely be taken as overwhelmingly likely that when they met they talked together about Jesus (Gal. 1.18f.; 2.9). In Dodd's famous phrase. 'We may presume that they did not spend all the time talking about the weather' (C. H. Dodd, *The Apostolic Preaching and its Developments* [London, 1936], p. 26). Further, since there is a very plausible link between Peter and the Evangelist Mark, one may also assume that the kind of traditions known to Paul were similar to those later incorporated in the Gospel of Mark. (See M. Hengel, *Studies in the Gospel of Mark* [London, 1985].) It can be argued that there is not much evidence of the influence of the Gospel tradition in the actual writings of Paul, but two points can be made in reply. One is that the extent of the Gospel allusions in Paul is greater than is often assumed, as P. Stuhlmacher has recently argued (P. Stuhlmacher, 'Jesustradition im Römerbrief', in *Theologische Beiträge*, 14, 1983, pp. 240-50). The other is that the situation with regard to Paul is the same as that with regard to John. The writer or school of writers responsible for the Johannine writings could produce letters in which there is nothing about the life of Jesus beyond a strong insistence that the Son of God truly came in the flesh, but this does not imply an ignorance of the life of Jesus or a lack of interest in it since we have the Gospel of John as positive evidence to the contrary.

We can take up Bultmann's third question at this point and claim that the life of the historical Jesus was significant for Paul despite this lack of overt reference in his Epistles. Reduced to its simplest essentials, Paul's message was that Christ died for our sins and rose from the dead (1 Cor. 15.3-5). For Paul these were historical events pregnant with theological significance. Even though some people might dispute the historicity of the resurrection of Jesus, Paul was quite clear that the resurrection was a historical event like any other event in the life of Jesus and not something that fell into a different category of happenings. To put the point in modern jargon, if we are to distinguish between the so-called 'Jesus of history' and the 'Christ of faith', then for Paul the fact of the resurrection was part of the story of the 'Jesus of history', although its significance was a matter of faith.

Further, Paul laid stress on the coming of the Son of God into the world as the man Jesus. If Jesus had not been born of a woman and had not lived under the law (Gal. 4.4), it is doubtful if he could have fulfilled the saving role Paul assigns to him. The human existence of Jesus with its concrete particularities was essential for Paul.

And, third, in principle Paul regarded the teaching of Jesus as an authoritative source for the way in which Christians ought to live, and he appealed to it in regard to specific questions on marriage and divorce, the subsistence of missionaries and the conduct of the Lord's Supper (1 Cor. 7.10; 9.14; 11.23-25).

All this shows that the suggestion that Paul was concerned only with the fact of the historical Jesus, and not with the content of the fact, is false and rests on a confusion in thinking. A fact is not a fact without some content. It is of considerable significance for what follows that for Paul the death and resurrection of Jesus, regarded as historical events within the career of the Jesus of history, had assumed overwhelming importance in comparison with the rest.

[13]Cf. R. Schnackenburg, *The Moral Teaching of the New Testament* (London, 1965), p. 13: 'In order to view Jesus' moral message in the right perspective it makes a difference what we regard as the leading idea from his preaching as a whole: the gospel of the goodness and mercy of God our Father, the salvation of souls, the call to discipleship, or the proclamation of the reign of God. In what follows we shall fit Jesus' moral demands principally (though not exclusively) within the framework of his gospel of the reign of God.'

[14]For this understanding of Paul as opposed to J. C. Beker's interpretation (see n. 10 above), see H. Ridderbos, Paul: *An Outline of his Theology* (London, 1977).

[15]Fraser, *Jesus and Paul*, pp. 23ff, 208.

[16]H. Schürmann, *Gottes Reich—Jesu Geschick: Jesu ureigener Tod im Licht seiner Basileia-Verkündigung* (Freiburg, 1983). (It gives me particular pleasure to refer to this book which its author has dedicated to the Faculty of Divinity in the University of Aberdeen.)

[17]We can ask the same questions about the relation between Jesus and John as Bultmann asked in the case of Jesus and Paul. First, was John influenced by the historical Jesus in his thinking? For upholders of the traditional theory that the Fourth Gospel was composed by the apostle John or by some other eye-witness of the ministry of Jesus, the answer is a straightforward one. But the question of authorship is controversial, and many scholars would deny that an eye-witness had any active part in the production of the Gospel. However, there is strong evidence that a broad stream of early tradition about the historical Jesus lies behind the Gospel, and that where John contains material similar to that in the other Gospels the source is not the writer's own knowledge of these Gospels, but his access to traditions closely related to the synoptic traditions (C. H. Dodd, *Historical Tradition in the Fourth Gospel* [Cambridge, 1963]). However much this tradition may have been modified in the process of composition, and however many stages of composition there may have been, the Gospel rests ultimately on a foundation of historical tradition about Jesus.

Second, how significant was the historical Jesus for John? The very fact that John wrote a Gospel shows that the historical Jesus had a great significance for him, and in this respect his theology is comparable with that of the other Evangelists who expressed their theology by writing Gospels. Moreover, as we have seen, the evidence of the Johannine Epistles demonstrates all the more powerfully that a writer or school of writers, who might be thought to have been interested only in theological evaluation of Jesus as the Son of God, had a central concern to present the story of the ministry of Jesus. It might be objected that the Jesus thus presented is really the risen Lord disguised in the lineaments of the earthly Jesus, but this would be a false assessment. The earthly Jesus has not been swallowed up in the risen Lord, but rather the full significance of the earthly Jesus, as John saw it, has been expressed by interpretation of his ministry and teaching in the light of post-Easter reflection. We are not dealing with a situation like that in some of the apocryphal writings, where revelation is placed in a post-Easter setting and has lost its links with the historical teaching of Jesus; on the contrary, the revelation is firmly grounded in the pre-Easter life of Jesus but is seen in the light of what followed. For John it was important to place the historical Jesus at the centre of his theology.

[18]J. D. G. Dunn, _Unity and Diversity in the New Testament_ (London, 1977), pp. 229 _et passim._
[19]On the unity of New Testament teaching, see especially A. M. Hunter, _The Unity of the New Testament_ (London, 1943).

3
Is Apocalyptic the Mother of Christian Theology?

I T WAS IN 1960 THAT E. KÄSEMANN ORIGINALLY PUBLISHED AN essay which subsequently appeared in English with the title 'The Beginnings of Christian Theology', in which he affirmed, 'Apocalyptic was the mother of all Christian theology'. The essay aroused controversy, and the author wrote a second essay in which he attempted to clarify and defend his position under the title 'On the Subject of Primitive Christian Apocalyptic'.[1]

The thesis stated

According to Käsemann, primitive Christian apocalyptic is to be defined as 'the expectation of an imminent parousia';[2] that is to say, it is the form of early Christianity which is dominated by the expectation of the impending return of Jesus. Käsemann begins from an analysis of certain sayings in Matthew which show the existence of two groups in the early Church, which shared belief in possessing the Spirit of God, but which differed in what they believed in other respects and attacked each other sharply, measuring each other by their lack of signs of the Spirit. One group was engaged in mission to the Gentiles and was associated with Stephen and his followers; it moved out to Antioch and prepared the way for Paul. The other was strongly Jewish Christian; it too was concerned with mission, but only to the Jews so as to bring about the restoration of Israel, and it insisted on strict adherence to the law. Both groups used what Käsemann calls 'sentences of holy law'[3] to set out their rules; these were sayings which set side by side earthly conduct and heavenly reward or judgement and were promulgated by Christian prophets. And behind the concern for mission, and the promises and threats in the holy law stood a fervent expectation of the coming of Jesus. The communities where this type of Christianity was to be found were 'the little congregations on the borders of Palestine and Syria'.[4]

Thus the marks of this type of Christianity were:

1. Fervent expectation of the coming of Jesus.
2. Enthusiastic Christianity associated with the presence of the Spirit.
3. Leadership by prophets who were the bearers of the Spirit.
4. Strong Jewish legalism.
5. Fierce opposition to the group of Christians who sought to convert Gentiles and who consequently took a less rigid attitude to the law.

Some comments must now be made on further details of this thesis.

1. Käsemann largely builds it on his understanding of various texts in Matthew in the light of what he calls 'form criticism', by which I take it that he means that from these texts we can discern their life-setting in the early Church. He draws attention to the polemical features in Matthew 7.22-23 (a group of enthusiastic prophets attacked by Matthew for failure to do the will of God); 23.8-10 (an attack on a Judaistic Christian rabbinate developing in the Church); 5.17-20 (an insistence on keeping every detail of the law, which Matthew himself does not share and has modified): 10.5-6 (an attack by Jewish Christians on an on-going mission to the Samaritans and Gentiles); 10.41 and 13.16, 17 (evidence for a division of the community into prophets and righteous men). The community saw itself as having the presence of the Spirit to such an extent that, whereas speaking against the Son of man was a venial offence, to speak against the Spirit working in the Church was unpardonable (Matt. 12.32). So too in Matthew 10.13-14 the tremendous authority of the missionary as the representative of Christ is portrayed. And overarching all is the authority of Christ who sits on the throne as the Son of man, the sign of the triumph of the righteousness of God. He will come again before the Church has completed its mission to Israel.

2. All the evidence that has been cited comes from the early Church and not from Jesus himself. When Käsemann says that apocalyptic is the mother of Christian theology, he adds, 'since we cannot really class the preaching of Jesus as theology'.[5] There are two points here. One is that the real beginning of Christian theology is after Easter—and here Käsemann is being loyal to the verdict of his teacher, R. Bultmann. But the other point is that the teaching of Jesus was not in fact apocalyptic. His teaching 'did not bear a fundamentally apocalyptic stamp but proclaimed the immediacy of the God who was near at hand'.[6] Although Jesus had links with John the Baptist whose message was apocalyptic, yet his own message was different.

At the decisive point it reverses the message of the Baptist by orientating the repentance which it, too, requires, not towards wrath but towards grace; consequently it calls man to the service of God in his daily life as if no shadow lay upon the world and God were not inaccessible. This service of God is then coupled with love of one's brother man as if there were no necessary distinction of cultus and ethic, and creation remained yet undisturbed. Love of one's brother, however, actually includes the far-off unknown and the enemy as if there were no world-renouncing piety required as the sign of the ineluctable will of God and no one could flee from this will. Though man may be in flight from God, yet God has never withdrawn himself from man. No 'works' are therefore required to call him back, just as there is no assurance in the face of his judgment. On the basis of this remarkable 'eschatology', which views all life as lived 'before God', it is easy to understand how Jesus, so far as we can see, did not baptize, built up no community as a holy remnant and as the nucleus of the messianic people of God and recognized no sharpening of the Torah other than the demand for obedience and love.[7]

Consequently Käsemann can conclude, 'I am convinced that no one who took this step can have been prepared to wait for the coming Son of Man, the restoration of the Twelve Tribes in the Messianic kingdom and the dawning of the Parousia (which was tied up with this) in order to experience the near presence of God. To combine the two would be, for me, to cease to make any kind of sense'.[8]

Thus for Käsemann the picture of Jesus is a non-apocalyptic one—but this is a picture which rests on the judgement that a considerable amount of gospel material does not go back to Jesus. However, it must be noted that Käsemann still wants to argue for some kind of continuity between the Church and Jesus: 'By designating Jesus as its Lord and as the Son of Man who was to come and by its consciousness of itself as being sent "in his name", the primitive community was laying claim to a continuity of history and of content. But this can only mean that after Easter eschatology, christology and ecclesiology were and are bound up with the message and activity of Jesus'.[9]

3. Käsemann argues that in the Hellenistic church and Paul one can see opposition to the earlier enthusiasm of the Jewish church. Paul shows a certain reserve against the eschatology of the enthusiasts, in that, while they believed that they were experiencing the resurrection life of Jesus, Paul believed that Christians possessed 'the reality of sonship only in the freedom of those under temptation—freedom which points forward to the resurrection of the dead as the truth and the completion of the reign of Christ'.[10]

Thus the apocalyptic enthusiasm of the Jewish church was shared by the Hellenistic church but in a different form, and Paul had to respond to it.

4. Finally, Käsemann has to allow that the theology of apocalyptic Christianity has been discredited by the delay of the parousia: 'We have to state clearly and without evasion that this hope proved to be a delusion and that with it there collapsed at the same time the whole theological framework of apocalyptic of the time after Easter, at the heart of which was the restoration of the Twelve Tribes but which also fought for the Mosaic Torah and against the practice of the Gentile mission'.[11] Nevertheless, Käsemann wants somehow to maintain this delusive hope, for he concludes his first essay by saying that the central motif of apocalyptic was 'in fact the hope of the manifestation of the Son of Man on his way to enthronement; and we have to ask ourselves whether Christian theology can ever survive in any legitimate form without this theme, which sprang from the Easter experience and determined the Easter faith'.[12]

I hope that this is a fair and adequate summary of a position that has certainly proved stimulating to subsequent scholars. As I have already indicated, Käsemann was moved to reply at some length to critical comments from some of his German colleagues. But, whatever else he achieved, he certainly contributed to the development of a fresh look at the nature of apocalyptic and its place in early Christianity. Consequently, when James Dunn came to write about the diversity of theological viewpoint in the New Testament, he singled out four main areas for discussion, namely, Jewish Christianity, Hellenistic Christianity, apocalyptic Christianity and early Catholicism. Dunn admits that these four areas are not the only ones that might be listed and emphasizes that they do not indicate separate segments but rather what he calls 'dimensions and emphases within first-century Christianity which all overlap and interact to some degree'.[13] Thus, when he talks about apocalyptic Christianity, he is talking about a particular strand of thought which might be found in many places.

Dunn begins by examining the characteristics of apocalyptic thinking and the apocalyptic writings, and this is a valuable point in his discussion when compared with that of Käsemann whose attempt at definition is really quite inadequate. He then proceeds to look for apocalyptic features in the New Testament, and he finds them in three areas: the teaching of John the Baptist, of Jesus, and of the earliest Christians. John looked forward to imminent judgement in the shape of a baptism by fire possibly carried out by a heavenly being, and only those who genuinely repented could hope to survive. Jesus too announced the coming of God's Kingdom, but saw its power already at work in his ministry. He anticipated a period of trials before the imminent end of the world, and his outlook was centred on Israel. But he refrained from detailed speculation and the drawing up of an apocalyptic calendar, and he emphasized that the Kingdom was already present in some way. With regard to the earliest Church, Dunn argues that the members saw the resurrection of Jesus as the beginning of the resurrection of the dead, that they lived in daily expectation of his parousia, and their common life centred around the temple and was thus Israel-centred. He sums up: *'Christianity began as an apocalyptic sect within Judaism, a sect which in its apocalypticism was in substantial continuity with the messages both of John the Baptist and of Jesus.* And since this is where Christianity all began, to that extent Käsemann is correct: apocalyptic *was* "the mother of all Christian theology".'[14]

But apocalyptic did not disappear without trace, and Dunn proceeds to look at its literary deposit in the New Testament, which he finds at three points in particular. First, the earliest New Testament documents in his opinion, 1 and 2 Thessalonians, demonstrate that Paul's teaching has strong apocalyptic features; some of the converts clearly thought that they were living in the last day itself, and Paul had to temper their enthusiasm. There is a note of sobriety alongside the hope of the imminent End. (We may note in parentheses that the extent of apocalyptic thinking in the writings of Paul may in fact be much greater. See the work of J. C. Beker, cited in n. 1.) Second, there is Mark 13, a composite document in which the author suggests that the imminent desecration of the temple in Jerusalem will be the beginning of the End. But, as in 1 and 2 Thessalonians, the centre of the imminent expectation is the coming of Jesus as the Son of man, and the exposition is marked by sobriety and earnestness. Finally, there is the Revelation of John which is a genuine apocalyptic document with a clear Christian content.

From this survey, Dunn concludes that apocalyptic was an integral part of first-century Christianity. It has continued within the Church, though it has always been a somewhat uncomfortable companion to orthodox theology. Positively, Dunn says, it is a valid part of Christianity, setting reality on a wide canvas, seeing history as having a purpose, and thus giving a proper evaluation to the present time and leading the believer to a new sense of responsibility to the world.

The thesis examined

So much by way of exposition of the case for apocalyptic as the mother of Christian theology. It is now time to cast a critical eye over it and to see what we are to make of it. The question, we remind ourselves, is whether apocalyptic is the mother of Christian theology.

The first point to be made is that the answer must depend to a great extent on the definition of the term 'apocalyptic'. We must start with Käsemann's definition, since it is primarily his statement that is under scrutiny. The obvious and necessary criticism is that he has given rather a special sense to the term apocalyptic. If we rewrite his thesis, then it would take the form that 'the expectation of an imminent parousia is the mother of Christian theology'. We shall examine that statement in a moment, but first of all I think that it is fair to say that this is not necessarily the meaning that most people would draw from the original statement. What is apocalyptic? Here Dunn is a much more sure guide when he distinguishes between the type of thinking we call apocalyptic and the sort of literature which belongs to this literary classification. For Dunn, apocalyptic theology is characterized by: belief in two ages with a sharp break between them; an attitude of pessimism toward the present age and hope with regard to the age to come; belief in an eschatological climax involving a time of severe tribulation, judgement on God's enemies, salvation for God's people, and resurrection; the belief that the End is imminent; a vision of reality that is cosmic in scope; and finally belief in the sovereignty of God who will bring about the fufilment of his people's hopes. It thus emerges that the End which is imminent is an End which has certain specific characteristics. Now I do not see that Käsemann would want to quarrel with this definition. What he has done is to draw attention to the characteristically Christian element, the parousia or coming of the Son of Man, that is—for Christians—of Jesus. That is perhaps fair enough, but I shall suggest in a moment that simply to talk of an imminent parousia can open the door to a wrong emphasis.

However, it would be wrong to pass over the fact that another, rather different, definition of apocalyptic has been given by C. Rowland. He agrees with G. Bornkamm that 'the disclosure of divine secrets is the true theme of later Jewish apocalyptic',[15] and cites other authors to the same effect. In his own words, 'Apocalyptic, therefore, is a type of religion whose distinguishing feature is a belief in a direct revelation of the things of God which was mediated through dream, vision or divine intermediary'.[16] Adopting this definition, he is able to show that apocalyptic did not have a special view of eschatology, and that, while apocalyptic is often concerned with eschatological issues, there is not a distinctive apocalyptic eschatology. Hence eschatology should not be made the basis of a definition of apocalyptic, and consequently some texts which are often said to be apocalyptic are not really so at all. However, this definition does do justice to a body of literature which can properly be called apocalyptic.

This is not the place to evaluate Rowland's work in detail, but I must confess that I find it generally persuasive. The point that emerges is that Käsemann has produced a definition of apocalyptic in terms of eschatology which is inappropriate. However, the effect of this point is not to make Käsemann's or Dunn's presentation immediately untenable. For we can still ask whether it is the case that 'the expectation of an imminent parousia is the mother of Christian theology', and obviously this statement may be true or false quite independently of whether this expectation has been incorrectly labelled as apocalyptic. We can also of course ask the separate question whether eschatology would be a better candidate for the motherhood of theology.[17]

Thus we find that Käsemann has really raised three possible questions. First, the place of the expectation of an imminent parousia in early Christianity. Second, the place of apocalyptic ideas and imagery in the traditional sense of that term. And third, the place of apocalyptic understood as belief in the direct revelation of the things of God.

The second point that I wish to make concerns the place of expectation of the imminent parousia in early Christianity. We saw that Käsemann reached his conclusions about this on the basis of a form-critical analysis of certain materials in Matthew which understood the texts primarily as witnesses to a life-setting in the early Church and denied that they brought us into direct contact with the historical Jesus. Let me make three comments on this point.

First, we observed that Dunn was able to show the presence of an apocalyptic, or, as we should better say, an eschatological strand in early Christianity which emphasized the imminence of the parousia without resorting to the sceptical estimate of the gospel material as authentic Jesus-tradition which was advocated by Käsemann. It is not necessary to share Käsemann's excessively sceptical attitude to the gospel tradition in order to show the presence of expectation of the imminent return of Jesus in the early Church.

Second, the evidence assembled by Dunn does demonstrate the existence and importance of this belief. There is no way in which the significant position of the hope of the imminent parousia in the early Church can be denied. There have certainly been attempts to do so, but they can hardly be pronounced successful.[18]

Third, in particular Käsemann's attempt to deny that Jesus shared a belief in the parousia is a failure. Even if the texts that he discusses from Matthew were church creations, there remains a sufficient basis of material in Mark and Q to disprove his contention. Dunn has pointed out the unlikelihood of a non-apocalyptic Jesus standing between an apocalyptic John the Baptist and an apocalyptic primitive Church. He has also argued that Jesus' message of the immediacy of God is integrally related to his doctrine of the imminent future of the kingly rule of God which is already being manifested in his own ministry. In short, the hope of the parousia is to be found right through the teaching of Jesus and of the early Church.[19]

But this conclusion raises the third point that I want to make. Granted that the imminent parousia was part of early Christian thinking, did it occupy such a place that it can rightly be called the mother of Christian theology? Again, the question of definition comes up, because Käsemann has used the metaphor of motherhood without indicating unambiguously what it is meant to convey. He could mean that this hope was the central, the most significant, belief in early Christianity. He could also mean that it was thinking about this belief which was the earliest kind of theological thinking carried on by the early Christians, and that it was out of this thinking that more developed theology arose. To prove the latter point, Käsemann would need to give some kind of demonstration of how Christian theology developed in this womb, and he has not done this. But the two questions need to be answered: 1. Was the imminent parousia the central motif in early Christian theology? 2. Can early Christian theology be shown to have developed from this matrix?

I should want to argue that, while the imminent parousia was an important motif in early Christian theology, it did not occupy the central position that Käsemann claims for it. First of all, E. Lohse has remarked how the earliest expressions of the gospel that we possess make little or no reference to the parousia. First Corinthians 15.3-5 is generally recognized to be a very early summary of the gospel, and it is concerned with the death, burial, resurrection and appearances of Christ, and not with his future coming. The same is true of other passages, such as Romans 1.3-4; 4.25; 10.9-10. If there is an eschatological event that is proclaimed here, it is the resurrection of Jesus, not his parousia. But this was an eschatological belief which was common to most of Judaism, and the Christian novelty was in believing that in the case of Jesus the resurrection had already happened.

From this fact Lohse concludes:

> It is clear that the origin of Christian theology is not to be found in apocalyptic—be it in Jewish expectation, or be it in primitive Christian enthusiasm—but it lies in the kerygma that preaches the crucified Christ as the risen Lord. Käsemann's thesis . . . receives no confirmation from the oldest expressions of Christian preaching and the confession of the earliest church. The origin and centre of primitive Christian theology lies rather from the beginning in the word of the cross.[20]

Second, there is a lot of evidence to show that the beginnings of Christian theology lie in study of the Old Testament Scriptures, a study that was much broader than being confined simply to the apocalyptic parts of the Old Testament. Although it is true that Daniel was an important text for the early Church, it was probably not the most important—even if M. Casey goes too far in playing down its influence.[21]

Third, we ask just how important a place expectation of the imminent parousia had in the thinking of the early Christians. Following Käsemann, various scholars have argued that the very earliest stage in Christianity was one of hoping for the return of Jesus as the Son of man, and that, for example, the earliest use of the Christological titles was in connection with the parousia. F. Hahn in particular has argued for an evolution in Christological thinking along these lines.[22] But what is the evidence? If we turn back to Dunn's summary, we note that first he mentions the use of apocalyptic category of resurrection by the early Christians to express their new faith.[23] What this shows, however, is that they were confronted by an experience for which there was no other explanation, rather than that they deliberately chose a category which arose out of their conviction that the End was at hand. One might say that their conviction that Jesus was risen led them to believe that they were living in the last days.[24] We may add to this the fact of their experience of the Spirit which, according to Acts 2.17-18, was seen as a sign of the fulfilment of prophecy and as a token that the last days had dawned. Second, Dunn mentions the daily expectation of the parousia. He cites as evidence the 'Maranatha' cry, the hope expressed in Acts 3.19-21, the sayings about the coming of the Son of man preserved in Q, and, we may add, the evidence of 1 Thessalonians about the content of Paul's preaching. This evidence certainly points to the hope of the parousia as imminent. The question is whether it signifies that there was a 'daily' expectation. Third, Dunn mentions the Israel-centredness of the early Christians with their hopes of eschatological renewal at the temple. But this evidence surely suggests rather that the early Christians regarded Jesus as establishing true Judaism, and that they naturally used the temple as he did—as the place for true worship of God and teaching about his Kingdom. To deduce that they had a 'very narrow' outlook[25] is unjustified.

What we may take from this evidence is that the expectation of the parousia must be seen in the context of belief in the resurrection and consequent vindication and exaltation of Jesus and in the context of the present experience of the Spirit. One can certainly conclude that the early Christians were apocalyptically minded in that they believed that they were living in the last days, but their horizon was not formed exclusively by the hope of the imminent parousia. The resurrection of Jesus and the gift of the Spirit as immediate experiences must have been of basic importance, and it was out of their present experience of Jesus that they were led to cry 'Maranatha'.

We may strengthen this argument further by observing that the parousia and the associated events are rarely the occasion of specific teaching in the New Testament. On the whole, the references are incidental and they occur in contexts that suggest that they may have had their home in Christian worship. We do not get the impression that teaching about the parousia was the central element in Christian instruction or in evangelism. Of course, we do have the apocalyptic material in the Gospels and the teaching of Paul about the parousia. But it must be noted that it is difficult to know just how the gospel material was related to the kerygma and catechetical instruction of the early Church. There are in fact two opposing errors in this area. On the one hand, Käsemann tends to emphasize the importance of the gospel material and to play down the kerygma in his discussion of the earliest Church. On the other hand, W. Schmithals has argued that the gospel tradition exerted little or no influence in the early Church and is largely a literary creation from a period later than Paul.[26] Somehow a balance between these extreme viewpoints must be achieved. As regards the Pauline evidence, it is noteworthy that his discussions of eschatology are largely concerned with the problem of the resurrection (1 Thess. 4; 1 Cor. 15; 2 Cor. 5), and when he does discuss the parousia specifically (2 Thess. 2), it is to correct people who imagined that it would happen immediately. The gospel apocalyptic material in its present form has a twofold concern: to warn people to be ready for what may take them unawares, and to warn them equally not to be misled by suggestions that the Day of the Lord is already present. The problems are how far the intense expectations which are combatted here represent any kind of 'mainstream' Christian thinking, and whether this element of caution goes back to the earliest days or reflects a later stage at which the delay of the parousia was a problem. I would claim that there is evidence in the Gospels that Jesus did allow for an interval before the parousia, and hence that the early Church had this element of caution right from the start.[27]

When all this has been said, it is of course undeniable that the gospel tradition contains statements—perhaps one should say numerous statements—which are future-related in one way or another. Whether or not they were spoken by Jesus exactly as we have them, they were handed down in the Church and known to the Church. It is important not to play down their significance, perhaps because we find them strange and want to construct a Jesus and an early Church that fit in with our preconceptions of what they ought to be like. However, the conclusion that I would want to draw at this stage is that, while the hope of the parousia formed an important part of the horizon of early Christianity, to speak of it as the mother of Christian theology is unjustified. Rowland puts the point well:

What Dunn has indicated is the way in which eschatology dominated early Christian theology. Most of the ideas he collects point to early Christianity as an eschatologically-orientated community, whose expectation about the future is distinguished, not so much by the so-called 'apocalyptic' elements, but by the earnest conviction that the hopes of Judaism were already in the process of being realized. They believed that the final climax of history was imminent, not because they had utilized a particular brand of eschatology, but because their beliefs about Jesus and their experience of the Spirit had led them to understand their circumstances in this particular way.[28]

Fourth, we saw that Käsemann regarded the apocalyptic theology of early Christianity as discredited by the fact that the parousia never happened. At the same time he wanted to hold on to this hope. Käsemann goes astray because he assumes 1. that the expectation of the early Church was delimited, i.e., one could set a kind of *terminus ante quem* for its occurrence, and 2. that a hope which has dragged out for 1,900 years must surely be a mistaken one. Various comments can be made about this. The first is that the fact that the time of waiting has turned out to be long is no indication that the early Church would have regarded the hope as unreal or illusory. It has often been pointed out that the hope still burns brightly in what are probably among the latest books of the New Testament, such as 2 Timothy, 2 Peter and Revelation. If we bear in mind that the early Christians regarded the prophecies of Isaiah and others as not finding fulfilment until their own time, centuries after they were given, we can assume that they may have been prepared for a period of waiting. There is, to be sure, a difference in that the early Christians did believe that they were living in the era of fulfilment, and one might ask just how long the time would have to drag on before Christians would regard the coming of Jesus not as the beginning of the End time but rather as the middle or centre point of history—and Käsemann would presumably argue that precisely this did happen. But I am dubious whether the idea of 'the middle of time' is a New Testament idea, and my impression is that the early Christians thought of themselves as living in the last days. Further, it is important to ask whether A. L. Moore is not right in arguing that the time of the parousia is not delimited in the New Testament; there is no place in which it is categorically affirmed that it must come within a definite time interval.[29] The real question is whether an interval of 1,900 years is not so far beyond the horizon of the New Testament writers as to alter seriously the whole content of the hope: can we in fact proclaim the imminence of the parousia in the same way as the first Christians did? May we sing 'Soon and very soon we are going to see the King' with the parousia rather than our own death and resurrection in mind?

It lies beyond the scope of this essay in New Testament criticism to defend the view that in the hope of the parousia we have an element of Christian faith and hope which we are too easily led to surrender or to keep quiet about. The passage of time has not disproved the hope of his coming. If the hope of the imminent parousia of Jesus is not the mother of Christian theology, it is certainly the near horizon. 'For now is our salvation nearer than when we first believed. The night is far gone; the day is at hand' (Rom. 13.11-12).

Notes

[1]E. Käsemann, 'The Beginnings of Christian Theology' and 'On the Subject of Primitive Christian Apocalyptic', in *New Testament Questions of Today* (London, 1969), pp. 82-107, 108-37. See the excellent summary and analysis of his work by W. G. Rollins, 'The New Testament and Apocalypic', *NTS* 17, 1970-71, pp. 454-76. For the original responses to Käsemann's views, see R. W. Funk (ed.), *Apocalypticism* (*JTC*, 6, New York, 1969), which includes essays by G. Ebeling, E. Fuchs and other scholars, together with reprints of Käsemann's two essays. See also the critical comments by R. Bultmann, 'Ist die Apokalyptik die Mutter der christlichen Theologie? Eine Auseinandersetzung mit Ernst Käsemann', in *Exegetica* (Tübingen, 1967), pp. 476-82. The more recent work by J. C. Beker, *Paul the Apostle: The Triumph of God in Life and Thought* (Edinburgh, 1980), is important for its claim that the theology of Paul is thoroughly apocalyptic in character; the issues raised by it are too wide to be discussed here, especially since our topic is the origin of Christian theology rather than its Pauline development.

[2]Käsemann, *Questions,* p. 109, n. 1.

[3]Käsemann, 'Sentences of Holy Law in the New Testament', in *Questions,* pp. 66-81.

[4]Käsemann, *Questions,* p. 92.

[5]Ibid., p. 102.

[6]Ibid., p. 101.

[7]Ibid., pp. 113-14.

[8]Ibid., pp. 101-2.

[9]Ibid., p. 121.

[10]Ibid., p. 137.

[11]Ibid., p. 106.

[12]Ibid., p. 107.

[13]J. D. G. Dunn, *Unity and Diversity in the New Testament* (London, 1977), p. 236.

[14]Ibid., p. 325.

[15]G. Bornkamm, *TDNT,* IV, p. 815.

[16]C. Rowland, *The Open Heaven* (London, 1982), p. 21.

[17]Ibid., p. 355.

[18]For attempts to play down the existence of the hope of the parousia in some areas of the early Church, see T. F. Glasson, *The Second Advent: The Origin of the New Testament Doctrine.* (London, 1945, 1963). *His Appearing and His Kingdom: The Christian Hope in the Light of its History* (London, 1953), J. A. T. Robinson, *Jesus and His Coming: The Emergence of a Doctrine*

(London, 1957).

[19]The fact that Jesus believed in the imminent future coming of the End and the Kingdom of God seems to me to be well established despite the critical doubts that exist about the authenticity of some of the sayings about the future activity of the Son of man.

[20]E. Lohse, 'Apokalyptik and Christologie', *ZNW*, 62, 1971, 48-67; citation from 58. Cf. W. Schneemelcher, *Das Urchristentum* (Stuttgart, 1981), pp. 113-14.

[21]M. Casey, *Son of Man: The Interpretation and Influence of Daniel 7* (London, 1980).

[22]F. Hahn, *The Titles of Jesus in Christology* (Guildford, 1969).

[23]Dunn, *Unity*, p. 323.

[24]G. Lohfink, 'Der Ablauf der Osterereignisse und die Anfänge der Urgemeinde', *TQ*, 160, 1980, pp. 167-76.

[25]Dunn, *Unity*, p. 324.

[26]W. Schmithals, *Das Evangelium nach Markus* (Gütersloh and Würzburg, 1979).

[27]G. R. Beasley-Murray, *Jesus and the Kingdom of God* (Grand Rapids, 1986).

[28]Rowland, *Open Heaven*, p. 355.

[29]A. L. Moore, *The Parousia in the New Testament* (Leiden, 1966).

Part II
The Person of Jesus

4
The Synoptic Son of Man Sayings in Recent Discussion

Ⅰ N RECENT YEARS THERE APPEARED TO HAVE DEVELOPED a
general consensus of opinion in the English-speaking world about the use
of the term 'Son of man' in the Synoptic Gospels which may be summed up
as follows: Jesus adopted the title 'Son of man' from Daniel 7, where it
signifies one who was destined to receive kingship from God, and used it
with reference to himself in three types of saying, namely, group A with
reference to his present activity in his earthly ministry; group B with reference to his suffering, death and resurrection; and group C with reference
to his future coming, exaltation and function at the last judgement.[1] Genuine
sayings of Jesus are to be found in each of these three categories, and together they give us a picture of Jesus as One destined for triumph and
sovereignty but achieving this destiny by the path of humiliation, rejection
and suffering which was prophesied for the Servant of Yahweh. It is often
held that Jesus' use of the title may have had a certain 'collective' nuance; just
as in Daniel 7 it indicated a representative or symbol of the saints of the Most
High, so in the Gospels it may refer to the people of God whose head Jesus
conceived himself to be.[2]

During the past seventy years and more this understanding of the title has
been subject to strong criticism in the German-speaking world, the effects
of which have begun to exercise a popular influence in England only within
the last few years.[3] We propose in the present essay to examine the validity
of the principles and presuppositions which govern this new approach and
to inquire how far the traditional English understanding of Jesus' use of the
title requires modification.

1. There has been considerable discussion whether the term 'Son of man' could be used as a title in Aramaic. The phrase ὁ υἱὸς τοῦ ἀνθρώπου, which is a monstrosity in Greek, was certainly understood as a title by the Evangelists, but was the underlying Aramaic phrase used as a title? In 1896 H. Lietzmann argued that the phrase *bar nash(a)* was a generic term meaning 'man' and did not have a titular sense. Later scholars have in general rejected Lietzmann's denial that the phrase could be used in a titular sense, but have accepted the possibility that in some cases the Evangelists may have misunderstood an original generic use of the term and made it into a title.[4]

A further point is of considerable importance: could the phrase be used as a circumlocution for 'I' or 'me', referring to the speaker himself? This view was championed for a number of sayings by T. W. Manson and J. Y. Campbell, but recently it has been strongly attacked by P. Vielhauer, who cites in his favour M. Black.[5] Vielhauer, however, has evidently overlooked the fact that Black has drawn attention to one example of *bar nash* meaning 'I who speak',[6] and consequently the possibility of a non-titular use to refer to the speaker cannot be ruled out of court. This means that the possibility of ambiguity in the use of the phrase by Jesus (as a circumlocution for 'I' or as a title) cannot be excluded.[7]

2. The attempt to deny Jesus' use of the title 'Son of man' on philological grounds is scarcely successful. A second method of attack, developed by W. Bousset, seeks to achieve the same end by psychological considerations: it is held to be psychologically impossible that Jesus could have referred to himself by the title of Son of man. 'If', wrote Bousset, 'the Son of man, according to what appears to be commonly accepted now, can denote only the supraterrestrial transcendent Messiah, it is inexplicable how Jesus could already in the present claim for himself the designation and the rights of the Son of Man'.[8] Nor, holds Bultmann, could Jesus have regarded himself as the 'Son of man designate': such an idea is 'too fantastic'.[9] To accept the title of Son of man would be tantamount to claiming divinity, and in the opinion of J. Knox this is something that no sane or good man could possibly claim.[10]

No doubt a sane or good *man* could not claim this title, but, if the evidence of early Christian faith is to be accepted, Jesus was raised from the dead and declared to be the Son of God (Rom. 1.4). Moreover, a critical scrutiny of the Gospels shows other evidence than the disputed use of 'Son of man', which demonstrates that Jesus was conscious of a unique position in the saving plan of God and of a unique relationship of Sonship to God. Within the limits of the present essay this point cannot be developed,[11] but we believe that there is enough evidence to forbid us to rule out *a priori* the possibility that Jesus could have used this title to refer to himself.

3. A third attempt to deny the authenticity of a considerable number of Son of man sayings must also be noted at this point. In his discussion of the sayings about death and resurrection (group B), R. Bultmann asked rhetorically, 'Can there be any doubt that they are all *vaticinia ex eventu?*'[12] A negative answer to this question has seemed to be so obvious to many critics that P. Vielhauer did not think it necessary even to analyse this group of sayings in either of his two articles on our theme.[13]

Such a wholesale rejection of this group of sayings depends upon the arguments that prophecy is impossible (all prophecy must take place after the event), that the sayings in question reflect in detail the passion narrative, that the surprise of the disciples at the course of events is inexplicable if they had already been forewarned by Jesus about his passion, and that the sayings show no contact with those in group C which speak of the exaltation (and not the resurrection) of the Son of man. What, then, is the origin of these sayings? Bultmann was inclined to attribute them to the inventive faculty of his hypothetical Hellenistic communities, but H. E. Tödt has argued from their language that a Palestinian background is more likely.[14]

We may note that a dogmatic denial of the possibility of genuine prophecy is not supported by all scholars, and there are some who are prepared to admit that Jesus did speak of his coming death and even of his resurrection, although the sayings may have been partially rewritten in the light of their fulfilment.[15] It would be a notable sign of lack of scholarly objectivity if an *a priori* denial of the possibility of prophecy were made a decisive argument against the authenticity of these sayings. The real arguments against these sayings are accordingly the third and fourth of those mentioned above.[16] We may postpone consideration of the fourth for the moment, but, with regard to the third, 'it may be replied that the disciples probably were quite unable really to accept what he said about his death, particularly perhaps about his dying rejected by the rulers of Israel. That they should be taken by surprise in spite of his teaching on the subject is surely not really surprising!'[17]

4. Although all the Son of man sayings were regarded by the Evangelists as referring to Jesus himself, despite the fact that they are expressed in the third person, it is not equally plain from the context that in every case Jesus was using a self-designation. In one saying, which has been handed down in two forms in the tradition, there is a *prima facie* differentiation between the speaker and another person who is to appear in the future: 'And I tell you, everyone who acknowledges me before men, the Son of man also will acknowledge before the angels of God; but he who denies me before men will be denied before the angels of God' (Luke 12.8f., par. Matt. 10.32, Q; cf. Mark 8.38 and pars.). In the light of this saying, which in the opinion of

most critics can hardly be an invention by the primitive Church, it has been suggested that Jesus distinguished between himself and a future Son of man.[18]

On the basis of these considerations a plausible theory concerning the Son of man sayings may now be erected. If Jesus did not refer to himself as the Son of man (point 2), it is possible to accept sayings of group C as authentic utterances of Jesus about his expectation of a coming Son of man not identified with himself; it goes without saying that the authenticity of each individual saying must be critically considered. Sayings in group B about Jesus as the suffering and rising Son of man are incompatible with those in group C in which Jesus is not identified with the Son of man, and must be creations of the early Church. Finally, the sayings in group A, which refer to the present activity of Jesus as the Son of man cannot be genuine since they also conflict with the ideas expressed in group C; they either are due to a misunderstanding of *bar nash(a)* used generically (point 1) or are community creations. This view, which is essentially that of R. Bultmann,[19] is confirmed by two further considerations.

5. Our oldest Gospel source, Q, contains no sayings from group B; it is the later source Mark which is the first to bring together sayings of all three types. Thus the suspicion that the passion and resurrection sayings are late creations is confirmed by the results of source criticism.

6. Moreover, as was indicated above, sayings of group C refer to exaltation but not to resurrection, but sayings of group B refer to resurrection but not to exaltation. This indicates the existence of two contradictory strands of tradition which have not been unified (except in such a secondary grouping of sayings as Luke 17.22 ff.), and since it is arguable that exaltation is a more primitive concept than the *(post eventum)* concept of resurrection, the priority of group C sayings is again confirmed.[20]

7. One final principle remains to be mentioned. In 1957 P. Vielhauer brought forward the argument that neither in Jewish teaching nor in the authentic teaching of Jesus are the concepts of the Kingdom of God and the Son of man brought into any kind of relationship with each other. There is no saying of Jesus which links the two concepts. Further, the two concepts are mutually exclusive and irreconcilable. Consequently, since the Kingdom of God formed a definite part of the teaching of Jesus, it follows that the concept of the Son of man played no part in his thought.

Recent discussion of the Son of man has had to reckon with these seven principles, and we may proceed to summarize the four main types of theory which have been expressed in the so-called post-Bultmannian era.

(a) P. Vielhauer has not hesitated to take his argument to its logical conclusion, and in his two articles cited above he has found grounds for denying the authenticity of all the Son of man sayings.[21] He has found notable followers in H. Conzelmann[22] and H. M. Teeple.[23]

(b) At the opposite extreme, a position very similar to that characteristic of the English-speaking world has been adopted by E. Stauffer, who holds that Jesus spoke of himself as the Son of man and accepts sayings from all three groups as authentic. In his more recent writings, however, Stauffer has shown himself to be increasingly suspicious of the presence of apocalyptic elements in the teaching of Jesus and would not accept many sayings in group C as authentic.[24] Stauffer's position is shared by his former pupil E. Bammel, who has faced up to the argument of P. Vielhauer regarding the Kingdom of God and the Son of man and adopted the novel answer of taking the other horn of the dilemma: i.e., he plays down the importance of the Kingdom of God in the teaching of Jesus and holds that the Son of man was his central theme.[25]

(c) What is essentially the position of Bultmann has been upheld by the writers of the two fullest contributions to the debate. A hint of what was to come was given by G. Bornkamm in 1956 in his book *Jesus von Nazareth*. Here great importance was attached to Luke 12.8f. as a saying in which Jesus distinguished the Son of man from himself but made a tremendous claim for the authority of his own teaching in that men's decision for or against Jesus would be ratified by the Son of man at the last judgement.[26] Then in 1959 came the full-length exposition of the same position by Bornkamm's pupil, H. E. Tödt. This work makes a number of notable contributions to our understanding of the concept.

First, Tödt is concerned primarily with the use of the Son of man concept in the Christology of the early Church rather than with the authenticity of the sayings of Jesus. He holds that our understanding of the synoptic presentation of Jesus has been governed too much by the influence of Philippians 2.5-11, a passage which speaks of the pre-existence, humiliation and exaltation of Jesus. The Son of man in the Gospels has been assumed to be pre-existent (cf. 1 Enoch for the basis of this idea); humiliated, in that his glory is concealed under the guise of an ordinary man and he is destined (as the suffering Servant of Yahweh) to suffer and die; and exalted, whether at his resurrection (group B) or his parousia (group C). So far as the teaching of Jesus himself is concerned, Tödt will have none of these things; the Son of man, as in Bultmann's exposition, is a figure other than Jesus.

Secondly, the basic notion in the Son of man sayings, as other scholars had dimly perceived earlier, is the authority and sovereignty of Jesus. In the genuine sayings from group C, Jesus demonstrated his own authority by the claim that the Son of man would be the heavenly guarantor of the validity of the fellowship now established between him and the disciples. The early Church then identified the risen Jesus with the coming Son of man and proceeded to read back the title into the earthly ministry of Jesus as a means of expressing his authority on earth (group A sayings). It did not clothe the earthly Jesus with the glorious trappings of the transcendent Son of man of apocalyptic tradition, but used the title creatively to express the earthly authority of Jesus as he confronted 'this generation'. A further stage in development was the use of the title to refer to the way in which the sovereign figure of Jesus was opposed by men and put to death (group B sayings).

Thirdly, this analysis is made the basis of a distinction between two types of Christology in the early Church. The one, found in Mark and Paul, depicted Jesus as Saviour in terms of the passion kerygma, and used the sayings in Mark 10.45 and 14.24 as links with the Son of man tradition. The other, found in Q, saw Jesus as the authoritative teacher. For the community that created Q, the significance of the resurrection was that it indicated the divine validation of the earthly authority of Jesus and confirmed the legitimacy of the community's task of gathering together and proclaiming the teaching of Jesus.

The significance of this approach is twofold. On the one hand, it represents a notable attempt to recreate the situation in the early Church in which the Son of man tradition was preserved and developed. Tödt recognizes clearly that he who denies a *Sitz im Leben* in the life of Jesus for a saying must produce a convincing substitute in the life of the early Church, and he deals with this problem meticulously. On the other hand, he has drawn attention to the importance of Q as a source which is all too easily dismissed from Christological discussion, and has tried to show that it contained a view of the person of Jesus quite different from that of Paul, which (if Tödt's case is sound) must be taken into careful consideration by dogmatic theology.

A similar position is adopted by A. J. B. Higgins, who has evidently written his book very much under the influence of Tödt. Certainly his earlier article surveying Son of man *Forschung*[27] contained little hint of the way in which his own decision would fall. His book has its own value alongside that of Tödt in that it chooses a wider area for investigation and brings the Johannine teaching into the picture—although only to show that it is irrelevant for the question of the teaching of the historical Jesus. He does not display the same interest as Tödt in examining the development of the concept of the Son of man in the early Church but rather concentrates his attention on the mind of Jesus himself. In so doing, he isolates a somewhat different set of authentic sayings from Tödt but they all come from the same category (group C), and he is also prepared to accept that a number of other sayings may have been spoken by Jesus in the first person, the substitution of 'Son of man' for 'I' being due to the early Church. Like Tödt he holds that the influence of Daniel 7 on Jesus was minimal. Where Higgins differs most from Tödt is in his estimate of the relation of Jesus to the Son of man. He expresses this by saying that 'the Son of man idea was adapted by Jesus to denote himself as the Son of God he already believed himself to be, reinstalled in his heavenly seat'.[28] Jesus expected a time in the future when he would perform 'Son of man' functions (the inverted commas are important), and it was not a difficult step for the early Church to think of him as actually the Son of man. In his attitude to the other teaching of Jesus, Higgins is basically conservative, and believes that many of the ideas which are expressed in the inauthentic Son of man sayings may be found elsewhere in the teaching of Jesus. Finally, we may note that he believes that he has solved Vielhauer's dilemma in that Jesus did not think of his mission in relation to the Kingdom of God in terms of the Son of man at all.[29]

(d) A quite different approach to the problem has been made by E. Schweizer, who has also reinvestigated the Son of man concept in the light of Vielhauer's thesis.[30] Schweizer begins by arguing that the fact that 'Son of man' is a phrase confined almost exclusively to the lips of Jesus is strong proof of the authenticity of at least some of the sayings. He then makes his own analysis of the material and finds that none of the sayings in group C is indisputably authentic, although there is evidence that Jesus referred to the functions of the Son of man as witness at the last judgement. Nor are the predictions of the passion (group B) authentic in their present form. The new element in Schweizer's presentation is his argument that the sayings about the earthly activity of Jesus as the Son of man (group A) have the strongest claims to authenticity. 'The Son of man described in those sayings which seem to be original is a man who lives a lowly life on earth, rejected, humiliated, handed over to his opponents, but eventually exalted by God and designed to be the chief witness in the last judgement'.[31] This picture is derived from the Jewish concept of the humiliation and exaltation of the righteous man. In this way the Son of man is seen to be a concept independent of that of the Kingdom, and so Vielhauer's dilemma is avoided.

It may be appropriate at this point to mention the contribution of M. Black, who has recently added to a series of distinguished essays on our theme[32] a survey of the work of T. W. Manson, P. Vielhauer and E. Schweizer. Black feels that the importance of Vielhauer's arguments can easily be overestimated and that Schweizer's list of genuine texts looks as if it has been tailored to fit a particular theory. In his earlier writings he himself upheld a much more traditional position. His new contribution is to carry further Schweizer's suggestion that the exaltation of Jesus is in some ways a more primitive idea than the resurrection; there was a pre-Pauline Christology of exaltation which has left widespread traces in the New Testament (including the 'hymn' in Phil. 2.5-11, which is thus, *pace* Tödt, linked to the Son of man Christology), and it may be that Jesus himself spoke in terms of exaltation rather than of resurrection (cf. John 3.14). Black is also prepared to find a collective sense in the references to the functions of the exalted Son of man at the last judgement.[33]

We may terminate our descriptive survey of recent work at this point. It has emerged that there is no consensus at present regarding the place of the Son of man in the teaching of Jesus. We have confined our attention to this point and not attempted to deal with the other problems at present under discussion, such as the sources of the term in Judaism and its meaning there, the relation of the Son of man to the 'Man' of much near-Eastern speculation, and the problems associated with the 'messianic' secret in the teaching of Jesus. But the area which has been isolated for survey is to some extent a unit capable of being examined by itself, and we may now proceed to examine it more critically.

As a preliminary step, it needs to be reiterated that here, as in all areas of biblical study, it is essential to avoid coming to the subject with fixed, preconceived notions. P. C. Hodgson has attempted to show that in earlier studies of our problem two presuppositions governed progress. First, on the basis of a particular theological judgement one group of sayings was declared authentic. Thus both R. Bultmann and J. Knox held to the authenticity of sayings in group C which fitted in with their ideas about the self-consciousness of Jesus. Then, secondly, 'invariably the argument for inauthenticity of one group of sayings rests upon a prior judgement that another group, or groups, *are* authentic'.[34] Hodgson commends Tödt for being free from this error. Serious advance can be made only by unbiased examination of the actual texts.

Closely linked with this danger is that of argument in a circle. In his examination of the sayings in Q, A. J. B. Higgins discusses the theory that Luke 9.58 (par. Matt. 8.20) may be a parallel to the passion sayings in Mark. But 'the understanding of the saying as an indirect passion prediction is greatly weakened by the absence from Q of any other sayings which could be so described'. He goes on to argue later, 'there are formidable difficulties in the way of taking Matthew 12.40 as the older form [sc. than Luke 11.30]. It would be the only allusion in Q to the death and resurrection of the Son of man'. But it would be equally logical to use these two texts to bolster up a passion interpretation in both of them. Moreover, we find with some astonishment that Higgins has in fact admitted that 'the passion did not lie completely outside the interests of Q', a reference to it being found in Luke 13.34f. (par. Matt. 23.37-39). One cannot therefore assume that texts in Q cannot refer to the passion, and it is equally clear that no weight can be attached to Higgins's further logical deduction: 'The upshot is that the absence of sayings of this category from a source which is almost entirely a collection of sayings may be adduced as further corroborative evidence for the inauthenticity of sayings about the passion of the Son of man elsewhere such as we have encountered in Mark and Luke'.[35] On the contrary, we may use the evidence of the sayings in Mark and Luke to strengthen the case for finding references to the passion in Q—that is, if we are going to place any weight on this sort of procedure at all.

More serious considerations than this must obviously guide us in forming a judgement about the place of the Son of man in the teaching of Jesus.

1. We may begin with the most radical argument, that of P. Vielhauer that the Kingdom of God and the Son of man are mutually irreconcilable concepts; they are not brought together in Jewish sources, and therefore it is unlikely that they could have been brought together in the teaching of Jesus—indeed they are never linked in his teaching. Three points may be made.

(a) Although both concepts are rare in apocalyptic and rabbinic Judaism, so that in the nature of things frequent contacts between them are unlikely, there are in fact links between them. We may remind ourselves of the wording in Daniel 7.13f: 'With the clouds of heaven there came one like a *son of man*, and he came to the Ancient of Days and was presented before him. And to him was given *dominion* and glory and *kingdom*, that all peoples, nations and languages should *serve* him; his *dominion* is an everlasting *dominion* which shall not pass away, and his *kingdom* one that shall not be destroyed.' One would have thought that comment on the juxtaposition of Son of man, dominion and kingdom in this text was entirely superfluous. Vielhauer, however, holds that the Son of man is not regarded in the vision or its interpretation as an individual, heavenly person, but is a symbol for the eternal heavenly kingdom.[36] This is a manifest misinterpretation of the text. So far as the interpretation of the vision is concerned, the Son of man is the representative or symbol of the saints of the Most High (Dan. 7.18, 22, 27). If he is their representative, he is most naturally thought of as their head, in which case we should probably see a 'messianic' reference here.[37] If, on the other hand, he is a symbol for the saints, we would have a basis for the 'collective' view of the Son of man advocated by T. W. Manson. The first of these alternatives is preferable, but in either case the Son of man is not a symbol of rule but of a ruler or rulers, and the desired link between the Kingdom of God and the Son of man is plainly made. Vielhauer's case rests upon an analysis of the chapter to determine its original form, but, whether or not his analysis is correct, it commits the basic error of failing to ask how a first-century Jew, unlearned in source criticism, would have understood the passage. It is strange that H. E. Tödt makes no attempt to counter Vielhauer's exegesis of this text; perhaps this is because of his (improbable) assumption that Daniel 7 exercised no influence on the mind of Jesus.[38]

It is true that the Kingdom does not figure in 4 Esdras 13, but it is hard to see how the idea of rule is to be excluded from 1 Enoch 69.26-28 where the Son of man sits upon a *throne*, abides forever, and eradicates sinners from the earth: could kingship be more emphatically asserted without using the word itself? It may not be irrelevant to note than in Revelation 14.14 the Son of man wears a *crown* and inaugurates the eschatalogical judgement, while in 1.13 he takes on the lineaments of the Ancient of Days.

There are of course Kingdom texts in both apocalyptic and rabbinic Judaism in which the Son of man is not mentioned. But this is because 'Son of man' was a rare concept, brought into connection with the Kingdom only in a limited part of the apocalyptic tradition. The Kingdom can certainly be described without reference to the Son of man; in rabbinic Judaism it is a transcendent, heavenly concept, and is not linked to the coming of the Messiah. But, since the Son of man is more of a heavenly, transcendent figure than the Messiah, there does not seem to be any compelling reason against his association with the Kingdom of God—an association which, as we have seen, is made in two of the texts.

(b) In any case, we have no right to limit what was and was not possible for the mind of Jesus by reference to current categories of thought. If Jesus was in any sense a creative thinker, he could easily transcend the categories of thought of his time, make new associations, and fill out old concepts with new meaning.[39] Even, then, if Vielhauer's estimate of the Jewish literature were correct, it would not greatly affect what Jesus himself was capable of thinking. If, further, Jesus was governed more by the apocalyptic than by the rabbinic concept of the Kingdom—a point made, admittedly with some exaggeration, by N. Perrin[40]—he would not have seen any incongruity in using the symbol of the Son of man.

(c) We may also ask whether there really would have been any tension in the mind of Jesus between the concepts of the Kingdom of God and the Son of man. Certainly no undisputed saying links together the Kingdom and the Son of man.[41] The most that can be shown is that Kingdom and Son of man sayings are juxtaposed in the same strata of Gospel tradition, whether originally or as a result of compilation.[42] But this shows that the Evangelists were certainly not conscious of any incongruity between the two types of saying. It may well be that the relationship between the two concepts did not demand their fusion with each other. E. Schweizer has noted that Jesus' teaching about the Kingdom and his ethical instruction are not always brought into close connection with each other.[43] Vielhauer has rendered the important service of raising the question of the relation between the Kingdom and the Son of man in the teaching of Jesus, but it is by no means obvious that his assessment of that relationship is the right one. We are at liberty to examine the Son of man sayings without presupposing the truth of his theory. Principle no. 7 in our original enumeration has been shown to be very hollow.

2. We must now ask whether Jesus identified himself with the Son of man or not. The view that the genuine sayings of Jesus (as admitted by Bultmann and his followers) refer to another person rests on the unlikelihood of Jesus identifing himself with the transcendent Son of man (principle 2) and on the sayings where a distinction appears to be drawn between Jesus and the future Son of man (principle 4). We examined the former of these two principles earlier and concluded that it represented an arbitrary and indeed a false assumption. We must now consider the second principle.

It is to be observed first of all that this principle has a singularly narrow basis in the evidence. The only texts that make this distinction are Luke 12.8f. (with Mark 8.38, which may be a variant form of the same saying), Mark 14.62 and Matthew 19.28, which is often held to be a community formation.[44] It has been noted by P. Vielhauer that these sayings come from group C, a category in which from the nature of the case there can be no contextual indications as to whether or not Jesus is identified with the Son of man.[45] It might be argued that the fact that the early Church preserved (or even created) the sayings in this form with *prima facie* differentiation between Jesus and the Son of man, although it itself identified Jesus with the Son of man, is strong evidence that the form of the sayings goes back to Jesus himself and that this unique differentiation must represent his original meaning. But it can equally well be held that the early Church preserved these sayings in this form because it saw in them nothing incompatible with the fact that Jesus himself claimed to be the Son of man; it was faithful to what was recognized as being Jesus' peculiar manner of referring to his future role.

Moreover, if the early Church could hold together statements in which Jesus was clearly identified with the Son of man along with others which might give a different impression—especially if it were the case that Matthew

19.28 is an early Church creation (which is by no means certain, however)—
we may well ask why its Master was not permitted to behave in the same way.

Thirdly, it is to be remembered that apart from these Son of man texts,
'there is no scrap of evidence that Jesus expected one greater than himself
to come, and there is much evidence to the contrary'.[46] A theory that is built
only upon a doubtful interpretation of at the most three or four sayings and
goes against the rest of the evidence rests upon most shaky foundations.

Fourthly, we must ask who Jesus expected this hypothetical Son of man
to be. If it be held that Daniel 7 exercised very little influence upon Jesus,
and that the apocalyptic tradition, in which the Son of man is in any case
a marginal figure, likewise was scarcely utilized by him—as H. E. Tödt
argues—why and how did Jesus take this unknown symbol and claim that
the Son of man would be the validator of the fellowship established between
the disciples and Jesus at the last judgement? Why did Jesus say so little
about this Son of man, and why did the early Church take this unimportant
figure from the teaching of Jesus and proceed to make it a key category in
its Christology? (And why did it confine the title to the mouth of Jesus alone,
and later drop the use of the title almost completely?)

Fifthly, if Tödt is right in his assertion that the Son of man sayings express
the authority of Jesus on earth, why does this authority need to be ratified
by a marginal figure of Jewish apocalyptic? This point becomes the more
pressing when we remember that Tödt stresses that in the sayings of group
A Jesus as the earthly Son of man displays not the transcendent *dunamis* of
the glorious eschatological judge, but the *exousia* of God's messenger; if the
tradition is so restrained at this point and refuses to turn Jesus into a *theios
anthropos,* what grounds are there for denying that Jesus may have spoken
of his authority in this way—other than the theory that he did not identify
himself with the Son of man, which is already manifestly showing signs of
wear? The restraint of the sayings in group A is surely a mark of genuineness.

Sixthly, Tödt regards the Son of man as the one who would uphold or
validate the decisions made by men *vis-à-vis* Jesus: 'Attachment to Jesus is not
an ephemeral bond on earth, but a fellowship which will be confirmed at the
coming of the Son of man.'[47] It is very hard to conceive the nature of such
a relationship. For Jesus certainly made the eternal destiny of man dependent
upon their earthly response to himself and his message, and presumably he
expected to be present at the last judgement himself. Is, then, the attachment
of men to him on earth a relationship which will be replaced at the last
judgement by some kind of relationship to the Son of man? In that case, what
is the eschatological role of Jesus? Does he simply cease to be of any further
account? Or is the attachment of men to him something that will continue

at the last judgement? Then we must ask what need there is of validation by the Son of man, and what precisely validation can mean. Whichever way we look at it, there is surely no room in the teaching of Jesus for an eschatological figure alongside himself in the manner depicted by Tödt; a much more coherent picture is obtained once the identification of Jesus and the Son of man is made.

We may, finally, argue the point from another angle. If there exist texts in which Jesus does identify himself with the Son of man, texts against whose authenticity there is no convincing evidence other than the supposition that Jesus could not have spoken of himself as the Son of man, then we are entitled to hold that the texts on which Tödt built his case have been wrongly interpreted. We shall therefore confront this handful of disputed texts with others which have good claims to authenticity. In effect this method of argument has already been used by E. Schweizer, but it will be necessary for us to reconsider the texts in the light of more recent discussion, particularly by P. Vielhauer and A. J. B. Higgins.

(a) Luke 7.34 (par. Matt. 11.19). 'The Son of man has come eating and drinking; and you say, "Behold a glutton and a drunkard, a friend of tax collectors and sinners".'

Since it is extremely unlikely that the early Church would have invented the comparison between John and Jesus found in Luke 7.33f. or created such scurrilous comments about him, there is every reason to accept the content of this saying as genuine.[48] P. Vielhauer has objected that the word 'came'[49] presupposes that the ministry of Jesus, like that of John, was completed, and that the authenticity of all the 'I' sayings is doubtful.[50] Neither of these arguments is convincing. A sweeping condemnation of all the 'I' sayings is methodologically unsound,[51] and the early Church was not aware that in placing a saying in the form 'I have come' or 'I came' on the lips of Jesus it was committing an anachronism.

Consequently, the only real argument against the authenticity of the saying is the use of the title 'Son of man'. Either, then, it is held, 'Son of man' may be an error in translation for *bar nash(a)* meaning 'I who speak',[52] or the early Church transformed a saying couched in the first person into a Son of man saying.[53] The sole reason for raising these possibilities is the *a priori* assumption that Jesus could not have used the title 'Son of man' to refer to himself; but this is precisely the point that requires to be proved. It is certainly possible to explain away the presence of 'Son of man' in this saying if one has a mind to do so, but it is equally clear that there is no necessity to do so.[54]

(b) Luke 9.58 (par. Matt. 8.20). 'Foxes have holes and birds of the air have nests; but the Son of man has nowhere to lay his head.'

R. Bultmann argued that this saying was a popular proverb, true of man in general, which the Hellenistic church applied to Jesus.[55] But the parallels that he cites to show that the saying applies to man in general have been rightly rejected as inadequate by many scholars.[56] A second line of attack is to argue that the saying was not literally true of Jesus, who often enjoyed the comfort of the homes of his friends; it was only for special reasons, such as prayer, that he was required to spend nights in the open.[57] This is an argument from the silence of the tradition and to that extent of doubtful validity, but in any case it is probably wrong to interpret the saying in an exclusively literal manner. It is more likely to be a metaphorical expression of the sense of rejection felt by Jesus which would also be experienced by his disciples.[58] There may even be an allusion to his passion and final rejection.[59] Vielhauer has objected to the insertion of the idea of rejection in order to obtain a suitable meaning for the saying, but the reasons for this objection are not clear; there is no doubt that Jesus was conscious of rejection by the people.[60]

Again, therefore, the sole weighty reason for not accepting the saying is its use of the title 'Son of man'. But the only argument that can be used in this connection is that of H. E. Tödt: 'An interpretation which assumed that Jesus in the *parousia* sayings spoke of the Son of Man as of a transcendent figure, whilst he formulated other sayings in which the Son of Man was devoid of all traditional attributes and conceived according to Jesus' own activity on earth, would face an unsurmountable difficulty.'[61] We have, however, already maintained that this argument is illegitimate. If it is right to see in this saying an expression of the authority of Jesus on earth and of his rejection by men, there is no good reason to deny that he could have used the title of 'Son of man' to describe both his present earthly authority and his future heavenly glory. In short, the arguments against the authenticity of this saying are not compelling.

(c) Mark 2.10. 'The Son of man has authority on earth to forgive sins.' The fact that 2.5b-10 is often, but not universally, held to be a later addition to the story of the paralytic man cannot be used to prove that the pericope is late or as a basis for conclusions about the origin of the saying.[62] Nor can the argument that the *Streitgespräche* are without exception late formations[63] be used to warrant a sweeping condemnation of their contents. Attempts to deny the authenticity of the saying must rest on firmer ground.[64] Difficulty has been found in the linking of the Son of man with forgiveness. Forgiveness is not linked with the Son of man in Jewish tradition, and it is rarely mentioned by Jesus himself; there is some ground for suspicion that the saying represents an attempt by the early Church to justify its own practice of forgiving sin by putting an ecclesiastical formula of absolution upon the lips of Jesus.[65] But, as E. Schweizer has convincingly argued, though forgiveness is often said to be a rare concept in the Gospels, it is not wholly absent, and Jesus' fellowship with sinners was a practical example of it.[66] In the light of our previous discussion, we need not tarry with the argument that the saying is out of harmony with the parousia sayings.[67]

J. Wellhausen held that the saying was a corruption of a statement referring originally to man in general,[68] but later scholars have rejected this theory on the excellent ground that it produces an untrue statement.[69] A much more plausible view would be that here the Son of man is a collective concept, so that the saying gives the disciples of Jesus the authority to forgive sin (cf. Matt. 16.19; 18.18; John 20.22f);[70] but this theory does not mitigate the 'difficulty' of the saying since the 'collective' concept of the Son of man must surely include Jesus himself, and in any case it is he who mediates this authority to the disciples. Two other possibilities remain. The view that the saying is a transformed 'I' saying[71] is simply a device to get rid of the unwanted 'Son of man' and is unlikely in a context where the authority of Jesus finds expression. C. E. B. Cranfield has suggested that the saying is really an editorial comment by the Evangelist on the healing, but it is difficult to see why Mark should have inserted the name of the Son of man at this early point in his Gospel.[72] On the whole, the view that in this saying Jesus expresses his authority as the earthly Son of man to forgive sins has much to commend it.[73]

(d) Luke 19.10. 'For the Son of man came to seek and to save the lost.' We may begin our consideration of this saying by noting that the presence of a similar saying, obviously based on this text, as a variant reading in two passages (Luke 9.56; Matt. 18.11) cannot be used as an argument against the authenticity of the saying.[74] Nor is it legitimate to argue from the resemblance of the saying to Mark 10.45 that its origin is suspicious.[75] The Palestinian origin of Luke 19.10 and Mark 10.45 is demonstrated by a comparison with 1 Timothy 1.15 and 2.5f. respectively, which are couched in more Hellenistic terms; Bultmann's view that our saying and Mark 10.45 are Hellenistic is thereby completely shattered.[76]

The real grounds for suspicion of the saying are the facts that it could be an addition to the story of Zacchaeus[77] and that (like Luke 7.34) it has the form of an 'I came' saying. The first of these two arguments proves no more than that the saying may originally have been an isolated or floating piece of tradition,[78] while the second is a gross *petitio principii*. There is no good reason why Jesus should not have understood his mission in terms of the bringing of salvation and made the creative link between the coming of the Son of man and the advent of salvation.[79] Once again, the best argument that can be offered against the saying is simply the circular one: 'By analogy with the other sayings about the present activity of the Son of man it is not to be assumed that we have here an authentic saying of Jesus.'[80]

We have now examined four sayings from a variety of Gospel sources and claim that cumulatively they establish a strong case that Jesus did speak of himself as the Son of man with reference to his earthly activity. The only really compelling argument against their authenticity was their alleged incompatibility with texts such as Luke 12.8f. Hence the result of our investigation is to show that the interpretation of sayings from group C to refer to a Son of man distinct from Jesus himself is to be rejected. We have, therefore, by this examination of the texts confirmed our suspicions regarding the interpretation offered by H. E. Tödt and A. J. B. Higgins. At the same time, we have demonstrated that Vielhauer's denial of the genuineness of any Son of man sayings is by no means compelling. We must not therefore use the argument that Jesus did not refer to himself as the Son of man to disprove the authenticity of other sayings whose authenticity is in doubt, nor must we argue that because Jesus spoke of a future Son of man he could not also speak of a present Son of man.

3. Is it possible to go any further than the point that we have now reached? We have argued for the authenticity of a number of sayings in group A referring to the present activity of Jesus as the Son of man.[81] This has brought us to the position of E. Schweizer. Can we go beyond him in accepting sayings from groups B and C as authentic teaching of Jesus?

Tödt and Higgins, as we have seen, were able to defend the authenticity of sayings in group C on the assumption that they referred to someone other than Jesus. But this method of defence is inadmissible once it is established that Jesus spoke of himself as the earthly Son of man; for it is clearly impossible that Jesus spoke of two Sons of men or that the early Church did so. We must, therefore, inquire whether Jesus referred to himself as the future Son of man. We shall consider four sayings.

(a) Luke 12.8f. 'And I tell you, every one who acknowledges me before men, the Son of man also will acknowledge before the angels of God; but he who denies me before men will be denied before the angels of God.'

In his discussion of this saying E. Schweizer is unable to pronounce definitely for or against its authenticity, but holds that it must come under the common suspicion which he attaches to sayings in group C. He puts forward the possibility that 'Son of man' may be an importation into the first half of a saying which spoke originally of acceptance and denial by God (the passive form of the verb may be used as a circumlocution in reference to divine actions).[82] This suggestion is unlikely since Mark 8.38 (par. Luke 9.26) preserves a parallel form to Luke 12.9 with mention of the Son of man, and the omission of 'Son of man' in verse 9 may have been due to a desire to achieve a smooth transition to verse 10.[83]

The most serious challenge to the authenticity of the saying is presented by P. Vielhauer. He argues that the saying speaks of confession and denial of Jesus in an earthly court (a forensic situation being depicted in both the protases and apodoses of the double statement); this presupposes a situation of persecution for the disciples of Jesus, and in particular a situation in which it is no longer the Kingdom of God but the person of Jesus that is the content of Christian proclamation. These three points indicate a post-Easter situation, and the saying is to be interpreted (with E. Käsemann) as a piece of early Christian legislation based on an eschatological *lex talionis*.[84]

Vielhauer denies categorically that Jesus could have looked forward to a period after his death when men might be persecuted for their allegiance to him; the most that he may have prophesied was eschatological tribulation. But it has been shown convincingly by E. Percy that Jesus regarded himself as the eschatological bringer of salvation,[85] and W. G. Kümmel has argued that Jesus expected a lapse of time between his death and the final coming of the Kingdom.[86] Further, it is questionable whether we should draw a line between persecution and the eschatological tribulation of the people of God; for Jesus persecution was an aspect of tribulation.[87] Consequently, it is by no means impossible that Jesus may have spoken of a future situation in which his disciples would be persecuted for their allegiance to him.

That the saying must be interpreted as referring to confession of Jesus before earthly courts is unlikely. Confession and denial are not exclusively forensic concepts, as a glance at the concordance will quickly show; Peter's denial of Jesus in his lifetime did not take place before a court.[88] Vielhauer argues that the forensic situation in the apodosis of Luke 12.8 demands by analogy a forensic situation in the protasis also. But it is to be observed that the only context in which heavenly confession and denial can be envisaged is that of the last judgement, whereas earthly confession and denial may take place in other contexts. In other words, the presence of a forensic context in the apodosis is due to the peculiar conditions of the heavenly situation, and therefore it is illegitimate to demand a forensic situation by analogy in the protasis also.[89]

Can Jesus, then, have uttered the saying? A possible line of interpretation is that he was saying that a person who confessed him, an apparently lowly person proclaiming the message of God, will be confessed by him when he appears as witness or judge at the last judgement in glory. The saying would then express pointedly the contrast between the present lowly condition of Jesus as 'I' and his future glory as the Son of man.[90] It may seem strange that in other sayings Jesus referred to himself in the present as the lowly and rejected Son of man, but this apparent inconsistency of usage may be due to reasons now hidden from us.[91]

(b) Luke 12.40 (par. Matt. 24.44). 'You also must be ready; for the Son of man is coming at an hour you do not expect.'

According to J. Jeremias, the parable of the burglar that this saying concludes originally referred to the coming of the End as the final catastrophe for the Jews; the early Church applied it to the parousia by seeing the burglar as the returning Son of man.[92] On the other hand, P. Vielhauer holds that the parable in its earliest form stems from the early Church as part of its attempt to deal with the problem of the delay of the parousia.[93]

I have discussed this parable elsewhere and argued that Jesus could well have spoken of the coming Son of man under the simile of a burglar (and hence with an element of warning and threat) even to his disciples, since they needed to be warned against the danger of falling away; should it be urged that the original context of the saying was preaching to the crowds, there is no good reason to deny that Jesus may have warned them of the sudden coming of the Son of man. We have already observed that the theory that Jesus did not expect an interval before the parousia goes against the evidence, and accordingly there is no good reason for denying that the saying may go back to Jesus himself.[94]

(c) Luke 18.8b. 'Nevertheless, when the Son of man comes, will he find faith on earth?'

In view of the recent defence of this saying by J. Jeremias, we may fairly claim it in support of our position.[95] The doubts against its authenticity raised by H. E. Tödt and A. J. B. Higgins are weak. They depend on the considerations that the mention of the Son of man is alien to the preceding parable and that the concepts of the Son of man and of faith are here linked.[96] In reply it may be urged that the saying is of pre-Lucan origin, and that the reference to faith is thoroughly in keeping with the teaching of Jesus.

(d) Mark 14.62. 'I am; and you will see the Son of man sitting at the right hand of Power, and coming with the clouds of heaven.'

A consideration of the possible authenticity of this text is closely bound up with the problem of its meaning. The saying applies to the Son of man the imagery of Psalm 110.1 and Daniel 7.13. It has often been regarded as referring to an act of exaltation in which the Son of man is enthroned and receives sovereignty,[97] but in fact no *act* of exaltation is described. What the hearers of Jesus will see is the Son of man already enthroned and coming on the clouds. The order of the two participles indicates clearly enough that the text is not describing a coming of the Son of man *to* the Ancient of Days,[98] and the use of the verb 'you will see' suggests that the scene of the parousia and final judgement is in mind. In other words, the emphasis of the saying is not upon 'exaltation as such but upon judgement. The basic thought comes from Daniel 7, which describes a scene of judgement and vindication, and this thought is developed with the aid of Psalm 110. The meaning is then that those who judged Jesus on earth will one day stand before the final judgement and see the Son of man vindicated and exalted by God and (it is implied) appearing in judgement against them.[99]

According to this interpretation, the meaning of the saying is very similar to that of Luke 12.8f. As in that saying, Jesus does not explicitly identify himself with the Son of man, but there can be little doubt that the identification is implicitly made. Yet the saying differs from others in group C in that it is preceded by what may be a claim of Jesus to messiahship.[100]

Can Jesus have uttered the saying? We may at once dismiss the argument of H. E. Tödt that Jesus would not have made use of the Old Testament Scriptures in the manner found in this saying.[101] P. Vielhauer has argued forcibly that this part of the Gospel of Mark shows strong signs of Christian influence, that (if the saying is genuine) it would be necessary to assume that Jesus took the unheard-of step of identifying the Messiah and the Son of man and that his disciples somehow managed to learn what he had said at the trial, and finally that Mark 14.55-64 is a later insertion into the passion narrative and of extremely doubtful historical value.[102] But to allow the presence of Christian influence in a section of a Gospel is by no means to prove that each individual item has suffered from this influence; each item must be examined individually from this point of view. Further, it is wrong to assert that the Son of man was not in some sense a messianic figure; the author of the Similitudes of Enoch made the identification,[103] and it is hard to see why Jesus could not have made the same identification. The theory that the court proceedings must have been held strictly *in camera* and their content never divulged to the outside world is quite improbable.[104] Anybody who has had any experience of working on committees will know that the most closely guarded secrets can easily become public knowledge; and in any case we have no reason to suppose that the trial of Jesus would be a closely guarded secret. As for the historicity of the trial scene, the fairest verdict at the moment can only be that the matter is still *sub judice*.[105] In short, the case against Mark 14.62, though strong, is not conclusive.

Space forbids a discussion of other sayings in group C, but sufficient has been said to show that in principle at least we may admit that Jesus spoke of himself as the future Son of man. The sayings that we have studied refer to the presence of the Son of man at the judgement or to his coming (Mark 8.38 combines these two thoughts) and thus express his future sovereignty and glory. It is interesting that they do not refer to the Son of man's assumption of this sovereignty and glory or to an act of exaltation. They do not connect the humble figure of Jesus and the transcendent Son of man by means of an act of exaltation, but take the position of the latter for granted.[106] This consideration leads to the important consequence that in the Gospels resurrection and parousia are not two alternative descriptions of the same reality. The resurrection of Jesus is the act by which he is exalted, and the future appearance of the Son of man is of one who already occupies an exalted position. Consequently, there is no conflict between the thought of the resurrection of Jesus and his future coming as the Son of man, although the two ideas are not brought into connection with each other in any of the sayings; we have indicated above a possible reason why this connection was not made.[107] It is therefore possible that the sayings of Jesus in group B do not represent a different stratum of tradition alongside a supposed older stratum in group C but form an integral part of his understanding of the Son of man.

4. So we are brought to the point where the question of the authenticity of the sayings in group B can be raised. We have already seen that the thought of rejection by men and even of death is probably to be found in the Q tradition. Moreover, it is a highly doubtful assumption that the teaching found in Mark is in general later than that found in Q. Tödt has given reason to believe that the passion sayings in Mark come from a Palestinian tradition, but it has yet to be proved that this tradition (or its component parts) is older or younger than that in Q. Consequently, principle 5 of our earlier discussion loses its force.[108]

We may also remind ourselves at this point of the argument of J. Jeremias that 'the assertion of the Gospels that Jesus expected a violent death has the strongest historical probability in its favour'.[109]

If these points are valid it becomes possible to ask whether the sayings that associate the Son of man with suffering and resurrection rest on authentic teaching of Jesus.

(a) The term 'Son of man' is brought into the passion narrative by Luke at 22.48. 'Judas, would you betray the Son of man with a kiss?' The saying is not discussed by H. E. Tödt, but A. J. B. Higgins has argued against its authenticity on the grounds that Jesus would not have referred to himself as the earthly Son of man in the hearing of non-disciples and that the saying represents a Lucan substitute for Mark 14.41 and a dramatic climax to the prophecies of betrayal.[110] The former of these arguments has already been shown to be unsound. As for the second, it has been argued by F. Rehkopf that the text comes from a special Lucan source and is not due to editorial modification of a Marcan source by Luke.[111] If this argument is sound, the saying rests on an early tradition. Higgins holds that this argument does nothing to salve the authenticity of the saying since he regards his first argument as being of overriding importance, but we have already seen that this argument is not sound.

(b) In his discussion of Mark 14.21, 'For the Son of man goes as it is written of him, but woe to that man by whom the Son of man is betrayed!', A. J. B. Higgins has upheld the view that although in its present form the saying is a community creation it is not a sheer invention. He notes the use of the word 'go' with reference to his passion by Jesus, and conjectures the existence of an original 'I' saying behind the present text.[112] In particular, the reference to scriptural necessity cannot go back to Jesus himself. But if the allusion to 'going' may be authentic, it is difficult to see why Jesus may not have used the term 'Son of man' in this connection, once we have rid ourselves of the prejudice that Jesus could not have referred to himself on earth as the Son of man. Moreover, the view that Jesus could not have referred to the scriptural necessity of his own path to the cross is surely to be rejected.[113]

The evidence of these two sayings, drawn as they probably are from two traditions of the passion, indicates the strong likelihood that Jesus did use the term 'Son of man' in relation to the passion. There is, therefore, good reason to hold that the use of the title in the earlier predictions of the passion may be genuine.

(c) The series of three predictions of the passion in Mark (8.31; 9.31; 10.33f.) shows a considerable variety of wording within a basically similar framework. H. E. Tödt limits his discussion of them at the outset by restricting his examination to the alternatives of their being formed by the Hellenistic or the Palestinian church, and argues for the latter alternative.[114] A number of points may be assembled to enable us to press backwards from the Palestinian church into the teaching of Jesus. First, the term 'to be delivered', which is characteristic of these sayings, is found linked only with Son of man, Lord Jesus and God's Son, and not with the title 'Christ'; in the pre-Pauline texts (Rom. 4.25; 8.32; 1 Cor. 11.23) a reference to Isaiah 53 is probable, but this is much less clear in the Gospels.[115] These two considerations indicate the very great age of the Gospel references to the delivery of the Son of man. Secondly, the idea of 'rejection' is to be traced back to Psalm 118. 22, a passage which was known to Jesus (Mark 12.10).[116] Thirdly, there is nothing in the description of the Jewish authorities which would be strange on the lips of Jesus, and the substitute phrase 'into the hands of men' is an Old Testament expression. Fourthly, the earliest forms of the prediction speak of death rather than of crucifixion. Fifthly, the sayings refer in their oldest forms to resurrection 'after three days', a form that is later altered to 'on the third day'. This change, attested in Matthew and Luke, shows that the Marcan form was ambiguous. Tödt's attempt to show that it could have been developed in the early Church before the later form is of doubtful validity. Our earliest reference in the kerygma, 1 Corinthians 15.4, has 'on the third day', and there is no evidence for use of the other phrase. It is much more likely that 'after three days' was the original, ambiguous wording used by Jesus; it could mean 'after a short time', but it was given unequivocal precision in the kerygma.

These considerations are not exhaustive, but together they indicate that the possibility of the authenticity of the predictions of the passion is not to be rejected out of hand.[117] The sayings show a close link with those in group A which depict the opposition faced by the Son of man and cohere closely with them.

5. If the results of this survey are valid, they indicate that Jesus used the term in two principal ways. On the one hand, he used it to refer to his earthly career as a figure of authority rejected by men, crucified and raised from the dead. On the other hand, he spoke of a coming Son of man who would act in sovereign power at the last judgement. These two types of saying are not brought into close relation with each other (except in Luke 17.22ff.), the reason for this being, as we have seen, that Jesus avoided overt identification of himself with the Son of man and so sought to preserve a certain mystery regarding his person. What this mystery was can now be indicated. It has always seemed remarkable that Jesus should have adopted a self-designation for himself which was, so far as we can tell, far from central in Jewish thought and whose use as a title in Aramaic is even a matter of some doubt. The reason for this may be found in the desire of Jesus to give cautious expression to his own unique relationship with God as his Son and agent of salvation. The title of 'Messiah' was both inadequate to express this relationship (since the Messiah tends to be an earthly figure of limited authority) and misleading (thanks to popular nationalistic interpretations), while that of Son was only too clear in its implications. But the title of 'Son of man' had distinct merits. It was admirably fitted to express Jesus' conception of his own person since it referred to a person closely linked with God and of heavenly origin.[118] In this respect it was superior to the title of Messiah.

Furthermore, it was not a current term and was capable of being moulded by Jesus to suit his own conceptions. Finally, there appears to have been the possibility of the ambiguous use of *bar nash(a)* in Aramaic as a circumlocution for the first person pronoun, so that its titular use would not in every instance be inescapably present to Jesus' hearers. 'Son of man' was thus a perfect vehicle for expressing the divine self-consciousness of Jesus while at the same time preserving the secrecy of his self-revelation from those who had blinded their eyes and closed their ears.[119] In the early Church the title rapidly dropped out of use[120] because of its unsuitability to express the fullness of the Church's belief about Jesus and especially because of its peculiarity in Greek translation. It was now possible to use the title of 'Son of God' without restraint as the term best fitted to express the supreme place occupied by Jesus.

Notes

[1]See the table in A. J. B. Higgins, *Jesus and the Son of Man* (London, 1964), p. 185 (cf. p. 26 for earlier discussions); also P. C. Hodgson, 'The Son of Man and the Problem of Historical Knowledge', *JR*, 41, 1961, pp. 91-108.

[2]T. W. Manson, *The Teaching of Jesus* (Cambridge, 1935), pp. 211-34; *The Servant-Messiah* (Cambridge, 1953), pp. 72-4; V. Taylor, *Jesus and His Sacrifice* (London, 1937), pp. 21-32; 'The Son of Man Sayings relating to the Parousia', *Exp. T.*, 58, 1946-47, pp. 12-15; *The Gospel according to St. Mark* (London, 1952), pp. 119ff.; *The Names of Jesus* (London, 1953), pp. 25-35; A. M. Hunter, *The Work and Words of Jesus* (London, 1950), pp. 84-7; H. E. W. Turner, *Jesus Master and Lord* (London, 1953), pp. 196-205; C. E. B. Cranfield, *St Mark* (Cambridge, 1963), pp. 272-7; similarly also O. Cullmann, *The Christology of the New Testament* (London, 1959), ch. 6. It need hardly be said that there are considerable differences in detail in the writings of these scholars.

[3]R. Bultmann, *Die Geschichte der synoptischen Tradition* (Göttingen, 1958) (Eng. tr. *The History of the Synoptic Tradition*, London, 1963); H. E. Tödt, *Der Menschensohn in der synoptischen Tradition* (Gütersloh, 1959) (Eng. tr. *The Son of Man in the Synoptic Tradition*, London, 1965); cf. Higgins, op. cit.; R. H. Fuller, *The Foundations of New Testament Christology* (London, 1965), pp. 119-25, 143-55.

[4]F. Hahn, *Christologische Hoheitstitel* (Göttingen, 1964), pp. 13-17, summarizes earlier discussion.

[5]Manson, *The Teaching of Jesus*, pp. 217 f.; J. Y. Campbell, 'The Origin and Meaning of the Term Son of Man', *JTS*, 48, 1947, pp. 145-55; E. Schweizer, 'Der Menschensohn', *ZNW*, 50, 1959, pp. 185-209 (p. 198); P. Vielhauer, 'Jesus und der Menschensohn', *ZTK*, 59, 1962, pp. 133-77 (pp. 157-9), who quotes M. Black, *An Aramaic Approach to the Gospels and Acts* (Oxford, 1946), pp. 246f.

[6]Black, ibid., p. 250 n. In a paper delivered at the Third International Congress of New Testament Studies (Oxford, 1965), G. Vermes, adduced a number of examples of the same usage in Aramaic and showed that they were used in situations of humiliation, danger and embarrassment. He also maintained, however, that the phrase was not used in Aramaic as a title and would indeed be totally unsuitable for this purpose. But the facts that a titular use is attested for the phrase in 1 Enoch and 4 Esdras and that the Palestinian church understood it as a title surely indicate that Jesus could have used this unsuitable phrase and moulded it to suit his own purpose. (For the published version of Vermes's paper see p. 115 n.15.)

[7]Schweizer, op. cit.; Cranfield, op. cit., pp. 273, 275 ff.

[8]W. Bousset, *Kyrios Christos* (Göttingen, 1921), p. 9, as cited by Tödt, op. cit. (Eng. tr.), p. 127.

[9]Bultmann, op. cit. (Eng. tr.), p. 137.

[10]J. Knox, *The Death of Christ* (London, 1959), pp. 52-77; cf. Higgins, op. cit., pp. 19, 199; Vielhauer, op. cit., p. 160.

[11]J. Jeremias, *The Central Message of the New Testament* (London, 1965), ch. 1.

[12]R. Bultmann, *Theology of the New Testament* (London, 1952), I, p. 30; *The History of the Synoptic Tradition*, p. 152.

[13]Vielhauer, op. cit.; earlier, 'Gottesreich und Menschensohn in der Verkündigung Jesu', in W. Schneemelcher (ed.), *Festschrift für Gunther Dehn* (München, 1957), pp. 51-79 (p. 56). Both essays are reprinted in P. Vielhauer, *Aufsätze zum Neuen Testament* (Neukirchen, 1965), pp. 55-91, 92-140.

[14]Tödt, op. cit., pp. 141-221.

[15]E. Stauffer, *New Testament Theology* (London, 1955), p. 110; J. Jeremias (and W. Zimmerli), *TDNT*, V, pp. 712-7; Schweizer, op. cit., pp. 195-7.

[16]A certain amount of assimilation of language between the predictions and the passion narrative is no proof that the predictions are secondary.

[17]Cranfield, op. cit., p. 267.

[18]R. Bultmann, *The History of the Synoptic Tradition*, p. 152; G. Bornkamm, *Jesus von Nazareth* (Stuttgart, 1956), pp. 161f.; Tödt, op. cit., pp. 55-60; Higgins, op. cit., pp. 24, 57-60.

[19]Summarized in Bultmann, *Theology of the New Testament*, I, pp. 28-32.

[20]Ibid.

[21]Vielhauer's position was anticipated by H. B. Sharman, *Son of Man and Kingdom of God* (New York, 1944).

[22]H. Conzelmann, 'Gegenwart und Zukunft in der synoptischen Tradition', *ZTK*, 54, 1957, pp. 277-96 (pp. 281ff.); 'Jesus', *RGG*, 1959, III, cols. 630f.

[23]H. M. Teeple, 'The Origin of the Son of Man Christology', *JBL*, 84, 1965, pp. 213-50.

[24]Stauffer, op. cit., pp. 108-11; *Jesus Gestalt und Geschichte* (Bern, 1957), pp. 122-4 (Eng. tr. *Jesus and His Story* [London, 1960], pp. 133-5).

[25]E. Bammel, 'Erwägungen zur Eschatologie Jesu', in F. L. Cross (ed.), *Studia Evangelica*, III *(TU*, 88, Berlin, 1964), pp. 3-32.

[26]Bornkamm, op. cit., pp. 160-3, 206-8 (Eng. tr. *Jesus of Nazareth*, London, 1960, pp. 175-8, 228-31).

[27]A. J. B. Higgins, 'Son of Man-*Forschung* since "The Teaching of Jesus" ', in *New Testament Essays: Studies in Memory of T. W. Manson* (Manchester, 1959), pp. 119-35.

[28]Higgins, *Jesus and the Son of Man*, p. 202.

[29]A position closely akin to that of Tödt is also adopted by Hahn, op. cit., pp. 13-53; Fuller, op. cit.

[30]E. Schweizer, 'Der Menschensohn'; 'The Son of Man', *JBL*, 79, 1960, pp. 119-29; 'The Son of Man Again', *NTS*, 10, 1962-3, pp. 256-61; cf. *Lordship and Discipleship* (London, 1960).

[31]Schweizer, 'The Son of Man', pp. 121f.

[32]M. Black, 'The "Son of Man" in the Old Biblical Literature', *Exp.T*, 60, 1948-9, pp. 11-15; 'The "Son of Man" in the Teaching of Jesus', ibid., pp. 32-6; 'The Eschatology of the Similitudes of Enoch', *JTS*, n.s. 3, 1952, pp. 1-10; 'The Servant of the Lord and the Son of Man,' *SJT*, 6, 1953, pp. 1-11.

[33]M. Black, 'The Son of Man Problem in Recent Research and Debate', *BJRL*, 45, 1962-3, pp. 305-18.

[34]Hodgson, op. cit., p. 91.

[35]Higgins, *Jesus and the Son of Man*, pp. 125f., 134, 133, 133 respectively.

[36]Vielhauer, 'Gottesreich and Menschensohn', pp. 71-3; Tödt, op. cit., p. 332.

[37]Compare F. F. Bruce, *Biblical Exegesis in the Qumran Texts* (London, 1960), p. 65: 'Daniel's

"one like a son of man" was from the first intended to be identical with the Isaianic Servant' Cranfield, op. cit., p. 273, notes that the rabbis always interpreted Daniel 7.13 of the Messiah.
[38]Tödt, op. cit., pp. 35f.
[39]Cf. W. G. Kümmel, *Heilsgeschehen und Geschichte* (Marburg, 1965), p. 468, n. 70.
[40]N. Perrin, *The Kingdom of God in the Teaching of Jesus* (London, 1963), pp. 160ff.
[41]Matthew 13.37ff. and 16.28 are usually held to be editorial.
[42]Tödt, op. cit., pp. 332-6.
[43]Schweizer, 'Der Menschensohn', pp. 186f.
[44]Tödt, op. cit., pp. 62-4.
[45]Vielhauer, 'Jesus und der Menschensohn', pp. 144-6.
[46]Cranfield, op. cit., p. 274.
[47]Tödt, op. cit., p. 45.
[48]Higgins, op. cit., p. 122; W. G. Kümmel, *Promise and Fulfilment* (London, 1957), p. 46, n. 93.
[49]Luke has the perfect tense; Matthew has the aorist tense.
[50]Vielhauer, 'Jesus und der Menschensohn', pp. 163-5, following Bultmann, *The History of the Synoptic Tradition*, op.cit., pp. 150-63 (p. 155); cf. Hahn, op. cit., p. 44.
[51]Schweizer, 'Der Menschensohn', p. 199; Higgins, op. cit., p. 122; Fuller, op. cit., pp. 127f.
[52]Manson, *The Teaching of Jesus*, pp. 217f.; *The Sayings of Jesus* (London, 1949), pp. 70f.; Jeremias, *The Parables of Jesus*, p. 160, n. 37.
[53]Higgins, op. cit., p. 123. Tödt, op. cit., pp. 114-18, appears to adopt the same position.
[54]The saying is accepted as genuine by Schweizer, op. cit., pp. 199f.
[55]Bultmann, op. cit., pp. 28, 98, followed by Vielhauer, op. cit., pp. 161-3; Hahn, op. cit., p. 44.
[56]Job 14 speaks of the weakness of man, but makes no contrast with the animals. Homer, *Odyssey*, 18. 136 ff., describes the plight of man when forsaken by the gods; Plutarch, *Tib. Gracchus 9*, p. 828 c, refers to men in the circumstances of war, cf. Manson, *The Sayings of Jesus*, p. 72; Schweizer, op. cit., p. 199; Higgins, op. cit., p. 124.
[57]Vielhauer, op. cit., pp. 161-3.
[58]The argument of Vielhauer that the setting of the saying in a context of discipleship is secondary since the saying itself makes no reference to discipleship, surely requires no refutation. Was Jesus never permitted to leave obvious logical deductions to the common sense of his hearers, or must he spell out every utterance in words of one syllable for the benefit of sceptical critics?
[59]R. H. Fuller, *The Mission and Achievement of Jesus* (London, 1954), pp. 104f.
[60]E.g., Mark 6.11 (par. Luke 9.5); Mark 6.4.
[61]Tödt, op. cit., p. 125; cf. p. 273; cf. Fuller, *The Foundations of New Testament Christology*, pp. 124f.
[62]Against Tödt, op. cit., p. 126; Hahn, op. cit., p. 43.
[63]Tödt, op. cit., p. 130.
[64]Vielhauer, op. cit., p. 159, argues that the saying presupposes a link between illness and sin which Jesus himself repudiated (Luke 13. 1-5; John 9. 1-3). Commentators, however, are agreed that this principle is not to be found in the story.
[65]Higgins, op. cit., pp. 27f.
[66]Schweizer, op. cit., p. 198.
[67]Tödt, op. cit., p. 130; Vielhauer, op. cit., p. 160.
[68]J. Wellhausen, *Das Evangelium Marci* (Berlin, 1903), pp. 17f.
[69]Tödt, op. cit., pp. 126 f.; Higgins, op. cit., p. 26.
[70]The view is discussed by Taylor, *The Gospel according to St. Mark*, pp. 199f.
[71]Bultmann, op. cit., p. 15 (but contrast p. 155).
[72]Cranfield, op. cit., p. 100. G. H. Boobyer, 'Mark II, 10a and the Interpretation of the Healing of the Paralytic', *HTR, 47*, 1954, pp. 115-20, regards the insertion as pre-Marcan.

[73]The saying is accepted as genuine by Taylor, op. cit., p. 200; Kümmel, *Heilsgeschehen und Geschichte*, pp. 435f., 468 n. 70.

[74]Higgins, op. cit., p. 76, mentions these variant readings, but it is not absolutely clear what deduction he wishes to make from them.

[75]Higgins, op. cit., p. 77.

[76]Bultmann, op. cit., p. 155. Hahn, op. cit., p. 45, objects that present 'salvation' as the purpose of the earthly work of Jesus is a late concept.

[77]Higgins, op. cit., p. 76; Hahn, op. cit., p. 270, n. 5.

[78]Cf. Tödt, op. cit., p. 133.

[79]Prof. A. M. Hunter has suggested to me that the verse is a 'shepherd' saying (cf. Ezek. 34.16), and fits in admirably with Jesus' use of this motif.

[80]Tödt, op. cit., p. 134.

[81]Within the limits of the present article, it is impracticable to discuss all the Son of man sayings; fuller consideration would not affect the results obtained above.

[82]Schweizer, op. cit., pp. 188, 192.

[83]Kümmel, Promise and Fulfilment, pp. 44f.

[84]Vielhauer, 'Gottesreich und Menschensohn', pp. 68-70; 'Jesus und der Menschensohn', pp. 141-7; E. Käsemann, 'Sätze heiligen Rechtes im Neuen Testament', *NTS*, 1, 1954-5, pp. 248-60 (pp. 256f.).

[85]E. Percy, *Die Botschaft Jesu* (Lund, 1953).

[86]Kümmel, Promise and Fulfilment, pp. 64-83; cf. my *Eschatology and the Parables* (London, 1963), pp. 19-21.

[87]Cranfield, op. cit., p. 161. Persecution is the normal lot of disciples and a sign of the end because the disciples already live in the last days.

[88]Tödt, op. cit., p. 342.

[89]Hahn, op. cit., p. 35, holds that the form of the saying as *heiliges Recht* can go back to Jesus himself.

[90]This interpretation is put forward by P. Vielhauer as the way in which the early Church understood the saying; cf. Teeple, op. cit., p. 218.

[91]There is no saying which speaks of both the present lowliness of the Son of man and his future glory, although these two ideas are brought together in what may be editorial compositions (Mark 8. 31-8; Luke 17. 22-30); for the passion sayings, which refer to the death and resurrection of the Son of man, see below. This means that it is possible that Jesus may have maintained a certain ambiguity in his use of the title: in the 'present' sayings 'Son of man' could have been a circumlocution for 'I', while in the 'future' sayings it could have referred to another person. It is also noteworthy that, according to Manson's analysis (*The Teaching of Jesus*, pp. 211-25), the great majority of the Son of man sayings were addressed to the disciples and not to the people at large.

[92]Jeremias, *The Parables of Jesus*, pp. 48-50.

[93]Vielhauer, 'Gottesreich und Menschensohn', p. 66; 'Jesus und der Menschensohn', pp. 147f.

[94]*Eschatology and the Parables*, pp. 16-24, 36-8. The saying is accepted as genuine by Kümmel, Promise and Fulfilment, pp. 54-6.

[95]Jeremias, *The Parables of Jesus*, pp. 153-7.

[96]Tödt, op. cit., pp. 99f.; Higgins, op. cit., pp. 91f; cf. Kümmel, *Heilsgeschehen und Geschichte*, p. 462, n. 28.

[97]Taylor, op. cit., p. 569.

[98]Cranfield, op. cit., pp. 444f. The view rejected in the text is developed especially by J. A. T. Robinson, *Jesus and His Coming* (London, 1957), pp. 43-52.

[99]Cranfield, ibid.; Higgins, op. cit., pp. 73f. Tödt, op. cit., p. 40, wrongly denies the judicial nature of the scene.

[100]It is not certain whether the 'I am' of Jesus represents acceptance or rejection of the status suggested by the high-priest's question. If the latter view is accepted, the thought in the saying

is very similar to that in Luke 12.8f. If the former view is accepted, then here we have a unique instance in the Synoptic Gospels of Jesus claiming an earthly messianic status. Cf. Cranfield, op. cit., pp. 443f.

[101]Tödt, op. cit., p. 36. Tödt's further remarks, pp. 266-9, do nothing to remove the impression that his argument is a circular one.

[102]Vielhauer, 'Gottesreich und Menschensohn', pp. 64f.

[103]Teeple, op. cit., p. 213, n. 7.

[104]See John 18.15, with C. H. Dodd, *Historical Tradition in the Fourth Gospel* (Cambridge, 1963), pp. 80, 86-8.

[105]Tödt, op. cit., p. 36, states categorically and without proof, 'It is improbable indeed that the community had at its disposal detailed reports about the course of the examination in which Jesus' words were repeated accurately. Besides, the community was not much interested in historical details, but preferred to describe the passion by means of the words of Scripture.' For another view, see Kümmel, *Promise and Fulfilment*, pp. 49-51; Higgins, op. cit., p. 67.

[106]Matt. 19.28 is a doubtful exception to the rule.

[107]The connection betwen resurrection and parousia in Mark 14.58, 62 is of a veiled nature. Note that our argument here disproves principle 6 for study of the Son of man concept.

[108]In addition to the Q tradition, the L tradition also contains references to the passion of Jesus which have good claims to authenticity; cf. especially Taylor, *Jesus and His Sacrifice*, pp. 164ff.

[109]Jeremias, *TDNT*, v, p. 713.

[110]Higgins, op. cit., pp. 80f.; Hahn, op. cit., p. 46 n.

[111]F. Rehkopf, *Die lukanische Sonderquelle* (Tübingen, 1959), pp. 50-6. The author complements the studies of H. Schürmann by finding traces of a non-Marcan source in Luke 22.21-3, 47-53. For the Proto-Luke theory in general, see the recent defence in G. B. Caird, *Saint Luke* (Harmsworth, 1963), pp. 23-7.

[112]Higgins, op. cit., pp. 50-2.

[113]B. Lindars, who stresses the creative use of the Old Testament by the Church, admits that in its references to Isaiah 53 it followed the lead of Jesus himself *(New Testament Apologetic* [London, 1961], p. 88).

[114]Tödt, op. cit., p. 156.

[115]Ibid., pp. 156-61. The presence of allusions to Isaiah 53 in the sayings of Jesus is a much-debated question which cannot be discussed here.

[116]For the genuineness of Mark 12. 10 see Cranfield, op. cit., pp. 386f.

[117]With regard to the much-discussed text, Mark 10.45, we can do no more here than express our belief in its authenticity. [1989] See P. Stuhlmacher, *Versöhnung, Gesetz und Gerechtigkeir* (Göttingen, 1981), pp. 27-42.

[118]Cf. Cullmann, op. cit., p. 162: 'by means of this very term Jesus spoke of his divine, heavenly character'; Higgins, op. cit., p. 202.

[119]We should probably not ignore also the way in which 'Son of man' was capable of a corporate reference, *pace* Hahn, op. cit., pp. 18f.

[120]It is beyond the scope of this essay to discuss the use in Acts 7.56 and in John.

**Nyack College
Eastman Library**

5
The Son of Man
in Contemporary Debate

O F THE VARIOUS CHRISTOLOGICAL TITLES THAT OCCUR IN the Gospels, the phrase 'Son of man' is of the greatest significance in contemporary study of the historical Jesus. Such titles as 'Messiah' (or 'Christ') and 'Son of God' appear infrequently in statements attributed to the lips of Jesus, but 'Son of Man' occurs comparatively often.[1] Further, while the authenticity of the other titles as self-designations of Jesus is highly debatable,[2] we are on much firmer ground in holding that Jesus did make use of the phrase 'Son of man' in a way which has important implications for his self-understanding, whether or not he meant to designate himself by this phrase. Consequently, in any attempt to discover what assessment Jesus made of himself and his relationship to the message which he preached, a consideration of the phrase 'Son of man' has more hope of fruitful results than discussion of other titles.[3]

Unfortunately, the problem of the meaning and use of this phrase is extremely complex, and there is a wide range of scholarly opinions about its solution. In 1959 A. J. B. Higgins produced a survey of 'Son of man-*Forschung* since "The Teaching of Jesus",[4] which described the many, varied contributions to the debate since T. W. Manson's important chapter in his book on *The Teaching of Jesus.*[5] Almost immediately afterwards a number of important studies of the theme appeared, and the present writer attempted to assess one aspect of this discussion in a paper composed four years ago.[6]

In brief, it emerged that one of the chief points of debate was whether Jesus used the phrase 'Son of man' or not, and, if he did, whether he was referring to himself or not. In order to analyse the various opinions of scholars on this point, we made use of a fairly generally accepted classification of the Synoptic sayings by their contents into three groups. Group A contains those sayings that refer to the Son of man as an earthly figure who eats and drinks, has nowhere to lay his head, has authority over the Sabbath, and so on. Group B contains sayings that speak of the suffering, death and resurrection of the Son of man. Group C refers to the future coming or parousia of the Son of man, his exaltation and his functions at the last judgement.

Making use of this classification we could distinguish the various scholarly contributions to the debate as follows: 1. The 'conservative' wing of scholarship, represented by O. Cullmann on the Continent and by British scholarship generally, accepted the authenticity of all three groups of sayings and believed that Jesus was speaking about himself. 2. The 'radical' wing, with P. Vielhauer as its most thorough advocate, ascribed all the sayings to the early Church; the 'Son of man' formulations do not go back to Jesus himself. In between these extremes there were two main mediating positions. 3. A position which goes back to R. Bultmann, and which was especially advocated by G. Bornkamm, H. E. Tödt and A. J. B. Higgins, was that only the sayings in Group C were authentic and that in them Jesus referred to an eschatological figure other than himself. 4. The other main position was that of E. Schweizer, who argued for the authenticity of the sayings in Group A as references to Jesus himself but was sceptical about the present form of the others, especially those in Group C.[7]

Although the position of Tödt and Higgins has perhaps gained the most support, it might well be thought that stalemate had been reached in a discussion which had divided the scholarly world into sharply conflicting groups. It may be that the inherent unsatisfactoriness of this situation has had something to do with fostering the extravaganza of further contributions to the debate which have appeared in the last four years. During this period there have been no less than three sizeable books on the theme and many smaller contributions. Our present purpose will be the modest one of chronicling this recent phase of study and attempting to assess where future progress may best be made.

Our procedure will be to mention the main contributions to the subject in broad terms, and then look at each of the main areas of debate; namely, the linguistic problem, the problem of origins, the usage in the Synoptic Gospels, and the usage in John.[8]

I
The year 1967 saw the publication of no less than six major contributions

to our subject. The first two of these were limited in their scope. N. Perrin's book, *Rediscovering the Teaching of Jesus*, was concerned to set out and illustrate the general principles of Gospel study, and it was notable for the much more sceptical attitude to the authenticity of the teaching ascribed to Jesus than might have been expected on the basis of the author's earlier work, *The Kingdom of God in the Teaching of Jesus* (London, 1963). In his study Perrin confines himself to the apocalyptic sayings in Group C, none of which he regards as authentic.[9] What is of interest, however, is not so much the adoption of this conclusion as the reasons which lead to it; these reasons lie in the previous history of the phrase 'Son of man' and in the author's use of the radical approach to the Gospels which does not accept any saying as authentic teaching of Jesus unless it can be proved to be such.

A different approach to the Gospel material was taken by M. D. Hooker in her book, *The Son of Man in Mark*. As its title indicates, the treatment is confined to one branch of the tradition. Although the author is interested in the theology of Mark, she nevertheless draws conclusions regarding the teaching of Jesus, and these are more traditional than those of Perrin. It is, however, a serious weakness in the argument of the book that the author has confined herself to the occurrence of the phrase 'Son of man' in Mark, and as a result has not considered such a text as Mark 3.28f. which in its Marcan form does not refer to the Son of man but whose parallel in the Q tradition does have such a reference.[10]

Closely related to the work of Hooker is that of C. K. Barrett. His book, *Jesus and the Gospel Tradition*, is a general study of the teaching of Jesus, but since the Son of man occupies an important place in that teaching the phrase is a central theme of the book.[11]

The fourth main work to appear in this *annus mirabilis* for study of the Son of man was the lengthy work by F. H. Borsch, *The Son of Man in Myth and History*. Borsch is particularly concerned with the background of thought behind the New Testament use of the phrase, and he examines a mass of unfamiliar evidence from many sources in great detail (177 pages) before turning to the New Testament itself. Unfortunately his style of writing is not blessed with lucidity, and his conclusions are not easy to find or to summarize.

Finally, there is the article on Son of man in Kittel's *Theologisches Wörterbuch zum Neuen Testament*, running to seventy-nine pages of closely packed material, clearly written but immensely detailed and very hard on the digestion. Some forty years ago the composition of this article was entrusted to J. Jeremias, but he has been content to limit his contribution to a significant article in the *Zeitschrift für N.T. Wissenschaft* and to hand over the composition of the Kittel article to his former pupil, C. Colpe. The latter is a foremost authority on *Religionsgeschichte*, well-qualified to deal with the difficult background problems of the Son of man, as well as a competent New Testament scholar of similar outlook to Jeremias. His article surveys the whole area of Son of man study, and it is noteworthy for its attempt to describe the history of the use of 'Son of man' during the period between the ministry of Jesus and the composition of the Gospels.

II

We now turn to the various problems associated with the phrase 'Son of man', and commence with the linguistic problem. A person who came to the phrase ὁ υἱὸς τοῦ ἀνθρώπου from the background of a Greek education would probably be tempted to take it in a 'genealogical' sense with the meaning of 'the physical son of a particular man'. It would be difficult to interpret the phrase as it occurs in the Gospels in this way,[12] and it is generally agreed that the Greek phrase is a literal translation of a Semitic phrase. Old Testament Hebrew uses the phrase *ben- 'ādām* to refer to a particular person or to mankind in general.[13] In Aramaic a set of similar phrases is used which can mean 'the man', 'a man', 'somebody' or 'mankind in general'.[14] There has been much argument whether any of these Aramaic phrases could be used (a) by a speaker to refer to himself, and (b) as a kind of title referring to a particular person.

This point was the subject of a paper at the International Congress on New Testament Studies held at Oxford in 1965 in which G. Vermes argued that the Aramaic phrases *bar nāsh* and *bar nāshā* could be used as a circumlocution for the first person singular in certain contexts.[15] This appears to be a sound conclusion, but there is some doubt about its significance. Vermes himself and M. Black apparently take the evidence to mean that the phrases can refer exclusively to the speaker, 'I and nobody else'.[16] But Jeremias and others argue that the phrases have an inclusive sense, so that the speaker says something which is true of humanity in general and hence also of himself in particular;[17] the meaning would then be, as A. Gelston puts it, 'I as a particular man' or 'I *qua* man'.[18]

On the whole, the balance of probability seems to favour this second interpretation of the evidence. If so, this would seem to make it unlikely that Jesus could have used the phrase 'Son of man' as a circumlocution for 'I' in statements which were true only of himself.

But the matter is complicated by the question of the use of the phrase as a title. Was this possible in Aramaic? It is a fact that there is no example of a titular use in Aramaic literature.[19] Thus in Daniel 7.13 what we have is not a reference to a person with the title 'the Son of man' who comes with the clouds of heaven, but rather a description of 'one like a son of man' (RSV), which should perhaps be translated simply as 'one like a man' or 'a human figure'. Here, therefore, is a case not of a fixed title but rather of a description akin to that in Ezekiel 1.26 of 'a likeness as it were of a human form'.

On the basis of this negative evidence, Vermes argued that 'Son of man' could not have been used as a title in the Aramaic sayings which lie behind the Gospels. But this conclusion is not compelling. Colpe argues, rightly in our opinion, that the phrase could have a titular meaning in apocalyptic contexts; that is to say, the background of the usage in Daniel 7.13 and elsewhere could make it refer to 'that well-known manlike figure of apocalyptic tradition'. Nevertheless, the non-technical use of the phrase made it possible for a titular example of the phrase to be misunderstood in a generalizing sense and vice versa.[20]

The conclusion appears to be, therefore, that the phrase could have been used in Aramaic to refer to the manlike figure of Daniel 7.13 and that it could also be used in a generalizing sense by a person referring to himself as a representative human being.[21]

III

From linguistics we turn to origins. Where did the concept of the 'Son of man' arise? If we begin by considering the immediate influences which may lie behind New Testament usage, we are at once led into fairly familiar country. Three Jewish sources are usually thought to shed some light on the spiritual milieu of the concept, namely, the vision and its interpretation given in Daniel 7, the extended references to the Son of man in the Similitudes of Enoch, and the apocalyptic vision in 4 Ezra.

Of these the third is too late in date to have been a direct influence upon New Testament usage, although it may contain earlier ideas which have also influenced the New Testament. The Similitudes of Enoch are usually assigned to the era B.C., but there are dissenting voices on the matter.[22] In any case, however, it is clear that in these writings the concept of the Son of man does not suddenly spring into existence without any previous history, and consequently recent study has concentrated its attention on the background of usage in these sources. There is the further consideration that, if the New Testament material cannot be adequately accounted for against the background of these sources, it may be that it is based independently upon the tradition which affected the Jewish material.

We start from Daniel 7. As the chapter stands, the Son of man is interpreted as a symbol or representative of 'the saints of the Most High' who are identified with the pious members of Israel.[23] This does not, however, necessarily mean that the man-like figure is merely a collective symbol; he may well have been a particular person.[24] The later history of the Son of man concept shows that it was taken to represent an individual and understood in what may be called a broadly messianic sense. It may well be the case that this later understanding of the concept betrays a memory of the origins of the Son of man figure which leads us to a correct interpretation of its meaning.[25]

The most careful survey of the origin of the Son of man concept as used in Daniel comes from C. Colpe.[26] He examines successively the possibilities of an adequate background in the Old Testament itself and then in a series of non-biblical figures, that of Gayomart in the Avestas, Adapa in Babylonian literature, the sun god in Egyptian mythology, Adam in Rabbinic speculation and the primal man in gnosticism. Each of these possibilities is rejected, and Colpe finally suggests a background in Canaanite mythology where we find the figure of a young god, Baal, who rides on the clouds to the supreme god, El, the father of years. Colpe admits that there are difficulties surrounding this hypothesis but holds that these are less than with any other theory.[27]

The other major survey in this area is that of F. H. Borsch who comes to somewhat different conclusions. Assembling material from a wide variety of sources, he attempts to show that these bear witness to a set of common ideas and motifs which have survived down the centuries in different, often fragmentary, forms. There were various legends involving the First Man, the king and Primordial Man which were inextricably bound up with each other and which are reflected in myth and dramatic ritual. Borsch ascribes the impulse for the later speculation about the Man (i.e., the Son of man) to this general mythical-ritual background with its ideology of kingship. He then argues that there were a number of Jewish or semi-Jewish groups which maintained such ideas into New Testament times. These sects

> practised various forms of baptism as an ordination/coronation rite and . . . were likely open to at least a measure of *foreign* (or simply indigenous but non-Jewish) influences. . . . For a number of these groups, and often in connection with their baptismal rites, speculation about or belief in the Man (in one or more of his guises) had a significant role to play. . . . The sources of both many of these water rites and of the concern with the Man, as well as the interrelation between the two, reach back to the ancient kingship ideologies.[28]

It is difficult to know what to make of this theory. Borsch moves so rapidly from one source to another and from one ideology to another, tracing common themes and establishing cross-links that his work may impress one critic as a master-stroke of synthesizing genius but another as a gigantic *tour de force*. The whole survey needs to be carefully examined by a competent *Religionsgeschichtlicher* and at present it remains *sub judice*.[29]

One other investigation in this area of early origins must be noted. M. D. Hooker finds the background of the concept in the Old Testament itself. She claims that there it is to be understood collectively of Israel as the heir of Adam. Destined to rule, the Son of man experiences loss of dominion and suffering, but will ultimately be vindicated by God. The phrase thus refers to a role rather than a person, although in 1 Enoch it has come to be used of a supernatural individual.[30]

This survey of the ultimate origins of the Son of man concept may well suggest that we are some distance from any sort of consensus of opinion on the matter. Nevertheless, there are two points on which several of our authorities are agreed. We have already observed that from a linguistic point of view it is doubtful whether we can speak of a fully titular use of the phrase 'Son of man' in the pre-Christian period. We may now complement this observation by noting that it is doubtful whether we can speak of one single, well-defined 'Son of man' concept. Thus N. Perrin has argued that what we find in the literature is a series of separate and independent exegetical uses of Daniel 7, making use of the human image described there.[31] Similarly, M. D. Hooker holds that the identification of the Son of man with Enoch which is made in the Similitudes was possible because 'Son of man' was not a title for a recognizable figure.[32] Finally, in this connection we must mention H. R. Balz, who has demonstrated that a considerable variety of ideas were associated with the phrase 'Son of man' so that it can hardly be regarded as a title with a specific content and reference.[33] This is a far cry from E. Stauffer's claim that 'Son of man' was 'just about the most pretentious piece of self-description that any man in the ancient East could possibly have used',[34] although the point should not be pressed unduly.

A second conclusion is that we are probably not to look to the extra-biblical apocalyptic writings for a direct influence upon the New Testament usage. Our authorities are, however, divided regarding where we should seek for the immediate influence upon the New Testament. For example, C. Colpe holds that in the Gospels we have testimony to an independent Jewish Son of man tradition which must be placed alongside the surviving Jewish sources,[35] but N. Perrin believes that the oldest New Testament texts rest upon a reinterpretation by the early Church of Daniel 7.[36]

This means that the scholars are far from being of one mind on the ultimate origins of the Son of man concept or the proximate influences upon the New Testament. What is of interest and importance as we turn to the next part of our theme will be the question how far these differences of opinion over background affect exegesis of the New Testament.

IV

The most comprehensive survey of the material in the Synoptic Gospels is afforded by Colpe.[37] Following Jeremias, he begins by bracketing off three sayings in which 'Son of man' meaning 'a man' has been misunderstood in the tradition as a title for Jesus. Mark 2.10 goes back to an original form which may be paraphrased, 'Not only God can forgive but also in the case of me, Jesus, a man'.[38] Similar originals are postulated for Matthew 11.19 = Luke 7.34, and Matthew 8.20 =Luke 9.58. In all three cases Colpe accepts forms of the sayings without the titular 'Son of man' as authentic sayings of Jesus.[39]

Having thus cleared the ground, Colpe next argues that there are eight sayings about the future coming of the Son of man which go back to Jesus himself: these are Matthew 24.27, 37 (=Luke 17.24, 26) Luke 17.30; 21.36; 18.8; 22.69; Matthew 10.23 and 24.30. His reasoning is that there are no compelling arguments against their genuineness, that the production of further Son of man sayings by the early Church would be unlikely if there was not already a core of authentic sayings of Jesus, and that these eight sayings offer a unified picture of the activity of the Son of man which is not dependent upon the surviving Jewish sources (Daniel, 1 Enoch and 4 Ezra). They speak of the sudden coming of the Son of man from heaven at the last day to judge men on the basis of their response to Jesus.

By accepting only this set of sayings as authentic teaching of Jesus, Colpe thus aligns himself with the view of R. Bultmann, G. Bornkamm, H. E. Tödt and A. J. B. Higgins that only the apocalyptic sayings in Group C are authentic teaching of Jesus. This raises the question whether Jesus identified himself with the Son of man.

Before answering this question, Colpe refers to four groups of sayings which originally did not use the term 'Son of man' but later had it added to them.[40] Here Colpe is closely following Jeremias who holds that in cases where there are two forms of a statement in the Gospels, the one with and the other without the term 'Son of man,' the latter is more primitive than the former. These groups of sayings are: 1. Luke 22.27 and 48 which speak of Jesus as the Servant of Yahweh and of his betrayal; 2. Mark 3.28f. and Matthew 5.11 which speak of men's rejection of Jesus; 3. Matthew 10.32f. and Luke 22.28-30 which refer to the eschatological significance of Jesus for his followers; and 4. Matthew 12.39 and Mark 9.9 and 31 which prophesy the 'perfecting' of Jesus on the third day after he has undergone the suffering which is the typical fate of the prophet. Colpe argues that in order to understand the Son of man sayings we must also take these sayings into consideration, since apart from them Jesus would appear as no more than a prophet of repentance. It was, therefore, entirely fitting that these sayings were later transformed into Son of man sayings.

According to Colpe, Jesus did not raise the question whether he was the Son of man. Rather he used three sets of parallel concepts, his own 'perfecting', the Kingdom of God and the Son of man, to refer to the breaking in of the eschatological future in the present time. These three sets of concepts were not brought into relationship with each other. Hence the Son of man is a symbol of Jesus' certainty of his own 'perfecting'. Colpe continues: 'With a shift from the assurance to the one who has it, the whole process may be interpreted as a dynamic and functional equating of Jesus and the coming Son of Man with the future perfecting of Jesus in view. On this view, the primitive community then made of it a static personal identification accomplished already in the present Jesus'.[41]

I find this conclusion difficult to accept, but proceed for the moment to expound Colpe's view of the subsequent development of the tradition. He gives a careful analysis of the various stages through which it passed, though he is careful to observe that this does not necessarily represent a chronological development. In brief, he distinguishes the period of oral tradition from that of the Gospels and their written sources. Within the former period he distinguishes three stages: 1. Once the Easter event had convinced the disciples that Jesus himself would return to them, the authentic sayings of Jesus about the coming Son of man were promptly understood to refer to himself. At the same time the sayings using 'Son of man' in a non-titular sense were given a messianic meaning and consequently the title was regarded as applying to Jesus during his earthly ministry. At this stage one or two other sayings (notably Matt. 10.32f. = Luke 12.8f. and Luke 12.10) were reformulated. 2. At a second stage this process was carried further. Statements about the suffering of Jesus were given a 'Son of man' form, and various eschatological sayings and other statements in the first person were reformulated in terms of the Son of man. 3. The third stage was characterized not so much by the reformulation of existing sayings of Jesus as by the creation of new sayings, including the Jonah saying (Luke 11.30) and the prophecy of the parousia in Mark 13.26.

We may terminate our summary of Colpe's analysis here. It has emerged that only eight occurrences of the title 'Son of man', all referring to the eschatological figure, go back to Jesus himself. The present form of all the other sayings is due to the early Church. Consequently, Jesus did not think of himself as being already the 'hidden' Son of man during his earthly ministry, nor did he use an ambiguous form of expression, meaning 'I' or 'Son of man' to describe himself.

The analysis of the Gospel material by N. Perrin takes its start from Mark 13.26.[42] Perrin holds that this text represents the earliest form of the hope of the future coming of the Son of man and also that it is a product of the early Church.[43] Consequently, Jesus himself could not have spoken at all of the coming Son of man; all the other texts in the Gospels are secondary to Mark 13.26. What happened was that the early Church understood the resurrection of Jesus in terms of Daniel 7.13 (along with Ps. 110), so that Jesus was seen as the Son of man who ascends to God. Then the application of Zechariah 12.10ff. led to the idea of the parousia of the Son of man. From this beginning in early Christian exegesis of Old Testament texts arose the whole Son of man speculation.

Perrin thus agrees with Colpe in finding the origins of the Son of man ideology in apocalyptic. He differs from him at two points. First, he denies, as we have already seen, the existence of a Jewish concept of the coming Son of man which Jesus and the early Church could have used, and consequently he has to show how this idea developed in the early Church by creative exegesis of the Old Testament.[44] Second, unlike Colpe, he holds that no sayings in the Gospels are authentic utterances of Jesus unless they can be positively proved to be such.[45]

The question now arises whether the postulation of a different, non-apocalyptic background leads to different results. M. D. Hooker adopts as her method of study a simple *seriatim* consideration of the sayings recorded in Mark. This means that her starting point is the two Group A sayings, Mark 2.10 and 28, and she finds no difficulty in demonstrating that in them Jesus acts as the Son of man with the authority of God on earth, and thus as Adam was originally intended to act. Further, the disciples are associated with Jesus in this authority, although 'the Son of man in the gospels . . . is not a truly corporate figure; rather it is true to say that the consequences of the Son of man's authority always extend to others'.[46]

Next there is a consideration of the passion prophecies; these refer to the denial of the Son of man's authority by men, but also speak of his vindication by God in terms of resurrection; only at his vindication will his authority and glory as the Son of God be revealed. Of particular interest is the theory that the suffering of the Son of man is not to be understood in the light of Isaiah 53, but rather in terms of the teaching in Daniel.[47]

Finally, the sayings in Mark 13.26 and 14.62 are held to refer to the vindication of the Son of man and his reception of authority rather than primarily to the fact of his coming on the clouds.

In her closing discussion M. D. Hooker concludes that the pattern of activity displayed in Mark goes back to Jesus himself, and pleads for an understanding of the Son of man which is 'messianic but *not* "supernatural".'[48]

It has already been observed that the views of C. K. Barrett are very close to those of Hooker. We may, therefore, content ourselves with noting three points which he makes:

1. The content of Mark 8.38 is such that it cuts across the traditional classification of the sayings into three groups; elements from each group are to be found in it.[49]

2. Barrett argues that Jesus spoke of his vindication in two ways, in terms of resurrection and of future glory. These were two alternative ways of designating one event, which Jesus expected to happen soon after his death. It was the early Church which interpreted the sayings to refer to a past resurrection and a future parousia.[50]

3. Barrett reaffirms that ideas of suffering and atonement are bound up with the figure of the Son of man in Daniel, and that the whole concept is to be understood from its Old Testament background; the Son of man is the representative of humanity and of Israel in particular.[51]

The general conclusion of these two writers is thus that the Son of man is less of an apocalyptic figure and more of a messianic figure, and that the substantial authenticity of the various aspects of this concept within the teaching of Jesus can be upheld.

Finally, in this section, we must briefly mention the views of F. H. Borsch. Unlike the other writers he treats the Synoptic material *after* the rest of the New Testament evidence, a procedure which may well raise doubts whether he has taken the development of thought sufficiently into account. He accepts the substantial authenticity of most of the sayings attributed to Jesus and holds that Jesus believed that he had 'been given the right to speak and act in the role of the Son of Man', but left his own relationship to the future, glorious Son of man undefined.[52] Borsch's main concern, however, is to show how the various features of the Man myth which he described earlier in his book can be traced in a broken and fragmentary form in the Gospel material. In the course of this attempt he draws in much Gospel material in which the title itself does not occur; thus the baptism, temptation and Transfiguration are all held to be related to the Man myth.[53]

The general impression that remains, however, is one of vagueness, and Borsch's defence of the general authenticity of the sayings as teaching of Jesus is the less convincing because his methods would seem to make it possible to prove almost anything.

V

Before we attempt to draw some conclusions on the basis of this survey, two other areas of study must be briefly mentioned for completeness' sake.

The investigation of the Son of man sayings in the Gospel of John is a wide field of research in itself.[54] The Johannine sayings present the same features as the Synoptic sayings, but in addition there is a new emphasis on the Son of man as a figure who ascends and descends. Now if this group of sayings be regarded as forming one coherent Son of man ideology,[55] the question arises whether this is simply a Johannine development of what is already present in the Synoptic Gospels,[56] or whether other, non-Christian traditions have exercised an influence. In particular, has Gnostic mythology been at work here?

Whereas earlier research was ready to find gnostic influence at this point, the general trend in the limited period of our investigation has been different. S. S. Smalley has argued that the case for Gnostic influence is weak, and holds that Johannine theology stands close to that of the Synoptic Gospels and the Hellenistic church.[57]

The other area of research is the writings of Paul. Here the question arises whether Paul's references to Jesus as 'the Man', which would be the correct Greek translation of *bar nāshā*, represent a Hellenistic formulation of 'Son of man'. It must suffice to note that recent study has given a cautious affirmative to this question.[58]

VI

So much by way of general survey. What conclusions may be drawn, and are there any pointers regarding profitable lines of future research?

A number of questions arise from our discussion. The first is concerned with the proper method of studying the Gospel material. We have seen that somewhat different results are achieved according to whether or not the so-called traditio-historical *(traditions-geschichtlich)* method is followed.[59] The general principle behind this method is that any sayings in the Gospels which might be derived from Judaism or ascribed to the primitive Church cannot, at least in the first instance, be ascribed to Jesus. In other words, sayings ascribed to Jesus are to be regarded as inauthentic unless they can be *proved* to be authentic. A radical application of this criterion leads to the denial that Jesus used the title 'Son of man' at all. A less radical application allows a minimum of sayings to him, usually those in Group C.

But the validity of this radical method is by no means universally acknowledged.[60] Those, like M. D. Hooker, who adopt the principle that the tradition may be taken as authentic unless there are compelling reasons against doing so ascribe a much greater proportion of the sayings to Jesus. Nevertheless, it should be noted that, although C. Colpe adopts the more conservative approach, he accepts only eight of the Group C sayings as authentic. He is, however, prepared to admit the substantial authenticity of many of the other sayings in a non-'Son of man' form, and his rejection of the 'Son of man' formulations rests upon other grounds. For ourselves we believe that there are good grounds for preferring the conservative approach.[61]

It may also be the case that the order in which the Gospel sayings are treated affects the results reached. Those scholars who start from the apocalyptic sayings find themselves rejecting the others as teaching of Jesus, but those who start from the Group A 'earthly' sayings, as the order of Mark requires M. D. Hooker to do, and as F. H. Borsch chooses to do, find themselves able to accept at least some of the apocalyptic teaching as well. Even with the apocalyptic sayings there are differences of judgement between N. Perrin who starts from the sayings which are dependent upon Daniel 7, and C. Colpe who starts from the sayings which, in his opinion, do not have this background. We may ask whether subjective considerations have influenced judgement here, and whether there is a proper starting point for study.[62]

A further problem arises with regard to the type of theological development postulated by the two main wings of scholarship. If we adopt a view like that of M. D. Hooker, the majority of the sayings must be attributed to Jesus himself; all the development, so to speak, took place in his mind, and he had a 'complete' doctrine of the Son of man. There is consequently less room for development within the early Church. If, however, we adopt the kind of view which has been most carefully worked out by C. Colpe, we find that a very considerable development must have taken place in the early Church. The coming Son of man was identified with Jesus, and then the earthly ministry of Jesus was understood in terms of the Son of man.

A number of considerations suggest that the former view is preferable. Apart from the Gospel sayings themselves, there is extraordinarily little evidence for a Son of man Christology in the early Church; unlike the other Christological categories, it has left little trace outside the Gospels. Further, Colpe never explains clearly why the early Church identified Jesus with the coming Son of man, nor why it proceeded to integrate certain aspects of his earthly ministry into a Son of man ideology.[63]

J. Jeremias has argued that the oldest group of Son of man sayings are those to which there are no parallel formations without the term 'Son of man'; where such parallel forms exist, 'Son of man' is a later insertion. It is, however, unsafe to postulate a general rule of this character, and the possibility of exceptions cannot be ruled out. Some of the alternative forms which are supposed to give parallels to the Son of man sayings are not very convincing.[64] Moreover, the effect of the argument is to cast doubt upon a number of sayings which are otherwise perfectly unexceptionable as sayings of Jesus.[65] We may, therefore, be permitted to doubt the validity of Jeremias's rule, and consequently of Colpe's use of it.

How, then, are we to view the sayings which are attributed to Jesus? We return to the other main consideration in our survey, that of background. There seems little doubt that a decision on this point does affect our attitude to the Gospel material. It does matter whether the background is to be found in Jewish apocalyptic, or in the Book of Daniel *simpliciter*, or more broadly in the Old Testament, or even in a wider amalgam of thought.[66] It seems to us more likely that the background to New Testament usage is to be found in the Old Testament with M. D. Hooker and C. K. Barrett rather than in the very shadowy and unsubstantiated apocalyptic tradition proposed by C. Colpe.[67]

If this point is allowed—and clearly it requires a much fuller discussion than is possible here—then we are brought up against the fact that the majority of Son of man sayings can be seen as forming one pattern in which the general theme of authority, its rejection and its vindication, is expressed.[68] It is much more likely that the basis at least of this pattern goes back to one mind, that of Jesus himself, than that it was the product of piecemeal evolution in the early Church.

We have also seen that it is reasonably certain that 'Son of man' should not be taken in too strict a titular sense: The use of it by Jesus with reference to himself would not clash with his general reticence with regard to titles. There is the problem that some of the uses seem more titular, whereas others seem more a form of self-designation. If it is unlikely that 'Son of man' was a simple circumlocution for 'I', the possibility remains that Jesus, taking over the use of the term from the Old Testament and especially from Daniel, made it his self-designation in a quasi-titular manner.[69] The reason for his adoption of this self-designation may lie in his consciousness of divine Sonship[70] and his unwillingness to reveal it openly; the phrase 'Son of man', referring in Daniel 7 to a heavenly, messianic being, could be used as a veil for his true title[71] and at the same time as a means of expressing his solidarity with the people of Israel.

These conclusions will show that we favour the kind of view advocated by M. D. Hooker and C. K. Barrett. It would be idle, however, to suggest that the problem is settled, and any conclusion must necessarily be tentative.

Further attention to the problems of method and background may lead to more assured results.[72]

Notes

[1]There are about forty possible occurrences of the title (excluding obvious parallels) in the Synoptic Gospels, and a further dozen in the Gospel of John.

[2]See O. Cullmann, *The Christology of the New Testament* (London, 1959); F. Hahn, *Christologische Hoheitstitel* (Göttingen, 1964; Eng. tr. *The Titles of Jesus in Christology*, London, 1969); R. H. Fuller, *The Foundations of New Testament Christology* (London, 1965).

[3]An increasing realization of the difficulty of the 'titular' approach and a recognition that this approach ignores an important area of evidence have combined to develop an interest in the Christological significance of the work of Jesus and of his non-titular sayings. See especially H. R. Balz, *Methodische Probleme der Neutestamentlichen Christologie* (Neukirchen-Vluyn, 1967).

[4]A. J. B. Higgins (ed.), *New Testament Essays: Studies in Memory of T. W. Manson* (Manchester, 1959), pp. 119-35.

[5]Cambridge, 1931, pp. 211-34.

[6]"The Synoptic Son of Man Sayings in Recent Discussion', *NTS*, 12, 1965-66, pp. 327-51 (see pp. 73-99 above). Other surveys include: G. Haufe, 'Das Menschensohn Probleme in der gegenwärtigen wissenschaftlichen Diskussion', *Ev. Theol.*, 26, 1966, pp. 130-41; R. Marlow, 'The *Son of Man* in Recent Journal Literature', *CBQ*, 28, 1966, pp. 20-30; J. N. Birdsall, 'Who Is This Son of Man?' *EQ*, 42, 1970, pp. 7-17.

[7]For view 1., see Cullmann, op. cit.; V. Taylor, *The Names of Jesus* (London, 1937), pp. 25-35.

For view 2., see P. Vielhauer, *Aufsätze zum Neuen Testament* (München, 1965), pp. 55-91, 92-140; H. Conzelmann, 'Gegenwart und Zukunft in der synoptischen Tradition', *ZTK*, 54, 1957, pp. 277-96; E. Käsemann, *Essays on New Testament Themes* (London, 1964), pp. 43f.; H. M. Teeple, 'The Origin of the Son of Man Christology', *JBL*, 84, 1965, pp. 213-50.

For view 3., see R. Bultmann, *Theology of the New Testament* (London, 1952), I, pp. 28-32; G. Bornkamm, *Jesus von Nazareth* (Stuttgart, 1956), pp. 160-3, 206-8; H. E. Tödt, *The Son of Man in the Synoptic Tradition* (London, 1965); A. J. B. Higgins, *Jesus and the Son of Man* (London, 1964).

For view 4., see E. Schweizer, *Neotestamentica* (Zurich, 1963), pp. 56ff.

For fuller bibliographical details, see the previous essay.

For further statements along the above lines, see for 1.: R. Maddox, 'The Function of the Son of Man according to the Synoptic Gospels', *NTS*, 15, 1968-69, pp. 45-74; F. F. Bruce, *This Is That* (Exeter, 1968), pp. 26-30, 96-9; for 2.: H. Conzelmann, *An Outline of the Theology of the New Testament* (London, 1969), pp. 131-7; for 3.: W. Pannenberg, *Jesus—God and Man* (London, 1968), pp. 58-66; for 4.: E. Schweizer, *Das Evangelium nach Markus* (Göttingen, 1967), pp. 94-6; cf. T. Boman, *Die Jesus-Überlieferung im Lichte der neueren Volkskunde* (Göttingen, 1967), pp. 148-83; R. Leivestad, 'Der apokalyptische Menschensohn ein theologisches Phantom', *ASTI*, 6, 1968, pp. 49-105; J. C. O'Neill, 'The Silence of Jesus', *NTS*, 15, 1968-69, pp. 153-67, finds authentic teaching of Jesus among those sayings in which 'Son of man' is a self-designation and not a title.

[8]The main works to be discussed here are: N. Perrin, *Rediscovering the Teaching of Jesus* (London, 1967); M. D. Hooker, *The Son of Man in Mark* (London, 1967); C. K. Barrett, *Jesus and the Gospel Tradition* (London, 1967); F. H. Borsch, *The Son of Man in Myth and History* (London, 1967); Colpe, ὁ υἱὸς τοῦ ἀνθρώπου, *TDNT*, VIII, pp. 400-77; J. Jeremias, 'Die älteste Schicht der Menschensohn-Logien', *ZNW*, 58, 1967, pp. 159-72.

A full bibliography up to 1967 is given by C. Colpe.

[9]Perrin, op. cit., pp. 164-202, cf. pp. 259f. Elsewhere Perrin has indicated that he does not regard any of the Son of man sayings as authentic teaching of Jesus ('Recent Trends in

Research in the Christology of the New Testament', in J. C. Rylaarsdam (ed.), *Transitions in Biblical Scholarship* (Chicago, 1968), pp. 217-33, especially p. 221).
[10]On this text see E. Lövestam, *Spiritus Blasphemia: Eine Studie zu Mk. 3, 28f par Mt. 12, 31f, Lk. 12, 10* (Lund, 1968).
[11]A similar view is defended by C. F. D. Moule, *The Phenomenon of the New Testament* (London, 1967), pp. 33-6.
[12]One or two scholars have argued that the 'particular man' is Adam (J. B. Cortes and F. M. Gatti, 'The Son of Man and the Son of Adam', *Biblica*, 49, 1968, pp. 457-502). The clear association of the phrase with Daniel 7.13 speaks against this interpretation.
Another view is that 'Son of man' is a euphemism for 'Son of God' (J. M. Ford, ' "The Son of Man"—A Euphemism?', *JBL*, 87, 1968, pp. 257-66). It is true that the Son of man has divine attributes and functions, but the linguistic suggestion is unproved and unlikely.
[13]C. Colpe (*TDNT*, VIII, 402), notes that the definite form is not attested in the Old Testament.
[14]According to C. Colpe (*TDNT*, VIII, pp. 402-5), the four expressions *'enash, 'enasha, bar ('e)nash* and *bar ('e)nasha* were used. Any of these could be used to mean 'the man', 'a man' or 'somebody'. The first two expressions could be used collectively to mean 'men'; the last two (those with *bar*) could be used in a generalizing sense.
[15]"The Use of *bar nash/bar nasha* in Jewish Aramaic', published as Appendix E in M. Black, *An Aramaic Approach to the Gospels and Acts* (Oxford, 1967[3]), pp. 310-28. According to Vermes, 'In most instances the sentence contains an allusion to humiliation, danger or death, but there are also examples where reference to the self in the third person is dictated by humility or modesty' (p. 327). The criticisms made by J. A. Fitzmyer in his review of the book (*CBQ*, 30, 1968, pp. 417-28) do not affect the main point at issue.
[16]Black, op. cit., pp. 328-30; cf. O'Neill, op. cit., p. 161, n. 1.
[17]Jeremias, op. cit., p. 165, n. 9; Colpe, op. cit., p. 403f.; R. Le Déaut, 'Le substrat araméen des Evangiles: scolies en marge de l'*Aramaic Approach* de Matthew Black', *Biblica*, 50, 1968, pp. 388-99 (especially 397-9). The phrase 'I and nobody else' would be expressed in Aramaic by *hahu gabra*.
[18]A. Gelston, 'A Sidelight on the "Son of Man",' *SJT*, 22, 1969, pp. 189-96, especially p. 189, n. 2.
[19]Vermes, op. cit., pp. 327f.
[20]Colpe, op. cit., pp. 404f.
[21]R. E. C. Formesyn ('Was there a Pronominal Connection for the Bar Nasha Selfdesignation?', *Nov.T*, 8, 1966, pp. 1-35) argues that the form *hahu bar nasha* was the actual expression for 'I'. He holds that the closeness of form between this expression and the title 'Son of man' led to the messianization of the former in the early Church. However, there is no positive evidence for the form postulated by Formesyn (cf. Vermes, op. cit., pp. 313f.).
[22]For the generally held view, see Colpe, op. cit., p. 423, n. 180. A date early in the second century AD is upheld by J. C. Hindley, 'Towards a Date for the Similitudes of Enoch: An Historical Approach', *NTS*, 14, 1967-68, pp. 551-65.
[23]For discussion of the view that originally the 'saints of the Most High' were angelic beings rather than pious Israelites, see Hooker, op. cit., p. 13, n. 3.
[24]We must distinguish between the original significance of the figure before it was taken over by Daniel and the use which Daniel makes of it. The original figure is clearly that of a man-like heavenly being, an angel or a god (Colpe, op. cit., p. 421). In Daniel it may retain this meaning or be a symbol for something else. 1. Many scholars take it to be simply a symbol for the saints of the Most High, in the way in which the female figure of Britannia symbolizes the British people (Hooker, op. cit., pp. 11-30, 184). 2. Following P. Vielhauer and H. E. Tödt, C. Colpe holds that the figure symbolizes the abstract concept of rule. This view is very unlikely. It places too much stress on the analogy with the beasts in the preceding part of the chapter (the beasts in any case represent *kings* as well as kingdoms), and it does not do justice to the form of v. 14 which speaks of dominion being given to the man-like figure. Further,

the prehistory of the concept suggests that a heavenly individual is meant. 3. We therefore prefer the view that the man-like figure is a heavenly being who is the representative or head of the saints, in the same way as a king or president can be said to 'represent' his subjects. Thus Daniel's use of the figure is in accord with its previous meaning. See Marshall, op. cit., p. 336 (= pp.81f. above), and, in addition to the authorities cited there, G. von Rad in *TDNT*, I, p. 567, n. 13; H. L. Ellison, *The Centrality of the Messianic Idea for the Old Testament* (London, 1953), pp. 13-15; E. J. Young, *Daniel's Vision of the Son of Man* (London, 1958); Bruce, op. cit., p. 26.

[25]To this extent, T. F. Glasson was right in suggesting that the concept in 1 Enoch 14 is older than that in Daniel 7 (*The Second Advent* [London, 1947], pp. 13-18). Literary dependence of Daniel on 1 Enoch is, however, unlikely.

[26]Colpe, op. cit., pp. 406-30.

[27]N. Perrin has indicated his acceptance of Colpe's thesis (op. cit., p. 166, n. 1).

[28]For the above summary, see Borsch, op. cit., pp. 132, 218f.

[29]As Borsch admits (op. cit., pp. 225-31), the existence of groups maintaining Son of man speculations in the time of Jesus has not been proved.

[30]In our opinion, Miss Hooker dismisses too easily the evidence for the Son of man as a heavenly individual being in Daniel.

[31]Perrin, op. cit., pp. 164-73.

[32]Hooker, op. cit., pp. 43-7. Other scholars who reject the view that 'Son of man' was a stereotyped apocalyptic title are Leivestad, op. cit., and O. Betz, *What do we know about Jesus?* (London, 1968), pp. 109-12.

[33]Balz, op. cit., pp. 61-112. Of special importance is Balz's demonstration that very much the same mixtures of attributes and functions are associated with other titles for eschatological Saviour figures. Thus the sharp distinction which is sometimes drawn between the titles of Messiah and Son of man is unjustified.

[34]E. Stauffer, *New Testament Theology* (London, 1955), p. 108.

It would, however, be wrong to deny completely the existence of any kind of Son of man figure in Judaism. Here Perrin plainly goes too far. The evidence shows that there was considerable fluidity in depicting the Son of man, not that there was no Son of man figure. See W. G. Kümmel's critical assessment of Perrin's book in *JR*, 49, 1969, pp. 59-66.

[35]Colpe, op. cit., p. 429.

[36]Perrin, op. cit., p. 173.

[37]Colpe, op. cit., pp. 430-61.

[38]The difficulty with this explanation of this and the other two sayings is that they are not general statements which are universally true; they refer to Jesus alone. It is therefore unlikely that an original reference to Jesus as a man has been misunderstood in the tradition as a reference to the Son of man. The reference to 'men' in Matthew 9.8 comes from Matthew himself and is not necessarily a clue to the original form of the saying. For the linking of the phrase 'Son of man' with forgiveness, see Maddox, op. cit., p. 57, who views forgiveness as a juridical function of the Son of man.

[39]Cf. Perrin, op. cit., pp. 119-21.

[40]Cf. Higgins, op. cit., for the same explanation of several sayings.

[41]Colpe, op. cit., p. 441. The original German is: 'Bezieht man es von dieser Gewissheit auf ihren Träger, dann kann man diesen Sachverhalt auch als dynamische, in seiner zukünftigen Vollendung intendierte und funktionale Gleichstellung Jesu mit dem kommenden Menschensohn interpretieren. Die Urgemeinde machte daraus eine statische, schon in Jesu Gegenwart realisierte und personale Identifikation' (C. Colpe, *TWNT*, VIII, p. 443). Colpe's conclusion is similar to that of A. J. B. Higgins who holds that Jesus spoke of 'performing Son of man functions in the future', but does not go as far as Higgins in claiming that Jesus expressly related himself to the Son of man (Higgins, op. cit., pp. 200-3).

[42]N. Perrin, 'Mark xiv. 62: The End Product of a Christian Pesher Tradition', *NTS*, 12, 1965-

66, pp. 150-5. See the reply by F. H. Borsch, 'Mark xiv. 62 and I Enoch lxii. 5', *NTS*, 14, 1967-68, pp. 565-7.

[43]Cf. Boman, op. cit., p. 152.

[44]Perrin notes that Colpe has to admit the lack of a Jewish background for the concept of the Son of man which he ascribes to Jesus, and therefore needs to postulate an otherwise unattested stream of apocalyptic tradition behind the usage of Jesus (Perrin, op. cit., p. 260). Perrin is correct in holding that the existing biblical and late Jewish material affords an adequate background for the New Testament usage, but is wrong in denying that this background could lead to the use of the Son of man concept by Jesus himself (cf. Kümmel, op. cit., pp. 64f.

[45]See C. Colpe's more conservative principle, op cit., p. 432.

[46]Hooker, op. cit., p. 181.

[47]Cf. M. D. Hooker, *Jesus and the Servant* (London, 1959). E. Best, *The Temptation and the Passion* (Cambridge, 1965), p. 164, also finds a suffering Son of man in Daniel. Bruce, op. cit., pp. 26-30, 97-9, rightly stresses the weakness of the allusions in Daniel to a suffering Son of man and reasserts the use by Jesus of the Suffering Servant imagery.

[48]Hooker, *The Son of Man in Mark*, p. 187.

[49]Barrett, op. cit., p. 32; cf. Maddox, op. cit., pp. 49f.

[50]Barrett, op. cit., pp. 77-87. A similar view is upheld by M. Black, 'The Son of Man Problem in Recent Research and Debate', *BJRL*, 45, 1962-63, pp. 305-18; 'The "Son of man" Passion Sayings in the Gospel Tradition', *ZNW*, 60, 1969, pp. 1-8.

[51]Barrett, op. cit., pp. 41-5.

[52]Borsch, op. cit., pp. 321, 360. The ambiguity postulated by Borsch is not satisfactory, especially since the Gospels themselves do not make a clear distinction between the earthly Son of man and the glorious Son of man. Borsch's difficulty is due to his overstress on the use of 'Son of man' as an apocalyptic title.

[53]We may compare the way in which E. Lohmeyer found a Son of man Christology embedded in parts of the Marcan narrative where the title itself is not found *(Das Evangelium des Markus* [Göttingen, 1959], *passim).*

[54]S. Schulz, *Untersuchungen zur Menschensohn-Christologie im Johannesevangelium* (Göttingen, 1957); R. Schnackenburg, 'Der Menschensohn im Johannesevangelium', *NTS*, 11, 1964-65, pp. 123-37 (cf. *The Gospel according to St John* [London, 1968] I, pp. 529-42).

[55]E. D. Freed, 'The Son of Man in the Fourth Gospel', *JBL*, 86, 1967, pp. 402-9, has argued that John uses Christological titles indiscriminately, and that consequently there are no special ideas bound up with the title 'Son of man' which are not part of a more general Christological conception; cf. Jeremias, op. cit., p. 170.

[56]For the view that much of Johannine theology is a development of synoptic themes, see C. K. Barrett, *The Gospel according to St John* (London, 1955). Barrett, however, saw the influence of speculations about the primal or archetypal Man on the Johannine concept of the Son of man (ibid., pp. 60f.).

[57]S. S. Smalley, 'The Johannine Son of Man Sayings', *NTS*, 15, 1968-69, pp. 278-301. See also E. M. Kinniburgh, 'The Johannine "Son of Man",' *Studia Evangelica*, IV = TU CII, 1968, pp. 64-71, who argues that in John the title is no longer apocalyptic but has become a term of realized eschatology. W. H. Cadman, *The Opened Heaven* (Oxford, 1969), pp. 26-42, holds that the imagery of the ascent of the Son of man to heaven symbolizes the close union between God and Jesus during his earthly life.

[58]Colpe, op. cit., pp. 470-3; Borsch, op. cit., pp. 232-56. The problem is part of the broader issue of Adam and 'man' in Paul's thought which cannot be raised here.

[59]For the basic principle, see (for example) Käsemann, op. cit., pp. 36f., and for the method see Perrin, op. cit., pp. 15-53. There is some doubt whether the principle should be called 'form-critical' (Fuller, *The Foundations of New Testament Christology*, p. 116) or 'traditio-historical' (cf. R. H. Fuller, *A Critical Introduction to the New Testament* [London, 1966], pp.

93f.). If the latter adjective is accepted, 'form-critical' loses its broad sense and refers purely to classification of the Gospel material by form; the study of the material thus classified in order to determine how it was modified in oral transmission and to determine the location of these modifications in the development of tradition is then 'traditio-historical'.

[60]Colpe, op. cit., p. 432; Hooker, op. cit., pp. 4-7, 79 et al.; Kümmel, op. cit., pp. 60f. From a radical viewpoint also the method is open to criticism: F. G. Downing, The Church and Jesus (London, 1968).

[61]See I. H. Marshall, review of R. H. Fuller, The Foundations of New Testament Christology, Themelios, 3, 2, 1966, pp. 25-34; 'Questions about the Gospels—II. History or Fiction?' TSF Bulletin, 53, spring 1969, pp. 3-9; I Believe in the Historical Jesus (London, 1977).

[62]The type of interpretation favoured by G. Bornkamm and H. E. Tödt has its basis in taking Luke 12.8f., with its apparent distinction between Jesus and the Son of man, as its point of departure (Bornkamm, op. cit., pp. 161f.). On this text, see G. Lindeskog, 'Das Rätsel des Menschensohns', Stud. Theol., 22, 1968, pp. 169-76.

[63]See the criticisms of this argument by Hooker, op. cit., pp. 185f.; Schweizer, Das Evangelium nach Markus, p. 94; cf. Teeple, op. cit., pp. 224-6.

[64]Jeremias's use of parallels from the Gospel of Thomas is of doubtful value; it is uncertain whether this document reflects an independent, primitive stream of tradition. Some of the parallels cited from the Gospels are from secondary material (Matt. 9.8 as a parallel to Mark 2.10). In others the lack of correspondence is so great as to raise doubt whether they are in fact alternative versions of the same sayings (Luke 13.32 as a parallel to Mark 8.31; Mark 14.24 as a parallel to Mark 10.45; Matt. 26.50 as a parallel to Luke 22.48; John 5.12 and 8.25 as parallels to John 12.34).

[65]See, for example, the defence of Luke 24.7 by M. Black in his article in ZNW, 60, 1969, pp. 2f. (See n. 50.)

[66]Leivestad, op. cit., pp. 98f.

[67]We would see a greater influence of Daniel upon the Synoptic tradition than C. Colpe allows. At the same time, we believe that there is no good reason for denying that Jesus knew and used the Book of Daniel.

[68]See especially Maddox, op. cit.

[69]Our view would be that 'Son of man' is used throughout the sayings of Jesus as a way of referring to himself in a manner intended to recall its use in the Old Testament. It would thus be a self-designation based on the quasi-titular use of the phrase rather than upon its putative use as a simple circumlocution for 'I'. At the same time, the phrase was ambiguous and would not necessarily be recognized as titular by Jesus' hearers.

[70]For Jesus' filial consciousness, see Higgins, op. cit., p. 207; 'The Son of Man Concept and the Historical Jesus', Studia Evangelica, V = TU CIII, 1968, pp. 14-20. For a defence of Jesus' use of the term 'Son' as a self-designation, see I. H. Marshall, 'The Divine Sonship of Jesus', Interpretation, 21, 1967, pp. 87-103 (reprinted below, pp. 134-49).

The question may be raised how far one's attitude to the person of Jesus as the Son of God affects a critical estimate of the Son of man sayings; the type of criticism which rules out the resurrection (understood in the traditional sense) as an object of historical study is bound to rule out the possibility of understanding Jesus in any other than purely human categories. Such a limitation of historical possibilities prevents an adequate assessment of the Gospels.

[71]Cf. our remarks above on Miss J. M. Ford's theory; cf. also E. Lohmeyer, Galiläa und Jerusalem (Göttingen, 1936), p. 35, who says of 'the Son of man', 'welcher Name nur verhüllt was der urchristliche Glaube vom Gottessohn bekennt'.

[72][1989] The immense volume of material on the 'Son of man' question published since 1970 makes any attempt at evaluation within the limits of this postscript quite impossible. The following brief comments are an updating of the relevant discussion in the 'Nachwort' to the German translation of my book The Origins of New Testament Christology (Leicester, 1976; Die Ursprünge der neutestamentlichen Christologie (Giessen, 1985):

A solid *Festschrift* in honour of A. Vögtle (R. Pesch and R. Schnackenburg (eds.), *Jesus und der Menschensohn* [Freiburg, 1975] contains a number of contributions to the use of the phrase in the Gospels. On the one hand, H. Schürmann and G. Schneider argue that the occurrences of the phrase in Q and the Lucan *Sondergut* are due not to Jesus but to the early Church. On the other hand, W. G. Kümmel and R. Pesch argue for the use of the phrase by Jesus in Luke 12.8f.; Mark 9.31 and 14.62. A. J. B. Higgins, who contributed to the same volume, has also written a further monograph defending the Tödt-Hahn interpretation (*The Son of Man in the Teaching of Jesus*, SNTS Monograph Series 39 [Cambridge, 1980]).

But the centre of interest in the English-speaking world is undoubtedly the further development of the kind of theory advanced by G. Vermes discussed above. Two main contributions must be noted. First, there is the detailed study of Daniel 7 and its influence by M. Casey (*Son of Man* [London, 1979]). Casey is primarily concerned with the original significance of Daniel 7; he argues that there is no 'Son of man' figure in the chapter, and that what we have is merely the use of a human figure as a symbol for Israel. In subsequent Jewish literature he finds (like Vermes and N. Perrin) that there is no Son of man concept. Then he looks at the Gospels. He argues that sayings which reflect the influence of Daniel 7 are not authentic teaching of Jesus. What survives is a set of some twelve texts, all of which can be translated back into Aramaic and which use the Aramaic idiom *bar 'enash(a)* to make general statements that were true of Jesus himself. Casey's discussion has the important merit of actually testing the possibility of Aramaic renditions of the texts. He has taken the discussion further in various essays ('The Jackals and the Son of Man Matt. 8.20//Luke 9.58', *JSNT*, 23, 1985, pp. 3-22; 'General, Generic and Indefinite: The Use of the Term "Son of Man" in Aramaic Sources and in the Teaching of Jesus', *JSNT*, 29, 1987, pp. 21-56).

Second, there is the study of B. Lindars (*Jesus the Son of Man* [London, 1983]) who differs from his predecessors in arguing that the Aramaic idiom *bar 'enash(a)* refers not to all people in general (and hence to the speaker in particular) but rather to a specific class of people with whom the speaker identifies himself. He then claims that there is a core of authentic sayings in the Gospels which can be understood in this way. For example, in Matthew 8.20 Jesus says that foxes have holes and birds have nests, but he and anybody who shares in the conditions of his missionary vocation have no place of rest. This is one of the few sayings where the hypothesis looks credible and could make good sense of a saying; but when, for example, we are told that Jesus said, 'just as Jonah was a sign to the Ninevites . . . so there is a man who will be a sign to the present generation', or, again, that, 'if anybody confesses or denies Jesus now, he will have an advocate or an accuser in the shape of his own response to Jesus at the last judgment', our credulity is stretched to breaking point.

This general type of view has now found its rather belated entry into the German-speaking world with the publication of a work by a Danish scholar, M. Müller, *Der Ausdruck 'Menschensohn' in den Evangelien*, Acta Theologica Danica 17 (Leiden, 1984).

The work of these scholars suggests that instead of the usual threefold classification of the Son of man sayings we should rather divide them into two basic groups—those that reflect an Aramaic idiom and those that show influence from Daniel 7. They would argue that only sayings in the former category can have a chance of being authentic sayings of Jesus. J. D. G. Dunn, however, holds that it was Jesus himself who made the jump from the use of the Aramaic idiom to the use of an allusion to Daniel 7, and that once this jump was made the way was open for further use of Daniel 7 (*Christology in the Making* [London, 1980], pp. 86-8).

It is a problem with the approach of Casey and Lindars that their understanding of *bar 'enasha* as generic leads to some rather unconvincing interpretations of the texts in the Gospels. Renewed attention needs to be given to the possibility of an indefinite sense for the idiom originally defended by G. Vermes and developed by R. J. Bauckham, 'The Son of man: "A man in my position" or "someone"?', *JSNT*, 23, pp. 23-33.

S. Kim has advanced the interesting thesis that Jesus used 'Son of man' in line with its

Danielic use (which was based in turn on Ezekiel 1) to refer to himself as a divine figure, the Son of God who is the head of the sons of God (*"The 'Son of Man' " as the Son of God* [Tübingen, 1983]). This hypothesis appeared independently of the works by Casey and Lindars and does not really come to terms with their discussion of the Aramaic background.

The view that the concept of Son of man is essentially messianic continues to be defended by different authors with reference to Daniel 7, and also to the use in the Gospels (G. R. Beasley-Murray, 'The Interpretation of Daniel 7', *CBQ*, 45, 1983, pp. 44-58; *Jesus and the Kingdom of God* (Grand Rapids, 1986); G. Gerleman, *Der Menschensohn*, Studia Biblica 1 (Leiden, 1983); W. Bittner, 'Gott—Menschensohn—Davidssohn: Eine Untersuchung zur Traditionsgeschichte von Daniel 7, 13f.', *Freiburger Zeitschrift für Philosophie und Theologie*, 22, 1985, pp. 343-72; W. Horbury, 'The Messianic Associations of "The Son of Man",' *JTS*, n.s. 36, 1985, pp. 34-55; C. C. Caragounis, *The Son of Man* (WUNT 38) (Tübingen, 1986). J. H. Charlesworth (*Jesus within Judaism* [London, 1988]) cautiously adopts the position that Jesus knew and was influenced by Daniel and 1 Enoch and that consequently Son of man sayings from all three traditional categories may go back to him).

We thus have two approaches to the problem, the one concentrating attention on the use of an Aramaic idiom and the other defending the influence of Daniel 7 and subsequent Jewish literature. There is clearly an unfinished debate here, and it can be urged that both sides need to engage more closely with each other's insights.

6
Son of God or Servant of Yahweh? – A Reconsideration of Mark 1.11

T HE WORDING OF THE DIVINE MESSAGE CONVEYED TO JESUS by a heavenly voice at his baptism is given in its most primitive form in Mark 1.11 Σὺ εἶ ὁ υἱός μου ὁ ἀγαπητός, ἐν σοὶ εὐδόκησα.[1] According to V. Taylor the language recalls that of Psalm 2.7 Υἱός μου εἶ σύ, ἐγὼ σήμερον γεγέννηκά σε and Isaiah 42.1 Ἰακὼβ ὁ παῖς μου, ἀντιλήμψομαι αὐτοῦ. Ἰσραὴλ ὁ ἐκλεκτός μου, προσεδέξατο αὐτὸν ἡ ψυχή μου, with echoes of other passages such as Genesis 22.2; Isaiah 44.2 and 62.4.[2] It thus suggests that Jesus is being addressed as the Son of God and the Servant of Yahweh.

One possible reason for the linking of the two primary passages was suggested by G. Dalman.[3] He noted that the word παῖς, which is found in Isaiah 42.1 LXX as a translation of עֶבֶד with the meaning 'servant', can also mean 'child' or 'son'; if the word is given the latter meaning, the text could be applied to the 'son' of Psalm 2.7. As evidence for this possibility, Dalman adduced Wisdom 2.13-18 and 12.19-20, where the parallelism shows that παῖς means 'child' although the source of Wisdom's language is Isaiah 40 ff., where the word means 'servant'. For Dalman, then, the ambiguity in the meaning of παῖς led to the application of Isaiah 42.1 to the Son of God in Psalm 2.7. It follows that the application of the title of 'Son' to Jesus was primary and, since the ambiguity arises only in Greek, that the combination must have taken place in a Greek-speaking environment.

A different explanation was developed by W. Bousset. In a footnote in *Kyrios Christos* he suggested that perhaps παῖς originally stood in the saying. This was altered to υἱός, and thus the first step was taken in a process which led to the complete assimilation of the saying to Psalm 2.7 in Luke 3.22 D.[4]

On this view, the original form of the saying was based purely upon Isaiah 42.1 and did not refer to Jesus as the Son. Bousset also observed that the presence of ἀγαπητός suggested dependence upon Isaiah 42.1 rather than upon Psalm 2.7.

What Bousset voiced as a suggestion has been developed into a carefully supported and fairly widely held theory. It has won the adhesion of O. Cullmann[5] and J. Jeremias,[6] both of whom have adduced further arguments in its favour, and it is accepted by a number of other scholars.[7] We may summarize the arguments in its favour as follows:

1. παῖς is ambiguous and can mean 'servant' or 'son'.

2. The use of ἐκλεκτός (said to be the more probable reading) in John 1.34, a verse closely associated with the baptismal saying, suggests that this was the 'highest' title applied to Jesus in this context. Moreover, ἐκλεκτός itself points to Isaiah 42.1.

3. In the baptismal text itself ἀγαπητός can be a translation variant for ἐκλεκτός, and its use is attested in the version of Isaiah 42.1 quoted in Matthew 12.18. Compare how ἐκλελεγμένος has replaced ἀγαπητός in Luke 9.35.

4. The reference in the context to the descent of the Spirit upon Jesus is paralleled in Isaiah 42.1b, and confirms that the thought of the passage can be largely explained from this text.

5. Since Jesus is unlikely to have been designated 'Son of God' in Palestinian Jewish Christianity, it is probable that the text (if it represents an early tradition) addressed Jesus by the less offensive title of 'Servant'.

6. Elsewhere in Mark, especially in the passion narrative, the concept of Jesus as the Servant of Yahweh is often expressed, and this makes it probable that a Servant Christology can be detected in the earlier chapters of Mark and specifically in the baptismal narrative.[8]

These arguments have not sufficed to convince all scholars,[9] and there would appear to be room for a reconsideration of the evidence.

II

(a) It may be worth observing at the outset that there is no trace of any other understanding of the passage in the early church than that offered by Mark. The same text is offered in the transfiguration story (Mark 9.7 and pars.), and the interpretation offered by the early Fathers is in terms of Psalm 2.7.[10] Of particular interest is the text in the Gospel of the Hebrews, 'My Son, in all the prophets was I waiting for thee that thou shouldest come and I might find rest in thee. For thou art my rest; thou art my first-begotten Son that reignest for ever.'[11]

Two texts may be thought to suggest a different view. One is Luke 9.35, where Luke has ὁ ἐκλελεγμένος in place of ὁ ἀγαπητός found in Mark 9.7.[12] The other is John 1.34 (cf. 2. above). In both of these cases, however, what we have is a variant for ἀγαπητός and not for υἱός; they cannot, therefore, be used as part of a proof that υἱός was not an original part of the text.[13] With regard to John 1.34 there is a variant reading υἱός, the existence of which might be thought to militate against the point just made. But it should be observed that it is not certain that ἐκλεκτός is the original reading in this text,[14] and, even if it is, the change in the MS tradition to υἱός rather than to ἀγαπητός would be inevitable in view of the usage of John elsewhere. The evidence, therefore, of Luke 9.35, and John 1.34 cannot be regarded as contradicting the exegetical tradition of the early church. It shows that the Servant motif was associated with the baptismal and transfiguration narratives, but not that the presence of the Son motif was denied.

(b) A second point is that arguments which indicate a substantial influence from Isaiah 42 upon the baptismal narrative in no way exclude the possibility that other Old Testament passages have also influenced the text. It is no part of our purpose to deny the influence of the Servant concept upon the mind of Jesus or of the Evangelists,[15] but simply to affirm that other influences may also be present, and indeed may be of primary importance.

It is true that an explanation of the saying in terms of one Old Testament source may be the simplest hypothesis, but it does not follow that it is the right hypothesis. On the contrary, the effect of much recent research has been to show that a multiplicity of Old Testament allusions may be detected in many late Jewish and New Testament texts. Moreover, the clusters of ideas around such 'messianic' titles as 'Son of God', 'Son of man', 'Messiah' and 'Servant' overlap at so many points that it is often hard to disentangle the original associations of any given title or to establish simply on the basis of a set of descriptive concepts which title is being used in a given passage. A case in point is the way in which 'Son of man' in 1 Enoch has attracted to itself language used to describe both the Messiah and the Servant. This phenomenon is common in the New Testament; full allowance must be made for a richness of Old Testament allusion in many texts.

This general point is sufficient to dispose of arguments 3. and 4. above. The fact that ἀγαπητός *may* be drawn from Isaiah 42.1 is no argument that the preceding phrase must come from the same place. A number of other possible sources for ἀγαπητός can in fact be listed, and we cannot even say that the word must have been drawn from Isaiah 42.1. Similarly, even if the descent of the Spirit in Mark 1.10 may echo Isaiah 42.1, it does not follow that the wording of Mark 1.11 must be derived from the same source. As in the case of ἀγαπητός, even the derivation of this feature from Isaiah 42.1 is not beyond question. The king or Messiah is the Lord's *anointed* (Ps. 2.2!), and the Spirit of the Lord rests upon him (Isa. 11.1f.; cf. 61.1, quoted in Luke 4.18).

Both of these particular examples show that a variety of sources (and not simply Isa. 42.1) may lie behind the baptismal saying. It is time to turn to the opening part of the saying and to ask whether we must postulate that its original form was dependent upon Isaiah 42.1.

(c) Our problem is whether a text which in its present form echoes Psalm 2.7,[16] which is framed in the second person (Isa. 42.1: third person!) and which contains the word υἱός (unattested in any version of Isa. 42.1) ever existed in a form with παῖς instead of υἱός.

The Hebrew word translated as παῖς in Isaiah 42.1 is עֶבֶד, which unequivocally means 'servant'. It occurs 807 times in the Massoretic Text, but only once is it said to be translated by υἱός (Deut. 32.43).[17] This exception, however, disappears on examination; the LXX is here not dependent upon the MT, but follows a different text which is attested in a Hebrew MS from Cave 4 at Qumran.[18] It may be taken as certain that the Hebrew word עֶבֶד would never be translated as υἱός, and it follows that ambiguity was possible only on Greek soil as a result of the genuine double meaning of παῖς.[19]

Conversely, the LXX scarcely ever used παῖς as a translation of בֵּן (only Prov. 4.1; 20.7).

Now Jeremias's argument is that the title of παῖς, with the meaning of 'servant', was perfectly acceptable in the Palestinian church where it arose, but was found offensive to the Gentile church because of its lowliness. He therefore holds that the ambiguous παῖς μου was clarified to υἱός μου in the pre-Marcan Hellenistic tradition, and argues that this suggestion would fit in with the way in which the phrase παῖς θεοῦ underwent a semantic change from 'servant of God' to 'child of God' at latest by the second century.[20]

This argument is open to various objections:

(i) According to Jeremias, originally only Isaiah 42.1 (Heb. text) would have been quoted.[21] If this is the case, we may be surprised that the interpretation of the ambiguous παῖς by the early Church was not governed by the memory of the original עֶבְדִּי. It may be argued that the author of Wisdom could misunderstand παῖς to mean 'child', but in this case we are dealing with a work dependent upon the Greek Old Testament.[22] As Jeremias himself observes, 'The further the distance from the original Hebrew text the more the second conception ("child of God") prevailed in the Jewish Hellenistic understanding of Isaiah 40 ff.'[23] It is interesting that early in the second century AD Greek-speaking Judaism began to translate עֶבֶד by δοῦλος instead of παῖς.²⁴ This shows not merely that παῖς was ambiguous, but also that the correct interpretation of עֶבֶד was known and maintained.

(ii) Lindars observes that the argument of Jeremias would carry more conviction if other examples of the change could be quoted.²⁵ Jeremias himself claimed that a similar process took place in John 1.34 if it is correct that ἐκλεκτός has there been replaced by υἱός.²⁶ Lindars, however, objects that this is not a true parallel, since this change was not necessitated by a semantic problem in the word itself. We may also note that in any case this hypothetical change occurred too late to offer a parallel to a change in the early, pre-Marcan tradition.

One other possible example must be discussed. It arises from a comparison of the story of the centurion's servant (Matt. 8.5-13, par. Luke 7.1-10) with that of the nobleman's son (John 4.46-54). The version in Matthew uses παῖς throughout, that in Luke uses παῖς and δοῦλος interchangeably, showing that Luke understood παῖς to mean 'servant', and the version in John uses παῖς, παιδίον and υἱός interchangeably. It has, therefore, been argued that an original story about a παῖς has been developed independently in terms of a δοῦλος (Luke) and a υἱός (John), the meaning of παῖς in Matthew being indeterminate.²⁷ Whatever be the truth in this suggestion, it does no more than show the ambiguity of παῖς when there is nothing to control the meaning. It does not provide a parallel to the doctrinal change made in Mark 1.11.

(iii) Although the word παῖς is ambiguous in New Testament usage, as has just been observed,²⁸ its meaning as a title is undoubtedly 'servant'. This is true in Matthew 12.18 (quotation of Isa. 42.1), Luke 1.54 (with reference to Israel; cf. Isa. 41.8f.); Luke 1.69 and Acts 4.25 (with reference to David). The analogy of these examples makes it likely that when the title is used of Jesus in Acts 3.13, 26; 4.27 and 30 it has the same meaning. This is confirmed for Acts 3.13 by the clear allusion to Isaiah 52.13, and Acts 3.26 takes up this reference when it explains the glorification of God's servant in terms of the resurrection. Difficulty arises, however, with Acts 4.27. The use of the term in Acts 4.25 and the analogy of the other references already considered would suggest that here also the word means 'servant'. This has been disputed by E. Haenchen and H. Conzelmann, who hold that the quotation from Psalm 2.1f. in verse 26 and the allusion to the (baptismal) anointing of Jesus (cf. Χριστοῦ, Ps. 2.2; and Luke 3.22; 4.18) demand the meaning 'son' here.²⁹ The objection is not convincing. It seems likely that Isaiah 61.1, quoted in Luke 4.18, was taken as a description of the anointing of the Servant of Yahweh.³⁰ Moreover, the fact that the παῖς is here identified with the Χριστός/υἱός of Psalm 2 does not mean that the word need lose its own meaning. The use of the adjective ἅγιος, which is closely associated with δίκαιος (Isa.

53.11) and παῖς in Acts 3.13f., is a further pointer that the Servant is 'in mind here also.[31] These considerations show that παῖς should be understood to mean 'servant' in the references in Acts.[32]

(iv) The problem of a semantic change now arises. If Jesus was given the title of παῖς with the meaning of 'servant', is it likely that the word developed the meaning of 'child' at this stage in the tradition? It is true that a development of this kind did take place at a later date; Jeremias is able to adduce Mart. Poly. 14.1 and 20.2 and (from before AD 100) 1 Clem. 59.2-4 as evidence for this change, but (as he admits) the change took place gradually and not everywhere at the same time. There does not seem to be any concrete evidence to justify us in the supposition that the change took place earlier. On the Jewish side, παῖς was correctly replaced by δοῦλος in translations of the Old Testament (see above). The fact that Luke himself preserves παῖς with the meaning of 'servant' likewise shows that the change had not taken place at the time and place where he wrote. Jeremias's argument is that παῖς was unpopular in Gentile Christian circles, but this is an over-statement. The title was used—in Acts, 1 Clem., and Mart. Poly. together with Did. 9.2f.; 10.2f.; 10.7 copt. (cf. Barn. 6. 1; 9.2)—and the fact that it survived at all, even in liturgical settings, shows that it was not so unpopular as not to be used at all. It was no doubt its ambiguity and its lowly content which led to its rather scanty use and to its replacement by other titles. The fact of its unpopularity, however, is no proof that an original παῖς was likely to be changed to υἱός rather than to δοῦλος. Evidence for this change is still lacking.

We may, finally, ask whether there are any other texts which conceal an original παῖς. So far as δοῦλος is concerned, there is one direct application of it to Jesus in the 'Carmen Christi' in Philippians 2.7. Although the point is disputed, it is probable that we have an allusion to the suffering Servant of Yahweh here,[33] but there is no evidence to suggest that the word has replaced an original παῖς. With regard to υἱός, Maurer has argued that the word expresses a Pais-Christology or is a free translation of עֶבֶד in Mark 14.61 and 15.39.[34] In the latter passage, however, the centurion's comment is surely to be understood in terms of divine sonship, and it is quite improbable that the saying ever referred to the Isaianic Servant. Similarly, in the former passage it is unlikely that the high priest would have been interested in Jesus' claim to be the Suffering Servant (even if 'Servant' was a current messianic designation). A survey of other texts does not suggest that in any case an original παῖς has been covered up. One small piece of evidence that points in the other direction has been noted by various scholars: although the form of the citation of Isaiah 42.1 in Matthew 12.18 has been conformed to the baptismal saying (Matt. 3.17), it is interesting that Matthew has not conformed the two titles to each other.[35]

In the light of this examination of the evidence, we submit that there is no reason to believe that παῖς has been replaced by υἱός in the original form of the baptismal saying. We must therefore attempt to account for the character of the saying in terms of an original use of υἱός.

III

There can be no doubt that, if υἱός is an original part of the saying, its closest Old Testament parallel is to be found in Psalm 2.7. The slight change from the LXX word-order is not of any great importance if the text is not dependent upon the LXX; it does, however, put the stress upon the naming of *this* σύ (Jesus) as God's Son, rather than (as in the Psalm) upon the choice of the addressee to be a son.[36]

The word ἀγαπητός is ambiguous in meaning. In the LXX it can be translated as 'beloved' or as 'only', and the latter is its undoubted meaning when used of a son or daughter.[37] In the latter case the adjective is connected with ἀγαπάω in its narrower meaning of 'to be content with' and thus means 'that wherewith one must be content, hence of only children'. There is no example of ἀγαπητός as a translation of בָּחִיר, 'elect', except in Matthew 12.18, where, however, the wording is probably to be explained as due to assimilation to the baptismal saying.[38] Attention has been drawn to the Lucan form of the saying at the Transfiguration which uses the form ἐκλελεγμένος. The variation is presumably due to Luke himself, but, since he omits both ἀγαπητός and ἐν σοὶ εὐδόκησα from the version of Mark, it is possible that he understood ἐκλελεγμένος as an equivalent to the latter phrase[39] or perhaps to both of them. As for John 1.34, we have indicated earlier that the text here is uncertain; if ἐκλεκτός is original, this shows the influence of Isaiah 42.1 upon the saying.[40] The most that can be shown is that ἀγαπητός and ἐκλεκτός were felt to be sufficiently close in meaning to draw Psalm 2.7 and Isaiah 42.1 to each other, so that to some extent the two terms were interchangeable in Greek. The evidence for taking ἀγαπητός as a translation of בָּחִיר cannot be said to be strong.

Of decisive importance is that in the present form of the text the adjective is closely linked with ὁ υἱός μου; it is not a separate title (see p. 131, n. 25). Its obvious meaning, therefore, is 'only'. What, then, is the origin of the adjective? Recent scholars have suggested the influence of the Targum on Psalm 2.7, which renders the first part of the verse as 'Beloved as a son to his father you are to me'.[41] The date of this version is uncertain; the form of wording is similar to that in the Targum on 2 Samuel 7.14, 'I shall be to him *as a father, and he shall be to me as* a son', where the relationship of the Messiah to God as his Son is clearly weakened,[42] possibly in reaction to Christian claims. In any case, the change of wording in the Targum with its removal of the direct statement of sonship found in the MT makes it most unlikely that it is a source for ἀγαπητός in the baptismal saying.

It is possible, therefore, that we should return to the older suggestion that the baptismal saying shows the influence of the description of Isaac in Genesis 22.2, 12, 16.[43] Here the wording of the LXX ὁ υἱός σου ὁ ἀγαπητός offers a close parallel to the text,[44] and is indeed closer to it than any of the various versions of Isaiah 42.1, in all of which the genitive of the possessive pronoun appears twice. If, however, the saying is not dependent on the LXX, this argument loses weight. An exposition of the baptismal story in terms of Isaac typology is found in the Testament of Levi 18 (cf. Test. Judah 24), although the words of the heavenly voice are not cited in this passage.[45] Other allusions to this typology in the New Testament (e.g., Rom. 8.32) may be taken as confirming its presence in the baptismal narrative or, alternatively, as indicating the source from which Test. Levi gained this insight for the understanding of the passage. It is, therefore, uncertain whether direct influence of Genesis 22 should be detected in the baptismal saying, but at the very least we are given a significant clue towards the meaning of the saying.

The final part of the saying is also open to derivation from a number of sources. One source, however, is ruled out in this case; no form of Psalm 2 offers a parallel to the wording. A number of passages in which God is said to take pleasure in his people and in David (2 Sam. 22.20) are listed by M. D. Hooker, and she comes to the conclusion that Jesus is regarded in this text as the 'True Israel'.[46] But the idea that Jesus is the True Israel is never stated explicitly in the New Testament, and there is a considerable leap in thought between the Old Testament passages which express the love of Yahweh for his people by means of the analogy of Fatherhood and the very direct use of the Father-Son relationship which is characteristic of the New Testament.[47] More weight should be given to E. Schweizer's preference for 2 Samuel 22.20 which would keep us in the realm of Davidic and messianic ideas. This passage, however, cannot be said to have exerted any great influence upon New Testament thought. We are, therefore, brought back to Isaiah 42.1 as a possible source, and on this occasion the evidence for its influence upon the baptismal saying is much more convincing. It is true that the wording of the LXX is quite different at this point (προσεδέξατο αὐτὸν ἡ ψυχή μου), but if we are correct in arguing that the baptismal saying need not be dependent upon the LXX this objection loses its weight. In fact, the use of εὐδοκέω instead of the LXX προσδέχομαι is attested as a translation-variant by Theodotion, Aquila and Symmachus and also by Matthew 12.18.[48] The real difficulty is that the third person construction in the MT with נַפְשִׁי as subject is replaced by a first person construction (εὐδόκησα); this, however, need be no more than a legitimate, free translation of the MT.[49] We may also adduce here the fact that Isaiah 42.1 was interpreted messianically in Judaism and that it was linked with Psalm 2.7.[50] In other words, granted that the baptismal saying contains a reference to the messianic Son of God, it is entirely fitting that it should develop this thought with the aid of language from Isaiah 42.1.

IV

The conclusion of our inquiry is a set of probabilities. It is impossible to say with absolute certainty that the baptismal saying directly reflects Psalm 2.7, Genesis 22.2 and Isaiah 42.1 in its three main components, but it can be claimed with a fair degree of probability that these three passages must be regarded as the background for its interpretation, and that a denial of the presence of ideas from either Psalm 2.7 or Isaiah 42.1 is to be rejected.[51]

The use of υἱός in the Gospels has aroused much controversy.[52] In view of the undoubted Palestinian Jewish character of many of its occurrences, the possibility of Hellenistic derivation can be once and for all ruled out, except perhaps as a marginal influence upon some sayings.[53] It is more common to understand the title in terms of messiahship. As the Davidic king in the last days, Jesus is installed as the Son of God, the title being understood in a functional sense.[54] This view of the title suggests that, because Jesus is the Messiah, therefore he receives the messianic title of Son. Further, the title is originally purely functional, and only at a developed stage of Christology is it taken to represent a more personal or metaphysical relationship to God. I have argued against the correctness of this hypothesis elsewhere, on the grounds that the personal relationship of Jesus to God as his Father is the basic stage in the development, and that it would be more correct to say that Jesus is the Messiah because He is the Son of God.[55] It may be urged that this view of the evidence both provides the best background for the baptismal saying and is confirmed by the interpretation of it. In short, the baptismal saying contains an expression of the basis for Jesus' personal relationship of Sonship to God the Father. It goes beyond a purely functional or messianic use of the title by the use of the qualifying adjective ἀγαπητός which indicates the unique relationship of Jesus to his Father. Thus the personal relationship expressed in Genesis 22 becomes important for the understanding of the text. At the same time, the closely allied ideas of Messiahship and Servanthood come to expression. As the Son of God,

Jesus is the Messiah, and the task to which he is appointed is that of the Servant. It then becomes clear that the temptation story provides confirmation of our understanding of the baptism. It is as the Son that Jesus is tempted, and the purpose of Satan is to destroy the relationship of trust and obedience between Jesus and his Father.[56]

If this interpretation of the saying is correct, it follows that the suggestion of Jeremias that the παῖς θεοῦ predication may have played an essential part in the emergence of the messianic title ὁ υἱός τοῦ θεοῦ which was unknown to late Judaism loses its basis.[57] Rather, the development of this unknown title is to be traced from the unique filial consciousness of Jesus, a factor which Jeremias more than anyone else has delineated and expounded.

The difficulty has of course been raised that the original use of Psalm 2. 7 was in connection with the resurrection (Acts 13.33 and elsewhere) as the point at which the early Church placed the installation of Jesus as the Son of God. The application of the Psalm and the title of 'Son of God' to Jesus at his baptism would then represent a later stage in the development of early Church theology.[58] It is, however, more probable that Acts 13.33 and allied passages should be understood in the sense that, because Jesus was God's Son, therefore God raised him from the dead. It was because the title of Son was already associated with Jesus that the early Church was able to apply Psalm 2.7 to his resurrection, interpreted as a raising to new life analogous to the begetting of a child.[59] There need, therefore, be no difficulty in assuming that Psalm 2.7 could be used in the baptismal saying before it was applied to the resurrection of the Son of God.

Notes

[1]The third person form, οὗτός ἐστιν, found in Matthew 3.17; John 1.34 and the Transfiguration narrative (Mark 9.7 and pars.; 2 Pet. 1.17) is secondary. The text of Luke 3.22D, which substitutes the wording of Psalm 2.7, is also secondary; cf. similar phenomena in the Western text of Acts 7.37; 13.33 (Ps. 2.8!). See J. Jeremias (with W. Zimmerli), *TDNT*, V, p. 701, n. 349. The New Testament section (pp. 698-713) of the original article (*TWNT*, V, pp. 653-713) appears in a revised form in J. Jeremias, *Abba* (Göttingen, 1966), pp. 191-216; references to this section are to the revised form. The English translation in *TDNT*, V, pp. 654-717, incorporates the revisions.

[2]V. Taylor, *The Gospel according to St Mark* (London, 1953), p. 162. Taylor's exegesis is that of many scholars.

[3]G. Dalman, *The Words of Jesus* (Edinburgh, 1909), pp. 276-80.

[4]W. Bousset, *Kyrios Christos* (Göttingen, 1926), p. 57, n. 2.

[5]O. Cullmann, *Baptism in The New Testament* (London, 1950), pp. 16-18; *The Christology of the New Testament* (London, 1959), p. 66.

[6]Jeremias, op. cit.

[7]R. H. Fuller, *The Mission and Achievement of Jesus* (London, 1954), p. 55; *The Foundations of New Testament Christology* (London, 1965), pp. 169f.; C. Maurer, 'Knecht Gottes und Sohn Gottes im Passionsbericht des Markusevangeliums', *ZTK*, 50, 1953, pp. 1-38; F. Hahn, *Chris-*

tologische Hoheitstitel (Göttingen, 1964), pp. 338, 340. B. Lindars, *New Testament Apologetic* (London, 1961), pp. 139f., holds that the reference to Psalm 2.7 was consciously added to the original text by the early Church; this avoids the suggestion that the change from παῖς to υἱός produced an allusion to Psalm 2.7 by sheer coincidence.

[8]For points 1. to 4., see Jeremias, op. cit.; for 2. see also R. Schnackenburg, *Das Johannesevangelium*, 1 (Freiburg, 1965), p. 305; for 5., Hahn, op. cit.; for 6., Maurer, op. cit.

[9]See the most recent discussion in R. H. Gundry, *The Use of the Old Testament in St Matthew's Gospel* (Leiden, 1967), pp. 29-32; cf. E. Lövestam, *Son and Saviour* (Lund, Copenhagen, 1961), pp. 94-7; U. Wilckens, *Die Missionsreden der Apostelgeschichte* (Neukirchen, 1963), p. 164. G. Vermes, *Scripture and Tradition in Judaism* (Leiden, 1961), pp. 222f., and E. Best, *The Temptation and the Passion* (Cambridge, 1965), pp. 169f., find one source of the title of Son in Genesis 22.2, and develop the suggestion of an Isaac typology. At the other extreme, M. D. Hooker, *Jesus and the Servant* (London, 1959), pp. 68-73, plays down the significance of the Servant Christology in the Gospels and in this text; cf. E. Schweizer, *TDNT*, VIII (article: υἱός, pp. 334-97), pp. 367f.

[10]Lindars, op. cit., p. 140, n. 2.

[11]Translation in Hennecke and Schneemelcher (eds.), *New Testament Apocrypha*, I (London, 1963), pp. 163f.

[12]The reading ἀγαπητός in Luke is probably due to assimilation to the parallels; cf. also Luke 23.35.

[13]Note that ἀγαπητός is an attribute of υἱός in the text and not an independent title (as ἐκλεκτός is in Isa. 42.1); cf. G. D. Kilpatrick, 'The Order of some Noun and Adjective Phrases in the New Testament', *Nov. T.*, 5, 1962, pp. 111-14.

[14]Gundry, op. cit., p. 30, argues that the Johannine preference for 'Son' makes it likely that ἐκλεκτός is a secondary reading due to assimilation to Isaiah 42.1 LXX and perhaps Luke 9.35; cf. G. Schrenk, *TDNT*, IV, p. 189, n. 18. *The Greek New Testament* (1966) gives to υἱός a 'B' grade of certainty. Note that the reading υἱός in **p**⁶⁶ and **p**⁷⁵ disproves the suggestion that this wording arose in the fourth century in the struggle against adoptionism (J. Jeremias, *TDNT*, V, p. 689, n. 260; followed by Schnackenburg, op. cit., p. 305).

[15]R. T. France, 'The Servant of the Lord in the Teaching of Jesus', *Tyndale Bulletin*, 19, 1968, pp. 26-52.

[16]For the difference in word order between the LXX of Psalm 2.7 and the baptismal saying see below.

[17]W. Zimmerli, *TDNT*, V, p. 673.

[18]P. W. Skehan, 'A Fragment of the "Song of Moses" (Deut. 32) from Qumran', *BASOR*, 136, December 1954, pp. 12-15; cf. F. F. Bruce, *Second Thoughts on the Dead Sea Scrolls* (Exeter, 1961), p. 67. In place of עֲבָדָיו־דַּם in the MT, the fragment has בני דם.

[19]The interpretation of παῖς as 'son' in Wisdom must rest on the Greek text of Isaiah and not on a misunderstanding or theological reinterpretation of the MT עֶבֶד. For the view that Wisdom has brought together the παῖς-tradition of 2 Isaiah and the υἱός-tradition of Psalm 2, see B. M. F. van Iersel, *Der Sohn' in den synoptischen Jesusworten* (Leiden, 1964), pp. 75-77.

[20]J. Jeremias, *TDNT*, V, pp. 699, 702f.

[21]Ibid. pp. 701, 704f.

[22]See, for example, L. H. Brockington, *A Critical Introduction to the Apocrypha* (London, 1961), pp. 58, 70.

[23]J. Jeremias, *TDNT*, V, p. 683.

[24]Ibid., pp. 683, 702, n. 356.

[25]Lindars, op. cit., p. 140.

[26]J. Jeremias, *TDNT*, V, p. 701, n. 350. See n. 14 above.

[27]R. Bultmann, *Das Evangelium des Johannes* (Göttingen, 1959), pp. 151f.; R. Schnackenburg, *Das Johannesevangelium*, I, 1965, pp. 502-6. According to Bultmann, παῖς in Matthew means 'child'; the word was misunderstood by Luke. It is, however, by no means certain that the Synoptic and

Johannine incidents should be identified; see C. H. Dodd, *Historical Tradition in the Fourth Gospel* (Cambridge, 1963), pp. 188-95, especially p. 194 and n. 2.

²⁸'Child': Matthew 2.16; 17.18; 21.15; Luke 2.43; 8.51 and 54 (both fem.); 9.42; John 4.51; Acts 20.12. 'Servant': Matthew 14.2; Luke 7.7; 12.45; 15.26; probably also Matthew 8.6, 8, 13.

²⁹E. Haenchen, *Die Apostelgeschichte* (Göttingen, 1959), p. 165 n. 4; H. Conzelmann, *Die Apostelgeschichte* (Tübingen, 1963), p. 37.

³⁰O. Procksch, *TDNT*, I, p. 102; Hooker, op. cit., pp. 67f., 85; E. E. Ellis, *The Gospel of Luke* (London, 1967), p. 97.

³¹Procksch, op. cit.

³²The argument of Wilckens, op. cit., pp. 163-8, that the Pais-Christology is of uncertain antiquity fails to take into account the evidence from other New Testament sources. But, even if Wilckens's view should be justified, this would simply indicate that a Pais-Christology (with παῖς in the sense of 'servant') was a possible creation in a gentile church when Luke was writing.

³³I. H. Marshall, 'The Development of Christology in the Early Church', *Tyndale Bulletin*, 18, 1967, pp. 77-93 (especially pp. 91f. [reprinted below, pp. 150-64, especially pp. 160f.]). More hesitant is R. P. Martin, *Carmen Christi* (Cambridge, 1967), p. 195.

³⁴Maurer, op. cit., pp. 24-8, 32.

³⁵Lövestam, op. cit., p. 95. A possible occurrence of παῖς in a baptismal context has been defended by Jeremias (*TDNT*, V, p. 702, n. 356) in John 1.29, 36 where ἀμνός may be a translation of Aramaic טַלְיָא which may also mean 'servant'. But it is hard to see why the change of meaning should have taken place. According to M. McNamara, *The New Testament and the Palestinian Targum to the Pentateuch* (Rome, 1966), p. 94, n. 62, the meaning of 'lamb' is very rare for טַלְיָא.

³⁶E. Lohmeyer, *Das Evangelium des Markus* (Göttingen, 1959), p. 23.

³⁷C. H. Turner, 'Ὁ υἱός μου ὁ ἀγαπητός', *JTS*, 27, 1925-6, pp. 113-29 (cf. *idem* in *JTS*, 28, 1926-7, p. 362, and A. Souter in *JTS*, 28, pp. 59f.).

³⁸G. Barth, in G. Bornkamm, G. Barth and H. J. Held, *Tradition and Interpretation in Matthew* (London, 1963), p. 126 (following K. Stendahl); E. Schweizer, *TDNT*, VIII, p. 368 n. 239; Gundry, op. cit., pp. 30, 112.

³⁹T. Zahn, *Das Evangelium des Lucas* (Leipzig, 1913), p. 386, n. 99.

⁴⁰John's use of μονογενής in 1.18 might equally well be taken as evidence that he interpreted an original ἀγαπητός in the baptismal saying in the sense of 'only' (Hooker, op. cit., p. 71).

⁴¹D. Plooij, 'The Baptism of Jesus', in H. G. Wood (ed.), *Amicitiae Corolla* (London, 1933), pp. 239-52 (especially pp. 248f.); Lövestam, op. cit., p. 96; E. Schweizer in *TDNT*, VIII, p. 368, n. 240; R. Gundry, op. cit., pp. 30 f. Gundry's reference to possible influence from Isaiah 41.8f.; 44.2 LXX is unlikely, since the √ἀγαπα of the Greek version has no direct Hebrew equivalent. Schweizer's reference to Targ. Isaiah 42.1 in the same connection is curious.

⁴²Lövestam, op. cit., p. 89; cf. p. 21, where the same tendency is demonstrated for the Midrash on Psalm 2; E. Lohse, *TDNT*, VIII, pp. 360-2.

⁴³Turner, op. cit., pp. 123f.; E. Best (see n. 9 above).

⁴⁴The MT, however, has the double possessive.

⁴⁵For the Christian character of Test. Levi 18, see M. de Jonge, *The Testaments of the Twelve Patriarchs* (Leiden, 1953), pp. 89f. It remains possible, however, that the section is pre-Christian, in which case it forms part of the background against which Mark 1.11 must be studied.

⁴⁶Hooker, op. cit., pp. 71-3.

⁴⁷To say that Jesus identifies himself with Israel or is the king of Israel is not quite the same thing as to say that he is the true Israel; cf. D. R. A. Hare, *The Theme of Jewish Persecution of Christians in the Gospel according to St Matthew* (Cambridge, 1967), p. 7.

⁴⁸The wording of Matthew 12.18 shows that its translation at this point is not due to assimilation to the baptismal saying.

⁴⁹The use of נַפְשִׁי is a circumlocution for the first person singular. For this usage see Job 30.25 the only example in the LXX.

⁵⁰J. Jeremias, *TDNT*, V, p. 693 and n. 292, pp. 695-7; Lövestam, op. cit., pp. 95f.

[51]P. G. Bretscher's article, 'Exodus 4.22-23 and the Voice from Heaven' (*JBL*, 87, 1968, pp. 301-12), appeared after the completion of the present study.

[52]Bibliography in *TDNT*, VIII, p. 334.

[53]Schweizer, loc. cit., p. 356f.

[54]Ibid., pp. 366-70. There is of course no thought of 'adoptionism' in the later sense of the term. Note also that the use of the same wording in the Transfiguration story (Mark 9.7) rules out the idea of installation into an office at the baptism.

[55]I. H. Marshall, 'The Divine Sonship of Jesus', *Interpretation*, 21, 1967, pp. 87-103 (reprinted below, pp. 134-49); cf. 'The Development of Christology in the Early Church' (see n. 33 above). See also K. H. Rengstorf, *Das Evangelium nach Lukas* (Göttingen, 1949), p. 59.

[56]Cf. Lövestam, op. cit., pp. 98-101. Even if the temptation narrative in Q should be secondary, as van Iersel argues (op. cit., pp. 165-71, cf. A. Feuillet, 'Le baptême de Jésus', *RB*, 71, 1964, p. 322 (pp. 321-52), it is an argument for the early existence of υἱός in the baptismal saying.

[57]J. Jeremias, *TDNT*, V, p. 702, n. 354.

[58]Lindars, op. cit., pp. 139-44. E. Schweizer, *TDNT*, VIII, pp. 367-9.

[59]Lövestam, op. cit., pp. 37-48; cf. also Gundry, op. cit., p. 161, n. 3.

7
The Divine Sonship of Jesus

T HE QUESTION WHETHER AND IN WHAT SENSE JESUS CON-
ceived himself to be the Son of God is one of extraordinary importance in
the discussion of New Testament Christology. If Jesus did regard himself
as the Son of God and conveyed this understanding of his person to his
disciples, it is clear that the common view that the title was first given to him
in the early Church stands in need of revision. According to a recent expression of this type of approach, the title of Son of God, understood as a means
of expressing the close relationship of the kingly Messiah to God, was first
attached by the early Church to the exalted and returning Jesus; only at a
later stage was it used to designate him in his earthly ministry as One
equipped with the power of the Spirit in the manner of a Hellenistic 'divine
man'; later still was it used to denote the physical nature of Jesus as the Son
of God born of the Virgin Mary.[1] The validity of this approach has been
challenged by a number of scholars, but there is certainly no unanimity as
to the correct solution of the problem.[2] We shall confine ourselves in what
follows to a re-examination of the evidence for the view that Jesus conceived
himself to be the Son of God, drawing into the discussion such evidence
from the early thought of the Church as is relevant to the question of what
he actually taught.

I
A question of terminology must be cleared up at the outset. Recent writers
have argued that there are two distinct titles which must be clearly distinguished from each other, 'the Son' used absolutely and 'the Son of God'.[3]

The former of these titles is found in the Synoptic Gospels (Mark 13.32; Matt. 11.27; Luke 10.22; Mark 12.6; Matt. 28.19), once in Paul (1 Cor. 15.28), five times in Hebrews (Heb. 1.2, 8; 3.6; 5.8; 7.28), and some twenty-three times in the Johannine literature, where, however, it is closely assimilated to the 'Son of God' title.

According to Ferdinand Hahn, the difference between the two titles is seen in the fact that the former title is used absolutely without God's being mentioned, while the latter is never used in conjunction with the term 'Father.' He also states, though without offering any justification for his statement, that the one title cannot be derived from the other, and then proceeds to investigate their origins separately and independently.

The validity of this distinction is very dubious. It is not unimportant that the later New Testament writers seem to have been unaware of it. This is true of John, who uses the two forms of expression indiscriminately, and it is also true of Mark who is obviously not aware that 'the Son' (Mark 13.32) has a different significance from 'the Son of God' used elsewhere in the Gospel. Further, when the forms 'his Son' or 'my Son' occur, it is not clear always whether 'God' or 'Father' is the antecedent.[4] A third point is that the absolute use of 'the Son' which is characteristic of Hebrews is to be explained in terms of the writer's own purposes and the influence of the Septuagint upon him rather than in terms of an inherited tradition.[5] Finally, it is simply not true that the title 'Father' is not used in conjunction with the title 'Son of God'.[6]

These points suggest that the alleged distinction is not well founded exegetically. If it can be shown that the usage of 'Son' in the New Testament can be explained without recourse to the theory of the parallel development of two independent concepts, it can be safely dismissed; a verdict on this point, however, depends on the remainder of this investigation.

II

Before we look at the usage of the title of 'Son' in the Synoptic Gospels, it will be wise to look at the correlative term 'Father'. The facts concerning the use of this title for God by Jesus have recently been summed up in an exhaustive and masterly survey by Joachim Jeremias on which we are heavily dependent.[7] The title is found some fifty-one times on the lips of Jesus in the Synoptic Gospels (excluding parallels). Of these occurrences seven are in prayer, thirteen times (eleven before the resurrection) Jesus spoke of 'the Father' or 'my Father', nine times of 'my heavenly Father', and on twenty-two occasions Jesus spoke to the disciples of 'your [heavenly] Father'.

A number of these sayings may not give the actual words of Jesus. In some seven cases a consideration of the parallels with Mark and Luke suggests that

Matthew has inserted the word 'Father' into his sources (Matt. 6.26; 10.29, 32, 33; 12.50; 20.23; 26.29); this is perhaps also the case in Matthew 5.45; 7.21; 10.20 and 18.10, though here the evidence is not decisive. A further point is that Matthew shows a decided fondness for the formula 'heavenly Father' and may well have inserted it at various points, although there are certain places where its use cannot be due to his editorial activity (Mark 11.25!), and suspicion regarding the adjective 'heavenly' does not mean that one should necessarily suspect the originality of 'Father' also in these phrases.[8]

From a study of the sayings which may reasonably be accepted as authentic, there can be no doubt that Jesus prayed to God as his Father and spoke to the disciples about God as their Father (Matt. 6.9; Luke 11.2), and the very word *'Abba'* that he himself used (Mark 14.36) was preserved in the early Church and used by Christians (Rom. 8.15; Gal. 4.6).[9] On the basis of this evidence, it might at first sight appear that Jesus and his disciples shared in an identical relationship of sonship to the Father and that there was nothing metaphysical about this relationship. There would then be nothing unique about the self-consciousness of Jesus in regard to this particular category of expression, and the whole terminology would find its adequate explanation as a natural development from the usage in the Old Testament and in Judaism.[10]

This would be a premature and erroneous conclusion. For, first, it must be observed that the relationship of which Jesus spoke was not one shared by all men,[11] or even by all Jews, but was the privilege only of disciples.[12] With the one very doubtful exception of the Sermon on the Mount, the context of all the sayings of Jesus on this relationship is teaching addressed to disciples.[13] There is no suggestion that all men are sons of God by physical birth or because he is their creator.

A second important fact is that no saying has been preserved in which Jesus linked the disciples with himself so that together they could say 'our Father'. The wording of Matthew 6.9 is for use by disciples only, and John 20.17 (if its evidence be permitted) explicitly distinguishes between 'my Father' and 'your Father', thus bringing out a distinction which is implicit elsewhere.[14] This suggests that there is a difference in the status of Jesus and his disciples which is not accidental.[15]

This leads to the third fact. Men are admitted by Jesus to a relationship with God which he himself already enjoys. This is demonstrated beyond all doubt by his use of *'Abba'* to address God in prayer. He dared to address God by an intimate word that no Jew had ever used, and he initiated his disciples into the same intimate relationship.[16] Jesus thus appears as the mediator of a new relationship with God.

These three points strongly suggest that Jesus had a consciousness of a unique relationship to God as his Father, and we must now see whether this view is supported by the texts in which Jesus spoke of God as his Father and of himself as the Son; these two categories of evidence cannot be rigidly distinguished from each other and will be treated together.

III

We begin with the saying found in Matthew 11.27 and its parallel in Luke 10.22: 'All things have been delivered to me by my Father, and nobody knows the Son except the Father, nor does anybody know the Father except the Son and he to whomsoever the Son wishes to reveal him.' The authenticity of this saying has been recently questioned by Hahn who argues that nowhere else does Jesus use the phrase 'my Father' and that the reference in 'all things have been delivered to me' is to the kind of authority and might mentioned in Matthew 28.18.[17]

The former of these two arguments may be set aside for the moment; if the saying proves to be genuine on other grounds, then we may rightly claim that the occurrence of 'my Father' in it is not an argument against its authenticity, but rather a point in favour of the authenticity of other sayings which contain this disputed expression. The latter argument is expressly taken up by Jeremias who points out that the whole context of the saying is governed by the thought of revelation rather than of authority and might, and that the use of the technical term *paradidōmi* requires this understanding of the phrase.[18] Jeremias also deals with other objections to the authenticity of the saying. Its Semitic character shows that it is not of Hellenistic origin; in particular, the formulation of the mutual relationship of Father and Son can be paralleled from Semitic sources as a type of expression necessary in languages which (unlike Greek) possess no reciprocal pronoun. As for the common charge that the saying has a Johannine character, Jeremias argues that it is not precisely paralleled in John, but represents a stage on the way to Johannine thought.[19]

In order, however, to defend the saying as a whole, Jeremias finds it necessary to argue that the words Father and Son have been given an absolute, titular sense in Greek although in the original Aramaic saying they had a generic sense: 'All things have been transmitted to me by my Father, And as only a father knows his son so also only a son knows his father and he to whom the son wants to reveal it.' When taken in this way, the saying does not apply the title of 'Son' to Jesus, although it contains the seed from which the titular use developed.

The reasons that Jeremias adduces for adopting this lexical possibility are two. First, he follows Gustaf Dalman in arguing that the use of the absolute form 'the Father' as a title for God is not found in Aramaic and that it is attested only at a late stage in Christian sources.[20] This argument is not securely based. While it is true that *abba* can be translated as 'the Father' or 'my Father', the evidence brought forward by Dalman does not mean that 'my Father' is the only legitimate translation; and indeed 'my Father' would be an impossible translation if 'the Son' stands alongside it. That 'the Father' is a late title is an argument based on silence; even if the title is a rare one in the Synoptics and in Paul, it is found in such an early written document as Romans and is frequent in the Johannine writings.[21]

More important is Jeremias's second contention that the title 'the Son' is never used in Jewish sources or in pre-Hellenistic Christian sources as a title for the Messiah.[22] Two points arise here. The first is whether the facts are as Jeremias states them. The evidence has been surveyed by R. H. Fuller who, along with other scholars, has drawn attention to the evidence of the Florilegium from Cave Four at Qumran. Here the important text, 2 Samuel 7.14: 'I will be his father and he shall be my son', is quoted and applied to the Branch of David. Admittedly this is not quite a titular use, but it would seem to be fair to agree with Fuller's conclusion: 'Son of God *was just coming into use* as a Messianic title in pre-Christian Judaism. . . . It meant not a metaphysical relationship, but adoption as God's vice-regent in his kingdom.'[23] There is, therefore, some reason to question the confidence of Jeremias's assertion.

But, secondly, whatever be the truth about the Jewish background, we must surely reckon with the possibility that Jesus may have used the title of 'Son' regardless of whether or not it was a current messianic title. It is, in our opinion, certain that Jesus spoke of himself as the Son of man, thereby using a title which was far from being commonly used in Judaism to express in a veiled manner the mystery of his own person,[24] and it is extremely likely that this title expressed his consciousness of divinity.[25] Now if Jesus did speak of God as his Father—as the evidence of his prayers decisively establishes— it is difficult to see why he could not take the further step of referring to himself as his Son. To put the point slightly differently: if Jesus could have uttered Matthew 11.27 in the form suggested by Jeremias, there is no reason in principle to deny that he could have spoken it in the form actually preserved in the Gospels.

What is of especial importance is that this use of the category of Sonship would be based upon Jesus' consciousness of a unique filial relationship to God rather than upon the conviction that as the Messiah he was the Son of

God. The evidence strongly suggests that the fundamental point in Jesus' self-understanding was his filial relationship to God and that it was from this basic conviction that he undertook the tasks variously assigned to the Messiah, Son of man and Servant of Yahweh, rather than that the basic datum was consciousness of being the Messiah. If this is so, the argument that 'the Son' was not a current messianic title becomes irrelevant. In any case, the Synoptic Gospels indicate that Jesus used this title only in his private teaching to his disciples, so that the question whether the people at large would have understood him to be using a current messianic title is further shown to be an irrelevant one.

Consideration of these points indicates that the traditional interpretation of this text is at least as likely as the view propounded by Dalman and Jeremias. As a final consideration in favour of the understanding of the saying given by the Evangelists, we may ask whether the father-son relationship that Jeremias detects in the text is in fact a common Jewish illustration of the transmission of revelation. The examples cited by Jeremias[26] come from 3 Enoch which was surely not the most popular of Jewish writings. They speak of a father's revealing secrets to a son rather than of the personal knowledge of the father possessed by the son, and they do not develop the thought of the exclusiveness of that relationship which is contained in the saying in the Gospels. On the whole, the saying in the Gospels seems to go beyond the kind of thought expressed in 3 Enoch and to express a relationship which is peculiar to the Father and the Son.

Our provisional conclusion is that we may safely follow those scholars who have argued for the authenticity of Matthew 11.27 and its parallel Luke 10.22 in its traditional form,[27] and we must now look at further texts to see whether they support this point of view.

The saying in Mark 13.32, 'But of that day or that hour no one knows, not even the angels in heaven, nor the Son, but only the Father', has been evaluated in three ways. Either it is genuine as it stands, or it is wholly a product of the early Church, or it is a distorted saying of Jesus.[28] The second of these two views is exposed to the old objection that one can scarcely imagine the early Church framing such a saying about its exalted Lord even under the pressure of delay in the parousia.[29] Since, however, the distortion in the text which is proposed by advocates of the third view is found in the words 'nor the Son', it is clear that this same argument is equally valid against this approach; if a saying existed which made no reference to the ignorance of the Son, it is hard, if not impossible, to conceive of the early Church's proceeding to transform an unexceptional saying into a 'hard' one. It may be argued that the early Church was forced to adopt this line as time went on in order to account for the seeming mistake of Jesus in prophesying an early parousia, but this argument is fallacious at every step. It must be insisted that it is far from being the case that Jesus announced the immediacy of his parousia and that in consequence the early Church soon felt disillusioned and had to reframe its theology;[30] and it must likewise be emphasized that there is no evidence to support the view that the early Church would have sought a way out of its difficulties by imputing ignorance, if not actual error, to its Lord. Hahn has suggested that the text is older than Matthew 11.27 and comes from a stage when the Son's subordination could be framed in this drastic manner,[31] but evidence for the existence of this stage is lacking.

Nevertheless, the use of the _title_ 'the Son' has caused difficulty for some critics, and suggestions have been made that the words 'nor the Son' are a Christian addition to the text, or (more plausibly) that they are a Christian interpretation of an original 'nor the Son of man'.[32] The former of these views is espoused by Jeremias who holds that once these words are deleted, the phrase 'the Father' can be replaced by 'my Father', which is an alternative rendering of the Aramaic _abba_. But the considerations that were urged above in discussion of Matthew 11.27 are equally valid here; we are once again dealing with the esoteric teaching of Jesus to his disciples, and the linguistic argument against the titles does not carry conviction. The latter view is very much a conjecture which gains credence from the apocalyptic context of the saying but is not supported by any other occurrences of the same phenomenon. In any case, 'Son' and 'Son of man' are very close in meaning. The conjecture, however, is probably unnecessary, and we may agree with Rudolf Schnackenburg that 'there are no grounds for striking out the final words ("nor the Son but the Father") as long as we accept the genuineness of Matthew 11.27—Luke 10.22'.[33]

In addition to the two basic texts which we have now considered, three others remain to be considered in the establishment of a cumulative case that Jesus spoke of God as his Father and knew himself to be his Son. The first and second of these sayings are concerned with the use of the phrase 'my Father' which we have already noticed in Matthew 11.27. They are treated very briefly by Jeremias,[34] and a fuller substantiation of the case for accepting them as genuine will not be out of place.

The saying in Matthew 16.17, 'Flesh and blood has not revealed this to you, but my Father who is in heaven', is passed over by van Iersel on the grounds that it belongs to the post-resurrection teaching of Jesus.[35] This is an unlikely setting, and the Caesarea Philippi context remains the most probable.[36] Hahn admits that the saying is old, but follows A. Vögtle in arguing that it is not so old as the rest of the section (vs. 18f.).[37] Vögtle regards verses 18 f. as words of Jesus, possibly spoken after his resurrection, but holds that verse 17 is an addition by Matthew in response to the confession made by Peter in verse 16. Nevertheless, it should be noted that he holds that the logion rests ultimately on a genuine teaching of Jesus.[38] It is accordingly possible that the saying is genuine, even if its present context is suspect; and in favour of this possibility it should be observed that its language is not characteristically Matthaean and the style is Semitic.[39] Jeremias notes that it falls into the same circle of ideas as Matthew 11.27. Within the present discussion it is impossible to discuss the Matthaean pericope as a whole, but enough has been said to show that the saying in Matthew 16.17 may well be genuine.

Equally great problems surround Luke 22.29: 'As my Father appointed a kingdom for me, so do I appoint for you.' These are due principally to the closeness of the saying as a whole (Luke 22.28-30) to a similar saying in Matthew 19.28 which at the point under consideration here diverges completely from the Lucan form. The Matthaean version has figured much in recent study because it contains a reference to the Son of man which is lacking from Luke. The variety of opinion among critics is extremely diverse. The most considerable discussion of the passage is by Heinz Schürmann who argues for the originality of Luke's version as compared with that of Matthew, and states that the passage, rather than being his own composition, is from Luke's special source.[40] In particular, the phrase 'my Father' is not one that Luke adds to his sources and is pre-Lucan.[41] Does this, however, justify us in accepting the authenticity of the reference? Hahn denies dogmatically that the saying is genuine, but we have to turn to F. W. Beare to find reasons for this view.[42] He finds difficulties in the idea of the disciples' sharing in the temptations of Jesus (which sounds reminiscent of later veneration of the apostles), in the use of *diatithēmi* which should mean 'to bequeath', and in the reference by Jesus to 'my table' and 'my kingdom'.

These three difficulties are not so weighty as may appear at first sight. Concerning the first, Schürmann has argued that the use of *peirasmoi* here is pre-Lucan and that Luke is unlikely to have created a passage in praise of the disciples and inserted it in this context.[43] The way in which the disciples are praised and promised thrones is decidedly primitive and is probably to be traced back to Jesus himself since we find no trace of the Twelve playing 'any special role either in Jerusalem or beyond' after the resurrection.[44] Second, there is no need to see any hint of the idea of a 'testament' in the use of *diatithēmi;* the verb means to ordain freely or to dispose authoritatively, and it cannot have the sense of making a will here since it is used of the Father as well as of Jesus.[45] There remains the authoritative use of 'my' by

Jesus. It is purely arbitrary to deny such authority to him, and Schürmann has amply shown that the thought of his kingly authority is by no means a late development.[46] Accordingly the case against Luke 22.29 is not proven, and this verse may be added to those which testify to Jesus' consciousness of God as his Father.

One other text must be considered in this connection. In the parable of the wicked husbandmen there is a reference to the son of the owner of the vineyard which is a fairly obvious allegorical allusion to Jesus himself as the Son of God (Mark 12.6). W. G. Kümmel in particular has argued that Jesus could not have used the title in this parable as a synonym for the Messiah since it was not a current messianic title and therefore would be meaningless to the hearers.[47] This reasoning is not convincing, since it is by no means obvious that Jesus did mean to speak directly about himself and his status to the people through this parable. It is more likely that he used a term which arose from his own filial consciousness and which might convey this meaning to his disciples but which did not flaunt the secret before the unbelieving people. Jeremias writes:

> We have to distinguish between what Jesus himself meant, and the way in which his audience understood him. There can be no doubt that in the sending of the son Jesus himself had his own sending in mind, but for the mass of his hearers the Messianic significance of the son could not be taken for granted. . . . The christological point of the parable would have been hidden from the audience.[48]

We may, therefore, add this saying to the texts already examined which throw light on the mind of Jesus.

IV

The evidence that has been assembled in the previous section has shown that there is a firm basis for the view that Jesus spoke of God as his Father and of himself as the Son. We have confined our attention to statements attributed to Jesus himself, and it has emerged that the teaching of Jesus about the Son is most intimately connected with his consciousness of God as his Father. As we observed earlier, the use of *abba* in prayer and of the phrase 'my Father' indicates that Jesus was conscious of a unique relationship to the Father, and even when he mediated a share in this relationship to his disciples he remained conscious of a distinction between their status and his. The fact that he spoke of *the* Son further strengthens this impression. All this suggests that Jesus' consciousness of being the Son arose out of his own personal relationship with the Father and belongs to this circle of ideas. We therefore find ourselves in close agreement with the position represented by Vincent

Taylor:
> Within the limitations of the human life of Jesus His consciousness of Sonship was gained through the knowledge that God was His Father, mediated by prayer and communion with Him in a process of growth and development which begins before the opening of the historic ministry and is consummated in decisive experiences of revelation and intuition.[49]

Before, however, we can go on with Taylor to claim that 'it is upon this historical foundation that Christological thinking must build', it is necessary to consider various pieces of evidence which might appear to support a different opinion.

There are two other main uses of the title of 'Son' in the Gospels which we have not yet discussed. On the one hand, there is the evidence of the divine Voice which addressed Jesus as 'my Son' at his baptism (Mark 1.11); and with this must be associated the way in which this title was taken up by Satan in the wilderness (Matt. 4.3, 6; Luke 4.3, 9) and the repetition of the heavenly message to the disciples at the Transfiguration (Mark 9.7). On the other hand, there is the way in which the demon-possessed acknowledged Jesus as 'the holy One of God' or the 'Son of the Most High' (Mark 1.24; 3.11; 5.7).[50]

In the former group of statements the sonship of Jesus is associated with Psalm 2.7, where the Lord's anointed is addressed with the words, 'You are my son, today I have begotten you'. It is a plausible argument that the primary factor in the application of the title of 'Son' to Jesus was his status as the Messiah; it was because of this status that the title of 'Son' was originally applied to him, and only later that the title was infused with a fuller content.

One may escape the force of this argument with the hypothesis that originally there was no reference to Psalm 2.7 in the baptismal narrative and that Jesus was addressed as the Servant of Yahweh rather than as the Son of God. In this case, the insertion of Psalm 2.7 in the narrative is an interpretation by the early Church and is of no significance for Jesus' own mind.[51] However, this suggestion is by no means free from difficulties. We may meet the problem in a different way by observing that there is very little stress, if any, on the thought of Jesus as the Messiah in the baptismal story. If messiahship is a thought present in the story at all, it would appear that Jesus is the Messiah because he is the Son of God rather than vice versa.[52] Sonship is the supreme category of interpretation of the person of Jesus in the Gospels, and messiahship occupies a subordinate place. The use of Psalm 2 at this point, therefore, need create no difficulty. It forms part of that revelation from the Father which took place in the secret communion of Jesus with him and which confirmed the existence of the relationship; through it Jesus was confirmed as the Son of God in carrying out the tasks of the Messiah and Servant of Yahweh.[53]

In the second group of statements the status of Jesus is often said to be conceived in terms of the Hellenistic idea of the 'divine man'. Great heroes were regarded as being divine, and in the stories of the exorcisms Jesus is presented in this guise. Thus the title of 'Son of God' would be applied to Jesus as the result of attempts to expound his significance in categories drawn from the Hellenistic world. If this were the case, the force of our argument would not be affected, for what would have taken place would be the Hellenistic elaboration of an idea already present in the Gospel material: it would be highly precarious to argue that the whole idea of sonship was a Hellenistic importation into the tradition at a late stage. In fact, however, the theory of Hellenistic influence suffers from certain weaknesses. The exorcism stories show Jewish traits, and there appear to be no parallels for the use of the title 'Son of God' in Jewish sources in this particular manner.[54] The suggestion that in these stories the title is secondary and has replaced some earlier designation of Jesus[55] is pure conjecture, and is not even supported by some plausible suggestion regarding what this earlier designation might have been.[56] Whatever be the origin of the title here, it is plain that this marginal use in the Gospels cannot have been the determining factor in the original application of the title to Jesus.

V

A more important challenge to the view which we have been upholding comes from a consideration of the theology of the early Church. We have evidence that the early Church associated the divine sonship of Jesus with his resurrection and exaltation.[57] Was this the earliest use of the title, and did its application to the earthly life of Jesus result from a later projection backwards? Or did the use by Jesus himself lead the Church to apply it to him in his exaltation? Can the early Church's use of the title be satisfactorily explained in the light of our earlier conclusions?

With regard to the Pauline material, Romans 1.3f.—or rather a reconstruction of a hypothetical original form of that text—is the only evidence that links the title of 'Son of God' with the resurrection and the thought of adoption. All the other Pauline texts which can reasonably be claimed to reflect pre-Pauline formulas and usage have been examined by Werner Kramer who has shown that the title is linked with the thought of God's sending or giving up his pre-existent Son for the salvation of men. Kramer links this usage with the Hellenistic Jewish church and thinks that the adoptionist use in Romans 1.3f. belongs to the Palestinian Jewish church.[58] Romans 1.3f. must, therefore, bear the brunt of the argument. Now it is universally agreed that Paul did not intend himself to be understood in an adoptionist manner here. The question is whether he has cited a formula which was originally intended to be understood in this way. The matter is complicated by the lack of agreement among scholars regarding the precise wording of this formula, but common to nearly all reconstructions are the words 'who was made of the seed of David . . . who was designated 'Son of God' by resurrection from the dead'.[59] If this text is to be understood as a contrast between the condition of Jesus before and after his resurrection, it must be observed that 'made of the seed of David' must have been a messianic expression from the beginning—for a statement that Jesus was simply a man descended from David is too banal to have formed part of a confessional formula—and that there is no Jewish evidence which would lead us to suppose that the early Church could have conceived of the Messiah as being adopted by God at some stage after the completion of his earthly work. If we also bear in mind that 'Son of God' was at least in process of becoming a messianic title, it becomes all the more unlikely that the early Church saw in the resurrection of Jesus his adoption by God to sonship.

The texts in Acts fit in with this conclusion. We begin with a text which does not mention sonship but employs different categories of Christology. In Acts 2.36 it is said that God has made Jesus who was crucified to be both Lord and Christ. It may be that we have been misled by the immediately preceding mention of the resurrection into thinking that this act of appointment by God took place after the crucifixion. The guilt of the Jews may well have been shown in their crucifixion of the One whom God had already made Lord and Christ. But if, as is more probable, the resurrection be regarded here as the point at which this act of exaltation took place (see Phil. 2.9-11), there is no suggestion that this in any way denied his previous status; the thought is similar to that in the 'hymn' in Philippians 2.5-11 where exaltation and pre-existence are not exclusive concepts. The titles of 'Lord' and 'Christ' are concerned with function and status rather than with essential nature, and consequently the question of Jesus' receiving a new nature at the resurrection simply does not arise. As in Romans 1.3f., the resurrection confirms and manifests an existing position.[60]

For the relation of sonship to the resurrection in Acts we must turn to 13.33. Here the problem arises through the specific quotation of Psalm 2.7 in its full form, 'Thou art my Son, today I have begotten thee.' The verb *anistēmi* is used elsewhere in Acts of God's raising up of men like the Mosaic prophet (Acts 3.22; 7.37) and of his resurrecting Jesus from the dead (Acts

2.24, 32; 13.34; 17.31). F. F. Bruce adopts the former possibility and holds that here, as in Acts 3.26, the reference is to the historical appearance of Jesus.[61] On this view the use of Psalm 2.7 here would be similar to the usage at the baptism (Luke 3.22). But the context and structure of the passage are perhaps more in favour of seeing a reference to the resurrection here.[62] If so, what is the function of Psalm 2.7 here? How was a declaration of *sonship* associated with an act of *resurrection*? A possible solution may be derived from Wisdom 2-3 where the claim of the righteous man that he is God's son is something to be tested and vindicated at his death: 'If the righteous man is God's son, he will help him, and will deliver him from the hand of his adversaries' (Wisd. 2.18).[63] Thus Psalm 2.7 could be fittingly applied to the risen Jesus because the resurrection proved that he, a just and righteous man (Acts 13.28), was treated as the Son of God in being raised from the dead. The reference to 'begetting' in the quotation is obviously not to be stressed; if any weight is to be given to it, it will refer metaphorically to the raising of Jesus to new life or (as in the original usage in the psalm) to the beginning of his reign. There is, therefore, no ground for finding any trace of adoptionism here, and consequently no reason to think that the idea of divine sonship was first applied to Jesus in this connection. Rather, the resurrection was the vindication of the status which Jesus had already claimed for himself.

We submit, therefore, that the evidence of early Church theology does not in any way run counter to the provisional conclusion established earlier in this essay that the roots of the New Testament designation of Jesus as the Son of God lie in his own consciousness of being uniquely related to the Father, a consciousness which he expressed both by speaking of God as 'my Father' and by referring to himself as 'the Son'. The task of exploring the use of this title in its further developments in the early Church lies beyond our present scope. It must suffice to have shown that the beginning of this development lies in the thought of Jesus himself, so that when the early Church proceeded to worship him as the divine Son of God, and to construct its theology on this basis it was not taking a step into Hellenistic mythology, but drawing out for itself the fuller implications of the historical self-understanding of Jesus.[64]

Notes

[1]F. Hahn, *Christologische Hoheitstitel*, 2nd edn. (Göttingen, 1964), ch. 5; see R. Fuller, *The Foundations of New Testament Christology* (New York, 1965) for a similar view.

[2]See the review of recent study in B. M. F. van Iersel, *'Der Sohn' in den synoptischen Jesusworten*, 2nd edn. (Leiden, 1964), pp. 3-28.

[3]Hahn, op. cit., p. 281. P. Vielhauer, *Aufsätze zum Neuen Testament* (München, 1965), pp. 194f.

[4]Mark 1.11; 9.7; 12.6; Col. 1.13; see Gal. 1.16.

[5]In Hebrews 1.2 the absolute use of 'Son' is due to the contrast between two types of revelation, revelation through a Son being contrasted with the variety of earlier channels of revelation; note that the word 'God' appears in the immediate context (Heb. 1.1). The use of 'my Son' in 1.5b is due to the writer's quoting a text from the LXX in which God is regarded as the speaker. In 1.8 'the Son' is a reference back to the mention of him in 1.5, and the addition of 'of God' would be stylistically awkward in a sentence of which God is the implied subject. In 3.6 the use is descriptive rather than titular, as also in 5.8. In 7.28 there is a quotation from the LXX.

[6]In Galatians 4.6 'God', 'his Son', and '*Abba*, Father' are juxtaposed. See Ephesians 4.6, 13; Revelation 2.18/27; 1 John 4.14f. In 1 Cor. 15.28 it would have been stylistically awkward to have added any qualification to 'the Son', and both 'Father' and 'God' appear in the context.

[7]J. Jeremias, *Abba* (Göttingen, 1966), pp. 15-67, especially pp. 33ff.

[8]Van Iersel, op. cit., pp. 97f., falls into this error.

[9]For the authenticity of this material, see Jeremias, op. cit.

[10]Exodus 4.22f.; Deuteronomy 32.6; Psalm 103.13; Isaiah 1.2; 30.1; Jeremiah 3.22; Isaiah 63.16; 64.8; Hosea 11.1; Malachi 3.17; Wisdom 2.16, 18; Sir. 4.10; Ps. Sol. 13. 8f.; 17.30; 18.4; Jub. 1.24f. For the type of interpretation given above, compare the view attributed to W. Grundmann by J. Bieneck, *Sohn Gottes als Christusbezeichnung der Synoptiker* (Zürich, 1951), pp. 53, 67; van Iersel, op. cit., pp. 23-6, notes that Grundmann has repudiated this view as a misunderstanding of his position.

[11]For the contrary view, see H. Montefiore, 'God as Father in the Synoptic Gospels', *NTS*, 3, 1956, pp. 31-46.

[12]T. W. Manson, *The Teaching of Jesus*, 2nd edn. (Cambridge, 1935), pp. 89-115; H. F. D. Sparks, 'The Doctrine of Divine Fatherhood in the Gospels', in D. E. Nineham (ed.), *Studies in the Gospels* (Oxford, 1955), pp. 241-62; Fuller, op. cit., p. 133; G. E. Ladd, *Jesus and the Kingdom* (New York, 1966), pp. 176-8. Van Iersel, op. cit., pp. 110-13, sides with Montefiore, but in fact holds that God is only potentially the Father of all men; men become his sons by response to the message of Jesus.

[13]Manson, ibid. His view is disputed by van Iersel and Hahn, op. cit., p. 320, n. 6, without any good reasons being advanced. Note that although the Sermon on the Mount was spoken in the presence of the crowds (Matt. 5.1; 7.28), its contents indicate that its teaching was meant for disciples or intending disciples (see Matt. 5.1b; Luke 6.20); this latter point will hold good whatever be our estimate of Matthew's setting.

[14]Jeremias, op. cit., p. 55, n. 106. See G. Dalman, *The Words of Jesus* (Edinburgh, 1909), pp. 190, 281.

[15]Against H. Weinel, quoted by G. Schrenk in *TDNT*, V, p. 987.

[16]See also the non-technical presentation of the evidence in J. Jeremias, *The Central Message of the New Testament* (New York, 1965), ch. 1.

[17]Hahn, op. cit., pp. 321-6. Earlier criticism is summarized by Bieneck, op. cit., pp. 75-87.

[18]Jeremias, *Abba*, p. 51.

[19]Ibid., pp. 47-50. See van Iersel, op. cit., pp. 146-61. Paul Winter has proposed a reconstruction of the text on the basis of mainly patristic evidence ('Matthew 11.27 and Luke 10.22 from the First to the Fifth Century', *Nov. T*, 1, 1956, pp. 112-48); his arguments are not sufficient justification for abandoning the almost unanimous witness of the Greek MSS (see Hahn, op. cit., p. 323).

[20]Dalman, op. cit., pp. 184-94, especially 193f.; Jeremias, *Abba*, p. 40.

[21]Romans 6.4 gives the earliest written evidence; O. Michel, *Der Brief an die Römer*, 11th edn. (Göttingen, 1957), p. 130 notes that the phrase 'through the glory of the Father' sounds confessional. The use of 'God the Father' in Philippians 2.11 probably goes back to an even earlier date in liturgical usage. The evidence of Acts 1.4, 7; 2.33 ought not to be dismissed out of hand as 'late'.

[22]Jeremias, *Abba*, p. 40; *The Parables of Jesus* (New York, 1965), p. 73, n. 86; van Iersel, op. cit.,

p. 4, n. 7; W. G. Kümmel, *Heilsgeschehen und Geschichte* (Marburg, 1965), pp. 215f.

[23] Fuller, op. cit., pp. 31-3. See the detailed discussion in O. Betz, 'Die Frage nach dem messianischen Bewusstsein Jesu', *Nov. T,* 6, 1963, pp. 20-48. Other rabbinic evidence is assembled by Hahn, op. cit., pp. 284-7, but see the criticisms of van Iersel, op. cit., pp. 185-90.

[24] I. H. Marshall, 'The Synoptic Son of Man Sayings in Recent Discussion', *NTS,* 12, 1965-6, pp. 327-51 (see above, pp. 73-99).

[25] For 'Son of Man' as a title concealing divine sonship, see E. Lohmeyer, *Galiläa und Jerusalem* (Göttingen, 1936), p. 35.

[26] Jeremias, *Abba,* pp. 52f.

[27] A. M. Hunter, 'Crux Criticorum—Matt. xi. 25-30—A Re-Appraisal', *NTS,* 8, 1961-2, pp. 241-9.

[28] The saying is accepted by van Iersel, op. cit., pp. 117-23. It is completely rejected by Hahn, op. cit., p. 327. It is regarded as distorted by Dalman, op. cit., p. 194. W. G. Kümmel, *Promise and Fulfilment* (Naperville, Ill., 1957), pp. 40-2; J. Jeremias, *Abba,* p. 40.

[29] See especially van Iersel, op. cit.

[30] I. H. Marshall, *Eschatology and the Parables* (London, 1963), pp. 16-24.

[31] Hahn, op. cit.

[32] Fuller, op. cit., p. 114. The suggestion that 'Son' here stands for 'Son of Man' was made by E. Lohmeyer, *Das Evangelium des Markus,* 15th edn. (Göttingen, 1959), p. 283, but he unhesitatingly accepted the saying as genuine.

[33] *God's Rule and Kingdom* (New York, 1963), p. 210.

[34] Jeremias, *Abba,* p. 54.

[35] Van Iersel, op. cit., p. 176, n. 5. Against the authenticity of the saying see especially W. G. Kümmel, *Heilsgeschehen und Geschichte,* pp. 56f., 290-308; R. Bultmann, *Die Geschichte der synoptischen Tradition,* 4th edn. (Göttingen, 1958), pp. 147-50, 277f., *Ergänzungsheft,* pp. 22, 36.

[36] R. H. Gundry, 'The Narrative Framework of Matthew xvi.17-19', *Nov.T,* 7, 1964, pp. 1-9, defends this setting against a setting in the context of the Last Supper.

[37] Hahn, op. cit., p. 321, n. 3; A. Vögtle, 'Messiasbekenntnis und Petrusverheissung', *BZ,* n.f. 1, 1957, pp. 252-72; 2, 1958, pp. 85-103.

[38] Vögtle, op. cit., p. 101.

[39] The narrative introduction to the saying is Matthaean. The form of the saying with *makarios* followed by *hoti* is paralleled in Matt. 13.16, but is not peculiarly Matthaean (Luke 14.14). All the other beatitudes in Matthew come from Q or are modelled on patterns in Q. The form *Bariōna* is strange, and its origin is unexplained; Matthew is unlikely to have invented it. *Sarx kai haima* and *apokalupto* are not words that Matthew himself has added elsewhere in the Gospel. The form 'my Father in heaven' may be Matthaean, but in fact only the words 'in heaven' are suspicious and they could be traditional; see above.

[40] H. Schürmann, *Jesu Abschiedsrede,* Lk. 22. 21-38 (Münster Westfallen, 1957), pp. 37-54.

[41] In Luke 2.49 the phrase is essential to the story. Only in Luke 24.49 does the possibility of redactional addition arise, but against this should be set the avoidance of the title in Luke 9.26; 22.42 in contrast with Mark 8.38 and 14.36 respectively.

[42] Hahn, op. cit., p. 321; F. W. Beare, *The Earliest Records of Jesus* (New York, 1962), pp. 227f.

[43] Schürmann, op. cit., p. 39f.

[44] K. H. Rengstorf in *TDNT,* II, pp. 326f.

[45] J. Behm in *TDNT,* II, pp. 104-6.

[46] Schürmann, op. cit., p. 44, n. 159; see pp. 42f. Schnackenburg, op. cit., p. 175f, is more cautious in his verdict but he seems to accept the text as based on authentic material.

[47] Kümmel, *Heilsgeschehen und Geschichte,* pp. 215f. With regard to the general authenticity of the parable, see Jeremias, *The Parables of Jesus,* pp. 70-7.

[48] Jeremias, op. cit., pp. 72f. The same author's caution about the use of this passage, expressed in *Abba,* p. 40, n. 37, is to be understood in the light of this quotation.

[49]*The Person of Christ in New Testament Teaching* (New York, 1958), p. 186. For other advocates of this view, see the lists in Hahn, op. cit., p. 280, n. 7; van Iersel, op. cit., pp. 13-20.

[50]It is generally thought that the centurion at the cross was not using the phrase 'Son of God' with its full Christian significance (Mark 15.39), although his words were true in a deeper sense than he intended.

[51]For this widely held view, see especially Jeremias, *TDNT*, V, p. 701 = *Abba*, pp. 192-4; O. Cullmann, *The Christology of the New Testament* (Philadelphia, 1959), p. 66.

[52]Bieneck, op. cit., p. 57.

[53]The similarities between the Son and Servant concepts have been especially noted by Lohmeyer, *Gottesknecht und Davidssohn*, 2nd edn. (Göttingen, 1953). It is precisely these similarities between the associations of the different titles that make it so difficult to decide which complex of ideas is uppermost in a given context.

[54]Fuller, op. cit., p. 69. On the other hand, the Gentile use of the phrase to indicate a godly man (not an exorciser of demons) is found in Mark 15.39.

[55]V. Taylor, *The Gospel according to St. Mark* (London, 1952), p. 228.

[56]The 'Holy One of God' is a possible candidate, but, if so, it is remarkable that it has survived in Mark 1.24. Its meaning is scarcely different from 'Son of God'. It should be borne in mind that the use of the appellation is regarded as supernatural by the Evangelists; this fact should not be *a priori* excluded from consideration. On the whole problem, see Cullmann, op. cit., pp. 276-8.

[57]Romans 1.3f.; Acts 13.33. The attempt of Hahn, op. cit., pp. 287-90, to show that the title of Son of God was first of all associated with the parousia has not met with critical approval; see the discussion in Fuller, op. cit., pp. 164-7; Vielhauer, op. cit., pp. 188-90.

[58]W. Kramer, *Christ, Lord, Son of God* (London, 1966), 24a-28c, pp. 108-26.

[59]Fuller, op. cit., p. 180.

[60]See W. C. van Unnik, 'Jesus the Christ', *NTS*, 8, 1961-62, pp. 101-16, especially p. 108. E. Schweizer, *Lordship and Discipleship* (London, 1960), pp. 36-8, offers a similar, but not identical, interpretation.

[61]F. F. Bruce, *The Acts of the Apostles* (London, 1951), p. 269.

[62]H. Conzelmann, *Die Apostelgeschichte* (Tübingen, 1963), p. 77.

[63]See E. Huntress,' "Son of God" in Jewish Writings Prior to the Christian Era', *JBL*, 14, 1935, pp. 117-23. The relation of early Christology to the Book of Wisdom is also discussed in D. Georgi, 'Der Vorpaulinische Hymnus Phil. 2. 6-11', in E. Dinkler, (ed.), *Zeit und Geschichte* (Tübingen, 1964), pp. 263-93.

[64][1989] The fullest recent discussion of Jesus as the Son of God is to be found in J. D. G. Dunn, *Christology in the Making* (London, 1980, ch. 2) (on which see my comments in *Trinity Journal*, 7, 2, 1981, pp. 241-5). The significance of *Abba* for understanding Jesus has been questioned by J. Barr ' "Abba" isn't "Daddy",' *JTS*, 39, 1988, pp. 28-47, but his questioning as to whether the term was a child's word for 'Daddy' does not basically affect the issue that Jesus spoke of God as his Father in a way that appears to have been unique, or at least extremely rare, in Palestinian Judaism.

8
The Development of Christology in the Early Church

EVEN IF *THEOLOGY* (IN THE STRICTEST SENSE OF THAT WORD as 'thought about God') cannot be reduced without remainder to *Christology*,[1] there is no doubt that the doctrine of the person of Jesus is of central importance in Christian thought. Traditional dogmatics have been based on the belief that the New Testament as a whole bears witness to the divine nature of Jesus as the Son of God. A full defence of this belief was provided in 1958 by Dr V. Taylor. The conclusions of his survey of the New Testament writers were as follows:

> All the Gospels affirm the divine Sonship of Jesus. . . . Although the designation 'the Son of God' does not belong to the vocabulary of the Acts, its religious values appear in the manner in which He is described. . . . The Son of God in Paul appears as a supramundane being standing in the closest metaphysical relationship to God. . . . In the mind of (John) Christ is the divine Son of God in a relationship which is fully ethical and spiritual, but also one of being and nature.'[2]

This doctrine of the person of Jesus is not peculiar to the writers of the New Testament, but is to be traced back to an earlier period. Even if the term 'Son' is found only rarely in the primitive preaching, its meaning was expressed in the use of the title of 'Lord'. 'We must accept the testimony of our sources that it is the Lordship of Christ to which prominence was given, and infer that the idea is far richer in Christological meaning than the name "Lord" might itself suggest'.[3] This view is confirmed by the fact that the idea of divine Sonship goes back to Jesus himself:

> Within the limitations of the human life of Jesus His consciousness of

Sonship was gained through the knowledge that God was His Father, mediated by prayer and communion with Him in a process of growth and development which begins before the opening of the historic ministry and is consummated in decisive experiences of revelation and intuition. It is upon this historical foundation that Christological thinking must build.[4] Taylor's view would seem to be that an understanding of the person of Jesus as the Son of God in a real or essential sense[5] is to be found 1. in the mind of Jesus and 2. in the thought of the early Church,[6] and 3. that this understanding can form the basis of a modern Christology. Taylor himself uses the New Testament data as the basis for a kenotic type of Christology.

More recent scholarship has questioned all three of these contentions. It has denied that Jesus spoke of himself as the Son of God, that the earliest Church spoke of him as the Son of God in any other than a functional manner, and that the ontological affirmations which are made of him in the various parts of the New Testament are fully consistent with each other or can be understood in any other than a mythological way by the modern theologian.[7]

We are concerned here not so much with the implications of this view for dogmatic theology as with the question whether it is a true reading of the New Testament evidence. There are in fact strong reasons for questioning whether the scholars who adopt this interpretation are doing full justice to the evidence.

I The teaching of Jesus
Our starting point must be the teaching of Jesus himself. Can his historical person sustain the weight of Christological interpretation which the early Church puts upon it? The issue has been put pointedly by J. W. Bowman: *'The Church cannot indefinitely continue to believe about Jesus what he did not know to be true about himself.'* The question, accordingly, of his Messianic consciousness is the most vital one the Christian faith has to face.'[8] It may be objected that we are unable to reach back by methods of scientific historical criticism to the 'Messianic consciousness' of Jesus, but both on general grounds and on the basis of specific investigations into the Gospel material we believe that this is a most pessimistic conclusion. The attempt can be made, and can be made fruitfully.[9]

In an earlier essay we discussed this question.[10] It emerged that Jesus was conscious of a unique filial relationship to God the Father. This was seen not merely in his use of *Abba* in prayer and in his reference to God as 'my Father', but also in his use of the terminology of 'Sonship'.[11] We suggested that the texts in which Jesus spoke of himself as 'the Son' (Matt. 11.27 par. Luke

10.22; Mark 12.6; 13.32) were genuine in their present form. Consideration was given to other texts in the Synoptic Gospels in which the title is given to Jesus by a heavenly voice or in the cries of demons, and it was argued that the evidence of these texts did not contradict our conclusion that in the use of the title by Jesus it was his awareness of a special relationship to God which was the determining factor rather than a messianic use of the title or the Hellenistic idea of the 'divine man'. Since it is often argued that the attribution of divine Sonship to Jesus was first made by the early Church which regarded the resurrection and exaltation of Jesus as the act in which God adopted him as his Son, an examination was made of Romans 1.3f. and Acts 13.33, and it was shown that the early Church regarded the resurrection as the vindication of a status which Jesus had already claimed for himself. One obvious objection to this theory is the suggestion that 'the Son' and 'the Son of God' are different Christological titles, with different origins and different histories until they were eventually brought together at a comparatively late stage in the development. We submitted, however, that the evidence for this theory was extremely tenuous and that it is most likely that Jesus' own manner of referring to himself formed the source of the Church's thought.

II Development in Christology
In this present essay we propose to take a closer look at the development of Christological thought in the early Church in order to see whether the purely functional use of the title 'Son of God' advocated by recent scholars is a satisfactory interpretation of the evidence. In a recent article, G. M. Styler has suggested that an interest in ontology is not to be found in the earliest forms of Christology; it appeared only at a late stage of the development, in the period of our written documents. Consequently, 'neither 'Son of God' nor 'Son of man' are [*sic*] originally ontological; their primary reference is not to nature but to function'.[12] Other writers, such as F. Hahn and R. H. Fuller, have strongly emphasized that in the earliest forms of Christology there was no idea that Jesus had a divine nature and that in a Palestinian milieu this idea would have been unthinkable.[13]

Now we are not seeking to establish a case that ontological considerations were of paramount importance in this early period. The question is rather whether the Christological affirmations made at this point possessed any ontological significance at all, even if the full implications were not realized at the time. Was the Christology of later periods a legitimate development from this period, and would the first Christians have agreed that later Christology expressed what was already implicit in their own affirmations? Or were there a number of competing and even contradictory Christologies in the early Church?[14] Did the ontological content of 'Son of God' remain constant throughout the development, or was there a significant change of meaning between the Jewish and the Gentile stages of thought?

In order to come to grips with this problem, it will be helpful to look at three presentations of the evidence. In his highly influential book *Kyrios Christos*, W. Bousset made a pioneer attempt to reconstruct the Christological thought of the early church. In his discussion of the title 'Son of God' he came to the conclusion that it was probably not used of Jesus in the earliest Church. His arguments were as follows:

1. The title is placed on the lips of Jesus only rarely in the earlier Gospel tradition and is not an authentic part of his teaching.

2. 'Son of God' was not a Jewish title for the Messiah, and its use would have endangered the strong monotheism of Jewish piety. It is therefore unlikely that the earliest Jewish Christians would have used it in their Christology.

3. The usage in the Gospels does not come from the earliest period. The use of the title in the temptation story is Hellenistic, and the use in Mark reflects the faith of Gentile Christians. In the baptismal and Transfiguration stories the word 'Son' is not used as a title.

4. In Acts the title is found but once (Acts 9.20), and it is unlikely that it would be used alongside the title of 'Servant' which has a firm place in the early tradition.[15]

Bousset did not discuss the use of 'Son of God' in the Hellenistic church. He was inclined to think that it was Paul himself who was responsible for a new development in the use of the title.[16] For a fuller study of this period we must turn to R. Bultmann.

In his *Theology of the New Testament*, Bultmann takes up the distinction between the earliest (Palestinian Jewish) church and the Hellenistic church which had been made by Bousset and W. Heitmüller.[17] Unlike Bousset, he believes that the title of 'Son of God' was used in the Palestinian church as a messianic or royal title. This possibility arises because Bultmann is not convinced that Psalm 2 was not already interpreted messianically in Judaism. The evidence for the use of the title is found in Romans 1.3f. (in its pre-Pauline form) and in the Transfiguration story (which Bultmann regards as an Easter story based on early tradition). These texts show that 'the earliest Church called Jesus Son of God (messianic) because that was what the resurrection made him. However, unlike the later Hellenistic church it did not regard the earthly Jesus as a Son of God (mythological).'[18]

In the Hellenistic church the title of 'Son' was regarded as being given to

Jesus at his exaltation (Heb. 1.4), but its use now developed to refer to the divinity of Jesus. The Hellenistic idea of salvation was based on the appearance of a divine figure who suffered the fate of a man. The title of 'Son of God' aptly stressed the divinity of Jesus in this type of understanding. Its use developed under three influences, the Hellenistic idea of 'divine men', the belief in 'son-divinities', and the Gnostic idea of a divine redeemer.[19]

Bultmann's scheme is sharpened and refined in the work of F. Hahn and R. H. Fuller. These two scholars operate with a threefold division in the early pre-Pauline Church—the Palestinian Jewish (Aramaic speaking) church, the Hellenistic Jewish church and the Hellenistic Gentile church. In the Palestinian Jewish church the title of 'Son of God' was applied not to the exalted Jesus but to the returning Jesus; it was a title which denoted Jesus in his future activity as the messianic king at the parousia. It is thus used in the same way as 'Son of man', 'Lord', 'Christ' and 'Son of David', which all referred originally to the future activity of Jesus. As evidence for this view Hahn cites Luke 1.32f., Mark 14.61f. and 1 Thessalonians 1.9f.

In the last mentioned of these three texts the thought of the resurrection is already present, and in the period of the Hellenistic Jewish mission the Church soon reached the stage of regarding the exalted and risen Jesus as the Son of God (Rom. 1.3f.; Acts 13.33; Heb. 1.5; 5.5; Col. 1.13; 1 Cor. 15.28).

One small difference between Fuller and Hahn should be noted at this point. According to Fuller, Romans 1.3f. in its earliest reconstructable form belongs to the Palestinian stage and speaks of Jesus as 'predetermined from the time of the resurrection to be the eschatological Son of God at the parousia'. This idea of Jesus being foreordained to perform eschatological functions finds support from Acts 3.20; 10.42; 17.31.[20]

It was at this same stage that elements of the 'divine man' concept were applied to the earthly life of Jesus, and the title of 'Son of God' was used to designate his earthly function as the bearer of the divine Spirit. The concept of the virgin birth was also developed at this stage to indicate that God's act of election of Jesus went back to the time of his birth.

Finally, in the Hellenistic Gentile church came the divinization of Jesus, as reflected in the Transfiguration and other epiphany stories. Jesus was now thought of as the pre-existent Son of God, and for the first time the title became an expression of his divine nature.[21]

From this brief survey of the work of representative scholars it will be apparent that there are considerable differences of detail in the schemes that they present. Bousset was so uncertain of his position that he admitted in 1916 that his conclusion that 'Son of God' was not used in the Palestinian church was perhaps too hasty.[22] But although there is a real consensus of opinion on the general process of development in the writers whom we have summarized, it is questionable whether this theory can stand up to critical analysis.

III Jesus' view of his person

Bousset's case rested upon the thesis that the title of 'Son of God' was not used by Jesus. We have, however, summarized above an argument to the contrary, and shown that Jesus did use the title of 'Son' to express his consciousness of a filial relationship to God the Father. The facts that Jesus had used this title, and that it was addressed to him during his earthly life, would surely have led to the use of this title to describe him in the early Church.

But can the use of the title by Jesus be described as ontological? It certainly expresses a function. We find that the title is used to describe Jesus as the One who reveals God to men (Matt. 11.27 par. Luke 10.22).[23] But two factors suggest that the usage is not simply functional. First, Jesus knew himself to be *the* Son. He occupied a position which was distinct from that of other men, and, even if he taught his disciples to call God their Father in the same intimate manner as he himself did, he stood on a different plane from them in his capacity of mediating this relationship to them. He was not, however, simply exercising a unique *function*. For, second, the revelatory function of Jesus was dependent upon the relationship of Sonship in which he stood towards the God. The title of 'Son' and the allied use of 'Father' express a relationship of communion in which revelation takes place so that the Son is able to reveal the Father to men. We may justifiably claim that what is thus predicated of Jesus is something more than a function or a status. It is more than a function because it expresses the hidden relationship with God which enabled Jesus to act as the Revealer. It is more than a status, for the use of the title is not to express a position of high honour which demands respect and even worship (as is the case with 'Lord'), but rather to express an essential relationship to God.

We have, therefore, in the teaching of Jesus a use of the title of 'Son' which certainly carries an ontological meaning capable of rich development. It would be most curious if the early Church had proceeded to use this title in a purely functional manner.

IV The time available for development

We must now observe that the length of time during which these extensive developments, stretching over as many as three stages in the spread of the

Church, took place is comparatively restricted. Jesus died in AD 30 at the earliest. The earliest letter of Paul which can be dated with certainty is 1 Thessalonians, which was written in or around AD 50. This means that in round figures we have to account for the postulated development within some twenty years. If in fact Galatians is earlier than 1 Thessalonians, the period is slightly shorter.

But we cannot assume that the Christology that Paul expresses in either of these Epistles sprang fully developed from his mind at the precise moment of writing. In 1 Thessalonians he writes about the person of Jesus in a way which expresses a very 'high' Christology. Jesus is named in close conjunction with God (1 Thess. 1.1, 3; 3.11, 13; 49; 5.18, 23), and the title of 'Lord' is given to him twenty-four times. In one passage he is described as the Son of God who is to come from heaven and whom God raised from the dead (1 Thess. 1.10). If we are to include Galatians in our evidence, we have here proof that Paul conceived of Jesus as the pre-existent Son of God (Gal. 4.4). The evidence of 1 Thessalonians, however, is adequate to give a fairly fixed date for the end of the development of a 'Son of God' Christology as a means of expressing the essential nature of Jesus. We are forced to ask whether the complicated development postulated by Hahn and Fuller could have taken place in this period.[24]

V Pre-Pauline Christology

(a) We must now consider what view of the person of Jesus was held in the Church before Paul. We begin by looking more closely at 1 Thessalonians 1.10. In his discussion of this text, Hahn found evidence for the use of the title of 'Son of God' to refer to the eschatological functions of Jesus, and suggested that here we have a piece of earlier mission preaching taken over by Paul.[25] This, however, cannot be the meaning of the text in Paul. W. Kramer's study of the use of 'Son of God' in those Pauline texts which may be regarded as containing pre-Pauline material has shown that the title is used in two ways.[26] It is used in formulae dealing with the resurrection and in formulae which speak of God 'giving' or 'sending' the pre-existent Son as the Saviour. With regard to the latter formulae he writes: 'This understanding of "Sonship" is distinctive in that its interest is not in any particular historical act but rather in describing Jesus' significance in terms of metaphysical and cosmological speculation, by introducing the notion of his pre-existence'.[27] The existence of this second class of formulae shows sufficiently that the idea of pre-existence was already present in the pre-Pauline Church. We must certainly reckon with it as one of the associations present in Paul's mind when he spoke of Jesus as the Son.

In 1 Thessalonians 1.10, however, this idea is not explicit. Paul's thought is of the status of Jesus in the period after the resurrection; we note in passing that Hahn's view that Sonship is here associated purely with the parousia is rendered untenable by the explicit mention of the resurrection.[28] But there is no suggestion anywhere in Paul that Jesus became the Son of God at the resurrection. Jesus did not become God's Son by being raised from the dead: it was *because* he was his Son that God raised him from the dead. This interpretation of the resurrection is confirmed by the Hellenistic Jewish interpretation of Sonship found in Wisdom 2.13-18. There the enemies of the righteous man acknowledge that 'He professes to have knowledge of God, and calls himself a child of the Lord . . . and boasts that God is his father'. Therefore they intend to test his claims. 'Let us see if his words are true, and let us test what will happen at the end of his life; for if the righteous man is God's son, he will help him, and will deliver him from the hand of his adversaries'. Paul's view of the Sonship of Jesus is thoroughly in line with this conception. The effect of the resurrection was to designate Jesus as 'Son of God in power' (Rom. 1.4), and therefore the idea of honour is bound up with the mention of Sonship, but the resurrection is not the appointment of Jesus to Sonship. Consequently 1 Thessalonians does not in any way contradict the texts which speak of Jesus as the pre-existent Son of God.

If this is the right interpretation of this text in its present Pauline context, there is no reason to suspect that Paul has in any way altered its meaning. We should be justified in thinking that a shift of meaning had taken place only if other pre-Pauline texts implied that Sonship was an honour conferred upon Jesus at his resurrection. This, however, is not the case.

(b) We have shown elsewhere that in Romans 1.3f. the primitive form of the text is not to be understood in an adoptionist manner. Nor is it to be taken, as Fuller suggests, to mean that Jesus was foreordained to be the Son at the parousia. The evidence cited by Fuller consists of three texts. We may dismiss Acts 10.42 and 17.31 as irrelevant, for in these verses the theme is that of judgement and the future function which is foreordained for Jesus is to act as judge. There is, however, no evidence that the idea of judgement was present in the formula in Romans 1.3f., and divine Sonship is only rarely linked to the thought of judgement; in John 5.23, 27 the Son is judge because he is the Son of man, Fuller's third text apparently offers better support for his case. He refers to Acts 3.20 where Peter speaks of God sending 'the Christ appointed for you, Jesus'. Fuller takes this to mean that Jesus has been foreordained to become the Christ at the parousia.[29] But the text may equally well mean that the One who has already been ordained as the Christ will return at the parousia. That this is the preferable view of the text is shown not only by the ascription of messiahship to the earthly life of Jesus in verse 18, but also by the peculiar use of ὑμῖν in verse 20; this use is to be seen in the light of the use in verse 26 where Peter speaks of God having raised up and sent his servant to the Jews. There is accordingly no reason to adopt Fuller's novel interpretation of Romans 1.3f.

In fact, Romans 1.3f is most plausibly understood as a statement about the nature of Jesus. If we adopt the basic minimum of wording common to all reconstructions of the text, we have two clauses in parallel to each other: '. . . who was descended from David . . . designated Son of God . . . by his resurrection from the dead'. Since the first clause contains a statement about the nature of Jesus, we may expect a similar statement in the second clause.[30] He is both the offspring of David, the earthly Messiah, and the heavenly Son of God. An ontological understanding of the person of Jesus is surely implicit here.

(c) Acts 13.33 has also been examined elsewhere, and it has been shown that the idea of adoption is also absent here. The theme of the passage in which the text occurs is the resurrection, and no special significance attaches to the use of the title; it occurs in an incidental manner in the quotation of a proof text from the Old Testament.

(d) But the question arises whether the use of this proof text (Ps. 2.7) does not imply that the early Church regarded the Sonship of Jesus as dating from his resurrection. This suggestion has also been made with reference to Hebrews 1.4f. and 5.5.[31] In the former of these two passages Jesus is said to have received a more excellent name than that of the angels. The more excellent name is clearly that of 'Son', and the immediately following quotations from Psalm 2.7 and 2 Samuel 7.14 (together with the allusion to Ps. 110.1 in verse 4 and the quotation in verse 13) have suggested that we have here a line of thought parallel to that in Philippians 2.9-11; on this view Jesus is here given the title of 'Son' at his exaltation, just as in the hymn in Philippians he is given the title of 'Lord'. But it is quite certain that the author of Hebrews did not think that Jesus received the title of 'Son' for the first time at his exaltation. On this point the commentators are unanimous. The author's 'wisdom' Christology shows plainly that the title of 'Son' belongs to the pre-existent Jesus.[32] When, therefore, the author assembles his testimonia regarding the exaltation of Jesus, there is no suggestion that he is thinking that Jesus was now appointed as Son for the first time.

Although, therefore, the use of Psalm 2.7 is associated with the resurrection, there is nowhere any evidence which compels us to think that the early Church regarded this as the moment at which Jesus became the Son of

God.[33] The usage is entirely consistent with the view that the resurrection was regarded as the moment in which God openly acknowledged Jesus as his Son and exalted him to his right hand. Indeed, when we ask what prompted the early Church to use Psalm 2.7 as a proof text it seems extremely unlikely that it was read as an allusion to the resurrection and then applied to Jesus; it is much more likely that the mention of the Lord's anointed and his Son led to the application to Jesus. It was the prophecy of Jesus' person in the psalm which led the early Church to see in it also a prophecy of the resurrection, and not vice versa. Consequently the use of the psalm presupposes that the early Church had already formed some estimate of the person of Jesus, whether as the Messiah or as the Son of God.[34]

VI   The Christology of the Jewish Church

The argument of the previous section has shown that the connection made in the early Church between the resurrection and the divine Sonship of Jesus does not imply that his Sonship was thought of as beginning from the resurrection. We must now ask whether there is any evidence which speaks positively in favour of an attribution of Sonship, understood in an ontological sense, to Jesus in this period. Here we must refer again to the work of W. Kramer who has demonstrated that pre-Pauline forms are to be traced in Galatians 4.4f.; Romans 8.3, 32; Galatians 2.20; Ephesians 5.2, 25 and possibly Romans 4.25. To these texts should also be added Philippians 2.6-8, although the title of 'Son' is not found in this passage.[35] Kramer holds that these forms, which express the pre-existence of Jesus, come from the Hellenistic Jewish church. On the one hand, he argues that the Jewish formulation present in the texts and the absence of any decisive allusion to the Gnostic myth of the ransomed redeemer speak against attributing these texts to the Hellenistic Gentile church.[36] On the other hand, the attribution of an adoptionist Christology to the Palestinian Jewish church prevents him from ascribing the doctrine of pre-existence to it. The presence of Jewish wisdom speculation in the pre-existence texts indicates rather that these forms must come from the Hellenistic Jewish church, and not from any earlier stage in Christological development.

Now we have already seen that the texts that Kramer adduces to support his theory of an adoptionist Christology in the Palestinian Jewish church do not bear out his view. From this point of view, there is no reason why a pre-existence type of Christology may not have developed in the Palestinian church. Is it possible that this happened? In investigating this question the Christological hymn in Philippians 2.6-8 is of great importance. Certainly the title of 'Son of God' is not present in the passage, and this has led Fuller to argue that the hymn originally spoke of the pre-existent 'Kyrios' rather than of the pre-existent Son.[37] But it is not certain that Fuller's is the right deduction from the facts. If Kramer is right, the title of 'Lord' is not found elsewhere in association with pre-existence in pre-Pauline texts.[38] If what we possess here is part of a hymn originally composed for a different context, it is by no means impossible that the title of 'Son' originally stood in the introduction to the hymn, and this suspicion may perhaps receive some confirmation from the use of 'God the Father' at the end of the hymn (Phil. 2.11). In any case, however, the hymn associates pre-existence with Jesus, and provides the atmosphere in which pre-existence could be linked to Sonship.[39] It is noteworthy how pre-existence is taken for granted; it is mentioned almost incidentally in verse 6a in a way which suggests that the idea was a familiar one.

The question of the date and origin of this hymn is therefore vital. The matter would be simplified if we were certain that the hymn reflects Aramaic linguistic and poetic usage. This was the view of E. Lohmeyer in his fundamental study of the passage,[40] and it is defended today by J. Jeremias.[41] Recently it has been attacked by Fuller. Fuller states that there are four phrases on which the case rests: '(i) "in the *form* of God" (verse 6), which is equated with *d'muth* or *ṣelem* from Gen. 1.26; (ii) "emptied himself" (verse 7), which is equated with "poured out his soul" (Isa. 53.12c) ; (iii) "servant" (δοῦλος), which has often been equated with *'ebhedh* (Isa. 53), etc.; (iv) "as a man" which has been equated with *k'bhar' 'naš* (Dan. 7.13), "one like a son of man".'[42] To these points should be added: (v) the use of participles for finite verbs, and perhaps (vi) the strophic, rhythmical and parallelistic arrangement characteristic of Semitic poetry.[43]

(i) Fuller argues that the concept of the first man is found only in Hellenistic Judaism, whereas the Son of man is found only in Palestinian Judaism. But we do not need to look to recondite 'first man' speculation in explaining the use of 'form of God' here. The most obvious parallel is with Adam, created in the image of God, who was tempted to 'be like God, knowing good and evil'. According to Jeremias, parallelism between the first man and the redeemer is to be found in Palestinian Judaism as well as in Hellenistic Judaism.[44]

(ii) The criticisms of Fuller and others[45] against the attempt to find an allusion to Isaiah 53.12c in verse 7 have been fully answered by J. Jeremias, whose arguments need not be repeated here.[46]

(iii) The equation of δοῦλος with *'ebhedh* has been denied for three reasons. First, 'everywhere else the Greek-speaking Christian church used παῖς ("servant") to translate *'ebhedh*'.[47] This is not strictly accurate, for in Mark

10.45 the verb διακονέω is used to express the concept of service in a text that has undoubted links with Isaiah 53, and the actual word δοῦλος is used in the preceding verse (Mark 10.44) of the position of a disciple. Morever, δουλεύω is found in Isaiah 53.11 to translate ʿebhedh, and δοῦλος itself, which is used on occasion to translate ʿebhedh in the LXX,[48] is found in Isaiah 52.13 Aquila. Second, it is argued that παῖς was a title of honour, expressing the special relationship between God and his Servant, whereas here the title expresses humiliation. But even if this be true of the use of δοῦλος in many of its occurrences in the LXX, it is by no means the case that it carries the idea of humiliation in Paul; on the contrary, it expresses the concept of a humble rather than a humiliating service, and because it is *God's* service it confers a certain status on the one who is called to be a servant.[49] There is, therefore, no objection to the use of δοῦλος here to translate ʿebhedh. Its purpose here is to provide a contrast to the κύριος status later given to Jesus because he was God's obedient servant (cf. Isa. 53.12a). A third point made by Fuller is that in this hymn the idea of servanthood is linked with the incarnation rather than with the earthly life and death of Jesus. This objection is nullified if we accept Jeremias's interpretation of 'he emptied himself' as a reference to the death of Jesus; even if this view is not accepted, there is no reason why this hymn should not represent a logical development of the idea of servanthood to cover the whole life of Jesus.

(iv) The equation of 'found in fashion as a man' with Daniel 7.13 is certainly doubtful, but the phrase is decidedly strange in Greek, and it is most plausibly explained as reflecting Semitic usage, such as is found in Daniel 7.13 and elsewhere.

We conclude that the case against authorship of this hymn by a person with a Semitic mother tongue has not been made out. On the other hand, it cannot be proved that the hymn was originally composed in Aramaic. It is, however, unnecessary to go to this length in an attempt to show that this hymn comes from an early stage in the development of Christology. For the distinction between a Palestinian Jewish and a Hellenistic Jewish church, which is the instrument used to effect a finer dating of material in the early period, is a most dubious one. On the one hand, we have learned that Palestine was subject to Hellenistic influences from the second century BC onwards, that Greek was spoken widely, and that Hellenistic Jews (e.g., Stephen in *Jerusalem!*) were present in the Church from an extremely early stage. To label a concept as 'Hellenistic' is not to prove that it must have emanated from outside Palestine.[50] On the other hand, we have found no evidence in the texts that we have studied to show that they cannot have come from the Palestinian church. Nor, indeed, is there any evidence to show that

Palestinian and Hellenistic Jewish Christians thought differently in matters of Christology.[51]

There remains the objection that the earliest Christians would not have spoken of Jesus as the Son of God, because this would have conflicted with Jewish monotheistic ideas. This argument fails to reckon with the facts that Jesus himself had given the impetus to this kind of expression, and that 'Son of God' does not mean δεύτερος Θεός. On the other hand, it must be borne in mind that the use of the title of 'Son of God' was comparatively rare in the earliest stages, and Acts 9.20 links its use with Paul himself; it may well be that the early Church did not make much use of it in preaching. It would be wrong to deduce from Acts 9.20 that Paul was alone in his use of 'Son of God', but it seems likely that it found little public expression in the early Church.[52]

VII Conclusion

The points that have now been assembled should be adequate to show that the view of Christological development in the early Church held by many scholars since Bousset is exposed to grave objection. If our arguments are sound, the thought of the early Church developed in the context of the self-witness of Jesus who knew himself to be the Son of God. At a very early date the evidence of Paul shows that a Christology with ontological implications had been developed. We were able to show that this Christology must have developed well before the time of the earliest written evidence, and that it was a Christology which was fully consonant with Jesus' consciousness of being the Son of God during his earthly life. Finally, we argued that within this period a distinction between Palestinian and Hellenistic Jewish Christianity is an unreal one, and that there is no evidence for a period in the early Church in which Jesus was not regarded as being the Son of God, not merely in function but in person. It is clear that during this stage of development the ontological aspects of the Son of God Christology were not developed for their own sake, but that such implications were none the less present.[53]

If these points are valid, they show that there was not such a drastic change in meaning between the use of 'Son of God' in the Jewish church and in the Gentile church as recent scholarship has supposed. The basic idea that Jesus stood in a special relation to God in his lifetime, a relation that stretched back to the period before his birth and that was confirmed by his exaltation and resurrection, was an essential ingredient of Jewish Christian Christology.

Notes

[1]T. Ogletree *(The 'Death of God' Controversy* [London, 1966], pp. 36, 57-9, 85) has demonstrat-

ed the failure of recent American writers to account for the transcendent features of the person of Jesus without reference to God.

²V. Taylor, *The Person of Christ in New Testament Teaching* (London, 1958), pp. 22, 31, 47, 103.

³Ibid., p. 197.

⁴Ibid., p. 186.

⁵The choice of a suitable adjective is difficult. 'Metaphysical', 'ontic', 'ontological' and even 'physical' are among possibilities used by various writers.

⁶It is generally agreed that the New Testament writers held such a view of the person of Jesus. What is in dispute is whether their predecessors in the early Church went beyond a purely functional interpretation of the person of Jesus and gave him ontological status, even if, as Taylor shows, the full implications were not worked out.

⁷For an exposition of this view, see R. H. Fuller, *The Foundations of New Testament Christology*, (London, 1965). I have reviewed this work in *Themelios*, 3, 2, 1966, pp. 25-34.

⁸J. W. Bowman, *The Intention of Jesus* (London, 1945), p. 108. Quoted by M. D. Hooker, *Jesus and the Servant* (London, 1967), ch. 6.

⁹F. F. Bruce, 'History and the Gospel', in C. F. H. Henry (ed.), *Jesus of Nazareth: Saviour and Lord* (London, 1967), ch. 6.

¹⁰I. H. Marshall, 'The Divine Sonship of Jesus', *Interpretation*, 21, 1677, pp. 87-103. See above, pp. 134-49.

¹¹See especially J. Jeremias, *Abba* (Göttingen, 1966), pp. 15-67. For other literature see article cited in n. 10.

¹²G. M. Styler, 'Stages in Christology in the Synoptic Gospels', in *NTS*, 10, 1963-64, pp. 398-409, especially p. 400.

¹³F. Hahn, *Christologische Hoheitstitel* (Göttingen, 1964), pp. 106, 288, 304, 308. Fuller, *Foundations*, pp. 205, 247ff.

¹⁴Cf. R. P. Casey, 'The Earliest Christologies', *JTS*, n.s. 9, 1958, pp. 53-77.

¹⁵W. Bousset, *Kyrios Christos* (Göttingen, 1926), pp. 52-7.

¹⁶Ibid., p. 151.

¹⁷W. Heitmüller, 'Zum Problem Paulus und Jesus', *ZNW*, 13, 1912, pp. 320-37.

¹⁸R. Bultmann, *Theology of the New Testament* (London, 1952), I, p. 50.

¹⁹Ibid., I, pp. 128-133.

²⁰Fuller, *Foundations*, pp. 164-7.

²¹Hahn, *Hoheitstitel*, pp. 280-333. Fuller, op. cit., pp. 187f., 192-7, 231f.

²²See B. M. F. van Iersel, *'Der Sohn' in den synoptischen Jesusworten* (Leiden, 1964), p. 10.

²³Mark 13.32 implies that even though Jesus is the Son, 'that Hour' has not been revealed to him.

²⁴Cf. E. L. Mascall, *The Secularisation of Christianity* (London, 1956), p. 228f.

²⁵Hahn, *Hoheitstitel*, pp. 289f. G. Friedrich ('Ein Tauflied hellenistischer Judenchristen, 1 Thess. 1 9f.', *Th.Z*, 21, 1965, pp. 502-16) has argued at length for the origin of the text in Jewish-Christian missionary teaching. He holds that 'his Son' was substituted for an original 'the Son of man' to make the hymn more intelligible to Gentiles.

²⁶W.Kramer, *Christ, Lord, Son of God* (London, 1966), 24a-28c = pp. 108-26.

²⁷Ibid., 29d, p. 127.

²⁸P. Vielhauer, *Aufsätze zum Neuen Testament* (München, 1965), pp. 189f.

²⁹Cf. J. A. T. Robinson, *Twelve New Testament Studies* (London, 1962), pp. 139-53, reproduced from 'The Most Primitive Christology of All?', *JTS*, n.s. 7, 1956, pp. 177-89. Against Robinson, see E. Schweizer, *Lordship and Discipleship* (London, 1960), pp. 57f.

³⁰W. Kramer, *Christ*, 24a, p. 108f.

³¹B. Lindars, *New Testament Apologetic* (London, 1961), pp. 139-44.

³²O. Michel, *Der Brief an die Hebräer* (Göttingen, 1960), p. 45, n. 6.

³³The same considerations apply to Hebrews 5.5. The other references to Jesus' exalted state

as the Son of God (Col. 1.13; 1 Cor. 15.28) say nothing about the moment when Jesus became the Son, nor do they show signs of pre-Pauline formulation.
[34]On the use of Psalm 2.7 in Acts 13.33, see also E. Schweizer, 'The Concept of the Davidic "Son of God" in Acts and Its Old Testament Background', in L. E. Keck and J. L. Martyn (eds.), *Studies in Luke-Acts* (Nashville and New York, 1966), pp. 186-93. I regret that this essay came to my notice too late for its arguments to be assessed in this article.
Consideration of the presence of ideas from Psalm 2.7 in the baptismal and Transfiguration stories must be deferred; if these belong to the original form of the stories, they afford further evidence that Psalm 2 was not first applied to Jesus in view of the resurrection.
[35]Cf. n. 26, and n. 27 above.
[36]These considerations dispose of F. Hahn's view *(Hoheitstitel,* 120f., 316) that the hymn comes from the Hellenistic Gentile church.
[37]Fuller, *Foundations,* p. 231f.
[38]Kramer, *Christ,* pp. 22a-g, 94-9.
[39]Cf. Hahn, *Hoheitstitel,* pp. 316, n. 2.
[40]E. Lohmeyer, *Kyrios Jesus* (Heidelberg, 1928), pp. 8-11.
[41]Jeremias, *Abba,* pp. 207-9, 275, 308-13.
[42]Fuller, *Foundations,* pp. 204-14, especially p. 204f.
[43]R. P. Martin, *An Early Christian Confession* (London, 1960), pp. 11f.; cf. 'The Form-analysis of Philippians 2, 5-11', *TU,* 87, 1964, pp. 611-20, where P. P. Levertoff's translation of the hymn into Aramaic is quoted. Note, however, that Lohmeyer did not hold that the hymn was originally composed in Aramaic, but only that it was the composition of a writer whose mother tongue was Semitic (Lohmeyer, op. cit., p. 9).
[44]J. Jeremias, *s.v.* 'Αδάμ, *TDNT,* I, p. 142.
[45]G. Bornkamm, *Studien zu Antike und Urchristentum* (München, 1963), p. 180; Hooker, *Jesus,* pp. 120f.; G. Strecker, 'Redaktion und Tradition im Christushymnus Phil 2.6-11', *ZNW,* 55, 1964, pp. 63-78 (p. 73, n. 41).
[46]See n. 41. A. Feuillet, 'L'hymne christologique de l'Épitrê aux Philippiens (II, 6-11)', *RB,* 72, 1965, pp. 352-80, 481-507.
[47]Fuller, *Foundations,* p. 205.
[48]J. Jeremias and W. Zimmerli, *TDNT,* V, pp. 673-7, 683.
[49]R. P. Martin, *The Epistle of Paul to the Philippians* (London, 1960), p. 56; cf. C. L. Mitton, *The Epistle of James* (London, 1966), pp. 12f.
[50]See, for example, W. D. Davies, *Christian Origins and Judaism* (London, 1962), pp. 105-8, 141; R. H. Gundry, 'The Language Milieu of First-Century Palestine. Its Bearing on the Authenticity of the Gospel Tradition', *JBL,* 83, 1964, pp. 404-8.
[51]A study of chapters 2 and 3 of R. Bultmann, *Theology,* I, will show how arbitrary is the division of material between the 'earliest Church' and the 'Hellenistic church'; cf. T. W. Manson's review in *JTS,* 50, 1949, pp. 202-6.
[52]Dr R. P. Martin has suggested to me that there may be a parallel in the scanty use of σωτήρ in the early Church.
[53]See further O. Cullmann, 'The Reply of Professor Cullmann to Roman Catholic Critics', *SJT,* 15, 1962, pp. 36-43.

9
Incarnational Christology
in the New Testament

ROM AN EARLY DATE BELIEF 'IN ONE GOD THE FATHER
Almighty, . . . And in one Lord Jesus Christ, the only-begotten Son of
God, . . . Who . . . came down from heaven, And was incarnate by the Holy
Ghost of the Virgin Mary' (the Nicene Creed) has been an accepted part of
Christian belief, as expressed in creeds and confessions. Within the last few
years, however, this belief has been subjected to strong criticism by a group
of British theologians who have argued that it is no longer a meaningful
belief for today, and that it can and ought to be jettisoned.[1] They have argued
that it is not a central doctrine in the New Testament, although they have
not succeeded in denying its presence altogether. More recently, the American Roman Catholic scholar R. E. Brown has stated that, while the incarnation is truly characteristic of Johannine Christianity, it is not characteristic
of about 90 per cent of the remainder of the New Testament.[2] Even so
conservative a scholar as J. D. G. Dunn has found a full-blown doctrine of
the incarnation present in only one passage in the New Testament.[3]

Assertions that the incarnation is not a New Testament doctrine or that
it is a dispensable doctrine in modern Christianity may be disquieting to
some of us, while to others they may simply give open expression to their
own secret uncertainties and doubts. Whatever be the frame of mind with
which we read such comments, however, they need to be taken seriously and
examined dispassionately. In the space at my disposal there is room simply
to take up one aspect of the problem, namely, how far there is a doctrine
of incarnation in the New Testament itself.

I

The word 'incarnation' is not a New Testament word any more than is Trinity or eschatology or Christology. Such words, however, have been found useful in the discussion of New Testament theology because they deal with identifiable subjects. Sometimes they are the names of concepts which became important in the later history of theology, so that it becomes profitable to compare later teaching with that of the New Testament and to correct the former by the latter. If dogmatics exists to test the preaching of the Church by the Word of God, so New Testament theology exists to test dogmatics by the Word of God as it is revealed in Scripture.

Some words used in later theology may not have a counterpart in New Testament teaching or may have a different connotation from that which they have in the New Testament. J. Carmignac has suggested with good reason that the common use of the term 'eschatology' can lead to misunderstanding of the teaching of the New Testament and wrong identification of its theological concerns.[4] A study of Christology in the light of the New Testament may show that the interests of the New Testament writers were different from those of later dogmaticians. A study of the New Testament to see what it says about 'incarnation' may possibly lead to the conclusion that 'incarnation' is an inappropriate category to use in analysing New Testament teaching, or that New Testament teaching suggests a different understanding and definition of the concept from that current in later centuries, or again that 'incarnation' is not a wholly satisfactory term to sum up this aspect of New Testament teaching and could be replaced by a more appropriate one. That is to say, the term 'incarnation' directs us to certain aspects of New Testament teaching which historically formed the basis for its use in the Church, but the teaching of the New Testament in these and other passages may lead us to a new apprehension of the concept and alterations in our existing ideas. We must always be alert to such possibilities, and also to the temptation to express New Testament ideas in our own way which does not in fact do justice to them.

II

The traditional basis of the doctrine of the incarnation is John 1.14 where the prologue of the Gospel comes to a climax in the statement that the Word who had been from the beginning with God and was active in the work of creation and was the light and life of men became flesh and dwelt among us. It is noteworthy that the subject of the passage is the Word or Logos. It is the career of the Logos which is being described, and not until verse 17 is the name Jesus Christ used for the first time, thereby identifying the

Word who became flesh with the historical figure of that name. From that point onwards John ceases to use the term Logos and writes about Jesus, using his name and a variety of Jewish messianic titles to refer to him.

For John, then, the Word became a particular person, Jesus, who existed in human form. The Word is clearly a personal being,[5] a phrase by which I mean that the qualities which we generally regard as being characteristic of human beings as persons are possessed by him. He has intelligence, emotions and will. He is like a person rather than like a dumb animal or a thing.[6] Above all, he is described as the only[7] (sc. Son) of God, so that, in so far as we think of the Father as a personal being, so also must we think of the Word as having the same sort of being. He is said to share the glory which is the prerogative of God. He is the Father's partner in his activities, and yet in some way he is subordinate to the Father.

To say that this being became flesh is the problematic statement, since John does not give us any immediate, nearer description of what he means. We have to consider the clause in the context of the Gospel as a whole. John does not mean that the Word turned into flesh or that it merely assumed a fleshly clothing like a Greek god who could instantly transform himself into a human bodily form and move about among men, his real nature and identity being hidden from them except, perhaps, when he demonstrated supernatural powers. It would be truer to say that John opposes such views. Rather, the Word took on a fleshly form of existence. He was, therefore, still the Word.

As such, he could display miraculous powers. We should not overlook this element, even though it has caused one writer to suggest that the Johannine Jesus walks through the world with his feet several inches from the ground.[8] In this way, it is implied, he was not a real man at all, but simply a heavenly being masquerading as a man. But in fact this same Gospel presents Jesus as a man who could ask questions to remove his own ignorance and who could feel such human emotions as hunger and sadness, and there is no suggestion that these emotions were faked for the occasion by somebody who was impassible. However, John suggests that the important evidences of divinity in Jesus are to be seen not so much in his mighty acts, though these are not unimportant, but in his revelation of divine glory through loving and humble service. It is the moral attributes that matter: grace and truth came through Jesus Christ. That is to say, the revelation of God in Jesus is seen primarily in his moral attributes and his teaching. Some would like to argue that, as the Word made flesh, Jesus should have been *in all respects* just like any other man, but this is surely an absurd presupposition. The problem, rather, is whether the evidence that he was the Logos constituted a denial of the real humanity of Jesus.

For John, then, Jesus is undoubtedly the personal Word of God now adopting a fleshly form of existence. When we talk of incarnation, this is what is meant by it, for it is here that the New Testament offers the closest linguistic equivalent to the term 'incarnation': *ho logos sarx egeneto*.

III

Our next task is to see whether similar teaching is to be found elsewhere. We must beware, of course, of assuming that similarity of expression necessarily means identity of ideas expressed, and so we must proceed with due caution.

The Epistles of John are commonly regarded as having been written, if not by the author of the Gospel himself, at least by somebody of a closely similar outlook, and subsequently to the Gospel. Here two things claim our interest.

First, there is a series of statements in which the writer defends the confession that Jesus is the Christ (1 John 2.22) or the Son (1 John 2.22f.) or that Jesus Christ has come in the flesh (1 John 4.2; cf. 2 John 7). There is general agreement that for the writer the terms 'Son' and 'Christ' are close in meaning, and that by these statements he wishes (i) to identify Jesus as the Son of God, and (ii) to affirm that this person Jesus Christ came in the flesh. The negative to these statements would be to deny that Jesus was the Son of God and that this person came in the flesh.

If we ask what such a denial would mean, it seems most likely that the deniers whom the writer had in mind held that a divine power, presumably a spiritual 'Son of God', came upon the man Jesus at his baptism and then departed before the crucifixion. This is the view combated in 1 John 5.6 where the writer emphasizes that Jesus Christ came with the water and with the blood.[9] If this interpretation is correct, John's opponents believed in a merely temporary possession of Jesus by a spiritual power, and they denied that it was the Son of God who died on the cross. Clearly John wished to say that this was not what he understood by the relation between Jesus and the Son. He obviously believed that there was a real and lasting union between the Son of God and the flesh of Jesus, while his opponents probably shared the later Gnostic disbelief in the impossibility of a real incarnation and laid stress on the importance of the divine spirit over against human materiality. Thus in the face of opposition to the idea, John affirmed the necessity of belief in Jesus Christ, the Son of God, as truly come in the flesh. It may well be also that John believed that even after the resurrection the union of the Son of God with the man Jesus still continued; the heavenly being worshipped by the Church was Jesus and not a disincarnate Son of

God.[10]

Second, 1 John begins with a statement about that which was from the beginning and which could be seen, heard and handled, namely the word of life. The language used is somewhat equivocal. The word of life could well mean the Christian message, the gospel, which conveys life to those who accept it, but the references to seeing and touching cannot refer to anything other than the concrete manifestation of the Word in Jesus. Both aspects of meaning are present, and it is probable that the writer has chosen this enigmatic and even awkward manner of expression in order to bring out the identity between the Word preached to his readers and the Word incarnate who had been personally known by the apostles.[11] If so, the important thing is that he writes about the Word being manifested in such a way as to be heard, seen and handled. He presupposes the concept of incarnation found in John 1.

Thus the same concept of incarnation as in the Gospel is present in 1 and 2 John, and indeed it is the principal Christological idea in these Epistles. This is a matter of great significance. The Gospel is concerned to present the historical, earthly person, Jesus, and it is in this context that the concept of incarnation might seem to be most at home. But the Epistles are written to people who had never known the earthly Jesus, whose belief was centred on the heavenly Son of God who would one day appear in glory; and it is in this context that the writer finds it necessary to stress that this Son of God truly came in the flesh and died as an atoning sacrifice for sin. For him there could be no separation of contemporary Christian belief and practice from its historical roots in the earthly manifestation of the Word or Son in Jesus in fleshly form. The concept of incarnation fundamentally shapes the Christology of the Johannine Epistles and forms the key idea around which John's other statements can be logically organized.

IV

Within the Pauline writings Philippians 2.6-11 is a passage which is often regarded as expressing an earlier formulation of Christian faith about Jesus, although this view is by no means firmly established.[12] The passage speaks of One who was in the form of God, but emptied himself, taking the form of a servant, being born in the likeness of men, and being found in human form. The word 'flesh' is not used here, but the equivalent term 'man' is used. A Being who was in the form of God became in likeness and appearance as a man.

Two different views have been taken of this statement. On the one hand, J. D. G. Dunn follows a number of scholars in arguing that the passage contrasts Jesus with Adam and refers to the way in which the man Jesus rejected the temptation to which Adam fell prey but rather took on himself the lot of fallen Adam. There is no reference to pre-existence or incarnation. On the other hand, S. Kim defends the more traditional interpretation of the passage as a reference to the act of choice of a pre-existent Being in becoming man and submitting to death.[13] For Kim the starting-point of Paul's thought is his conviction, born of his experience at his conversion, that he saw the exalted Christ in glory as the image of God; it was from this experience that he came to see Christ as the Last Adam and also as personified Wisdom. In the light of the total evidence from Paul's writings adduced by Kim, there seems to be no reason to deny the traditional interpretation of Philippians 2.6-11 and adopt Dunn's view unless there are convincing reasons for excluding the former possibility and preferring the latter. But Dunn's case is not compelling.[14] In particular, his interpretation does not do justice to the force of the recapitulatory phrase 'and being found in form as man' (Phil. 2.8), which is very odd if it refers to a person who had never been anything else but a man; again the *contrast* clearly expressed between 'being in the form of God' and 'becoming in the form of men' is extremely odd if the contrast is between two stages in the career of a man. We accept, therefore, the traditional view of the passage.

The fact that Christ is said to have become *like* a man is not to be taken to mean that the Being merely took on the outward form of a man, but rather to indicate that in becoming a man he did not cease to be what he originally was. To say that the Being was transformed into a man would have been misleading. In order to become like a man he had to empty himself, a verb which is best taken to refer to the abandonment of the glorious and lordly prerogatives which go along with equality with God in order to take on the humble form of a servant and to die. The point is, not that Christ gave up any divine attributes, but simply that he did not behave as one who was equal with God might have been expected to behave, but as a humble servant.

Our modern tendency is to insist that Jesus was every bit a man, just the same as one of us. This may perhaps cause us to do less than justice to the New Testament representation of him as primarily the Son of God who took on the form of man. Where modern discussion emphasizes the fullness of his humanity, the New Testament emphasizes the fullness of his divinity.

Other Pauline passages speak of Jesus in similar terms. In 2 Corinthians 8.9 we have the same thought in a different terminology. Here again Dunn wishes to reinterpret the passage in terms of the man Jesus deliberately renouncing his spiritual communion with God in order to endure the 'poverty' of desolation on the cross for our sakes.[15] But Dunn ignores the way in which heavenly glory can be described in terms of riches (Phil. 4.19; cf. Eph. 1.18; 3.16; Col. 1.27), and this provides the more obvious background for Paul's statement.

Galatians 4.4 states that God sent his Son, born of a woman. Similarly, in Romans 8.3 God sent his own Son in the likeness of sinful flesh. Both statements are taken by Dunn to refer simply to the oneness of Jesus with the human race so that he might deliver mankind from bondage and sin and grant them his own sonship in exchange; the language of 'sending' is like that in Mark 12.6 and need not refer to pre-existence—indeed, it is unlikely to do so, argues Dunn, since these statements are soteriological and do not give the necessary theological backing for presenting the novel idea of in-carnation to Paul's readers.[16] But this reinterpretation does not do justice to the texts. In his earliest Epistles Paul assumes that the exalted Jesus is on a par with the Father in a way which suggests that a lofty Christology formed part of his missionary preaching and catechetical instruction. To say that God sent his *Son, born* of a woman, suggests a different 'field of meaning' for 'sent' from that in Mark 12.6. Further, as Dunn admits, Galatians 4.4 contains language similar to that used in Wisdom 9.10 about the pre-existent figure of Wisdom. Even if this passage contains nothing more than a literary personification of Wisdom, there was nothing to prevent Paul using it to express the real pre-existence of the Son of God. Again, if Dunn's view is correct, it raises problems as to the point of time at which the Son of God came into existence for Paul. The background of Jewish thought about heavenly intermediaries argues strongly against the possibility that the com-ing into existence of the Son of God and the birth of Jesus (still less his resurrection) were simultaneous.

The evidence, then, favours the view that for Paul the Son of God existed before his earthly manifestation through his birth as a man. It is against this background of thought that the use of the term 'flesh' in Romans 8.3 takes on significance. In the New Testament generally 'flesh' is the physical sub-stance of which human beings and animals are made; it is variously associated with bones and blood and sometimes contrasted with spirit. It is the stuff of which we are made and thus indicates our corporeality; to be flesh is the opposite of being a ghost or a spirit (Luke 24.39). In this sense the term is ethically neutral, although it conveys the ideas of physical corruptibility and mortality. But, since the body, made of flesh, is the seat of passions and desires which can lead a person into sin, the term 'flesh' came to be used, especially by Paul, in an ethically bad sense, so that 'to live according to the flesh' is Pauline terminology for living a sinful life in disobedience to God. In Romans 8.3 Paul makes it clear that he is thinking of the flesh as that aspect of man which is prone to sinfulness, and he emphasizes that it was in the likeness of this flesh that God's own Son came in order that he might condemn sin in the flesh. Since elsewhere Paul makes it quite clear that Jesus himself did not sin, we are right to take this verse to mean that he assumed a nature that was like our human sinful nature, and yet did not himself sin (2 Cor. 5.21).[17]

We find the same thought in Colossians 1.22 where Paul states that the One who was in the image of God and through whom all things were created reconciled us to God *in his body of flesh* by death. He had a fully physical, human body, and it was in this incarnate form that he died.[18] The reference to this physical body would be uncalled for if Jesus were simply a man; the phrase is meaningful only as a way of emphasizing the fact that the One described in the preceding 'hymn' became incarnate in order to die on the cross. Further on in the same letter Christ is said to be the One in whom the whole fullness of deity dwells bodily (Col. 2.9). The tense here is present, indicating that the reference is to the heavenly Lord. Over against any suggestion that the power of God was scattered among several beings Paul emphasizes that it is all to be found in Christ, and in him in bodily fashion, that is, assuming a bodily form. Here, then, we certainly have the concept of incarnation, of all the nature and power of God being present in a human person.[19] Neither Colossians 1.22 nor 2.9 taken by itself necessarily points to the personal pre-existence of the divine Being incarnate in Jesus, but this thought is demanded by the language of the 'hymn' in 1.15-20; here it is extremely difficult to take the language to refer to anything other than the personal activity of the One who is the image of God in creation; Dunn's attempt to make the wording mean merely that the power which God exercised in creation is now fully revealed and embodied in Christ is quite unconvincing.[20]

It is clear that Paul uses incarnational language of Jesus; he uses the actual word 'flesh' to refer to the manner of the Son's presence in Jesus, and he identifies the Son as the personal agent of God in creation. But was this a central concept for Paul? The following points may be made.

First, Paul rarely discusses the person of Jesus as a topic in its own right. Not until we come to Colossians was this one of the points at issue between Paul and his readers. It follows that the amount of material in Paul which is directly Christological is scanty; Paul's Christological statements are made almost casually and implicitly in discussions of other topics.

Second, although Paul does not use the term 'Son' very often, it is a major Christological term for him. He uses it when he wishes to make important assertions about Jesus and especially to express his relationship to the Father.[21] When he does not use this term, he speaks of Jesus as the first-born of God or as being in the divine image.

Third, Paul thinks of the Son as coming into the world from the Father and as having been active in the creation of the world.[22]

Fourth, Paul speaks of Jesus as the Son of God and as a man who was born into a human family, with a human mother, physically descended from a human ancestor, David, and having human brothers. Paul does not stress the humanity of Jesus as such; he can simply assume it. Where he does direct attention to it is when he draws contrasts between the fatal results of Adam's sin for the human race and the beneficial results of Jesus' act of righteousness, and here he contrasts the one man Adam and 'that one man Jesus Christ' (Rom. 5.15, 17-19). The thought is hammered home by deliberate repetition, and Dunn is right to stress that for Paul the contrast between Adam and Christ was of central significance. Similarly, Paul contrasts the way in which the first man Adam merely became a living being, whereas the last Adam, the second man, became a source of life for others (1 Cor. 15.46-48). Here, however, it is plain that Jesus is more than just a man, for he is a life-giving spirit, the man from heaven. This phrase incidentally shows that for Paul, as for John, the heavenly Lord remains a man.

Fifth, this tension between Jesus as the Son of God and as the second man finds its resolution in a doctrine of incarnation, that is, that the Son of God has come into the world as a man. This suggests that here we have an organizing principle which not only enables us to make sense of Paul's theology but also is of theological importance to him. Paul emphasizes both that it was as a man that Jesus died in solidarity with us and at the same time that it was God who was active in Christ reconciling the world to himself.

V

The same understanding of Jesus is to be found in the Pastoral Epistles, although these writings have an ecclesiastical and pastoral concern and are not directly theological.[23] Incarnational language is found in 1 Timothy 3.16 which describes how 'he was manifested in the flesh'. Although no subject is expressed (the AV 'God was manifest' follows a late text), the language is based on that used elsewhere to describe how the Son of God was incarnate. The thought is of an epiphany in human form, and the implication is that a divine or heavenly subject is intended. The reference is certainly to the earthly life of Jesus and not to his resurrection appearances.[24] In the light of this verse the saying that Christ Jesus came into the world to save sinners (1 Tim. 1.15) probably also implies the pre-existence of the Saviour. The writer also takes over the common Christian belief in the human descent of

Jesus from David (2 Tim. 2.8). The heavenly and earthly origins of the Saviour can thus be mentioned on different occasions without any sense of conflict or incongruity. The factor binding these two aspects of his person together is the manifestation of the Son of God in the flesh.

Hebrews also teaches both the divine sonship and the humanity of Jesus. The pre-existent, creative activity of the Son is dominant in the opening verses of the book (1.1-3) and is quickly followed by a description of how he himself took the same nature of flesh and blood as the people whom he came to deliver. He had to be made, says the author, like his brothers in every respect. The Son experienced 'the days of his flesh' and shared in human suffering on the cross before being exalted to heaven. The pattern of thought is the same as we have found elsewhere, but there is an increased stress on the suffering of Jesus in the flesh and his consequent qualification to be sympathetic to mankind in its weakness. For the author it is important that the Saviour is both the Son, God's final messenger to mankind, and also truly man, able to stand alongside his brothers. Since the Son is regarded as pre-existent, his entry into the world is by partaking of flesh and blood, that is by incarnation.[25]

Finally, in our survey of the Epistles we may note that 1 Peter states that Christ suffered and died in the flesh (3.18; 4.1). The writer also speaks of him as One who was predestined before the foundation of the world, but made manifest at the end of the times (1.20). This appears to be a remnant of incarnational language; Peter does not lay stress on it, but simply makes use of a stereotyped traditional terminology which reflects an existing incarnational theology.[26]

VI

We have found substantial evidence of incarnational language and thinking in the Epistles. But what of the Synoptic Gospels and Acts? Although the Gospels are essentially accounts of the earthly life of Jesus, nevertheless they are written from a post-resurrection standpoint and may be expected to reflect the Church's theological understanding of Jesus. Is this expectation justified?

There is frankly little that can be called incarnational, in the sense of teaching the incarnation of a pre-existent Being, in Mark. The writer presents an account of the ministry and death of Jesus in which a key issue is whether he is the Messiah of Jewish expectation, a ruler descended from David. He shows how Jesus understood himself in terms of the Son of man, but in my view none of the statements made about the Son of man are concerned with his pre-existence or incarnation, unless we are entitled to assume that the phrase itself must have carried these associations.[27] Jesus is also declared to be the Son of God, and clearly this is a very significant term for Mark, but again the title is not used in a way which demands that we think of pre-existence. Mark's Gospel in effect asks: How can this man be the Son of God? It does not solve the problem.

It is different with the other Synoptic Gospels, both of which preface their accounts of the ministry with stories of the birth of Jesus. The account in Luke, which is, one might say, logically prior to that in Matthew, is concerned to show how Mary's son would be a holy child, the Son of God, and does so by means of the annunciation narrative which indicates that through the coming of the Holy Spirit upon the Virgin Mary her child would be God's Son. Here we have clearly a doctrine of incarnation, of the physical birth of the Son of God; nothing, however, is said about the pre-existence of the Son. Matthew's account has nothing to add at this point; he justifies the title 'God with us' (Immanuel) for Jesus in that he was Mary's son, conceived by the Holy Spirit.

As for Acts, here Jesus is a man, anointed by God with the Spirit and appointed by him as judge of all men (2.22; 10.38; 17.31). For Acts, Jesus is a man whose life follows a career ordained by God which leads him through crucifixion to exaltation. At the same time this Jesus is God's Son (9.20; 13.33), and it is because he is God's Son, the Holy One, that he does not see corruption but is raised up to new life (2.27). Yet how Jesus can be both man and God's Son is not discussed in Acts. This silence may partly reveal the lack of reflection on it in the evangelistic discourses of the early Church, but in the context of Luke's work as a whole it is more probable that the explanation given at the outset of the two-volume work in the birth narrative is meant to provide the background for subsequent Christological statements: Jesus is both the Son of God and the earthly descendant of David, a real man, in virtue of his Spirit-conception in the womb of Mary.

VII

We must now try to draw some conclusions from this material and see what further questions it raises.

1. We have found that the concept of incarnation, that is, that Jesus Christ is the Son of God made flesh, is the principle of Christological explanation in the writings of John, the writings of Paul including the Pastoral Epistles, the Epistle to the Hebrews and 1 Peter. The view that it is found merely on the fringe of the New Testament is a complete travesty of the facts. In the writers who are concerned with theological reflection about the person of Jesus, incarnational thinking is of central importance and forms indeed the

organizing principle of their Christology. Moreover, in the case of these writers we have found good reason to believe that for them the Son of God who became incarnate was a pre-existent Being. Here we have found ourselves compelled to part company with the conclusions of J. D. G. Dunn who argues that much of the apparently incarnational language refers not to a pre-existent Being becoming man but rather to the creative and saving power of God, given literary personification by Jewish writers in such concepts as Wisdom and Word, now being fully embodied in Jesus so that he represents all that God is in his relationship to mankind.[28]

2. Such incarnational thinking begins with the pre-existent Son of God and states that he became man or became flesh. It thus deals with the question of how the Son of God became man rather than how a particular man, Jesus, could be the Son of God. Thus this way of thinking arose in a community where Jesus was already confessed as the Son of God. In incarnational theology the Son of God is the subject and Jesus is, as it were, the predicate. The direction of thought gives a Christology 'from above' rather than one 'from below'.[29] It is presupposed that Jesus is the Son of God—an assumption that Paul (for example) takes for granted and never attempts to prove, and which has a firm foundation in the teaching of Jesus, whose filial consciousness is the probable starting-point for the Church's thinking.

3. Over against this type of thinking we have that of the Synoptic Gospels and Acts. They share the conviction that Jesus is the Son of God, and indeed provide the evidence from his teaching which led to this confession, but they have nothing corresponding to 'the Word became flesh'. For Matthew and Luke, Jesus is the Son of God in virtue of his birth by the Spirit; Mark does not raise the question. This poses the problem of whether the New Testament contains two alternative and possibly mutually exclusive explanations of the person of Jesus in terms of incarnation and Spirit-conception. The issue is sharpened by the fact that Jesus does not appear in the Synoptic Gospels to have any consciousness of his pre-existence.

If these two explanations are mutually exclusive, the conclusion might be that both are mythological statements of the mystery of the person of Jesus. It is in fact this kind of suggestion which has led some scholars to argue that incarnational language is not to be taken seriously, still less literally, but is merely one—dispensable—mythological expression of early Christian thinking about Jesus.

The question of the status of incarnational language is too large to be discussed here,[30] and we shall remain on an exegetical level. The basic point that needs to be made is that at least some of the New Testament writers did not regard the two types of approach as mutually exclusive. Thus Paul, who is clearly an incarnationalist, knows and affirms that Jesus was born of a woman. Whatever be the truth in the view of some scholars that this phrase betrays a knowledge of the virgin birth,[31] it is unquestionable that Paul believed that Jesus was born of a human mother, and that he did not simply appear in the world like a Greek god turning himself into a human messenger. The same can be said of John who has the figure of Mary, the mother of Jesus, in his Gospel, and notes the sarcastic Jewish comment 'We were not born of fornication' (8.41), which may be used with irony by John to express what he and his readers knew otherwise about Jesus. John also knows that the Christ was to be descended from David. The tradition of Jesus' human birth and descent from David is thus entirely compatible with an incarnational understanding of him. Indeed, a thinker who held to incarnationalism would surely see nothing incompatible in Spirit-conception, and indeed is extremely likely to have accepted some such explanation (if he thought about it at all) of how the man Jesus could be the incarnate Son of God. If, then, we start from incarnationalism, there is no great problem about the Spirit-conception of Jesus.

If we start from the other side, from the Spirit-conception and virgin birth, the way is perhaps not so clear. But so far as the birth-stories are concerned, the problem may be that a different question is being asked. Here the centre of interest or starting-point is the child who is to be born. Mary is about to bear a child without having had intercourse with her husband, and the question is: How can this be? The answer is that she is to be the mother of a child who is to be God's Son, and this is to be accomplished by the activity of the Spirit. The question is 'from below': how can this baby be the Son of God? The incarnational type of question is absent.

Despite the lack of interest in this question, the Synoptic Gospels certainly present Jesus as the Son of God and they guide us to the centre of his self-consciousness as such. It is precisely this self-consciousness which, even in the absence of any consciousness of pre-existence, makes it unsatisfactory to think of Jesus as merely the embodiment of God's creative and saving power and which drives us on to an incarnational understanding of him as the personal Son of God. The evidence in the Synoptic Gospels not only fits an incarnational understanding of Jesus but positively cries out for it.

4. It is here in all probability that we are to find the origin of the concept of the incarnation. The nearest concept that we have in Judaism is that of Wisdom coming to dwell among mankind. In Sirach 24, Wisdom is personified and describes how she is the word which was spoken by God and dwelt in heaven. She looked for a place in which to settle, and the Creator commanded her: 'Make your home in Jacob; find your heritage in Israel'. So

Wisdom settled in Jerusalem. Later in the chapter it is made clear that 'all this is the covenant-book of God Most High, the law which Moses enacted to be the heritage of the assemblies of Jacob.' This shows that Wisdom is a personification of the Torah. Similarly, in 1 Enoch 42 we are told that 'wisdom went forth to make her dwelling among the children of men, and found no dwelling place. Wisdom returned to her place, and took her seat among the angels.' There is, however, here nothing that resembles the idea of incarnation. The idea of Wisdom entering into holy souls and making them God's friends and prophets (Wisd. 7.27) is not comparable. At best we can say that language used of Wisdom has come to be used of Jesus.

We shall do better to seek the origin of the doctrine in the Church's knowledge of the filial consciousness of Jesus. The recognition that Jesus was the Son of God was the starting-point for reflection which made use of Wisdom and Logos language. At the same time the resurrection of Jesus and the Church's understanding of this as his exaltation to the right hand of God exercised a decisive effect in leading to the interpretation of his person in the most exalted terms. Here the comments of C. F. D. Moule on the significance of Jesus' 'post-existence' are extremely important.[32]

5. The theological importance of the incarnation cannot be developed here. On the one hand, the divine Sonship of Jesus is crucial in establishing his role as the representative of God, demonstrating his active, sin-bearing love. On the other hand, his real humanity is equally crucial in that through it he is joined to mankind, bearing human sin as man's substitute and conveying to mankind a share in his own personal relationship with God. He became what we are in order that we might become what he is. But there would have been no point in his becoming what we are if he was not what he is, the eternal Son of God, God incarnate reconciling the world to himself.[33]

Notes

[1]J. Hick (ed.), The Myth of God Incarnate (London, 1977).
[2]R. E. Brown, review in *CBQ*, 42, 1980, p. 413. Cf. M. Wiles: 'Incarnation, in its full and proper sense, is not something directly presented in scripture' (Hick, op. cit., p. 3).
[3]J. D. G. Dunn, *Christology in the Making* (London, 1980), p. 241.
[4]J. Carmignac, 'Les Dangers de l'Eschatologie', *NTS*, 17, 1970-71, pp. 365-90.
[5]This is true at least for the prologue in its present form. We are not concerned here with possible earlier stages in composition.
[6]The language of persons, as applied to God, is analogical. The point is that analogies drawn from our experience of persons are far more appropriate than those drawn from experience of other entities, whether or not they are entirely adequate to express the nature of God. Put otherwise, we in fact possess no better language than that of persons to express our understanding of God, and nothing in our experience of God suggests that this language is misleading.

[7]Despite the retention of 'only begotten' by some biblical translations and commentators, the translation 'only' for *monogenēs* is probably to be preferred. See I. H. Marshall, *The Epistles of John* (Grand Rapids, 1978), p. 214, n. 8.

[8]E. Käsemann, *The Testament of Jesus* (London, 1968).

[9]K. Wengst, *Häresie und Orthodoxie im Spiegel des ersten Johannesbriefes* (Gütersloh: 1976), gives the latest defence of this view.

[10]For the theological importance of this doctrine see D. M. Baillie, *God Was in Christ* (Faber, 1948), pp. 96-8.

[11]Marshall, op. cit., pp. 99-108.

[12]For Pauline authorship of the hymn see S. Kim, *The Origin of Paul's Gospel* (Tübingen, 1981), pp. 147-9.

[13]Dunn, op. cit., pp. 114-21; Kim, op. cit., ch. 6.

[14]See N. T. Wright's review in *Churchman*, 95, 2, 1981, pp. 170-2.

[15]Dunn, op. cit., pp. 121-3.

[16]Ibid., pp. 36-44.

[17]"While the Son of God truly assumed *sarx humartias*, He never became *sarx humartias* and nothing more, nor even *sarx hamartias* indwelt by the Holy Spirit and nothing more (as a Christian might be described as being), but always remained Himself.' C. E. B. Cranfield, *The Epistle to the Romans* 1 (Edinburgh, 1975), p. 381.

[18]The same thought appears in Ephesians 2.16 where Christ reconciled us to God *in one body* through the cross.

[19]Colossians 2.10 adds 'and you have come to fulness of life in him' (literally, 'and in him you are made full'), but the fact that Paul can write in such terms of believers in no way weakens the force of what he says in the previous verse about Christ or suggests that he sees no difference between Christ and Christians.

[20]Dunn, op. cit., pp. 187-94.

[21]M. Hengel, *The Son of God* (London, 1976), pp. 7-15.

[22]1 Corinthians 8.6 should probably be taken in this sense, despite the attempt by Dunn, op. cit., pp. 179-83, to deny that Christ is here being identified with a pre-existent being who was active at creation.

[23]The Pastoral Epistles are treated separately from the other Pauline Epistles in view of the doubts of many scholars that they stem directly from Paul; see, however, D. Guthrie, *The Pastoral Epistles* (London, 1957) for a defence of their Pauline authorship.

[24]See R. H. Gundry, 'The Form, Meaning and Background of the Hymn quoted in 1 Timothy 3:16', in W. W. Gasque and R. P. Martin (eds), *Apostolic History and the Gospel* (Exeter, 1970), pp. 203-22.

[25]J. D. G. Dunn again attempts to argue that in Hebrews the pre-existence of the Son is 'perhaps more of an idea and purpose in the mind of God than of a personal divine being' (p. 56)— in other words, Hebrews displays an understanding of pre-existence which is more Platonic than Johannine. When Hebrews uses Wisdom language in 1.1-3, 'it is the act and power of God which properly speaking is what pre-exists; Christ is not so much the pre-existent act and power of God as its eschatological embodiment' (p. 209). This impersonal type of understanding seems very alien to the biblical understanding of God as personal, quite apart from imposing a very artificial interpretation upon the biblical text.

[26]Strictly speaking, 1 Peter does not speak of the pre-existence of Christ, but rather of God's predestination of him as a person to fulfil certain functions.

[27]For a detailed discussion of the pre-existence of the Son of man, see Dunn, op. cit., ch. 3; in opposition to R. G. Hamerton-Kelly, *Pre-existence, Wisdom and the Son of Man* (Cambridge, 1973), he concludes that the Son of man is not pre-existent in the Synoptic Gospels. I am not sure that we can so easily reject the possibility that the Evangelists and their readers may have interpreted the Son of man as an individual, pre-existent figure (as in 4 Ezra and 1 Enoch) who came from God into the world, but this thought is not made explicit in the

Synoptic Gospels (as it is in John).
[28]See especially Dunn, op. cit., pp. 211f. I am very conscious that my brief comments in this essay cannot do justice to the detailed arguments of this highly stimulating book.
[29]For this way of putting things, see W. Pannenberg, *Jesus—God and Man* (London, 1964). The statement above is not meant to suggest that a modern approach to Christology 'from below' is wrong; it is only when Jesus has been identified as the Son of God that it becomes possible to look at things 'from above'—but this step was taken in the earliest days of the Church before our written documents.
[30]It is one of the merits of Dunn's book that he demonstrates conclusively that Christian incarnational thinking was not derived from mythological concepts and is therefore not itself mythological in character. However, he goes too far in defending incarnationalism against this charge by reducing the content of the biblical statements to such propositions as that Jesus fully embodies the creative power and purpose of God. Dunn comes near to denying that divine sonship is a personal category (see further, pp. 181-96).
[31]J. G. Machen, *The Virgin Birth of Christ* (London, 1930), pp. 259-63, holds that we cannot tell from the evidence whether or not Paul knew of the virgin birth. Some Roman Catholic authors take a more positive view of the evidence; see J. McHugh, *The Mother of Jesus in the New Testament* (London, 1975), pp. 273-7.
[32]C. F. D. Moule, *The Origin of Christology* (Cambridge, 1977).
[33][1989] In the second edition of his book Dunn has responded to criticisms (*Christology in the Making* [1989²], pp. xi-xxxi; cf. id., 'In Defense of a Methodology', *Exp.T,* 95, 10, 1984, pp. 295-9.

10
God Incarnate: Myth or What?

HE PUBLICATION OF THE SYMPOSIUM ENTITLED *THE MYTH of God Incarnate,*[1] and the various rejoinders which it has evoked, may turn out in the long run to be an event of comparatively little importance; there is no doubt, however, that we who live at the present time must come to terms with the issues raised by this book and re-think our understanding of Jesus Christ in the light of them.

There is a good case that in the days of the early Church doctrinal progress was to some extent indebted to the rise of heresy. It was not necessarily the case that the heresies contained a deeper insight into the truth, but rather that they exposed the weaknesses in more orthodox viewpoints and stirred up traditionally minded Christians to probe more deeply into what they believed, and thus to arrive at a fuller conception of the truth than they might otherwise have reached. Certainly Paul's thinking about the Christian faith was stimulated by his encounters with the Judaizers who insisted that circumcision and other works of the law were needed alongside faith, and he was led to insist all the more clearly and forcefully on the all-sufficiency of faith, and to deny that circumcision or uncircumcision was of any significance in the eyes of God. Similarly, Paul's conflict with the advocates of a Gnosticizing type of Christology in Colossae led him to express in a more adequate fashion the supremacy of Christ in creation and redemption. In both cases it is probably true to say that Paul was simply unfolding more explicitly the full content of his earlier beliefs, but it needed the stimulus of opposition to bring him to this deeper affirmation of Christian doctrine. At the same time he probably learned things from his opponents and was prepared to integrate them, if they were true, into his theological system.

In a sense, therefore, the Church ought to be grateful to its opponents and to heretics for forcing it to take its own beliefs more seriously and to subject them to critical examination and careful reformulation.

Whether or not the writers of *The Myth of God Incarnate* should be regarded as heretics is not my concern. Certainly they are conscious of expressing their views in a manner that differs significantly from Christian orthodoxy, and a dialogue with them ought to be fruitful for us.

Their general viewpoint can be summed up in some half-a-dozen main propositions:

1. The presentation of Jesus as God incarnate is only one of many ways in which Jesus is portrayed in the New Testament, and is not central in New Testament thought.

2. This particular presentation is to be regarded as 'myth'; that is to say, it is not to be taken 'literally', but as a way of underlining the great significance that early Christians attached to Jesus, just as we might say of a lover, 'He worships the very ground she treads on'.

3. The development of this particular myth can be accounted for in terms of the ordinary human evolution of ideas within a world which made use of mythological categories of thinking (although the symposiasts are not agreed regarding the details of the development); consequently it cannot be regarded as a heavenly revelation of the significance of Jesus.

4. The myth of the incarnation is not a valid myth for us today, and we ought to drop it as an inappropriate way of speaking about the significance of Jesus.

5. We ought to find other ways of expressing the significance of Jesuss which will speak meaningfully to the modern world.

6. It may well be that if we drop the idea of the incarnation, we shall also find ourselves dropping some of the other theological motifs that are closely tied to it, especially the idea that Jesus is the unique and only Saviour of mankind.

My approach to this thesis is that of a student of the New Testament and of a Christian believer, and therefore I am interested in all its aspects. But within the present limited space for discussion I shall have to concentrate my attention on certain aspects of the theme, and I shall therefore look at it primarily as a student of the New Testament. My question will be: does this approach represent a fair interpretation of the New Testament? This question really divides up into two: 1. What does the New Testament actually teach about Jesus on its own terms? 2. Is the category of 'myth' the right one to use in evaluating this teaching? In other words, we are concerned with

the facts about the New Testament presentation of Jesus and their significance.

I
Since the whole of the New Testament is about Jesus, it is clearly impossible
to discuss this theme adequately in a few pages, and there is a danger that
I shall simply present my own biased reading of it. The risk, however, must
be taken. I want to examine briefly the forms in which the New Testament
teaching is presented, and then their content.

1 The forms of New Testament teaching
The New Testament contains several overlapping groups of statements about
Jesus:

(a) He is described in terms of *specific titles,* such as 'Son of man', 'Christ',
'Lord' and 'Son of God'. These have been exhaustively discussed, and it is
fairly clear what they mean in the New Testament itself, although the paths
by which they developed remain somewhat obscure.[1] They have been aptly
called 'titles of dignity',[3] without necessarily being titles expressive of divinity. Nevertheless, it is indubitable that what we would call divinity had come
to be expressed with some of the uses of these titles by the time that they
came to be used in the New Testament documents, even if at earlier stages
these overtones were not so clear. Undoubtedly the application of the titles
to *Jesus* altered and deepened their significance by a well-known semantic
process. We may compare how a fairly neutral title like *Der Führer,* the
Leader, has once and for all acquired a particular significance as a result of
its application to Hitler. As a result of the resurrection, the titles of 'Son of
God', and 'Lord' in particular, developed in significance, the former expressing the relation of Jesus to God the Father in terms of unique sonship, and
the latter applying to him the actual title of 'God' used in the LXX.

(b) Closely associated with the use of titles is the language used of Jesus
in *credal statements* and similar formulations.[4] Christians expressed their belief in Jesus and their commitment to him in statements which took on
stereotyped forms as a result of frequent usage, Such statements often employed the titles just mentioned (e.g., Rom. 10.9; I Cor. 8.6; 12.3; 1 John
4.2, 15). Although the context of such statements was Christian worship,
this does not diminish them but rather heightens the seriousness with which
they were used. Their language is no less measured and deliberate than the
language of a textbook on dogmatics. This point is sometimes denied, as if
the language of worship is more loose than the language of the theological
textbook, but it must be remembered that, whether or not theological text-

books express their authors' convictions, the language of worship does do so. In any case, the credal language was taken over into the New Testament writings which represent careful reflection on the substance of the Christian faith, Such statements go beyond the titles in that they represent careful, sometimes detailed formulations which present the career of Jesus from his pre-existence to his exaltation (Phil. 2.5-11; Col. 1.15-20; 1 Tim. 3.16).

(c) A third highly significant feature is the use of *casual statements* which take for granted the position of Jesus alongside God the Father and express it as a matter of course that needs no exposition or defence. The Father and the Son are named together as the source of salvation and the attributes of the one are ascribed to the other (Gal. 1.3; 1 Thess. 1.1 are examples from the earliest New Testament writings); Old Testament texts that originally referred to Yahweh are applied to Jesus (Rom. 14.11/Phil. 2.10f.). Within a comparatively short period of time it had become natural to ascribe to Jesus the highest place in the universe.

(d) Next we have *deliberate discussions* of the person of Jesus by the New Testament writers, whether in narrative statement (cf. Phil. 2.5-11) or by doctrinal statement (e.g., John 1; Heb. 1). Very often these statements take up and weld together the earlier types of material to give a more comprehensive presentation.

(e) Finally, we may list separately those *statements ascribed to the earthly Jesus* in which he gives teaching which reveals something of how he regarded himself in relation to God. Throughout his sayings and actions there runs a note of high authority, but there are also a few statements where the basis of his authority becomes more explicit (Matt. 10.25-27; Mark 12.6; 12.35-37; 14.36; perhaps some of the texts in John may be added to this collection). Such texts are comparatively few, so that, if we had to base a case for the divinity of Jesus on what he himself said, we should not have an easy task. It is in fact this gap between what Jesus said and what the early Church thought about him that constitutes the basic problem in Christology. What needs to be asked is whether the historical character of Jesus' person provides an adequate foundation for the Church's elaboration of his person in the light of the resurrection.

2 The content of the New Testament teaching

We must now turn to the question of what these statements actually teach about Jesus. I begin with some negative statements:

(a) The New Testament writers were chary of calling Jesus 'God'. For them the Father was God, and as strict Jewish monotheists they found it hard to think otherwise. This perhaps makes it all the more significant that in a number of places this step is actually taken. Jesus had the religious value of God, and this comes to expression especially, but not exclusively, in the later New Testament writings (John 1.18; 20.28; Rom. 9.5; Titus 2.13; Heb. 1.8; 2 Pet. 2.1; 1 John 5.20).

(b) The term 'divine' is used only marginally in the New Testament (Acts 17.29; 2 Pet. 1.3f.; cf. Rom. 1.20), and is not applied to Jesus, again probably because of the strict monotheism of the writers.

(c) It follows that the phrase 'God incarnate' is hardly a New Testament phrase. It belongs more to the language of later dogmatics, and so the same question arises as in the case of the term 'Trinity': granted that it is not a New Testament term, does it express what is implicit in New Testament teaching? What we can say is that *the idea of incarnation* is present in the New Testament. It is found in John 1.14 which speaks of the Word becoming flesh, and in Colossians 2.9 which states that the fullness of divinity dwells in Jesus bodily (see further 1 John 4.2; 5.6; 2 John 7). Further, the New Testament teaches not so much that God became incarnate as that the Son of God or the Word became incarnate. It identifies Jesus as the Son of God. This term might merely imply a particularly close human relationship to God, such as might be enjoyed by devout men who obeyed God and were the objects of his loving care As a result, however, of Jesus' expression of his close personal relation to God, and especially of his resurrection, the early Christians came to realize that there was more than this to his being the Son of God. They recognized that he stood on the same side of reality as God. He had the same religious value for them as God. But they did not identify him with the Father. Nor, on the other hand, did they regard him simply as a human Messiah or prophet, or even as an angel. They found that their experience of Jesus burst their existing ideas of God and led them into a new concept of God which finally crystallized in the doctrine of the Trinity.

(d) It must be insisted that this concept of Jesus as being functionally on a level with God, intimately associated with the Father, and sharing his nature, is *woven into the fabric of the New Testament*. To some extent we can trace the development of this consciousness on the part of the early Christians; what is significant, however, is that by the time of writing of the earliest New Testament documents it is accepted thinking on every side. The five types of statement which we discussed form an interlocking web of evidence.

Further, this consciousness is not necessarily expressed in the precise language of incarnation, although this language is not absent. The symposium affords a helpful corrective to the view that the language of Jesus as 'God incarnate' is frequent in the New Testament. It is more characteristic of the

New Testament writers to speak of Jesus as the Son of God or as the Lord. The term 'incarnate' came into the discussion in order to clarify the character of the earthly Jesus. When the New Testament writers are speaking of the risen, exalted Jesus, there is less need to describe him as a man or to use the word 'incarnate', although the central affirmation of New Testament theology has been recently identified as the conviction of the continuity between the earthly Jesus and the exalted Christ.[5] Nevertheless, it can be insisted that the risen Lord is truly man (Luke 24.39; 2 John 7). In other ways, however, the idea of incarnation is clearly expressed. This is seen in statements of the pre-existence of the Son of God who is identified with Jesus (John 13.3; 16.27f.; 17.3-5; Gal. 4.4f.), and in the concept of his birth by the Spirit, as a result of which he is the Son of God (Luke 1.31-35) and bears the name Immanuel, 'God with us' (Matt. 1.24). To see Jesus is to see the Father (John 14.9), although Jesus and the Father are not identified. Thus it can be argued that, although the language of incarnation is not employed in every case, the substance of the concept is certainly widely present.

(e) In the light of this discussion, we can ask whether the phrase 'the incarnate Word' or 'the Son of God' is an apt summary of New Testament teaching and whether it represents a significant emphasis, indeed the central emphasis, in New Testament teaching about Jesus. It seems doubtful to me whether the symposium has properly faced up to these questions. There is no careful exploration of the New Testament use of the language and concept of incarnation. One or two of the writers claim that Jesus is 'as-if-God' for them personally, and imply that this is what they take the New Testament to be teaching.[6] This is obviously true as far as it goes. Jesus is regarded as the channel through which God operates with regard to men; he is functionally equal with God, and he is paid the same honour as God (subject to a certain element of subordination which preserves the ultimate, superior status of the Father). But does the New Testament go beyond this? Clearly the New Testament writers do speak of Jesus as the Son of God and Lord, and it does not require much argument to show that this is their central way of understanding Jesus. It is certainly the case for Matthew, Mark, Luke, John, Paul, Paul's successors, and the writer to the Hebrews. Each in his own way affirms that the earthly Jesus is the Son of God and the Lord of glory, whether or not they use the actual terminology of incarnation. And it certainly appears at first sight as though they meant more than simply that Jesus is 'as-if-God': they meant that he actually is the Son of God. Moreover, there is no evidence that they entertained any other concept of his person except marginally. (Thus there may be traces of an angel-Christology in the New Testament, but these are faint; there is no evidence that any New Testament writer thought of Jesus as a mere man, although some of them had to contend with advocates of such a position.)

I would, therefore, contend that the concept of incarnation is used in the New Testament, and that it is widely present and represents the central, unifying manner of describing the person of Jesus. However tentative may be my further remarks, I would regard my conclusions so far as unassailable.

II

However, this only completes the first part of our task. In what way is the language of incarnation to be interpreted? Is it simply a way of expressing the significance of Jesus 'as-if-God'? Is it simply an expressive way of saying 'Jesus is of ultimate importance'? Is it mythological language expressing some concept that we would want to express otherwise? There are two points to be raised here, the first of which can be dealt with fairly briefly.

(a) We may attempt *to explain the historical process* by which this language came to be used. This is done by M. Goulder, who outlines a hypothesis as to how incarnational language could have arisen; namely, from tendencies in Samaritan theology developed by Simon Magus who thought of himself as a divine incarnation. The significance of this is not altogether clears. Goulder's hypothesis has manifestly not convinced one of his fellow-symposiasts, F. Young.[7] Whether or not it is correct, Goulder himself affirms that 'historical study does not disprove divine activity: it just renders the old inspiration model implausible'.[8] I take this to mean that if we can account for the development of an idea in terms of natural causes, this makes it less plausible that it arose as a result of divine inspiration. Clearly, Goulder is saying that an idea which can be explained in this way did not arise as a result of a direct revelation from heaven. That is fair enough. But the question is whether God may not be working to reveal himself through a chain of apparently purely human causes. Goulder is careful to say that historical study cannot disprove this possibility. There cannot be a simple either/or between divine inspiration (in the broad sense) and the human evolution of ideas. To account for ideas in terms of human development is not to exclude that possibility that God was active in the process, leading men to the insights that he wanted them to reach. But Goulder is trying to say that equally we cannot prove that God was present in the process and that the ideas are therefore binding on us: we are free to jettison them if we will. We should then have to ask by what criterion Goulder feels free to accept certain New Testament ideas and to jettison others. His apparent criterion is that the latter are 'not believable today', and it is at that point that we should want to probe his doctrine of religious authority.

(b) The same kind of point is put slightly differently by F. Young. As I have said, she rejects Goulder's particular historical hypothesis about the origin of the concept of incarnation: 'The theological position discussed in this book does not depend upon any specific theory proving to be impervious to scholarly criticism'.[9] Instead she argues that the New Testament writers operated against *a background of mythological language*, and specifically: the use of phrases like 'Son of God' which had a wide range of implications and could be applied to human or superhuman beings; the concept of apotheosis, that is, the ascent of exceptional men to the heavenly realm; and belief in heavenly beings or intermediaries who might come and help mankind. Such terminology provided a ready means for early Christians to express their belief in Jesus and his significance. But all this belongs to a world-view which is not that of the twentieth century and must be classed as mythological. It must be laid aside if we are to speak meaningfully of Jesus today.

There are two or three questions implicit here. There is the question as to whether New Testament Christology rests on pagan mythology, and there is the question whether it itself is mythological and needs to be expressed in a different way today. We therefore turn to the question of how the New Testament language is to be understood, and we must begin by discussing the term 'myth', since it is a highly slippery term.

III

There is a helpful discussion of the concept of 'myth in the symposium, but a slightly different approach may be more useful for us. I want to suggest that the term has three aspects.

(a) First, there is the *primal* or *aetiological* use of the term to refer to myths that depict the origin of the world, or of the human race, or of some particular institution. Various primitive societies have 'creation myths' which tell in an unscientific manner how the universe came to be. In this sense of the term, 'mythical' tends to stand over against scientific or historical explanation, and myths belong to a society in which such thinking was simply not possible.

(b) Second, a myth may express some aspect of human experience or understanding of the world in story form. For example, it may be easier to explain the nature of human society or government not by explaining how it actually functions, or by giving a philosophical justification, but by telling a story of a 'human contract', describing how men originally formed societies and established institutions of government which they agreed to respect and obey. People who tell this kind of story may or may not believe that it actually happened like this. If they adopt the former view, they may claim to be giving a historical justification of the institutions of society. (They will not then succeed in giving a philosophical justification of why *we* should obey the government.) If they adopt the latter, more sophisticated view, then the myth is a historicization of what is actually happening, and tells in story form what it really means to live in society now. In the same way other aspects of human experience may be expressed in myth and this may on occasion be the most effective means of expressing deep human convictions about the nature of things.

(c) Third, a myth may tell *a story which involves the gods* or other supernatural actors who are envisaged as taking part in human affairs and are described anthropomorphically, even though their behaviour may burst the bounds of ordinary natural cause and effect.

We may see an illustration of all three aspects of myth in the story of the Fall of man in Genesis 3. Here we have, first, an account of the temptation of the first human couple by the serpent. It is a story that attempts to explain the origin of evil in the world. Most people would not think of it as literally true, but as an aetiological myth to show how evil began and death came into the world, or, as a very subsidiary feature, why the serpent has no legs but must crawl on its belly. Such a story does not rest on scientific or historical knowledge. It is true that some Christians would claim that it does describe what actually happened, revealed by supernatural agency to the author of Genesis, but in any case it is hardly based on historical or scientific investigation. But there is more to the story than this. A Jewish writer commented, 'Each of us has been the Adam of his own soul' (2 Baruch 54.19), and thereby suggested that the Fall narrative is a mythological description of our present human situation and helps us towards self-understanding. It describes my condition as a sinner, and thus expresses a deep insight into human nature. I am Adam. The third aspect of the story is the appearance of God in the Garden, able to talk with Adam and Eve, and of a serpent who can talk and is meant to represent the source of temptation. Supernatural forces appear on the stage of history and behave in miraculous ways.

Now these three elements may be present in myths each to greater or lesser extent. Not all three elements are to be found in each myth. Nor is any myth necessarily an expression of only one element. The 'social contract' myth, for example, does not contain the third element, supernatural action. On the other hand, when somebody suggests that the Fall myth is 'nothing but' a dramatization of the present state of man, he may be right as regards *our* understanding of it, but it seems quite certain to me that the narrator of Genesis thought that he was explaining what happened in the past; you cannot turn to the writer of Genesis and say, 'You've got it wrong; it is simply a dramatization of contemporary experience'; for him, and he should know, it was meant as imaginative history.

It appears to be inherent in all uses of the word 'myth' that the story in question is not factual, in the sense that everything in it is a description of what actually happened in the way that it actually happened. There may be a historical core, or a historical fringe of greater or less dimensions, but the story as a whole is not factual. It may be obviously a work of the imagination, composed by an author who had no access to historical or scientific information, or it may contain features that, to a modern reader, are frankly incredible. Various careful writers would insist that in its proper use the term 'mythical' does not necessarily imply the unhistorical nature of the story; it could be a story that is literally true, but it serves one or other of the functions of myth. Thus a story that is told as a parable may be a true story, but the point of a parable is independent of the truth of the story as such. Nevertheless, the popular use of the term 'mythical' certainly carries the implication that the story is factually untrue, and this is a source of confusion.

It follows that from the point of view of its function as myth, the question of the factual truth or falsity of the story is irrelevant. The important question is whether as myth the story is true or false, valid or invalid. Whether or not Genesis 3 relates what actually happened, the question is whether the story is a valid or true depiction of the human situation, or one particular aspect of it. For example, a 'myth of the Fall is surely more appropriate and valid with respect to human experience than a myth which suggests the continuing moral perfection of humanity. To speak of these terms, however, raises the question of how we decide whether a particular myth is valid or otherwise; are we reduced to the subjective level of determining what has for us 'the ring of truth'? Or is there some way, perhaps, in which some myths are reflections of deep human insights into the nature of things, or even a form of divine revelation?

Let me sum up this part of the discussion in the following five statements:

1. We must be extremely careful when using the term 'myth' to indicate precisely what we mean by it. There is a case that the word is used in a slipshod way in the symposium.

2. There is nothing illegitimate about the use of myth as a literary category in religious and other discourse. The use of myth is as valid as the use of history or parable, and I should not want to go along with people who would exclude myth from serious consideration as a vehicle of religious truth.

3. To state that a particular story is a myth is not to pronounce on its literal truth or falsity, or its ultimate validity or invalidity. The story may be partly

or wholly unhistorical, but its ultimate truth or validity does not depend on its historicity.

4. To speak of God at all by means of human language is to use language that is by definition 'mythological'; we cannot avoid such language, but we shall have to ask whether this particular definition is a helpful or appropriate one.

5. The question of 'myth' is closely tied up with the question of the supernatural.

IV

To say that the incarnation is a myth is manifestly to say something that is closer to aspects 2 and 3 of our definition of myth than to aspect 1. The confession of Jesus as the incarnate Son of God is not a piece of prescientific speculation about the distant past, nor did it arise independently of the historical events of the life and death of Jesus and of the belief in his resurrection. Aspect 1 of myth is thus absent here, unless we want to say that the myth of the incarnation is similar in character to creation and Fall myths.

But what about aspect 2? If we narrowly define aspect 2 as relating to myths that attempt to explain deep truths about the human situation, then we must doubt whether the incarnation falls into this category. For the incarnation is an attempt to explain an action of *God*, not of man. It is true that some theologians would claim that statements about God are really statements about man, representing an objectification of human values in terms of divine being or something of the sort. This seems perverse to me. It represents a transformation of the view that theological statements about God are usually—or, as some would say, always—statements about God in his significance for man, and are therefore simultaneously about God and man, into the view that theological statements are really only about man; this logical leap is not justified. The incarnation is a way of accounting for Jesus in his relationship to God; it carries implications for the relationship of man to God, but there is no indication that this is how the doctrine arose or that this is what it 'really' means. Historically, the doctrine of incarnation arose in close conjunction with the doctrine of the work of Christ. Some would go so far as to say that the early Church at first thought of Jesus in purely functional terms, and only at a later stage asked, 'What kind of status must Jesus have in order to perform these functions of Saviour, and so on?'[10] This does not mean that the doctrine of the incarnation is simply a graphical expression in personal terms of the significance of the work of Jesus as Saviour. It rather means that the doctrine of the incarnation is concerned with the sort of person who was qualified to do this work. And I would contend that both functional and ontological interpretation of Jesus went on from an early stage. The main point, however, is that the doctrine of the incarnation is about Jesus as the Son of God, and is not an expression of some timeless truth about the nature of man in general. So aspect 2 of myth is less appropriate for describing the doctrine of the incarnation than appeared at first sight.

We have, therefore, to discuss whether aspect 3 of myth is an appropriate category for describing the incarnation. I want to approach the matter by a broader consideration of the use of religious language. When we talk about God, we invariably find ourselves using language that is to some extent metaphorical and symbolical. To speak with a psalmist of God as 'my rock and my fortress' is to make a metaphorical statement about his dependability as the object of faith, and it brings home this fact in a vivid and evocative manner that perhaps goes further than a plain statement. But the statement remains a metaphor; not all that is true of rocks or fortresses is true of God, and in particular such a statement tends to reduce God to the level of a material object. If, however, we speak of God as 'Father', we make use of a picture drawn from human relationships, and within the context of Christian theology we would want to affirm that this is a less metaphorical way of describing the living God. Nevertheless, it is still metaphorical, in that not all the associations of fatherhood in ordinary discourse, such as physical generation, are present. To speak of God as 'Father' is to employ a language that has a limited applicability. We accept this fact in talking about God, recognizing the ultimate inadequacy of human language to describe him. At the same time, we are prepared to put up with these limitations, recognizing that if we do not use human terms to describe God we are reduced to an intolerable silence.

It may be objected that if *all* our language about God is metaphorical or analogical, we cannot know whether anything is directly true of God. This is an important point, and to discuss it properly lies outside my competence. I would claim in broad terms that within Christian theology we can operate with the so-called *analogia entis,* the belief that there is a real similarity between the Creator and his creatures, in terms of which it is possible to use creature-language analogically about the Creator. Hence, despite the metaphorical nature of our language about God, it is possible to make true statements about him.

But this does mean that there are limits to our capacity to talk directly about God. The language breaks down and produces antinomies when it is pressed too far. This is particularly evident when we deal with matters of creation, consummation and incarnation.

Thus, when we are discussing creation, we are trying to conceive of a situation in which the universe, with its space-time framework, did not exist. We are trying to think without the use of the categories of space and time which make thinking and expression possible. And we cannot in the nature of things do so. I think there may be some analogy to this in the so-called uncertainty principle in physics. My layman's understanding of this is that in certain submicroscopic situations it is not possible to insert a measuring tool to measure a particular magnitude without destroying the observed phenomenon. This impossibility is built into the nature of things; it is not something that may be overcome by more refined instrumentation. In an analogous sort of way, the more we try to focus on the creation, the more impossible it becomes to make an observation of it. In such a situation we have to resort to language that is pictorial, or that is content to state a fact without being able to explain it.

This sort of language may be called 'mythological', but, in view of the slipperiness of this term, I am suggesting that to describe it as metaphorical or analogical may be more useful and helpful. Let us now try to look at the incarnation in the light of this suggestion. This doctrine can be regarded as the early Church's attempt to account for the historical facts of the life of Jesus and his continuing influence. The early Christians claimed not merely that God was active through Jesus, but that somehow God was to be identified with him. The Church could not, however, identify him with the God about whom he spoke in the third person as his Father; but it took up his own manner of speaking and regarded him as the Son of God. In doing so, the Church seems to have gone beyond affirming that he was merely 'as-if-God', especially in view of its continued experience of the risen, exalted Jesus as the One through whom God is encountered. It is beyond doubt that the New Testament writers meant to affirm that Jesus was personally identifiable as the Son of God, and they remoulded their doctrine of God accordingly.

The way in which this identification was expressed was in terms of incarnation, the Son of God appearing in the form of man. To say this is not to explain what happened, but rather to affirm that it did happen. Later theology speculated on the questions involved, and debated how a person could be God and man at one and the same time, and whether the Son of God had a full human personality, and so on. These are questions that cannot be ducked, but they are not within the sphere of the New Testament writers' statements. Like the statements of creation and consummation, they affirm facts but do not offer explanations of what must be inexplicable within human categories of thought.

Is this way of speaking about Jesus defensible? I have argued that it is to be understood as a type of language which is analogical ('As a son is to a father, so is Jesus related as the Son of God to God the Father') and expressive rather than explanatory (Jesus is the incarnate Son of God, that is, the Son of God in human form, but how this happens is beyond our comprehension). Let us consider the difficulties raised by the symposium.

1. It is argued that the language causes intellectual difficulties for modern man, since we cannot understand how incarnation is possible. Therefore it should be scrapped. It seems to me that the symposiasts have run into difficulty here by regarding the concept of incarnation as an explanation rather than as a statement of the person of Jesus, and then claiming that as an explanation it causes difficulties. But my contention is that it is not meant, and was never meant, as an explanation. Just as we affirm a belief in creation without being able to explain it, so we can accept the incarnation without being able to explain it. In principle, explanation is impossible, since it is beyond the scope of human language to explain how the Creator can become a creature. This difficulty is inherent in Christian belief and applies to all Christian thought. I do not see that it rules out the possibility of Christian belief, for it is of the nature of belief that it cannot explain everything. What we are to believe as Christians is not to be measured by what modern man cannot accept; the early Church faced the same problem with its contemporaries to whom Christ crucified was foolishness.

2. It is argued that the language of incarnation represents the mythological thinking of a culture that we cannot share. It arose against a background of belief in divine intermediaries, semi-divine men, ascents to heaven, and the like. Faced by the significant figure of Jesus, the early Christians simply made use of the conceptual stock of the time, and did for Jesus what their admirers did for Plato or Alexander the Great. We may make various points by way of comment here. First, it is widely agreed that the traces of mythological language, in the sense of crude stories about divine actors, in the Bible are very sparse, both in the Old Testament and in the New Testament. The actual word 'myth' is used in the New Testament only in a pejorative sense, and the use of myth is marginal. G. Stählin puts the point emphatically when he says, 'The firm rejection of myth is one of the decisions characteristic of the New Testament.'[11] Second, the links between the presentation of the incarnation in the New Testament and pagan myths are scanty. There are of course parallels, just as there are parallels between many things in the New Testament and in the ancient world, but the differences are very marked. Third, if we are to abandon so-called 'mythological' language *in toto*, we are required to jettison the biblical concept of the living God as part of the myth. In this sense the teaching of the Bible is irreducibly mythological. The sym-

posiasts are plainly unwilling to take this step, although there are other people who do take it. But if one persists in belief in the living God, then it is hard to see how one can abandon belief in the incarnation. For it is by the incarnation that we come to belief in the living God, and without the incarnation God is dead. It is in the last analysis impossible to believe in the living God and to deny the incarnation. Fourth, it is arguable that the incarnation language was providentially available for the early Christians to express the significance of Jesus. The conceptual tool was ready to be developed.

3. Finally, the question arises whether the incarnation language can be demythologized and replaced by something else. Can we make do with such statements as 'Jesus has the religious value of God' or 'Jesus is as-if-God'? The symposiasts are prepared to experiment with this type of language. Against this possibility it must be urged that this is a very attenuated type of language, and it does not get round the difficulty of speaking about God, unless we are reduced simply to saying 'Jesus was the most remarkable man who ever lived'; but that is scarcely what it means to make a Christian affirmation about Jesus. No viable alternative to the Christian language of incarnation has yet been offered.

In his first Letter, John criticized people who denied that Jesus was the Christ, the Son of God come in the flesh, and declared, 'No one who denies the 'Son has the Father' (1 John 2.23). I believe that his comment still stands. To speak of Jesus as the incarnate Son of God is to use language that is metaphorical rather than mythological, language that cannot be jettisoned without abandoning belief in the truth of Christianity.

Notes

[1]J. Hick (ed.), *The Myth of God Incarnate* (London, 1977); M. Green (ed.), *The Truth of God Incarnate* (London, 1977); G. Carey, *God Incarnate* (Leicester, 1977). For subsequent discussion of the issue, see M. Goulder, *Incarnation and Myth: The Debate Continued* (London, 1979).

[2]For a general survey, see I. H. Marshall, *The Origins of New Testament Christology* (Leicester, 1977).

[3]F. Hahn, *Christologische Hoheitstitel* (Göttingen, 1964). The point is lost in the title of the English translation: *The Titles of Jesus in Christology* (London, 1969).

[4]For the need to go beyond titles and to determine the Christological significance of other aspects of the New Testament witness, see J. Ernst, *Anfänge der Christologie* (Stuttgart, 1972); L. E. Keck, 'Toward the Renewal of New Testament Christology', *NTS*, 32, 1986, pp. 362-77.

[5]J. D. G. Dunn, *Unity and Diversity in the New Testament* (London, 1977).

[6]Hick, op. cit., p. 39.

[7]Ibid., p. 117.

[8]Ibid., p. 84.

[9]Ibid., p. 117.

[10]This position is especially associated with O. Cullmann, *The Christology of the New Testament* (London, 1959).
[11]G. Stählin, in *TDNT,* IV, p. 793.

11
Jesus as Lord:
The Development of the Concept

IN THE PREACHING AND TEACHING OF THE EARLY CHURCH the concept expressed by Jesus' use of the phrase 'the Kingdom of God' was given fresh expression in a variety of ways, and one of them was the proclamation of Jesus himself as Messiah and Lord.[1] The Kingdom was in effect replaced by the King. The Christological title most used to express this motif was that of Lord, and in this essay I want to explore the development and usage of this title for Jesus in the early Church.[2]

There can be no doubt regarding the central importance of this concept. When Paul wanted to describe what made a person a Christian in Romans 10.9 he said, 'If you confess with your lips that Jesus is Lord and believe in your heart that God raised him from the dead, you will be saved.' This verse shows that the decisive mark of being a Christian was public confession of Jesus as Lord, and it is generally agreed that this confession was bound up with baptism. The evidence suggests that a person publicly expressed acceptance of Jesus as Lord at baptism. Obviously the outward confession was not enough, and two further factors entered into the picture. The first was that coupled with the outward confession with the mouth was the inward act of faith. Alongside confession of Jesus as Lord there is the faith that he really is the Lord, a fact that, as we shall see, is related to his resurrection. The second factor comes from 1 Corinthians 12.3, where Paul tells us that nobody can say that Jesus is Lord apart from the Holy Spirit. In other words, only the action of the Spirit can persuade us that Jesus is Lord and enable us to make our confession meaningfully. This is not surprising because faith and the Holy Spirit are like two sides of the same coin. What God does in

us by his Spirit corresponds to what we do by faith. The important point
is that the work of the Spirit at conversion is to lead us to confess that Jesus
is Lord. Other Christian confessions existed, but this seems to have been the
primitive one.

The meaning of 'Lord' in the Greek language

What would this term 'Lord' have signified to people who used it? If we
confine ourselves to the Greek language in which the New Testament was
written, the word κύριος could be used in a variety of contexts and ways.

1. One of its most frequent uses is simply as a title of respect in addressing
other people. In English we use 'Sir' in this kind of way, sometimes simply
as a mark of politeness to people whom we don't know or with whom we
have only a rather formal relationship, at other times as a mark of respect
for the dignity of somebody else. The word was clearly used in this way in
Greek (Matt. 27.63).

2. In particular, it could be used in this way to address an older person
or somebody of a higher social class. It appears to have been the word used
by pupils to address a teacher, and it corresponded to the use of 'teacher'
or 'rabbi' by the Jews (Matt. 8.25 diff. Mark 4.38; Matt. 17.15 diff. Mark
9.17).

3. Next it could be used to mean a master, the owner of property (Mark
12.9; Luke 19.33) or slaves (Luke 12.42f.; Eph. 6.5) or even a husband in
relation to his wife (1 Pet. 3.6). Anybody who stood in a legal relationship
of superiority or ownership was a 'lord' or 'master' to the people beneath
him.

4. It could be used of political rulers, and in the first century it was
particularly used of the Roman emperor (Acts 25.26) and expressed his
absolute authority. It corresponded to the Latin term *dominus*. It did not in
itself mean that the ruler was divine, but it could be used so closely with
divine terms that it probably acquired something of the flavour of divinity.

5. Finally, the term was used of the gods who have power and rights over
humankind (1 Cor. 8.5), and it could express a personal relationship to
them. One particular usage was very important, and for this we now have
to look at the Jewish background. In the Jewish Scriptures the name of God
was expressed by the four Hebrew letters 'YHWH', which were vocalized as
'Yahweh'. Over the years, however, the Jews became extremely reverential
towards God and were frightened even to say his name aloud for fear of
blasphemy. So they did not pronounce it, and in course of time the pronun-
ciation was forgotten. There was another Hebrew word *('ādōn)* which meant
'lord' and was often used to describe God. Accordingly, when the Jews came

to the name of God in Scripture, they substituted a form of this word for lord, *'ădōnāy*. When the Jewish Bible was translated into Greek, they replaced *'ădōnāy* with the corresponding Greek word for Lord, κύριος . They may not have done so with complete consistency in early days, but it seems probable that by New Testament times this was the word that was used.[3]

The application of 'Lord' to Jesus

Next we must summarize the ways in which the word 'Lord' was used when it was applied to Jesus.

1. The word was used as a polite form of address to Jesus, just as it was to other people. For example, the Samaritan woman in John 4 so addressed Jesus at a point in the conversation when he is still simply an unknown stranger (John 4.11).

2. During his earthly life Jesus was addressed by various people as 'Lord' or 'Sir', often in the context of his being known as a teacher. Sometimes he was addressed in Jewish fashion as 'Teacher' (Mark 4.38) or 'Rabbi' (Mark 9.5), and this term is then rendered in another Gospel by the Greek word 'Lord' (Matt. 7.28). It is Matthew and Luke who used it more frequently, and the question arises whether what was actually said was 'Rabbi' (which was simply a title for a teacher) or rather the Aramaic word *mār*, which means Lord and was a more general term of respect for a lord or master.[4] But whichever word was used, it need not have been more than a term of respect for a teacher or a religious leader. However, sometimes the word is used by people who come to Jesus asking him to perform a mighty work, and such usage may include the thought of the authority that Jesus possessed and that enabled him to do such things.

3. It is not likely that Jesus was thought of as a master of slaves, although in his parables he often has slaves addressing their masters with this term. In some of the parables the master may be a metaphorical picture for himself. One interesting point is when Jesus sends the disciples to get the animal on which he rode into Jerusalem; they are to say 'The lord needs it' (Mark 11.3); it is not absolutely clear how the term is to be understood, especially when in the same story Luke tells how the disciples spoke to the animal's 'masters', using the same Greek word.

4. We saw that the word was used for political rulers. Jesus was not regarded as a political ruler, and indeed in his teaching he distanced himself and his disciples from the behaviour of political rulers who sought power and glory. Nevertheless, the use of 'lord' for political rulers is relevant to us because political rulers could demand loyalty, reverence, and even worship from their subjects, which in the eyes of Christians conflicted with the loyalty

they felt to Jesus. Outside the New Testament we know that Christians refused to accept the dominion and divinity of the Roman emperor, and there can be little doubt that they saw opposition between calling Jesus 'Lord' and calling the emperor 'Lord' in any absolute sense. When Jesus is called 'King of kings and Lord of lords' (Rev. 17.14; 19.16), his supreme lordship is expressed. However, it does not seem likely that Christians called Jesus 'Lord' in imitation of political rulers; rather, it was because they regarded Jesus as their religious lord that they began to define his lordship as superior to that of political rulers.

5. Finally in this survey of usage we have the use of 'lord' for objects of religious veneration. This could have happened in two ways. On the one hand, Paul tells us that there were many so-called gods and lords in the world of his time, but for Christians there was one God, the Father, and one Lord, namely, Jesus Christ (1 Cor. 8.5f.). Here the rivalry between Jesus and pagan gods is expressed, and it is evident that Jesus is thought of as superior to pagan gods; indeed, in Paul's view they are not gods and lords at all, that honour being reserved for the objects of Christian worship. On the other hand, the title of 'Lord' ranged Jesus alongside God the Father. The New Testament does not often call Jesus God directly, but it certainly takes over the Old Testament use of κύριος to refer to God and reapplies it to Jesus. Passages of Scripture that originally applied to God are reapplied to Jesus, thereby showing a tacit identification of Jesus with the Lord spoken of in the Old Testament. So much so is this the case that it is true to say that the word 'Lord' in a religious sense is applied to Jesus more often than to God the Father in the New Testament. It appears that the Christians needed a new terminology to express the place of Jesus alongside God. They had two solutions. One was to speak of Jesus as the Son alongside the Father; the other was to appropriate one of the titles for God, namely Lord, for him and to reserve the title of God for the Father, and by and large they kept to this use of the titles.

The functions of Jesus as Lord

Having surveyed briefly the ways in which the term Lord could be applied to Jesus in relation to the existing uses of the word, we must now ask what were the implications of the title when it was applied to Jesus. What was it used to convey?

1. When we look at the developed thought of the New Testament, it is clear that Jesus was regarded as Lord in relation to the act of creation. 1 Corinthians 8.6 tells us that there is one Lord through whom are all things and through whom we exist. Although some scholars take this to refer to

the present lordship of Christ over creation—and that in itself is a staggering thought—I take it that the text refers to creation and contains the assertion that the pre-existent Christ had a part in the work of creation.[5] It is the same thought as in Hebrews 1.2 where creation is associated with the status of Jesus as Son.

2. It follows that at this stage in thinking Jesus is regarded as Lord over the whole of creation. There will come a point when all the powers in the universe will be finally subjected to him, even though at present they may still be in active rebellion. In Philippians 2.9-11 Jesus is granted the name that is above every name; this is surely the name of 'Lord'. By virtue of it everything in creation will bow before him and confess that he is Lord. The confession made by Christians here and now will one day be made by all creation, although it is not said that this will be the means of their salvation. The thought is of triumph rather than of redemption.

3. In a more personal way Jesus is the Lord of those who believe in him. They confess him as Lord at their conversion and baptism. He is their Lord by virtue of the fact that he has redeemed them and bought them to be his own. Using a different Greek word, 2 Peter 2.1 criticizes those who deny the Lord (δεσπότης) who bought them. A sense of personal devotion emerges in Thomas's cry to Jesus, 'My Lord and my God' (John 20.20) or when Paul speaks of the surpassing worth of knowing Christ Jesus 'my Lord' (Phil. 3.8). Adoring worship and communion characterize such phrases.

4. As a result, Paul particularly can speak to Christians 'in the Lord'. This phrase has much the same force as 'in Christ' and expresses the fact that the life of the believer is determined by the fact of Christ, the crucified and risen Lord. Thus Paul can command his readers to do certain things 'in the Lord' (Eph. 6.1; Col. 3.17; 2 Thess. 3.12), and it is thus with the Lord's authority that he issues his commands to believers. Here is the outworking of their personal acceptance of Jesus as their Lord: they must do what he says.

5. Finally, the hope of Christians is tied up with the coming of the Lord. They pray 'Maranatha' ('Our Lord, come'[6]), and it is this hope that fills their horizon (1 Cor. 16.22). The New Testament ends with the call to Jesus, 'Come, Lord Jesus' (Rev. 22.20), both as the object of personal devotion and as the Lord who will bring all war and opposition to an end.

The development of the belief that Jesus is Lord

Our next question is concerned with the way in which the understanding of Jesus as Lord developed in the early Church. What was it that led to this remarkable estimate of Jesus? How did a man who had been crucified come to be regarded within a few years as the Lord of all creation, on a level with

God himself? We must investigate the way in which the Church was led under the inspiration and guidance of the Spirit to this full acknowledgement of the status and nature of Jesus.

The theory of W. Bousset

Bousset argued that it was in effect the influence of the Hellenistic world that led the Christians to see Jesus as the Lord. He postulated that increasingly they began to see Jesus in the light of the pagan cults from which some of them had been converted. The person who had originally been revered simply as a teacher and prophet was increasingly assimilated to the kind of figure worshipped in pagan cults and so began to be regarded as spiritually present with his worshippers and as a person worthy of worship (1 Cor. 8.5f.). Thus the recognition of Jesus as Lord was a second stage in the development of Christology; this was preceded by a first stage in which Jesus was not regarded in so lofty a manner.[7]

This theory is implausible, and one of the main reasons why it is implausible is that it cannot account satisfactorily for another text from 1 Corinthians, the verse that records the early Christian cry, 'Maranatha'. This cry has been preserved in Aramaic, and it was evidently used in a Greek-speaking church in that language. Bousset was forced to argue that its use arose in Antioch where the church was bilingual. But it is much more probable that it arose in a church that normally spoke Aramaic and where the decisive theological development took place in an Aramaic-speaking culture. Moreover, we can trace a probable background for it in the book of 1 Enoch, which is cited in Jude 14. Here Enoch prophesies that the Lord will come with his holy ones to execute judgement. No doubt the writer of Enoch was thinking of God as the Lord (cf. Zech. 14.5). But early Christians applied the wording to Jesus, and prophesied and prayed that he would come in judgement. The point is that this text shows that Jesus was regarded as the coming Lord in the early Aramaic-speaking Church, and this takes us back into an area influenced by Jewish ideas rather than Greek ideas. Consequently, Bousset's view places the development too late and in the wrong cultural environment.[8]

The theory of F. Hahn

The contemporary scholar F. Hahn has argued from the evidence of phrases like 'Maranatha' that when the early Church first used various titles for Jesus they were limited in reference to the future activity that it expected of him. That is to say, the Church spoke of Jesus as Lord first of all in the context of his future coming, and it did so on the analogy of the future coming of the Son of man. Then, in Hahn's view, the Church began to realize that if Jesus was to come as Lord, he was not merely the Lord-designate, but was already the Lord; he had been enthroned since his resurrection. Thus the Church began to apply the title of 'Lord' to the risen Jesus, and then eventually to the earthly life of Jesus.[9]

This view is part of a larger theory that is unsatisfactory at many points. The objection to it in the present context is that it does not explain how it was that the title of Lord came to be applied to Jesus as the future Coming One. It is easy to see the connection between the Son of man and the future coming of Jesus, since we have Daniel 7.13f. to give us the link. But why did the early Church proceed from the future coming of Jesus to giving him the title of 'Lord'? It is surely more probable that the process was the other way round, namely, that the Church began by believing that Jesus was Lord and then prophesied that the Lord would come. Thus we still have to explain why the Church believed that Jesus was the Lord.

A possible solution
1 The teaching of Jesus
If we turn to the accounts of the earthly life of Jesus we may find some material to indicate what started this process. We have already seen that the disciples addressed Jesus as 'Sir' or 'Lord', but this in itself is hardly the starting-point for the process, since this phrase could be used to address any human being who occupied a position of superiority or honour. Even if Jesus said to his disciples, 'You call me Teacher and Lord' (in words ascribed to him in John 13.13),[10] it is doubtful how much we are to read into the title. However, various other bits of evidence may be significant.

(a) In Mark 2.28 Jesus says that the Son of man is lord of the Sabbath. Here 'lord' is not a title but more a description of a function. Nor is it used absolutely to mean 'the lord' but relatively to refer to the lord of the Sabbath. Yet it is a tremendous assertion to make. What kind of man is it who can claim lordship over the Sabbath? Was not this the prerogative of God? Moreover, it is the Son of man of whom this is said. Here we have a link between Son of man and κύριος that could be significant.

However, it must be noted that there is some doubt whether this is actually a saying of Jesus. Even so conservative a writer as C. E. B. Cranfield thinks that this is a comment by the author of the Gospel about the significance of the incident and was not meant to be understood as a saying of Jesus.[11] Other scholars suggest that Jesus was making a statement that is true of humankind in general; they understand 'Son of man' to mean 'a man like me', 'a man in my position', and not as an exclusive title.[12] Consequently, we must be cautious about our use of this verse, but it may well indicate that Jesus referred to lordship over the Sabbath in a way that was understood at an early stage in the Church to signify his own position as Lord.

(b) In a number of parables Jesus refers to the absence of a householder who may come back unexpectedly and find his servants either doing their duty as they should or else taking advantage of his absence to misbehave. The disciples are to be like men waiting for their master to return (Luke 12.36, 37, 42, 43, 45, 46, 47; Matt. 25.18, 19, 21, 23, 26). Here it is interesting that when Mark 13.35 has 'You do not know when *the* master *of the house* is coming', Matthew 24.42 has 'you do not know on what day *your* master is coming'. The point is that it would be very natural to transfer the name 'master' out of its parabolic setting where it means the master of the slaves in a household to its application where it means the master of the disciples and specifically the Son of man who is to come in the future. We can see this transfer actually taking place in Matthew, and it could obviously have taken place long before the Gospel was written. Indeed it is implicit in Mark where the application of the parable is expressed in parabolic rather than direct terms: 'Watch therefore—for you do not know when the master of the house will come . . . lest he come suddenly and find you asleep. And what I say to you I say to all: Watch' (Mark 13.35-37). I see no reason to dispute the authenticity of this parabolic material and would argue that this use of 'master' (though not necessarily the precise wording) can go back to Jesus.[13] Whether or not this claim can be sustained, it is obvious that, as soon as the early Church recognized Jesus as the coming Son of man, it would be natural for the term κύριος to be applied to him as the returning lord.

(c) Perhaps most significant is a brief dialogue in which Jesus asks the scribes how they can say that the Messiah is David's descendant, this being the popularly held view. Jesus saw an objection. In a Psalm attributed to David, the author said, 'The Lord said to my lord, "Sit at my right hand till I put your enemies below your feet" ' (Mark 12.35-37; Ps. 110.1).

A word of explanation is necessary. The English and the Greek forms of the Psalm both use the same word ('lord' and κύριος respectively) to refer both to the speaker and to the person addressed. However, in the Hebrew version the speaker ('the Lord') is 'Yahweh' (for which *'ădōnāy* would have been substituted in reading aloud) and the person addressed ('my lord') is *'ădōni* which means 'my lord' or 'my master'. The confusion is avoided in printed English versions of the Old Testament which use 'lord' both times but print the first occurrence in capital letters ('LORD') to indicate that the original had Yahweh. We might show the difference in spoken English by some such translation as 'The Lord said to my master'. There is no way of showing the difference in Greek unless one knows the context.

The point, then, is that the person addressed is called 'my master' by David. Hence the problem for Jesus' hearers: on the assumption that a man does not normally regard his son or descendant as superior to him, how can the Messiah be David's descendant, if, as the Psalm says, he is superior to him? Jesus is making a novel point, namely, that the Messiah is David's lord. Furthermore, he asks how the traditional scribal understanding of the Messiah as a human descendant of David can be maintained in the light of it.

A simple way of understanding this question—or rather of answering it—would be to say that what Jesus is doing is to pose an insuperable obstacle to the scribes' view of the Messiah: the Messiah is not in fact a descendant of David, whether in the sense of literal descent or in the sense of being a person of Davidic character and rule. This solution is unlikely, however, since the early Church firmly believed in the Davidic descent of Jesus, and this belief is found in early traditional material (Rom. 1.3f.). The pericope as it stands, therefore, cannot have this sense. Nor is it likely that it did so at an earlier stage in the history of the tradition; the early Church's firm belief that Jesus was Messiah can hardly have arisen if it was known that he himself had firmly ruled out this possibility.

Second, if the question were inverted, the answer would again be easy. How can the Messiah be superior to David if he is his son? That question can be answered either by saying, 'The son of David is superior to David because God raised him from the dead and exalted him to be lord'—an answer that could only be given after Easter—or by saying 'The son of David is superior to David because he is not only David's son but also the Son of man or the Son of God'; or one might combine the two answers.

Now if we go back to the original form of the question, perhaps the answer is essentially the same. We can paraphrase the question as, 'How can the Messiah be, as the scribes say [merely], a descendant of David, if as the Psalm says, he is superior to David?' And the answer is, he can still be what the scribes say he is, namely, the son of David by human descent, but it is more important to say that he is David's lord, inasmuch as he is also the Son of God/Son of man and/or he is specially exalted by God. It follows, incidentally, that if the Messiah is David's lord he is also the lord of people in general.

The significant points for our present purpose are: (i) Jesus here declares that the Messiah carries the title of 'Lord'; (ii) Jesus finds the evidence for this title in Psalm 110; (iii) Jesus holds that what was said to David's Lord in Psalm 110 must be regarded as a prophecy to be fulfilled in the case of the Messiah.

Again the question of authenticity arises, and I would argue that the objections to this being a genuine saying of Jesus are unconvincing.[14] Yet even if this point is not granted, the pericope was probably in circulation at an early date.

From these three pieces of evidence we can now see that Jesus spoke in such a way about lordship that the question would probably arise for his disciples as they pondered on what he had said. If, however, the authenticity of these texts is questioned, they will still testify to a very early stage of thinking in the Church.

2 The significance of the resurrection

The next step comes with the resurrection of Jesus. There can be no doubt that the emergence of the Christian Church was due to the belief of the disciples that Jesus had risen from the dead and had appeared to them. How did they interpret this event? They saw it not only as the return of Jesus to life and not only as his raising up to heaven by the power of God, but also as his exaltation. A key text in interpreting what had happened was Psalm 110.1, which they took as a prophecy of the exaltation of Jesus. The influence of this text is widespread in the New Testament. It is quoted in Acts 2.34 and Hebrews 1.13, and its influence lies behind the numerous places where Jesus is said to be at the right hand of God (Acts 2.33; 7.55f.; Rom. 8.34; Eph. 1.20; Col. 3.1; Heb. 1.3; 8.1; 10.12; 12.2; 1 Pet. 3.22; Rev. 5.1). It was cited by Jesus in Mark 12.35-37, the passage we have just discussed, and it also appears on his lips in Mark 14.62, where Jesus prophesies that the Son of man will sit on the right hand of Power and come with the clouds of heaven. The simplest explanation of all this is that Jesus himself spoke of the exaltation of the Son of man to the right hand of God, and that the early Church then interpreted his saying as being fulfilled in his resurrection and continued to use the text that he had cited as expressing this belief. Therefore, once the resurrection had occurred, the recognition that Jesus was indeed Messiah and Lord was fairly automatic, and this is precisely what Peter asserts of Jesus in Acts 2.36. Furthermore, a parallel line of thought, starting from Jesus' claim to be the Son of God, led to the interpretation of Psalm 2.7 as a prophecy of the begetting of the Messiah to new life (Acts 13.33).

But is this 'simple' explanation defensible? The main difficulty is the unwillingness of many scholars to allow the authenticity of the various sayings attributed to Jesus, especially his use of Psalm 110 at his trial. But if this is not authentic, it is difficult to see what put the quotation in the minds of the early Christians and led them to interpret the resurrection as glorification and vindication.

3 Growth in understanding in the early Church

Once this step had been taken, the rest of the development can be traced. If Psalm 110 is seen to be fulfilled in Jesus' resurrection, then this confirms that he is the Lord spoken of in the Psalm and the Messiah, and also that he is the exalted Son of man. Hence the dying Stephen speaks of seeing Jesus as the Son of man standing at the right hand of God. But it is the use of 'Lord' that interests us, and here various strands of thought can be traced.

(a) There is a direct path to the earliest Christian confession. We recollect that the inward faith that accompanied the outward confession that Jesus is Lord was the belief that God had raised him from the dead (Rom. 10.9). This confirms the evidence of Acts that it was the resurrection that was associated with recognition of Jesus' lordship.

(b) From this confession stems the personal relationship of the believer to Jesus as his Lord, which finds particular expression in Paul's use of the term 'in the Lord' and in the general use of 'the Lord' simply to mean 'Jesus'. Thus there also develops the use of the compound phrases, 'the Lord Jesus' and 'the Lord Jesus Christ', which encapsulate this confession and can become merely formal language if care is not taken. The title of 'Lord' adds dignity to the name 'Jesus' and to the compound 'Jesus Christ'.

(c) If Jesus is Lord after his resurrection, it is obvious that he must also have been Lord before it. The early Church saw the resurrection as essentially the confirming of a status rather than the conferral of a new status. Admittedly some texts may suggest the latter. Thus Philippians 2.9-11 suggests that the name of 'Lord' was conferred on Jesus at his exaltation, and Acts 2.36 might be thought to point in the same direction. But alongside these we must put verses like 1 Corinthians 9.5 and 11.23, which see Jesus as lord in his earthly life. Hence it is not surprising that Luke can refer to Jesus as 'the Lord' when describing what he said and did in his earthly life; this usage is in fact probably older than Luke. But it is significant that 'Lord' as a formal title does not come into statements made by Jesus or his followers before his resurrection, in correspondence with the historical facts. One might compare how in John it is only after the resurrection that Jesus is spoken of as the Lord by his followers (John 20.2, 13; etc.; cf. Luke 24.3, 34).

(d) If Jesus is Lord, it also follows that he will return as Lord. Hence we have the Maranatha cry. Jesus is not addressed or spoken of as Son of man, but the Church uses the title that signifies his victory. But here another factor is becoming evident. We have noted the suggestion that Maranatha may reflect Jewish wording that originally spoke of God as the Lord who will come in judgement. This brings us to the fact that the early Church saw Jesus as the Lord who was spoken of in various Old Testament texts where it was

God who was originally meant. That is to say: sooner or later the title of 'Lord', which originally referred to the exalted and victorious position of Jesus, was extended in meaning by applying to Jesus texts that originally spoke of God as the Lord. We can see this in the following examples: In 1 Thessalonians 1.8 Paul refers to 'the word of the Lord' (cf. 2 Thess. 3.1; Acts 8.25; 12.24; 19.10, 20) by which he must mean the message about or from Jesus. This is an extremely common Old Testament phrase which refers to *God's* word to the prophets. In 1 Thessalonians 4.6 Paul says that the Lord, namely Jesus, is an avenger, and he is probably alluding to Psalm 94.1, which originally referred explicitly to the Lord as the God of vengeance. In 1 Thessalonians 5.2 he speaks of the day of the Lord, another familiar Old Testament phrase that now means the day of the parousia of Jesus (see 1 Cor. 1.8; 5.5; 2 Cor. 1.14; Phil. 1.6, 10; 2.16; 2 Thess. 2.2; 2 Pet. 3.10). In Philippians 2.10f. Paul applies to Jesus the words of Isaiah 45.23, 'To me every knee shall bow', which originally referred to God, the Lord, and it is interesting that in Romans 14.11 he uses the same text of judgement by God. In 1 Peter 2.3 Christians are said to have tasted that the Lord is good, an allusion to Psalm 34.9 which originally applied to God. Christians are those who call on the name of the Lord (1 Cor. 1.2, alluding to Joel 3.5).

What led to this process? Clearly it was facilitated by the ambiguity of κύριος in Greek, but in a passage like Psalm 110 anybody who knew the Old Testament knew the difference between 'the Lord', namely, God, and 'my Lord', namely, the Messiah. The same ease of transfer may have been linguistically possible in Aramaic if Lord was translated as *mār*, a word that was used both of God as Lord and of human lords. But how did the Christians come to apply Yahweh-texts to Jesus? The process started fairly early, as 1 Thessalonians shows, although it is manifestly not the most primitive understanding of the title. Probably such phrases as 'the word of the Lord' and 'the day of the Lord', which were simply Old Testament allusions and not explicit citations of specific texts, were the first to be used, and this led to the recognition that what was said of Yahweh in the Old Testament found some of its fulfilment in Jesus. Once the day of the Lord became the day of Jesus, the path was open to assert that the future functions of God would be carried out by Jesus. And of course this development was facilitated by the recognition that Jesus was the Son of God, the One who was the image and first-born of God.

All this development must have taken place quite early because we find that it is fully complete by the time Paul wrote 1 Thessalonians and Galatians. Thus he is able to say in Galatians 1.1 that he did not receive his apostleship from man but through Jesus Christ and God the Father. Not only does he closely juxtapose Jesus and God, but he also contrasts them with men, thereby showing that for him Jesus is on the divine side of reality. Thus a number of factors will have contributed to the process whereby the functions of Yahweh were seen as fulfilled by Jesus, and so Jesus was given an appropriate status.

(e) Does this then mean that the title of Lord when applied to Jesus in the New Testament eventually came to denote his divinity? To put the question in this form is inappropriate. The term 'divine' is not used in the New Testament in any significant way. Further, Jesus is never identified *simpliciter* with God, since the early Christians were not likely to confuse Jesus with God the Father. Rather, they thought of Jesus as the Son of the Father, existing in his image, sharing his glory, and this means that they held that whatever was true of God in his nature and functions was also true of the Son, with the important qualification that ultimately the Son is subordinate to the Father. Now the title 'Son of God' obviously expresses this point, at least in some of its uses. The question is whether the use of Lord carries the same implications. From our preceding survey it will be obvious that in many of its uses Lord does not have this deeper content. But when Jesus is called 'the Lord' absolutely and when reference is made to his being given honour that puts him immediately below God the Father (Phil. 2.11), then it is hard to resist the view that Jesus is being given a title that is tantamount to divinity as we understand it. But the number of places where this implication is present is limited.

Conclusion
The concept of Jesus as Lord brings out his sovereignty. He is King of kings and Lord of lords. The title of 'king' was rarely used for him (only in Acts 17.7; Rev. 17.14; 19.16) and equally rare for God (1 Tim. 1.27; 6.15). It meant 'the emperor' in secular speech, as Acts 17.7 and 1 Peter 2.13 make plain. It is not clear whether this existing usage may have hindered its use. Because the kingship of Jesus was on a different plane from that of the emperor, there was no point in provoking trouble by suggesting rivalry. On the other hand, if 'Lord' was a title used of the emperor, the same objections would surely have applied to using it. The term 'Messiah' or 'Christ' should have meant a ruler, God's agent in establishing a Kingdom. But the term had this meaning only for Jews and could be taken to refer to a kingship that encompassed only the Jews or under which the Jews had superiority over the Gentiles. For whatever reason, the term lost the connotation of kingship and sovereignty, and it appears to have been understood more in the sense of redeemer or saviour. The sense of kingship was preserved in the title of

'Lord', which would have been intelligible to all kinds of people. However, we should note that there could be a narrowing of meaning here, in that 'Lord' tends to have a passive meaning; it signifies somebody who is to be obeyed and treated with honour, and it perhaps does not bring out sufficiently the active element of the exercise of kingship and dominion and indeed of granting salvation. Jesus is not merely the Lord to be obeyed; he is also the Saviour, the Messiah who suffers, and therefore the full New Testament confession must be 'Jesus *Christ* is the *Lord*', emphasizing that Jesus is both the Christ who saves us and the Lord whom we obey.

Notes

[1] I. H. Marshall, 'Preaching the Kingdom of God', *Exp.T,* 89, 1977-78; pp. 13-16. On the whole topic, see now G. R. Beasley-Murray, *Jesus and the Kingdom of God* (Grand Rapids, 1986).

[2] For bibliography, see H. Bietenhard, 'Lord, Master', in C. Brown (ed.), *The New International Dictionary of New Testament Theology,* 3 vols. (Exeter, 1976), II, pp. 519f., with *Addenda* (1982), 10.

[3] J. A. Fitzmyer, 'Der semitische Hintergrund des neutestamentlichen Kyriostitels', in G. Strecker (ed.), *Jesus Christus in Historie und Theologie* (Tübingen, 1975), pp. 267-98.

[4] See F. Hahn, *The Titles of Jesus in Christology* (Guildford, 1969), pp. 73-89; Ph. Vielhauer, *Aufsätze zum Neuen Testament* (München, 1965), pp. 150-7.

[5] J. D. G. Dunn, *Christology in the Making* (London, 1980), pp. 179-83.

[6] It is difficult to be certain whether the Aramaic phrases represented by 'Maranatha' should be understood as a statement or as a prayer, but the point being made is not affected.

[7] W. Bousset, *Kyrios Christos* (Nashville, 1970).

[8] M. Black, 'The Maranatha Invocation and Jude 14, 15 (1 Enoch 1:9)', in B. Lindars and S. S. Smalley (eds.), *Christ and Spirit in the New Testament* (Cambridge, 1973), pp. 189-96.

[9] Hahn, *Titles,* pp. 89-103.

[10] Whether or not John 13.13 represents the *ipsissima vox* of Jesus, it accurately describes how his disciples spoke of him during his earthly lifetime.

[11] C. E. B. Cranfield, *The Gospel According to St. Mark* (Cambridge, 1959).

[12] M. Casey, *Son of Man* (London, 1979), pp. 228f.; B. Lindars, *Jesus Son of Man* (London, 1983), pp. 102-6, regards the saying as composed by Mark on the pattern of Mark 2.10.

[13] The core of the parable at least goes back to Jesus: R. Pesch, *Das Markusevangelium* (Freiburg: 1977), 2, pp. 316f.

[14] I. H. Marshall, *The Gospel of Luke,* NIGTC (Exeter, 1978), pp. 746f.

Part III
The Work of Jesus

12
The Hope of a New Age: The Kingdom of God in the New Testament

C̲HRISTIAN HOPE IS MANIFESTLY BASED ON THE PROMISES and actions of God, and therefore it is not surprising that a discussion of the Kingdom of God (henceforward abbreviated in this essay as KG) should figure in a symposium on 'The Spirit and the New Age'. Although the phrase has been the subject 'of much biblical research in recent years, and although it is banded about with great frequency in discussions of Christian social action, it is unfortunately often the case that it is used in a very vague manner and that there is a lack of clear biblical exposition in the churches on the meaning of the term. Our aim in this essay will be to harvest and assess some of the recent scholarly discussion with a view to showing how an understanding of the KG can give fresh vigour to our Christian hope in God.

Introduction
Discussion of the KG was particularly spirited up to about 1965, and by that date a certain consensus appeared to be developing about the meaning and significance of the KG, especially as the phrase appears in the Synoptic Gospels.[1] Some of the main points that emerged can be summed up as follows:

1. The writers of the Gospels regarded the KG as being the central theme of the teaching of Jesus. This can be seen from the frequency with which the phrase appears on the lips of Jesus as compared with other theological concepts,[2] as well as from the way in which the Evangelists themselves iden-

tify it as the burden of Jesus' message.[3] Consequently, scholars tended to regard the KG as being in fact the principal concept in the actual teaching of Jesus.[4]

2. Among scholars who approached the Gospel records with a rigorously critical methodology for separating off what they regarded as the authentic teaching of Jesus from later elements wrongly ascribed to him, it was agreed that some of the texts about the KG must belong to any critically established 'irreducible minimum' of the teaching of Jesus.[5]

3. According to the Evangelists, Jesus announced both that the KG would come in the near future as the consummation of God's purpose and that it was already present in some way during his ministry as the fulfilment of God's promises. One is tempted to say that there was an increasing consensus on how this evidence ought to be interpreted, namely that both of these elements were to be taken at their face value as authentic aspects of the teaching of Jesus; the only problem that then remained was to explain how these two elements could be integrated with each other, one important suggestion being that the promise of the KG was *fulfilled* in the ministry of Jesus and would be *consummated* in the future.[6] Nevertheless, there was a continuing powerful body of opinion that accepted that the KG was an entirely future entity in the proclamation of Jesus and that it was regarded as present only in the sense that an event that is known to be impending can have decisive effects on how people see the time just before its arrival.[7]

4. The term 'KG' refers primarily to the sovereign activity of God as ruler or king and only secondarily to the realm over which he rules.[8] Its content is the saving and judging action of God.

5. In so far as the KG could be regarded as being present, it was so in and through the proclamation and activity of Jesus, and its presence (or, for upholders of the alternative view, its imminence) was evidenced in his parables and mighty works.[9]

Some twenty years later the mood of scholarship on these points has not undergone any substantial changes. However, there remain a number of questions where further precision is desirable, and some progress in answering them has been made. Some of these questions are:

1. Can we be more precise about the actual ways in which Jesus used the term 'KG'? For example, did he use it simply in ways familiar to his audience, or did he implicitly transform its content, just as he appears to have done with other theological concepts?

2. How is the KG related to other concepts that appear in the teaching of Jesus?

3. How did Jesus see his own role in relation to the KG? This question

needs to be asked quite specifically with reference to Jesus' self-understanding of his identity and role as well as with reference to his premonition of his own death.

4. What did Jesus envisage as the results of his proclamation of the KG? To what extent did his message have a communal or corporate dimension so far as his own lifetime was concerned?

5. In what ways did Jesus envisage the future dimension of the KG? Had he any place in his thinking for what we know as the Church?

6. Granted that the early Church stood in some kind of continuity with Jesus and his teaching, what happened to the KG in its proclamation and its theology? This is a question that can be raised in two contexts. First, there is the theology of the Church reflected in the New Testament epistles which is not overtly based on the sayings of Jesus. Second, there is the tradition of the teaching of Jesus which was handed down at first by word of mouth and then incorporated in the written Gospels. What did the early Church make of the KG?

These points constitute a formidable agenda, and it will not be possible to treat any of them in an adequate way in a brief essay, still less to deal with all of them. It will, however, be clear that the answers to some of them are very relevant to the topic of Christian hope in that the questions force us to explore different aspects of the nature of the hope held by Jesus. Further, if we can see how the early church appropriated and made use of the teaching of Jesus, this may help us in turn as we seek to understand and apply the teaching of Jesus and his followers for today.

The meaning of 'Kingdom of God'
As has been indicated already, there is a growing agreement that the phrase 'KG' should be taken to refer primarily to God's sovereignty rather than to the realm over which he is sovereign. It will then refer to God's sovereignty in contrast to that of Satan (Luke 11.18), who is the ruler of 'this world' (John 12.31; 14.30). Those who adopt this view tend on the whole to assume that the reference must be to a specific act of divine rule, so that one can ask, when is *the* Kingdom of God coming? (cf. Luke 17.20). It is this assumption that causes problems when the teaching of Jesus that the KG is both present and future is examined, and it is understandable that some scholars should want to explain away either the present or the future dimension.

A possible way out of the impasse has been suggested by N. Perrin. His contribution is to show that KG may be a 'symbol' for 'God acting in sovereign power' (i.e., God acting with might and imposing his authority so that people obey him). If KG functions in this way as a symbol, then it need not refer simply to a promised future realm or to a single mighty act by God. Rather, by the use of the words 'Jesus is deliberately evoking the myth of the activity of God on behalf of his people the exorcisms are a manifestation of that activity in the experience of his hearers. . . . KG is here a symbol, and it is used in this saying because of its evocative power. The saying is a challenge to the hearers to take the ancient myth with renewed seriousness, and to begin to anticipate the manifestation of the reality of which it speaks in the concrete actuality of their experience.' Again, 'the symbol of the kingly activity of God on behalf of his people confronts the hearers of Jesus as a true tensive symbol with its evocation of a whole set of meanings, and . . . the myth is, in the message of Jesus, true myth with its power to mediate the experience of existential reality'.[10]

Perrin is here making use of a distinction between symbols that have a one-to-one relationship to what they signify (as, for example, the mathematical symbol *pi* signifies a precise, unique quantity) and symbols that 'can have a set of meanings that can neither be exhausted nor adequately expressed by any one referent',[11] and he is claiming that KG falls into the latter category. When Jesus uses the term 'KG' he is pointing beyond the phrase to that which it signifies, namely the powerful action of God that can be expressed in a whole range of situations.

In a similar way, B. D. Chilton has argued that KG is an expression for 'the saving revelation of God himself' or 'God in strength', and that it refers to 'a personal God revealed'. This means that the KG need not be tied down in time; it can refer 'in the first place to God's self-revelation and derivatively to the joy of men in his presence', and hence it can further be used to refer to 'the reward held ready' in Luke 12.32.[12] Chilton's view is based on an exhaustive discussion of a set of texts in the Gospels that he examines in the light of their Jewish background, especially in the diction of the Targums.

The approach of Perrin and Chilton is a very attractive one in that it offers a way out of the present/future dilemma that has shaped discussion of the KG for so long. It suggests that the dilemma is a false one, since a reference to 'God acting in power' is clearly not to be tied down to any one particular manifestation of the power of God.

Nevertheless, closer scrutiny of it leads to some critical comments and some doubts as to its viability. First, it must be noted that Perrin does not seem to be too sure of the ontological status of what is represented by the symbol. He speaks of the 'myth' that is evoked by the symbol. Now it is certainly not the case that the use of the word 'myth' should automatically arouse suspicion in the minds of evangelical Christians, for the category of 'myth' can have a valid and proper use in Christian theology just like any other literary genre that is in itself neutral. Admittedly Perrin may be adopting a position near to that of R. Bultmann, whose influence on his thinking is freely admitted, but it should be observed that in this particular book he is critical of some aspects of Bultmann's position. Rather one may appropriate Perrin's insights by saying that the 'story' of God acting in power is the correct interpretation of, say, the exorcisms performed by Jesus, events that might be understood otherwise but that are in fact pointers to a correct understanding of the activity of Jesus as a manifestation of God's saving power. The position of Perrin is thus somewhat ambiguous. However, this observation does not apply to the work of Chilton, who interprets the Gospels in the context of an orthodox understanding of the Christian faith.

Much more to the point is our second critical comment. In both cases the interpreters gain their understanding of the meaning of KG from the examination of a limited group of texts that they believe can be shown to be authentic sayings of Jesus.[13] One is tempted to say that any saying of Jesus that Perrin accepts as authentic *must* be authentic, for he belongs to a particularly sceptical group of scholars. Consequently, our understanding of KG must do justice to the texts that Perrin invokes. However, this leaves us with two problems. On the one hand, Perrin has to admit that for the most part the Jews to whom Jesus spoke saw KG as a symbol with a single reference; we must ask, then, whether Jesus would have been speaking meaningfully to them if he had shifted the force of the term significantly. On the other hand, we have to face the problem of the remaining KG texts in the Gospels. If a wider group of texts than those examined by Perrin and Chilton proves to be authentic, then we must ask whether they burst open the definition that has been offered and lead us to a different one. Even, however, if the other usages in the Gospels are to be attributed to the followers of Jesus rather than to himself, it may still be the case that this is a pointer to the fact that they understood Jesus differently from Perrin and Chilton, and we shall have to ask whether this makes the view of the modern scholars doubtful. In short, we have to ask whether Perrin and Chilton's view still holds when a wider body of relevant evidence is taken into account.

Consequently, in understanding such an examination we must begin by asking how Jesus' audience would have understood him. Now Perrin himself has shown that the background of the teaching of Jesus lies in the apocalyptic understanding of the KG as God's action rather than in the Rabbinic concept of the KG as the expression of God's demands upon his people enshrined in the Torah, or Law.[14] KG was not all that common a term in Judaism but it appears to have been used for that future state of affairs when God's rule would be established and would bring peace and happiness for his people.

Sometimes the idea is close to that of the 'age to come' that will succeed this age and that will be ushered in by the resurrection of the dead.[15] The important point is that God brings about this new era by his own mighty action. Although the Jews spoke of 'the age to come', they did not regard it as being 'beyond history' but rather as being the next stage in history, brought into being by God's action in history, bringing the rule of Satan to an end and commencing his own rule. Thus the KG is the full and powerful manifestation of the sovereignty that God already exercises over the world.

Various texts in the Gospels speak of the KG as this future state of affairs to be established by God. The KG as the future state of the righteous is contrasted with Gehenna, the abode of the unrighteous dead (Mark 9.47). The righteous will enter the Kingdom prepared for them while the unrighteous are cast into outer darkness (Matt. 25.34). It will be a time of surprises for Jesus' contemporaries when they see the patriarchs admitted while they themselves are excluded (Matt. 8.11/Luke 13.29 Q). Jesus talks in the future tense about entry into this realm (Matt. 7.21), and he himself looks forward to sharing in eating and drinking in the new situation after the KG has come (Mark 14.25; Luke 22.16, 18). In all this Jesus reflects Jewish expectations (Luke 14.25).

Jesus' audience would have understood and accepted this basic expectation. He was operating with the same framework of ideas as they did, and if he had not done so, his teaching would have been unintelligible to them. One area of surprise would have been in his statements about who would be present in the KG; he shattered the easy assumption that any members of the people of Israel would qualify for entrance simply on the basis of their scrupulous observance of the Pharisaic legislation.

More significant is the question of time. According to Luke, the nature of Jesus' activity must have been such as to lead people to think that the KG would appear 'immediately' (Luke 19.11) and to cause some Pharisees to ask when the KG was coming (Luke 17.20).[16] The interpretation of the crucial statements in Matthew 10.7/Luke 10.9 Q and Mark 1.15 is disputed;[17] they can be taken to mean either that the KG has already arrived or that its coming is imminent; were these sayings perhaps genuinely ambiguous? In Mark 9.1 Jesus refers to people who would not die before they saw that the KG had come; the authenticity of the saying is disputed, as is its interpretation.[18] In Luke 21.31 Jesus refers to a future point at which people will know that the KG is near.[19] In addition, there are various texts that suggest that the day of judgement or the coming of the Son of man is imminent.[20] The thought of the imminence of the end is firmly embedded in the gospel tradition, but direct references to the imminence of the KG are not very frequent, and it is difficult to say that the distinctive teaching of Jesus lies here.

What is much more strongly attested is Jesus' teaching that the KG was already in some sense present in his ministry. The evidence for this has often been discussed and need not be rehearsed here in detail; the key texts are Matthew 11.12/Luke 16.16 Q; Matthew 12.28/Luke 11.20 Q; and Luke 17.21 together with Matthew 10.7/Luke 10.9 (11) Q and Mark 1.15, which in my opinion belong here rather than with the futurist texts.[21] These verses indicate that the action of God in bringing in the KG has already begun, so that Jesus can declare quite simply and plainly that the KG has arrived. So strong is this impression that C. H. Dodd could see no room for any teaching about a future coming in the outlook of Jesus; while he undoubtedly did not do justice to the future elements in the teaching of Jesus, the point to be stressed here is that he established the fundamental importance of the texts that testify to the presence of the KG.[22] It is these texts that convey the distinctive element in the teaching of Jesus about the KG. To say that the End was near was not unprecedented. To say that the future KG was *already* present was unparalleled.

The crucial question in interpretation is now whether this remarkable strand of teaching stands in genuine continuity with that about the future reign of God. Essentially the options reduce to two. The one is to say that the link lies in the concept of imminence or 'nearness': for Jesus the KG was so close in time that the whole of present life was coloured by its imminence. Whether he spoke of the KG as being virtually present and saw his mighty works as the precursors of its coming, or whether he could say that there was a sense in which the near Kingdom was already operative, the point is that his ministry derived its impetus and validity from the belief that the KG was very near, and with it the coming of the Son of man and the end of the present age. This view, which is that of scholars such as E. Grässer, who is its most consistent and able advocate, faces insurmountable difficulties. Those who hold this view have to admit that Jesus was mistaken in regard to the specific form of this hope that he held. The KG did not come in the way he prophesied, and consequently the validity of his whole message, inasmuch as it was based on this hope, is completely taken away. Scholars who interpret the teaching of Jesus in this way agree that this is so, and they then have to show how the early Church had to modify the tradition of the teaching of Jesus to take account of the 'delay of the parousia' and so produce an alternative theology in which the hope of the future coming of the KG is given little or no place and is replaced by an emphasis on the present working of God by the Spirit in the Church.[23] But this is highly unsatisfactory. Some people may be prepared to allow that Jesus was a mistaken prophet, but, if so, it is not clear that attempts to revamp his teaching can carry much conviction, and it looks rather as though one mistaken mythology is simply being replaced by another dubious mythology of the Spirit. The basic problem remains as to how the teaching of Jesus can in any way be valid when it rests on a set of mistaken assumptions. Nor were these assumptions peripheral ones; they were concerned with the central theme of his message.

The second type of option is to recognize that the essential or distinctive element in the teaching of Jesus was his proclamation that the KG which his hearers expected to come in the future was already present in his ministry. God's purpose, prophesied in the Old Testament, was being brought to fulfilment in an unexpected manner. The best way to express this is probably in terms of concealment or veiled manifestation.[24] What this means is that the popular expectation of the KG was of an open, public, and final act of sovereignty by God that would establish his rule in the world and bring its benefits to his people, but Jesus believed and taught that God was already acting in his ministry powerfully but secretly to establish that realm and to initiate a chain of events that would lead up to and include the End of popular expectation. There was thus a real and genuine manifestation of God's power, but it was in a sense veiled and secret.

If this view is sound, then it means that the basis of the proclamation of Jesus was a valid one, the belief that God was already fulfilling the prophecy of the coming of the KG. Or rather, the validity of Jesus' proclamation depends not on whether he was correct or mistaken about the nearness of the KG in the future, but on whether he was correct or mistaken about the reality of God's action in the present.

Further, the problem of continuity between the present and the future aspects of Jesus' teaching is solved. What Jesus taught was that the KG which the Jews expected in the future was already a reality. God was acting in power and consequently his realm was already in existence. Thus Jesus retained the traditional understanding of the KG as God's future realm initiated by his powerful action, but he transformed it 1. by declaring that the point in time at which it was to appear had already arrived, and 2. by indicating that the way in which it was appearing was different from what was traditionally expected.

By understanding the teaching of Jesus in this way we can give a satisfactory and coherent account of a larger corpus of sayings than Perrin and Chilton and place the teaching of Jesus within the structures of Jewish thinking—structures that he transformed in an intelligible way. Such an understanding, it should be emphasized, is not an arbitrary one imposed on the evidence at the cost of straining some texts to make them fit into the pattern. Rather, starting from texts that in our opinion have strong claims to being authentic, we have been able to achieve a consistent and coherent understanding of the teaching of Jesus into which other texts whose authenticity might otherwise perhaps be suspect can be fitted by the so-called criterion of coherence.

Moreover, we have established a vital point for our understanding of Christian hope that will be developed as we proceed further. Christian hope is often thought of as being somehow based on the future. Such hope is in danger of remaining precisely that and nothing more—hope. For hope to have substance it must be rooted in and related to something else—a conviction about the character of God, such as, for example, that he keeps his promises or that he has done certain things in the past. The teaching of Jesus about the KG enshrines the conviction that God has already begun to act in the world and will complete what he has begun. Thus the validity of the hope depends upon the validity of the conviction that God is already at work in the world.

What Jesus taught about the Kingdom

In the discussion of a concept such as the KG it is important to distinguish between the meaning of the phrase itself and what is said about it. The distinction is not always easy to observe in practice, and in the previous section we have had to transgress it. There we were concerned primarily with the meaning of the phrase in itself, but it was impossible to establish this without paying attention to the way in which it was used and to the contexts in which it appeared. The result of our investigation so far has been to show that KG did not simply function as a symbol for 'God acting in sovereign power' but rather that it referred to that realm that the Jews expected to be set up by the sovereign power of God in fulfilment of prophecy. Starting from this point we can give a coherent account of the use of the term by Jesus, and we can see that he began to use the term in a new way by claiming that the KG had already come and that it was present in an unexpected manner. We must now explore further what Jesus said about the KG. How did he use the term?

The way in which Jesus used the term 'KG' in a new way has been helpfully explored by J. Riches in *Jesus and the Transformation of Judaism*.[25] He tries to show how Jesus could take over a term like KG and retain its core meaning, while ridding it of some of its conventional associations and substituting others. Essentially his argument is that Jesus referred to the KG in the context of actions by himself that related it to his belief in a forgiving and merciful God who willed that people should love one another. Thus the concept was purged of its nationalist and martial associations and was linked to ideas of mercy and forgiveness extended to people of all kinds. The essential point that is being made here is a sound one that had of course been recognized by earlier scholars. The merit of Riches's presentation is that he is able to link what Jesus was doing in the case of the KG with his transformation of the ideas of purity and of God himself and thus to give a coherent account of the teaching of Jesus.

In this way the KG clearly becomes a symbol of hope for the downtrodden in society. It expresses the attitude of God to such people and declares that his concern is for them. Jesus' teaching is that God is at work to establish a new community. The bliss that is associated with the age to come is already being experienced, and this bliss is not just for the people who think they are entitled to it by virtue of their religious orthodoxy and adherence to the Jewish law.

At the same time, however, Jesus purged the concept of its nationalistic associations. We should be clear about what was actually happening here. It is commonly thought that the Jewish concept of the KG was a nationalistic and military one, and that Jesus replaced this image with a spiritual one. In fact, however, the Jewish concept was both nationalistic and spiritual. The description of the KG in Psalms of Solomon 17 combines both elements:

> Behold, O Lord, and raise up unto them their king, the son of David, at the time in which you see, O God, that he may reign over Israel your servant. Gird him with strength, that he may shatter unrighteous rulers, and that he may purge Jerusalem from nations that trample her down to destruction. Wisely, righteously, he shall thrust out sinners from the inheritance. He shall destroy the pride of the sinner as a potter's vessel. With a rod of iron he shall break in pieces all their substance. He shall destroy the godless nations with the word of his mouth. At his rebuke nations shall flee before him, and he shall reprove sinners for the thoughts of their heart. He shall gather together a holy people, whom he shall lead in righteousness, and he shall judge the tribes of the people that has been sanctified by the Lord his God. He shall not suffer unrighteousness to lodge any more in their midst, nor shall there dwell with them any man that knows wickedness. For he shall know them, that they are all sons of their God.[26]

Here vengeance on the godless nations and holiness among the people of Israel are closely linked together. Jesus, therefore, has to purge away the nationalist elements in the Jewish concept of the KG and to lay stress on the spiritual elements.

Now this approach is not without its problems as soon as we try to apply it to the situation of the downtrodden. On the one hand, the plight of the downtrodden is often due to the violent and ungodly in the nation itself and, on the other hand, it may be due to the violent and ungodly people of other nations. In first-century Palestine both types of oppression existed, just as they do today in many parts of the world. In what ways did Jesus envisage the KG as the solution to the needs of the people?

There is no programme of social action in the teaching of Jesus about the KG. He is concerned with the relationships of individuals to God and the behaviour that will result from that. On the one side, he offered to the needy forgiveness, integration into the community of God's people, and physical healing. On the other side, he called those who followed him to a life in which their total attitude must be one of love to God and their neighbour and of commitment to himself as Teacher and Master. His teaching about non-violence did not, in my opinion, forbid the use of restrained *force* (as opposed to *violence*) to preserve law and order, but it certainly forbade the excesses of armed conflict and insurrection. Nevertheless, in his preaching Jesus certainly condemned verbally the hypocrisy and greed of those who oppressed the poor and the outcasts of society, and he attacked the people of Israel as a whole for their failure to live as the people of God.

But how effective are words, even if accompanied by a few beneficial miracles? People might well have concluded that nothing much was happening. Jesus took care of this point in his teaching. The so-called parables of growth depicted the secret, quiet beginnings of the KG and gave the assurance that what was scarcely visible in its beginnings would grow, like a plant from a seed, until its effects were manifest and great (Mark 4.26-29, 30-32). Consequently, Jesus could speak about the 'mystery' of the KG (Mark 4.11; 'mysteries' in Matt. 13.11 and Luke 8.10). A 'mystery' is a divine secret that God reveals to the people who are able to understand it, such as his prophets in Old Testament times. Jesus told his followers that it was they who were privileged to be the recipients of his revelation concerning the KG. The mystery or secret was that the KG had come in the person, deeds, and words of Jesus. For those with the eyes to see, things were happening, but others could easily persuade themselves that nothing of significance was happening. Within the community formed by Jesus, new relationships did exist in which the needy could find a love that expressed itself both in material provision and in loving acceptance. This was something that was visible—'See how these Christians love one another' presumably reflects what some pagans actually said, even if the wording stems from a Christian apologist. At the same time there is no doubting that the early Christian groups were on occasion characterized by a lack of love and by material greed (see 1 Cor.), so that outsiders might also be tempted to think that there was nothing distinctive about them.

We can now move on to suggest some additional features that arise out of the teaching of Jesus on the KG when it is put in the total context of his teaching.

The Kingdom of God and the Father

The first is that with the concept of the KG there is closely associated Jesus' understanding of God. The KG is specifically linked with the thought of God as Father in Luke 12.32; 22.29ff. (contrast Matt. 19.28); Matthew 13.43; 25.34. In the references in Luke it is God as the Father who bestows the KG on the disciples and Jesus respectively. The two references in Matthew also occur in material addressed to disciples. This is congruent with the fact established by T. W. Manson that Jesus did not preach about God as Father to all and sundry but revealed him to his disciples.[27] Of crucial significance in this connection is the fact that the Lord's Prayer begins with the words, 'Father, may your name be hallowed, may your kingdom come', thus linking closely the name of 'Father' and the KG. Jesus starts from the situation of Jewish piety in which people were accustomed to pray to God, and he directs his disciples into his understanding of God as Father. We observe, first, that the prayer is one for God to act to establish his rule. It was common ground between Jesus and his audience that the coming of the KG is the act of God and not of persons, even though God would use persons in the fulfilment of his purpose. Jewish literature of the time shows that here Jesus was saying nothing new.[28]

Second, the God who establishes his rule is the God whom Jesus addresses as 'Father'. The fact that Jesus used an intimate form of address that appears to be unparalleled in contemporary Palestinian Judaism and that he taught his followers to know God in the same intimate manner as he himself enjoyed needs no further elaboration here.[29] This has an important consequence for the understanding of the KG. As A. M. Hunter put it, 'The King in the Kingdom is a Father.'[30] This fact indicates that the KG is primarily concerned with the creation of a family; the character of the King is the model for the character of the members (Matt. 5.48/Luke 6.36 Q).

Third, in this context it is God the Father who is at the centre of Jesus' teaching. The petition for the KG to come is preceded by the petition that God will cause his name to be hallowed. This is important because it shows that the coming of the KG and the hallowing of God's name are parallel concepts and indeed that they are very closely associated.[31] It is by concentrating attention on the Lord's Prayer as the critically assured minimum of

Jesus' teaching that H Schürmann is able to insist that Jesus' message was primarily about God and puts him at the centre.[32] The suggestion here is that God himself rather than the KG was primary for Jesus. I am rather doubtful whether this is a helpful distinction; it would be more cogent if it could be shown that teaching about God himself characterized the message of Jesus, but this is scarcely the case. Nevertheless, the significant fact emerges that the character of the KG is determined by the character and activity of God the Father.

The Kingdom of God and the Spirit
The second important element that must be brought into the picture is the Holy Spirit. The Evangelists were conscious that Jesus carried out his ministry in the power of the Spirit who was bestowed upon him at his baptism. That Jesus himself was aware of the source of his power is to be seen in the extremely significant text Matthew 12.28/Luke 11.20 Q where he comments that it is by the Spirit/finger of God that he does his mighty works and the KG has arrived. Whether we take 'Spirit' or 'finger' to be the original word used by Jesus and paraphrased by the use of the alternative word in one of the Gospels,[33] the text testifies to the realization of divine power active in the ministry of Jesus to enable him to carry out his exorcisms. In another saying Jesus attributes his mighty works to the power of the Spirit and warns unbelievers against the danger of blaspheming or speaking against the Spirit (Mark 3.29/Matt. 12.21b; Matt. 12.32b/ Luke 12.10 Q). Again, there is some doubt about the precise wording used by Jesus, but the basic point is not in any doubt, namely that Jesus recognized that his mighty works were performed in the power of the Spirit.

The obvious conclusion to be drawn is that for Jesus the coming of the KG and the activity of the Spirit were tightly connected, so much so that we may suggest that it was the working of the Spirit in and through Jesus that constituted the actual coming of the KG.[34] It is interesting that this connection is maintained outside the Synoptic Gospels, especially when we remember that references to the KG are less common. Birth by the Spirit and entry to the KG are linked together in John 3.3, 5, and Paul links the Spirit with the KG in Romans 14.17 and Galatians 5.21ff.; we may compare 1 Corinthians 4.20 where the KG is linked with power.

Three points emerge here. The first is that the KG is brought directly into conflict with the evil rule of Satan whose power is placed over against that of the Spirit. The Evangelists recognize that this motif was a dominant one in the ministry of Jesus when they relate at the outset of the story how Jesus, immediately after he had received the Spirit, was straightway sent into the desert to face Satan. Luke and John note how the events leading up to the passion and death of Jesus were instigated by the action of Satan through Judas (Luke 22.3; John 13.2, 27). It has sometimes been suggested that for Luke at least the period of Jesus' ministry between the temptation in the desert and the passion was free from temptation by Satan, but this hypothesis will not stand up to examination, especially in the light of Luke 22.28.

The second point is that the KG is associated with power. It is brought into being by the exercise of divine might, the 'finger' of God (cf. Exod. 8.16-19). As Paul says, the KG is not (simply) a matter of talking but of power (1 Cor. 4.20). A divine reality is at work in the world, and an important saying suggests that this power would become all the more evident after the ministry of Jesus (Mark 9.1).

A third point to be noted is that the Spirit was promised in the Old Testament as a gift for the last days in the same way as the KG (Joel 2.28ff.). The KG and the Spirit are thus both signs of the eschatological activity of God now realized in the ministry of Jesus.

The effect of these considerations is to underline the element of power in the KG as God's activity in Jesus which extends beyond mere prophetic inspiration expressed in words.

The Kingdom of God and Jesus

The fact that God's power is revealed in the KG in and through Jesus inevitably leads us to consider more closely his relation to the KG. It is the weakness of several treatments of the KG that they do not adequately consider the concept of messiahship. This is regrettable. For the word 'messiah' retained the sense of 'anointed' and was used to refer to a person endowed with the *Spirit* for a particular purpose authorized by *God*. We can leave aside the view that the background to the use of the term in the Gospels is anointing to priesthood[35] and take it for granted that the reference is to an anointed ruler or *king*. Thus the term 'messiah' is implicitly associated with the three terms that we have already considered: *God* sets up his rule (the KG) through a *king* anointed by the *Spirit*.

The question whether Jesus thought of himself as the Messiah is one that arouses much controversy. Since the early Church believed without question that he was the Messiah, the tendency to read back this title into his earthly ministry was obviously strong and therefore the texts must be examined with care. Yet the surprising fact is that, according to the Gospels, Jesus rarely used the word 'messiah' and rarely spoke in a way that suggests that he thought of himself as the Messiah. This fact, which helped to lead to the theory that Jesus did not think of himself as the Messiah and that such references as there are in the Gospels do not represent his teaching, ought rather to be evaluated as indicating the historical verisimilitude of the Evangelists and should encourage us to view the actual texts in the Gospels where the term occurs with greater respect. Alongside these texts must be placed three other pieces of evidence. First, there is the way in which Jesus was addressed as 'Son of David', an appellation that is firmly present in the tradition (Mark 10.47ff.), although Jesus himself taught that it was an inadequate way of thinking of the Messiah (Mark 12.35-7). 'Son of David' was a synonym for 'Messiah'.[36] Second, there is the use of the term 'Son of man' by Jesus. This term was not taken up by the early Church to any appreciable extent and is characteristic of the diction ascribed to Jesus. Within the scope of the present essay it is not possible to bring together the evidence for the writer's view that Jesus used this term as a messianic self-designation that draws its meaning from Daniel 7 where a figure like a man is given rule and authority by God.[37] Third, there is the fact that Jesus acted as an agent of God's rule and did not merely announce it as a prophet might have done. Various of his actions could be regarded as messianic in the strict sense of the term.[38] The cumulative effect of these three considerations is to show that Jesus did act messianically and that he must have been conscious that in doing so he was fulfilling the role of the Messiah. That is to say, the precise form that the KG took in the mind of Jesus was a messianic form as opposed to the kind of conception of the KG where a Messiah is not specifically present.[39]

If so, we face the question as to why Jesus did not publicly use the actual term 'messiah' of himself. The reason usually advanced is that he wished to avoid the misleading implications of a term that would lead people to expect a war-like leader. It has often been thought that this danger lurked behind the wish of the people to make Jesus king in John 6.15. This cannot be the whole story, however. Even if Jesus was reticent about using the term 'messiah', he was prepared to use the term 'KG' which, as we saw, contained a blend of political, military, and more spiritual associations for his contemporaries. It is, therefore, uncertain whether Jesus was simply trying to avoid political misunderstanding. Two other reasons may be suggested. If we are correct in assuming that Jesus used the term 'Son of man' by preference, then it can be argued, first, that this phrase expressed better the divine origin of the bearer of the title. For the Jews, 'messiah' seems to have connoted a purely human figure on the whole, but 'Son of man' in Daniel 7 connoted a heavenly figure 'like a man', and therefore it was better suited to express the true nature of Jesus. There is a case that 'Son of man' was tantamount to 'Son of God', and, if this suggestion can be upheld, it will explain why

Jesus preferred this term. But here our second consideration comes in: Son of man was also an idiomatic term in Aramaic that may possibly have meant much the same as 'I' in certain contexts, and there is much to be said for the view that Jesus used a deliberately ambiguous term as part of his 'veiled manifestation' of himself.[40] Now, if this is a correct suggestion, then we have a phenomenon similar to that which we found in the proclamation of the KG by Jesus. Jesus is concerned with authority and rule that will be revealed openly in the future, but at present it is hidden and partly secret. The fact that we can detect this same pattern in the use of both concepts, KG and 'Son of man', is surely significant. It would appear to support the authenticity of Jesus' teaching in both areas, since it is highly unlikely that the early Church would deliberately create the same motif in both areas.

Our discussion has shown that KG and 'Messiah' are correlative concepts, each belonging to the other and implying the other. Jesus thus appears as the divine agent to whom God has entrusted dominion and power, and it is thus in Jesus that the KG becomes a reality. As T. W. Manson put it, the KG is the messianic ministry; it is in the activity of Jesus that we see the activity of God that brings about his rule.[41]

The Kingdom of God and Israel

We must next ask what Jesus envisaged as the result of the establishment of the KG. The traditional hope was, as we have seen, for the setting up of a new kingdom in the presence of God at the end of the age in a cosmic setting; it would be composed of people who loved and served God and who lived together in righteousness and peace under the rule of God and his agent the Messiah. The Jews believed that they themselves would compose this people. The KG is thus a corporate entity and consists of people. Hence the mission of Jesus involved the creation of a people who would be the objects of God's rule and who would receive the benefits of his rule. Since Jesus warned the people of Israel that as a nation they were in danger of being rejected by God, he must have envisaged the creation of a new people, incorporating elements of the old people but also open more widely and constituted by a new allegiance. Along with his proclamation of the KG, he also called people to personal allegiance to himself as disciples and taught them that they must obey his words. The conclusion is irresistible that re-sponse to the message of the KG was identical with acceptance of Jesus as Master. The new Israel is constituted by its allegiance to the Messiah. The recognition that Jesus was concerned with the creation of a new Israel is not new. Again we owe to A. M. Hunter the lapidary statement that 'the King-dom of God implies a new Israel',[42] but it is Ben F. Meyer who has given the most concentrated expression to this thought in recent writing. He asks: 'Why indeed should the reign of God have been the object of a proclamation to Israel as such unless it bore on the destiny of Israel as such?'[43] Here two key texts must be mentioned. The first is the enigmatic saying recorded in differing forms by Matthew and Luke (Matt. 19.28/Luke 22.29f. Q):

> Truly, I say to you, in the new world, when the Son of man shall sit on his glorious throne, you who have followed me will also sit on twelve thrones, judging the twelve tribes of Israel.
>
> As my Father appointed a kingdom for me, so do I appoint for you that you may eat and drink at my table in my kingdom, and sit on thrones judging the twelve tribes of Israel.

Common to both forms of the saying is the idea of rule by Jesus which will be shared in the world to come by the twelve disciples as they sit on thrones and judge the tribes of Israel. There must be an element of symbolism in the saying, recorded as it is by Luke in the context of the prophecy of the betrayal by Judas (though Luke later records the appointment of a replacement for Judas). But a literal understanding of the saying is unlikely since it takes no account of the place of the Gentiles (whether in the eyes of Jesus or of the Evangelists). The thought is of privilege for the faithful followers of Jesus who have shared in his earthly ministry to Israel, and the privilege appears to be that of sharing in the judgement on the unbelieving people of Israel rather than of ruling over a reconstituted Israel. Is the saying, then, anything more than a symbolical way of stating that the disciples will share in the KG but unbelieving Israel will be condemned, or, rather, that a division will be carried through among the Jews on the basis of belief and unbelief? It is not likely, then, that this text speaks of a 'new' physical Israel ruled by the twelve, but it certainly prophesies the end of the old Israel.[44]

The other crucial text is Matthew 16.18 where Jesus prophesies that he will build his Church on 'this rock' and that it will not be overcome by the powers of death. The authenticity of this saying is much disputed, and we owe to Ben F. Meyer a spirited defence of it.[45] In the light of the Dead Sea Scrolls the language has been shown to be definitely Palestinian, and there are no conceptual reasons for denying it to Jesus. In effect, the sole remaining reason for not accepting it is its absence from the other Gospels, especially from Mark and Q; but it is curious reasoning that would reject a saying simply because it is not attested in the other Gospels or their sources.[46] If the saying is genuine, it expresses the purpose of Jesus to establish a people whom he describes as 'my people'. Coming immediately after Peter's confession of Jesus as the Messiah, this must mean 'the people of myself as Messiah'. Here, therefore, we have an express statement of the intention of Jesus to form a people to whom is given a name used of Israel as the people of God; compare how Stephen could refer to 'the church in the wilderness' (Acts 7.38). Moreover, the statement has a cosmic dimension with its reference to 'the powers of death', and Jesus goes on to speak of the keys of the Kingdom of heaven entrusted to Peter, which suggests that in some way the people and the KG are closely related. After the disastrous effect of the medieval equation of the KG with the Church, seen in the increasingly secular and unchristian expression of authority claimed by church leaders and in the refusal to recognize the saving rule of God outside the Catholic Church, there has been a strong reaction against the identification of the KG as the Church. Indeed, the current understanding of the KG as God's *activity* of ruling rather than as the area or people over whom he rules has strengthened the case. But we have seen that this modern understanding of the phrase 'KG' is one-sided and inadequate. The KG is not just the sovereign activity of God; it is also the set-up created by the activity of God, and that set-up consists of people. Hence the people created by Jesus is a manifestation of the KG: ideally they are the people who accept the rule of God through Jesus and on whom he bestows the blessings of his rule. The Church as the people of God is the object of his rule and is therefore his Kingdom, or at least an expression of it, imperfect and sinful though it is. We should not be afraid of recognizing this fact, despite the misuse of it in the past. Although the Church has the promise of sitting in judgement on the world (1 Cor. 6.2), which may be in effect a reinterpretation of the saying about the Twelve sitting in judgement on the tribes of Israel, this is a purely future role, and there is no justification for exercising it here and now. Indeed, the danger is already guarded against by the sayings of Jesus which insist that leadership is a matter of humble service and which warn the disciples categorically against desiring position and privilege. It is true, of course, that there will be leaders in the Church, but they have been given the pattern of humility and service that they must follow by Jesus.[47]

The Kingdom and the new age

After our rapid survey of some of the salient features in the teaching of Jesus, it is now time for us to try to assess their significance for today.

The first point to be noted is that the early Church did two things with the teaching of Jesus. On the one hand, it retained a record of it in the traditions that eventually received definitive form in the Gospels. This indicates that the teaching of Jesus continued to be influential in the Church, and, as we noted, the Evangelists appear to have recognized that the main theme of Jesus was the KG. On the other hand, the uses of the term KG outside the Gospels are much more thin on the ground. This suggests that while the early Church faithfully preserved the account of what Jesus actually said, it also moved on beyond his teaching and interpreted it for its new situation in the post-resurrection period in the Hellenistic world. Thus, although the mode of expression was varied, the central importance of the message expressed by Jesus in terms of the KG remained constant. Elsewhere I have tried to show how the emphasis shifted from the Kingdom to the King himself in his functions as Lord and Saviour and how the experience of the blessings of the Kingdom found apt expression as eternal life.[48] This does not mean that we should completely abandon the term KG and express the concept in other ways: rather, just as the early Church retained the term and used other forms of expression, so too we should retain and explain the biblical terms as well as look for new ways of expression that will be meaningful in our contemporary society.

Perhaps the most fundamental fact that we discovered in Jesus' teaching about the KG was the way in which he looked forward to the future full manifestation of God's rule but at the same time proclaimed and brought into being that same rule during his ministry. For Jesus the future had already commenced in the present time. The Old Testament had prophesied the hope of God's future action as king, and it expressed its hope on the basis of the mighty acts of God that had already been experienced, especially at the Exodus. The early Church was conscious of living in the era of fulfilment. Its hope for the future was based on what it already knew of the present working of God. This is an observation of the utmost importance. Christianity is not built upon a hope of what God may do in the future; on the contrary, the hope is built on the experience of what he has already done and is doing in the present time. And this hope is that God will bring to completion what he has already begun. He will continue to work in character with his past and present work.

Consequently, when we talk about the KG we are talking about something that is actually happening here and now, inaugurated by the ministry of Jesus, and now 'come in power' since his death and resurrection (Mark 9.1).[49] The KG is now 'incarnated' in Jesus himself. Through his death and resurrection he has been shown to be both Lord and Messiah (Acts 2.38). The hope of a new age is thus a hope that has been coming true ever since Jesus first began to proclaim, 'The time is fulfilled, and the kingdom of God is at hand' (Mark 1.15). The hope is no longer hope but present reality. To be sure, it is incomplete; we live 'between the times', but our assurance, based on our present experience, is that in the future we shall know in fuller measure the experience of divine power.

The terminology makes this clear. Jesus used one and the same term, 'the Kingdom of God', for the present and the future of God's rule. The Holy Spirit is described by Paul as the 'first instalment' of what God intends to give his people (2 Cor. 1.22; Eph. 1.14). The power that makes for newness is already making things new. In Johannine terminology, eternal life is a present experience stretching into the future. All this demonstrates that the message of the KG is that the age to come has already dawned. God is now at work in the world. This point needs some emphasis, for too often people talk as though the activity of the KG ceased with the termination of the earthly ministry of Jesus, or as though it is something purely heavenly or spiritual. Those who have spoken of the KG as present in the world today have often thought of it either in a purely humanistic manner as the reali-zation of a moral state of society through human effort or in terms of the establishment of some kind of ecclesiastical organization. But the language of the KG stresses that it is God who is presently exercising his powerful lordship in the world in which we live.

There might seem to be one decisive difference between the coming of the KG in the ministry of Jesus and its presence now. We saw that the manifes-tation in his ministry was veiled in certain respects, although Jesus could accuse his contemporaries of blindness when they failed to perceive the significance of the signs of the times. But now the situation appears to be different in that God has raised Jesus from the dead and thus declared him to be the Judge and Saviour of humankind. Does this not mean that the presence of the KG should now be manifest and open to everybody? On the whole, the New Testament suggests that the situation in fact is no different. The God of this world has blinded the eyes of those who do not believe. Christians walk by faith and not by sight. The fact of the resurrection—and the interpretation to be placed upon it—are not matters that can be proved in a way that will be universally compelling. Hence the presence and progress of the KG is still a matter for faith. The signs pointing to it are, however, stronger than they were before; the person who does not believe has to reject a stronger body of evidence.

The relation of the present of the KG to its future requires some consid-eration. The New Testament teaching about the future KG is cast in apoc-alyptic terms; it presents the picture of a cataclysmic end to the present world-order followed by a new order characterized by incorruptibility and permanence. Does this mean that there is no continuity between present and future? The tendency in much evangelical teaching has been to emphasize the disjunction between the two ages with the world getting worse and worse until eventually God steps in and makes a totally fresh start by taking his people away from the corrupt earth and raising the dead in Christ to share with them in the new world. Certainly the biblical picture is of a world in which evil gets worse and worse and the godly remnant suffers much persecution. Moreover, the world in which we live presents an equivocal face with the achievements of science and technology on the one hand and the potential for nuclear destruction and other evils on the other. Are there any grounds for hope in the message of the KG?

It is the merit of Ian Murray to have drawn attention to *The Puritan Hope*[50] that before the end of the age there would be widespread revival and the conversion of unbelievers, a hope based exegetically on Romans 11 and other passages. The significance of this hope has perhaps been missed because it has been entangled with questions about the millennium and its timing. Advocates of the Puritan view have linked it to postmillennialism, the doctrine that the millennium will precede the parousia and prepare the way for it. But postmillennialism is a doubtfully based option, and it would be better to recognize that the hope of revival in the last days is something to be distinguished from the millennium.

Can this hope be taken as something realistic? Does Jesus' preaching of the KG give us any basis for hope for the future? Certainly there is a pattern that must be observed. Scholars have often found it difficult to accommodate the expectation of the cross by Jesus in his proclamation of the KG: how can Jesus have announced the presence of God's rule and yet faced apparent defeat and the need to give his life as a ransom for many? The solution to the problem lies in the resurrection and his triumphant vindication by God. But this means that there was a pattern in the ministry of Jesus in which there was a genuine experience of opposition by the powers of evil that led to his crucifixion; the death of Jesus was real, but it was only apparent defeat, for it was itself part of God's plan and it was followed by a display of divine power and victory. This pattern was repeated in the early Church in its experience of strength in the midst of weakness. May we not then say that on a cosmic scale the KG comes in weakness and grows in weakness but that there will be a triumphant vindication at the parousia of the Lord? The pattern of crucifixion and resurrection enacted in the experience of Jesus will be followed in the case of the Church as it dies now in order to be resurrected with its Lord at the parousia. Thus the Church can proclaim the KG now in the sure hope of its final triumph. And yet at the same time it must be affirmed that the triumph is not merely future. The biblical teaching is not that God's strength is experienced after weakness, but rather that it is known in weakness. The cross itself was the place of glorification of Jesus according to the Fourth Gospel (John 3.31ff.). The Church rejoices in and during its sufferings, and, although death may be at work in its messengers who proclaim the good news, there is life for those who respond to the gospel here and now (2 Cor. 4.12). Thus the picture is one of veiled triumph now and open triumph to come.

If the Church possess this sure hope, what can we say about the activity of the KG here and now and the church's relationship to it? Here we may start with the well-known words of Vincent Taylor:

> One important feature His teaching does share with Apocalyptic: from first to last the *Basileia* is supernatural; man does not strive for it or bring it into being. Our modern idea of labouring for the coming of the Kingdom is a noble conception, fully baptized into Christ and expressive of His Spirit; but it is not His teaching regarding the *Basileia*.[51]

Taylor is of course right in what he says about the teaching of Jesus: the coming of the KG is the act of God; he acts to establish his rule over the community to whom he gives the blessings of his rule. Rightly, therefore, does Taylor go on to emphasize that we are to pray for its coming, and this surely remains a primary obligation. Yet this is surely not the whole story. For we have seen that God acted in Jesus to establish his rule and that the concepts of the Messiah/Son of man and the KG are indivisibly joined together. But the Messiah or Son of man is the leader of a group who are not only subject to God as King but also act in unison to spread the KG. The idea that the KG expands of its own accord independently of the action of God's agents is thoroughly false. Jesus called the Twelve and the Seventy (-two) to share in his work, and he told them to preach that the KG had drawn near and to perform the signs of its presence. The KG extends as it is proclaimed and as the signs of its presence are performed. If Jesus came to bring the KG, we must also conclude that his followers were commissioned by him to carry out the same task. It must be questioned, therefore, whether Taylor is right in saying that 'labouring for the coming of the Kingdom' is not the teaching of Jesus himself. On the contrary, this is precisely what he called his followers to do. To proclaim the Kingship of God is to preach the KG, for it opens up to people the possibility of responding to the message by acknowledging God as their king.

One can understand the position Taylor adopted. It was no doubt a reaction against the nineteenth-century liberals and the social gospellers who thought of a KG that was little more than a glorified human community bound together through action inspired by love. Such a conception is dangerously secular and leaves God out of consideration, to say nothing of Christ. Equally, it is possible and necessary to react against the autocratic claims of a Church that claims that it incarnates the KG and is in danger of implying that submission to a supreme pontiff is the same thing as accepting the kingship of God. It is good to be able to report that contemporary Roman Catholic scholarship now repudiates any such ideas.[52] However, we can learn from these dangers that the KG is not simply an ethical community among humankind or an ecclesiastical institution. But at the same time it must be insisted that the KG is concerned with moral issues; as Taylor again says, the moral renewal of humanity follows from the presence of the KG.[53] Nor must we forget that the KG is concerned with the formation of a Christian community and it is not simply a collection of isolated Christian individuals.

The Church consists of people who acknowledge God as king and who are committed to proclaiming his kingship and witnessing to his reality in their own lives as individuals and as a community. Put in other words, this means that a primary task of the Church is evangelism carried out in the power of the Spirit. But such proclamation is not simply aimed at the conversion of individuals. The Church must also spell out the nature of obedience to God both spiritually and morally, just as Jesus did. The proclamation of the KG will include the declaration of God's condemnation of what is evil and hypocritical in the lives of people both as individuals and as members of communal bodies in business and government. To say this obviously raises questions about the extent to which protest in the name of God should be carried out in action as well as in words, but there is no room here to take up the point. We must be guided by the example of Jesus, who forbade his followers to use violence, but who did things, like associating with tax collectors and sinners, that outraged his opponents and made them even plot to kill him.

Thus we conclude that the Church is called to participate in the realization of the KG here and now. To do so will arouse opposition; like its Lord it will experience weakness and crucifixion. But it will bear these things in firm hope because of the victory already achieved by God in Christ and because of his faithful promise to complete what he has begun. The promise of the KG signifies that 'in the Lord your labour is not in vain' (1 Cor. 15.58).[54]

Notes

[1]W. G. Kümmel, *Promise and Fulfilment* (London, 1957); G. E. Ladd, *Jesus and the Kingdom* (London, 1966); N. Perrin, *The Kingdom of God in the Teaching of Jesus* (Philadelphia, 1963); R. Schnackenburg, *God's Rule and Kingdom* (London, 1963). For summaries of the discussion, see O. E. Evans in *The Interpreter's Dictionary of the Bible* (Nashville, 1962), II, pp. 17-26; B. Klappert in *The New International Dictionary of New Testament Theology* (Exeter, 1976), II, pp. 372-90; G. Klein, 'The Biblical Understanding of the Kingdom of God', *Interpretation*, 26, 1972, pp. 387-418; I. H. Marshall in *The Zondervan Pictorial Encyclopedia of the Bible* (Grand

Rapids, 1975), III, pp. 801-9. For more recent studies, see H. Merklein, *Jesu Botschaft von der Gottesherrschaft* (Stuttgart, 1983), and G. R. Beasley-Murray, *The Coming of God* (Exeter, 1983); *Jesus and the Kingdom of God* (Grand Rapids, 1986).

[2]The following comparison may be instructive:

	Matthew	Mark	Luke
Kingdom of God	50	15	39
Believe, faith	24	20	26
Father (used of God)	44	4	17
Love	12	8	16
Parable	17	13	18
Son of man	26	14	24
Spirit, Holy	12	6	17

[3]See Matthew 4.23; 9.35; cf. 13.19; 24.14; Mark 1.15; Luke 4.43; 8.1; 9.2, 11, 60.

[4]A significant non-conformist on this point is E. Bammel, 'Erwägungen zur Eschatologie Jesu', in F. L. Cross (ed.), *Studia Evangelica III (TU 88*, Berlin, 1964), pp. 3-32.

[5]N. Perrin's book *Rediscovering the Teaching of Jesus* (London, 1967) is more ruthless than the author's earlier work listed above and may be regarded as fixing the low-water mark for English-speaking scholars; yet even he insists that there are strong arguments for the authenticity of Matthew 12.28/Luke 11.29 Q; Luke 17.20ff.; Matthew 11.12/Luke 16.16 Q and for other, parabolic sayings. The Continental low-water mark is fixed by H. Schürmann, *Gottes Reich—Jesu Geschick* (Freiburg, 1983), p. 135, who feels reasonably secure in holding only to Luke 11.2-4; 6-20; 11.20; 12.31 and 13.18ff. (with parallels as appropriate).

[6]See especially the works of G. E. Ladd and R. Schnackenburg cited above; L. Goppelt, *New Testament Theology* (Grand Rapids, 1981), I, pp. 51-67.

[7]J. Jeremias, *New Testament Theology* (London, 1971), I, p. 102: '(Jesus') meaning is that the eschatological hour of God, the victory of God, the consummation of the world, is near. Indeed it is very near.' Similarly, H. Conzelmann, *An Outline of the Theology of the New Testament* (London, 1969), pp. 106-15; R. H. Hiers, *The Kingdom of God in the Synoptic Tradition* (Gainesville, 1970).

[8]The need to think again about this point was shown by S. Aalen,' "Reign" and "House" in the Kingdom of God in the Gospels', *NTS*, 8, 1961-62, pp. 215-40.

[9]The basic study of the present sayings is Kümmel, *Promise and Fulfilment.* He argues that, 'Jesus saw the Kingdom of God to be present before the parousia, which he thought to be imminent, only in his own person and his works; he knew no other realization of the eschatological consummation' (p. 140).

[10]N. Perrin, *Jesus and the Language of the Kingdom* (Philadelphia, 1976), pp. 43, 45.

[11]Ibid., p. 30.

[12]B. D. Chilton, *God in Strength* (Freistadt, 1979), pp. 285ff.; 'Regnum Dei Deus Est', *SJT*, 31, 1978, pp. 261-70.

[13]Thus H. Merklein, *Jesu Botschaft von der Gottesherrschaft*, p. 38, argues that sayings in which KG is a spatial term all come from a stratum in the gospel tradition that is later than Jesus, and that he used the term only in a dynamic sense.

[14]Perrin, *The Kingdom of God,* pp. 56ff.

[15]See Ps. Sol. 17; Ass. Moses 10.1-10; Sib. Orac. 3.46-56, 652-4, 767-89; Qaddish; Tg. Gn. 49.10ff. Other references in the apocalyptic literature are to the present sovereignty of God over Israel and the nations (Ps. Sol. 5.21; Jub. 12.19; 1 En. 84.2f.; T. Reub. 6; T. Jud. 21; 1QM 6.6; Shemoneh Esreh 14).

[16]Even if Luke himself created the situation in Luke 17.20, the question attributed to the Pharisees is entirely credible. See I. H. Marshall, *The Gospel of Luke* (Exeter, 1978), pp. 653 ff.

[17]See ibid., pp. 422 ff.

[18]Ibid., pp. 377-9.

[19]Only Luke has supplied 'the Kingdom of God' as the subject of the verb 'is near' (cf. Mark 13.9); Mark may have thought that the reference was to the coming of the Son of man, but there is no essential difference.

[20]Mark 13.32; Matthew 24.42, 50/Luke 12.46 Q; Matthew 25.13; 10.23; 24.44; Luke 18.8; 21.36. Some of these formulations may belong to the Evangelists.

[21]See Marshall, *The Gospel of Luke*, pp. 628-30, 475ff., 655ff. and 422ff.

[22]C. H. Dodd, *The Parables of the Kingdom* (London, 1961).

[23]E. Grässer, *Das Problem der Parusieverzögerung in den synoptischen Evangelien und in der Apostelgeschichte* (Berlin, 1977).

[24]See especially C. E. B. Cranfield, *The Gospel according to St Mark* (Cambridge, 1977), pp. 63-8; H. Ridderbos, *The Coming of the Kingdom* (Philadelphia, 1962).

[25]J. Riches, *Jesus and the Transformation of Judaism* (London, 1980), pp 87-111.

[26]Ps. Sol. 17.23-30.

[27]T. W. Manson, *The Teaching of Jesus* (Cambridge, 1935), pp. 89-115.

[28]See Ps. Sol. (cited in n. 26); Ass. Moses 10.1; Sib. Orac. 3.47f., 767f.; Qaddish Prayer ('May he set up his kingdom'). Jesus need not be referring exclusively to the future, imminent Kingdom; his words can refer to God's action *now*.

[29]Jeremias, *New Testament Theology* I, pp. 61-8. See now J. Barr (above, p. 169, n. 64).

[30]A. M. Hunter, *Introducing New Testament Theology* (London, 1957), p. 31.

[31]For a profound discussion of the similarities and differences between the two petitions see E. Lohmeyer, *The Lord's Prayer* (London, 1965), pp. 100-10.

[32]H. Schürmann, *Traditionsgeschichtliche Untersuchungen* (Dusseldorf, 1968), pp. 13-35; *Das Gebet des Herrn* (Leipzig, 1981), n. 222.

[33]See Marshall, *The Gospel of Luke*, pp. 475ff.

[34]J. D. G. Dunn, *Jesus and the Spirit* (London, 1975), pt 1.

[35]The view of G. Friedrich, 'Beobachtungen zur messianischen Hoherpriesterwartung in den Synoptikern', *ZTK*, 53, 1956, pp. 265-311, has been refuted by F. Hahn, *Christologische Hoheitstitel* (Göttingen, 1964), pp. 231-41.

[36]See C. Burger, *Jesus als Davidssohn* (Göttingen, 1970); he does not regard the tradition as historical. On Mark 12.35-37 see Marshall, *The Gospel of Luke*, pp. 743-9.

[37]I. H. Marshall, *The Origins of New Testament Christology* (London, 1976), ch. 4.

[38]J. D. G. Dunn, 'The Messianic Secret in Mark', *Tyndale Bulletin*, 21, 1970, pp. 92-117.

[39]Jewish messianic expectations in the time of Jesus are extremely difficult to unravel. In some of the literature future expectations are expressed without mention of a messianic figure (e.g., Ass. Moses 10).

[40]See S. Kim, *'The "Son of Man" as the Son of God'* (Tübingen. 1983), pp. 35ff.

[41]T. W. Manson, 'Realized Eschatology and the Messianic Secret', in D. E. Nineham (ed.), *Studies in the Gospel Essays in Memory of R. H. Lightfoot* (Oxford, 1957), pp. 209-22; *The Servant-Messiah* (Cambridge, 1953), p. 63.

[42]Hunter, *Introducing New Testament Theology*, p. 34.

[43]B. F. Meyer, *The Aims of Jesus* (London, 1979), p. 133.

[44]So A. Plummer, *The Gospel according to Saint Luke* (Edinburgh, 1901), pp. 502ff.; J. Dupont, 'Le logion des douze trônes (Mt. 19, 28; Lc 22, 28-30)', *Biblica*, 45, 1964, pp. 355-92. Here I alter the opinion expressed in *The Gospel of Luke*, p. 818.

[45]Meyer, *The Aims of Jesus*, pp. 185-97; Jeremias, *New Testament Theology*, pp. 167-70.

[46]If we did this, we would have to reject large areas of teaching found only in any one Gospel— which would be patently absurd.

[47]The practical problem lies in how to combine force and love (1 Cor. 4.21).

[48]I. H. Marshall, 'Preaching the Kingdom of God', *Exp. T*, 89, 1977-78, pp. 13-16.

[49]On this saying, see the discussion of the various interpretations in Marshall, *The Gospel of Luke*, pp. 377-9.

[50]I. Murray, *The Puritan Hope* (Edinburgh, 1971).
[51]V. Taylor, *Jesus and His Sacrifice* (London, 1937), p. 10.
[52]Schnackenburg, *God's Rule and Kingdom,* p. 233.
[53]Taylor, *Jesus and His Sacrifice,* p. 8.
[54]This essay was originally published in *Themelios,* 11, 1, September 1985, pp. 5-15. [1989] See the detailed discussion of the material outside the Gospels in G. S. Shogren, 'The Pauline Proclamation of the Kingdom of God and the Kingdom of Christ within its New Testament Setting', unpublished Ph.D. thesis, Aberdeen, 1986.

13
The Development of the Concept
of Redemption in the New Testament

POSTERITY MAY WELL RECKON THAT THE MOST IMPORTANT contribution of Leon Morris to New Testament scholarship is his study of the vocabulary of atonement. His careful linguistic scholarship provides the exegetical foundation for a systematic statement of the meaning of the death of Christ, and the work of subsequent scholars has shown that the foundation is essentially secure. For example, his discussion of the meaning of the ἱλάσκομαι word group, in which he demonstrated that it refers to propitiation rather than to expiation,[1] has been confirmed by the work of R. Nicole and D. Hill.[2] Similarly, his interpretation of the terminology of redemption,[3] though open to some correction, is essentially sound, and there is not much more to be said on the matter.[4] Since, however, his treatment is concerned mainly with the *linguistics* of the word group, there is room for a consideration of the *concept* of redemption in the New Testament, tracing its origins and development.[5] Our aim will be to discover how the concept is used by Luke, by Paul and other writers, by the writer to the Hebrews and by Jesus, and then to frame a hypothesis regarding the development of the usage.

I

Like many other terms in New Testament theology, the concept of redemption has its roots in the Old Testament. The divine act of deliverance from Egypt became the 'type' for understanding God's future acts of salvation for his people. In Luke 24.21 the disciples 'clearly are using "redeem" in the typically Jewish manner of the long awaited intervention by Almighty God when his power would free his people from all their enemies and bring in a period of blessing and prosperity'.[6] This Jewish hope finds further expression in Luke 1.68 where God redeems his people by delivering them from the hand of their enemies, a thought which is not purely material in content, for in the same context there is reference to the forgiveness of sins (Luke 1.77). Similarly, in Luke 2.38 the author himself speaks of those who were awaiting deliverance for Jerusalem; the phrase should be taken with Luke 2.25 where Simeon is said to be waiting for the comfort of Israel, and behind both phrases should be seen Isaiah 52.9: 'For the Lord has comforted his people, he has redeemed Jerusalem'.[7] What is of significance is that this redemption is linked to the coming of the Messiah, the 'horn of salvation . . . in the house of his servant David' (Luke 1.69). Deliverance requires a deliverer; just as Moses was called a deliverer (Acts 7.35),[8] so Jesus is the deliverer, and the role ascribed to God in the Old Testament is transferred to him.[9] For Luke this hope of deliverance has been actually fulfilled in the coming of Jesus.[10]

Elements of future redemption are also to be found. In Acts 3.19-21 there is a reference to future times of refreshing and the establishment of 'all that God spoke by the mouth of his holy prophets from of old', a phrase which gives a verbal link with Luke 1.70. Thus the future completion of salvation is tied to the person of Christ who is to come again. The link between past and future redemption is to be found in the person of Christ rather than in an implicit reference to the cross.[11]

This leaves Luke 21.28 for consideration. The verse has no parallels in the other versions of the apocalyptic discourse, and the vocabulary and style are distinctively Lucan.[12] Although, therefore, the verse may be based on a source other than Mark, it appears to be a Lucan formulation,[13] and the idea of redemption here should be discussed against the background of Luke's thought. The reference is to the deliverance of God's people from the tribulation and distress of the last days by the coming of the Son of man (cf. 1 En. 51.2). It is noteworthy that Luke here uses the compound ἀπολύτρωσις, whereas in his other references he uses the simple forms. The compound form is found only once in the LXX (Dan. 4.32, with no Hebrew equivalent). It seems likely that normally Luke has used the common LXX terminology, but here he has used a word which was in fairly common Christian use.[14] The difference in terminology may simply be due to Luke's source (if he had one), but it may also be intended to reflect a distinction between the redemption inaugurated and achieved by the first coming of Christ and the final redemption consummated by his second coming.[15]

To sum up: Luke takes up the Old Testament idea of deliverance from tribulation by Yahweh and finds it fulfilled typologically in Jesus Christ who fulfilled Jewish hopes by his incarnation, suffering and entry into glory and who will bring about final redemption and 'times of refreshing' at his second coming. The language is that of Old Testament piety, and there is little reflection over the means of redemption.

II

A much more concrete use of the terminology is found elsewhere in the New Textament, especially in Paul. There are some grounds for thinking that Galatians is the earliest of the Pauline Epistles.[16] In 3.13 and 4.5 Paul uses ἐξαγοράζω to describe the action of Christ in redeeming believers. The word is found with this sense only here in the New Testament, and it has no background in LXX usage. The fact that the usual terminology of redemption has an Old Testament background makes the choice of word here all the more significant, and suggests that Paul had some definite reason for it.

The picture is one of release from a state of slavery under the law or the 'elements' (Gal. 4.3f.), as a result of which men are under the curse of the law (Gal. 3.10). The curse is pronounced upon those who fail to keep the law (Gal. 3.13) and consists in the sentence of death. But Christ has delivered men from the curse by himself being crucified, since to be crucified is a sign of standing under the curse of the law (Deut. 21.23). The verb used indicates that a purchase has taken place, leading to the release of slaves. The idea of 'cost' is definitely present. So also is the idea that a ransom or 'price' has been paid. A background may be sought in Old Testament ideas of the redemption of a life that is forfeit by a payment of money,[17] but in this case it is the life of another man that is the ransom. If we are right in seeing the notion of 'price' here, there remains the problem of the recipient, and there can be no doubt that it is God, if anybody, who receives the ransom.[18]

As a result of this act, men are justified (Gal. 3.8, 11); they receive the gift of the Spirit (Gal. 3.14; 4.6), and they are set free from slavery to become the free sons of God (Gal. 4:5-7; cf. 5.1).[19] Thus the accent lies on the deliverance of sinners and their entry into freedom, and the metaphor used is that of the ransoming of slaves.[20]

In 1 Corinthians 1.30 Paul uses the same kind of abstract language as in Galatians 3.13 (Christ becoming 'a curse', i.e., accursed) by speaking of Christ becoming 'our wisdom, our righteousness and sanctification and redemption'. The use of 'wisdom' arises from the context (1 Cor. 1.18ff.), but the reason for the introduction of the other terms is less obvious.[21] It seems probable that Paul has utilized a set of familiar concepts in order to make the meaning of wisdom clearer. For Paul true wisdom is associated with the cross and its effects. It is significant that righteousness and redemption occur together in Galatians 3.22 and also in Romans 3.24. Paul does not give any further explanation of these terms, and hence it may be concluded that they were familiar to his readers from his preaching. They all clearly refer to what Christ means in the present time to his people (cf. the use of ἐγενήθη). A redemption achieved by the cross is clearly indicated, although the precise content attaching to the word is no longer clear to us.

A fresh term is used in 1 Corinthians 6.20; 7.23 in what is evidently another stereotyped phrase, no doubt so familiar to the readers that this brief allusion was an adequate means of expression:[23] ἠγοράσθητε τιμῆς. The implication is that previously believers served themselves and men. Now they have been bought for a price, a word that suggests that an irrevocable trans-action has taken place,[24] and that can refer only to the death of Christ. Consequently, they belong to God, so that paradoxically they are God's slaves and yet at the same time his freedmen (1 Cor. 7.22).[25] The emphasis, however, is not on deliverance leading to freedom, but on purchase leading to slavery.[26]

The concept of redemption here is found in the Old Testament and Ju-daism[27] but also stands close to secular analogies. A. Deissmann compared the process to sacral manumission whereby a slave was purchased from his earthly master by a god and thus became the fictitious property of the god.[28] The analogy is highly suggestive, but it has come under attack, In the com-mercial sphere the price was actually paid by the slave himself to the god who then used it to buy the slave from his master, but in Paul it is Christ who pays the price; moreover, the slave was only in a fictitious sense the property of the god—the point of the transaction being that he no longer had an earthly master—but the Christian is the slave of God in a real sense. These differences may be readily admitted, but they are in no way a decisive ob-jection to the use of this metaphor.[29] A preacher would surely have delighted to point out the differences between sacral manumission and Christian re-demption, and especially to contrast the price paid by the slave in the secular world with the free gift of God in Christ.[30]

W. Elert has proposed that a different idea may be present, namely, *redemp-tio ab hostibus*.[31] In the ancient world the normal fate of prisoners of war was to become slaves, but it was possible for them to be released and returned to their native land on payment of a ransom by a fellow-citizen. The freedman stood under certain obligations to the person who had redeemed him, as a *libertus* to his *patronus*, until he had paid back the cost of his ransom.[32] So the Christian has been delivered from bondage to an enemy by Christ and now stands under obligation to him.

It is difficult to make an exclusive choice between these two possible backgrounds. Nor, in the present case, should one rule out the further possibilities of ordinary (non-sacral) manumission or even of simple sale of a slave from one master to another.[33] Thus it may be wrong to look for one specialized background to the New Testament concept of redemption; rather, the general concept of manumission forms the background, and different aspects of it contribute to the detailed understanding of the various New Testament passages. What is important is that along with the Old Testament background this secular background is certainly present, so that redemption in these passages is to be thought of in terms of change of ownership as a result of payment of a price. Whereas in Galatians the rationale of the price in relation to the former state of the Christian is clear, in 1 Corinthians the former state of the Christian has retreated into the background, and the stress is now on the payment of the price as a sign that the Christian now belongs to a new master.

This stress on redemption as a change of ownership rather than as simply the setting free of slaves lived on. It is present in 2 Peter 2.1 where Christ is described as the slave-master (δεσπότης; cf. Jude 4) who has purchased Christians for himself.[34] But the most important development is in Revelation where a series of references (1.5; 5.9; 14.3f.) take up the idea. The verb ἀγοράζω is used in 5.9 to describe the act of Christ in purchasing Christians from every race[35] for God. Here again the thought of service to God is expressed, notably in the idea of men as priests (Rev. 1.6, 5.10) and as an offering of first-fruits to God (Rev. 14.4).[36] At the same time, however, the release of Christians from sin (Rev. 1.5)[37] and their privilege of reigning (Rev. 1.6; 5.10) are stressed.

The association here of redemption with release from sin is based on Psalm 130.8: 'And he will redeem Israel from all his iniquities'.[38] The means is the death of Christ. The verb used, σφάζω, conveys the sense of a sacrificial offering (cf. Rev. 6:9 with reference to the martyrs),[39] especially since Jesus is presented as the lamb who is slain (Rev. 5.6, 12; 13.8). This introduces us to the fundamental point that redemption is accomplished by the offering of a sacrifice.

At first sight the collocation of redemption and sacrifice appears to indicate a confusion of imagery. In fact it is strongly rooted in the Old Testament and Judaism. The following three factors are relevant: 1. The death of the Passover lambs was seen as an element in the redemption of Israel from Egypt: 'May we eat there of the sacrifices and of the passover-offerings whose blood has reached with acceptance the wall of thy Altar, and let us praise thee for our redemption and for the ransoming of our soul' (Pesahim 10.6).[40] Hence J. Jeremias comments: 'As once the blood of the Passover lambs played a part in the redemption from Egypt, so by the atoning power of His blood He has accomplished redemption . . . from the bondage of sin . . .'[41] 2. L. Morris claims that the Hebrew verb _kipper_ often has the denominative sense 'to offer a _koper_'. Atonement is thus made by the payment of a ransom or the offering of a gift to Yahweh.[42] Admittedly the way in which atonement and ransom are here brought together is not the same thing as the idea of redemption by the offering of a sacrifice, but it shows that the two ideas were closely associated in the Hebrew mind. 3. The thought of the deliverance of Israel from its sin and its consequences by the death of the martyrs, conceived as a propitiatory offering to God, developed in Judaism and is to be seen in 4 Maccabees 17.22.

This complex of ideas lies behind the imagery in Revelation. Jesus is the slain lamb, and we should probably think of him as specifically the Passover lamb.[43] He is also described as 'the faithful witness' (Rev. 1.5), a phrase which implies his death as well as his testimony by word of mouth.[44] Hence the comparison of Jesus' death to that of a martyr and its understanding in sacrificial terms has already taken place. We have moved beyond the simple idea of a commercial ransom price to the Jewish concept of redemption by means of a sacrificial offering to God.

It follows that the phrase 'by his blood' in Revelation 1.5; 5.9 must be understood in sacrificial terms, just as in 4 Maccabees 17.22. It expresses the 'cost' of redemption[45] in terms of laying down of life, and the 'price' is paid to God, if to anybody.

We are moving in the same circle of ideas when we turn to 1 Peter 1.18 where the readers are told that they were redeemed from their former (sinful) way of life not with silver and gold but with the precious blood of Christ, as of a lamb without blemish or spot. Again the thought of deliverance from a past state of captivity and entry into sonship is linked to that of belonging to God (1 Pet. 2.9) and rendering him service. Martyrological ideas are not explicitly present here, and Christ's death is compared directly to that of a sacrificial lamb. In all probability the Passover lamb is meant,[46] and this is confirmed by the presence of other Exodus terminology in the Epistle.[47] The verb λυτρόω takes us into the realm of Old Testament ideas, especially the deliverance from Egypt.[48] The greatness of the sacrifice thus rendered by Christ ought to move the readers to godly fear (1 Pet. 1.17), and the contrast with silver and gold[49] shows that the idea of a ransom 'price' is well to the fore.

The same thought of believers becoming the possession of God through redemption is found in Acts 20.28 where we read of the Church of God which he obtained (περιποιέομαι) with the blood of his own One.[50] The verb is found in the LXX, but it translates a variety of Hebrew words, none of which is closely connected with redemption.[51] But the corresponding noun, περιποίησις, is used in stereotyped phraseology to signify Israel as Yahweh's special possession.[52] As Israel became God's special people at the Exodus, so he has acquired the Church to be his people. That this is indeed the background may be deduced from the use of the noun in 1 Peter 2.9; in both passages we may see the influence of Isaiah 43.20, and it seems that a piece of imagery traditional in the church is being used (cf. Titus 2.14). J. B. Bauer has linked the concept of redemption here with that of the covenant whereby God made Israel his people.[53]

Ephesians 1.14 now claims our attention. There are two main ways of understanding the passage. Some hold that it speaks of the way in which believers have received the Spirit as an earnest or foretaste (v. 14a) of the inheritance which will become fully their possession at the future day of full redemption (Eph. 4.30).[54] Others argue that it refers to the way in which believers have been sealed with the Spirit (v. 13) as the sign that God will one day enter upon full possession of the property which has already become his. There is little doubt that this second view is better. It alone does justice to the background of the term περιποίησις; it fits in neatly with the idea of the saints being God's portion (Eph. 1.11) whom he purposes to make holy (Eph. 1.4) in order that his glory may be praised (Eph. 1.14).[55] There will thus be a day of final redemption when God enters into full possession of his people.

It must be noted, however, that this future sense is not the primary one in Pauline thought. The idea is of the completion of an act already begun by God's sealing of believers with the Spirit; the same is true in Romans 8.23 where it is those who already possess the first-fruits of the Spirit who look forward to the redemption of the body. The point is strengthened by the fact that here the promised redemption is equated with divine sonship which, as we have already seen, was the gift of God to believers when they were justified and redeemed from the curse of the law (Gal. 4.5-7). For the believer future redemption means the deliverance of the body from the corruption and pain of the world into the glorious freedom of the children of God (Rom. 8.18-22); for God it means the completion of the process whereby believers become his possession.

In none of the passages just discussed is redemption directly related to the death of Christ; the thought is primarily of deliverance, and neither the agent nor the means is stated. Nevertheless, the use of the term forces us back to a consideration of that which is primary in Pauline thought, namely, the redemption already wrought by Christ and received by believers.

We come finally in this section to the passages in which Paul uses the term ἀπολύτρωσις in connection with the cross. We have already seen that 1 Corinthians 1.30 should be interpreted of the redemption already achieved by Christ, although the meaning of the term is not spelled out in any detail. In Romans 3.24 Paul explicitly applies it to the cross in a context which is so closely similar to Galatians 3 that we are justified in considering the one passage in the light of the other, and hence seeing ἀπολύτρωσις here as in some sense equivalent to ἐξαγοράζω in the earlier passage. The context in Romans 3 is one of universal sinfulness and liability to judgement, inability to keep the law, and the impossibility of being saved by the law anyhow. The thought of being in bondage under the law is not expressed here (see, however, Rom. 6.15), and it is the idea of slavery to sin which is to the fore; men are under bondage to sin (Rom. 7.14; cf. 6.16-23) and hence to death.[56] Their need is justification, and this is made possible, as in Galatians 3, by means of an act of redemption. Justification is provided freely by divine grace; there is nothing for us to pay (δωρεάν), from which we may conclude that the cost has been borne by God. Redemption is secured 'in Christ', that is, by God's action in him, and the means is his being offered as a propitiation by his blood. The language here is close to the martyrological terminology in 4 Maccabees 17.21, which D. Hill thinks may have directly influenced Paul.[57] Hence the death of Christ, viewed as that of a martyr, is expounded in sacrificial terms,[58] redemption being secured by means of the offering of a sacrifice through which sin is forgiven and men are delivered from its power.[59] The 'cost' of redemption is thus the death of Christ, seen as the gift of divine grace, and the 'price' of it is the sacrificial offering made to God. Thus we find again the paradox that the redemption terminology can be used to express a 'cost' borne by God and an offering or 'price' made to God.

The question arises whether Paul is here using a traditional formulation upon which he has superimposed his own comments.[60] Opinions vary regarding the precise content of such a formulation. As we have seen, similar ideas are expressed by Paul himself in Galatians 3 but the fact that here he uses the term ἀπολύτρωσις rather than ἐξαγοράζω suggests that he is using a piece of traditional terminology; again the fact that he does not need to explain the meaning of ἀπολύτρωσις in 1 Corinthians 1.30 indicates that a familiar idea is being used. There is, however, no good reason for believing that the term 'redemption' had a different meaning in its pre-Pauline use from that which Paul himself assigns to it; the use of the word here fits in with the general pattern of thought which we have already discovered in 1 Peter and Revelation, as well as with Paul's own usage in Galatians 3. Hence, if traditional formulations are being used here, this is evidence for the early currency of the idea of redemption, but not for the existence of a concept different in content from the Pauline one.[61]

Two Pauline passages remain for consideration, Colossians 1.14 and Ephesians 1.7. In Colossians 1.14 redemption is linked with deliverance from the power of darkness into the Kingdom of God's Son,[62] but it is stressed that redemption is to be equated with the forgiveness of sins.[63] It is thus a present possession of believers (ἔχομεν), and it is linked to a concept which is closely related to justification. But, as in Romans 3.24, the thought of redemption is mentioned in passing, and Paul moves on to the idea of reconciliation by means of the blood of the cross. If vs. 15-20 form part of a pre-Pauline hymn,[64] then Paul's introduction of the reference to the blood of the cross in v. 20 may be more closely related to the idea of redemption—as is certainly the case in Ephesians 1.7 where redemption is directly linked to the blood of Christ. The parallels elsewhere justify us in regarding the blood as a reference to the sacrificial death of Jesus; it indicates the cost of redemption, especially since the grace of God is also mentioned in the context (cf. Rom. 3.24), and it also indicates the 'price' paid to God in terms of sacrifice.[65] It is against this background that the idea of future redemption in Ephesians 1.14 should be seen; it refers to the consummation of what has already been achieved.

III

The Epistle to the Hebrews uses the concept in two passages. In 11.35 we read of the martyrs who refused to accept deliverance for themselves in order that they might attain to a better resurrection. The word thus relates to deliverance from death and the captivity which was associated with it at the 'cost' or 'price' of denying their faith. Here the elements of 'cost' and 'price' are clearly present, although the use is obviously metaphorical.

The other passage is 9.11ff. Christ entered into the 'holy place' above, like the high priest on the day of atonement, not with the blood of animals but with his own blood and 'found' eternal redemption.[66] Similarly, the writer says that a death has taken place for the redemption of sins (9.15). Here redemption is closely associated with the forgiveness of sins; believers are delivered from their sins, that is from their penal effects.[67] The means of deliverance is the death of Christ, 'blood' being clearly used in a sacrificial sense. As in 1 Peter 1.18, any thoughts of martyrdom have passed completely into the background, and the idea of redemption has been fully assimilated into the author's sacrificial thinking. The influence of other ideas tradition-ally associated with redemption may be seen in the references to the covenant and inheritance (9.15). The idea of the 'mediator' may also form part of this traditional complex in view of its reappearance in 1 Timothy 2.6.

Hebrews shows us an individual development of the idea of redemption in which it is closely linked with the sacrificial ritual of the tabernacle (rather than with the Passover sacrifice, as in Revelation and 1 Peter). It shows the continuing strength of the idea, although to some extent it has lost its original force.

IV

The 'ransom' saying of Jesus (Mark 10.45)[68] reappears in 1 Timothy 2.6 in a text which has been demonstrated to be a less Semitic form of expression[69] It has become one of the fixed formulae used by the author of the Pastoral Epistles, and he offers us his own further interpretation of the text in Titus 2.14. In 1 Timothy 2.6 Christ acts as mediator between God and man,[70] and performs his task by giving himself as a ransom for the lives of all. His death is an offering to God and serves as a ransom payment to free all men from death and so to reconcile them to God. The author's understanding of this is made clearer in Titus 2.14 where the word ἀντίλυτρον is replaced by ἵνα λυτρώσηται, using language based on Psalm 130 (129 LXX).8 (cf. Rev. 1.5). Men are thus delivered from lawlessness, that is, they receive forgiveness and deliverance from the power and penalty of sin, and they are cleansed in order to become God's special people (λαὸς περιούσιος); hence the redemption has the effect of purchasing men to be the property of God. All this is achieved by Christ who is described as 'Saviour', thus linking the concept of deliverance with the closely associated one of salvation.[71] The further linking of redemption with cleansing suggests that behind the author's thought lies the idea of the sacrificial blood of Christ which liberates and cleanses men (cf. Heb. 9.12-14).

Behind these developments lies the simpler wording in Mark 10.45 in which Jesus serves men by giving his life as a ransom for many. Mark no doubt intends the saying to be seen against the background of 8.37 where the question is raised whether a man can give any exchange for his life. Behind the question lies Psalm 49 (48). 7-9: 'Truly no man can ransom himself, or give to God the price of his life, for the ransom of his life is costly, and can never suffice, that he should continue to live on for ever, and never see the Pit'. What man cannot do has been done by Christ. We are surely justified in discerning here the thought of human mortality as the result of human sin, and in seeing in the death of Christ the ransom 'price' paid to God[72] for the redemption of mankind from death.[73] We may also see here a reference to the death of the Suffering Servant which benefits the 'many' when he makes himself an offering for sin.[74] The saying may thus contain a sacrificial idea, since the ransom is an offering to God for the lives of others, and the intermediate link may be found in the idea of martyrdom.[75]

V

It is time to draw together the threads of our discussion and see whether we can sketch the development of the idea of redemption more precisely.

In his book on the atonement in the New Testament, E. Lohse has argued that the theology of the earliest Church regarding the death of Christ is to be found in the kerygma in 1 Corinthians 15.3-5; the 'sayings of the Lord' in Mark 10.45 and 14.24; the formal statements based on these; the use of the term 'blood'; and the comparison of Jesus with the Passover lamb. Behind these various uses Lohse finds the influence of Isaiah 53. He claims that the oldest form of the cup-saying omitted the reference to the covenant and spoke of the death of Jesus in terms of Isaiah 53 as the giving of his life for many. Originally the thought was not sacrificial, but referred to the atoning death of the Servant. Then at a very early stage the thought of the covenant was attached to the saying, and hence the blood of Jesus was interpreted in terms of the covenant sacrifice.[76]

Whatever be the truth regarding the details of this description, there is sufficient substance in it for us to build upon it and to claim that in this material available to the early Church we have the necessary and sufficient presuppositions for the development of the concept of redemption. The decisive point is the association of Mark 10.45 with 14.24, an association that lay easily to hand in their common dependence on Isaiah 53. This association would be all the easier if Mark 10.45 were also linked with the Lord's Supper.[77]

From Mark 10.45b a direct line leads to the formal expressions in the Pastoral Epistles. The saying itself speaks of the martyr death of the Servant, and hence gave rise to (a) sayings that speak of Christ giving himself or handing himself over (John 6.51; Gal. 1.4; 2.20; Eph. 5.2, 25; cf. 'laying down one's life', John 10.11, 15, 17f.); (b) sayings that interpret the death of Jesus as having the atoning power of a martyr's death (Rom. 3.24).

The association with Mark 14.24 brings in the idea of the blood of Christ, again taken in a martyrological sense. Again two lines of thought develop: (a) Paul uses the idea of manumission to express the idea of redemption in a more tangible form, perhaps especially for Christians in the Hellenistic world. The same idea is found in Revelation and 1 Peter. (b) Once the martyr death of Jesus has been seen to have atoning power, the way lies open for a further understanding of it in terms of the Jewish sacrificial system. This operated in three ways: (i) Sacrificial ideas (ἱλαστήριον) were already bound up with the idea of martyrdom (4 Macc.; Rom. 3.24); (ii) The concept of the covenant, already associated with the cup-saying, led to the understanding of the death of Jesus in terms of the sacrifices associated with the Exodus, namely, the sacrifice of the Passover, which in Jewish thought wrought redemption for Israel, and also the covenant sacrifice (1 Pet. 1.2); (iii) The death of Jesus was associated with the sacrificial ritual of the tabernacle on the day of atonement, and this sacrifice was thus regarded as a means of redemption.

The motif that does not fit into this development is the concept of a still future redemption (Luke 21.28; Rom. 8.23; Eph. 1.14; 4.30). This may serve as a warning against trying to force the evidence into one rigid pattern.[78] It is best to see here a development from the Jewish idea of eschatological redemption, quite distinct from the Christian idea based on the theology of the cross. It takes two forms. In Luke the eschatology is seen to be essentially 'realized' in the coming of Jesus, and hence this idea of redemption can be easily linked to the main line of development. But the thought of a future redemption also persisted, though in a specialized sense, and it plays a modest part in New Testament thought; again, however, the terminology leads to the future redemption being seen to some extent in the light of the past redemption at the cross.

On this view, Mark 10.45 represents the simplest form of the concept and lies at the base of the development. The saying is free from ideas of blood, covenant, sacrifice and manumission, but depends on Isaiah 53, a text which is not taken up elsewhere in the development. Again, the saying undoubtedly comes from the earliest tradition of the Church, as is shown by its Semitic form and the fact that it has been handed down as a Son of man saying; there is in fact good reason to argue that it is an authentic saying of Jesus.[79]

It may be objected that the influence of Mark 10.45 is attested only in the Pastorals, and that Paul's terminology is different. In fact, however, Paul's choice of ἀπολύτρωσις, a word with no significant precedent in the LXX, and other associated words, suggests that the λύτρον saying lies at the root of the development. Paul's vocabulary expresses the result of Christ's death rather than its character, and this fits in with New Testament thought in general, which is more concerned with the nature of salvation than the precise way in which it has been achieved. Moreover, if ἀπολύτρωσις is a traditional term in Paul, this pushes the date of the entry of the idea into Christian theology still earlier.[80]

Thus the concept of redemption is to be traced back to the teaching of Jesus[81] and has undergone a rich development, leading to its use with various shades of meaning and in different associations of thought. It is one of the most frequently used categories of interpretation of the death of Jesus in the New Testament and excellently expresses its meaning. We may cordially agree with L. Morris: 'In the Scripture we see the price paid, the curse borne, in order that those who are redeemed should be brought into the liberty of the sons of God, a liberty which may paradoxically be called slavery to God. The whole point of this redemption is that sin no longer has dominion; the redeemed are those saved to do the will of their Master'.[82]

Notes

[1]L. L. Morris, *The Apostolic Preaching of the Cross* (London, 1955), pp. 125-85; the third edition (1965[3], pp. 144-213), incorporates his article 'The Meaning of Ἱλαστήριον in Romans iii.25', *NTS*, 2, 1955-56, pp. 33-43.
[2]R. Nicole, 'C. H. Dodd and the Doctrine of Propitiation', *WTJ*, 17, 1954-55, pp. 117-57; D. Hill, *Greek Words and Hebrew Meanings* (Cambridge, 1967), pp. 23-48. The opposite view was defended by C. H. Dodd, ' Ἱλάσκεσθαι, its cognates, derivatives and synonyms in the Septuagint', *JTS*, 32, 1931, pp. 352-60, reprinted in *The Bible and the Greeks* (London, 1935), pp. 82-95.
[3]Morris, op. cit., pp. 9-59 (3rd. edn. references are added in brackets, here 11-64); 'The Vocabulary of Atonement 1. Redemption', *Themelios*, 1.1, 1962, pp. 24-30.
[4]Following the example of B. B. Warfield ('Redeemer' and 'Redemption', *PTR*, 14, 1916, pp. 177-201; 'The New Testament Terminology of Redemption', *PTR*, 15, 1917, pp. 201-49 (both essays reprinted in *The Person and Work of Christ* [Philadelphia, 1950], pp. 325-48, 429-75; the latter also in *Biblical Foundations* [London, 1958] 199-245); art. 'Redemption' in *HDAC*, II, pp. 302-9), Morris is particularly concerned to show that the terminology of redemption invariably conveys the idea of release on payment of a price or ransom. He concludes: 'Both inside and outside the New Testament writings the payment of a price is a necessary component of the redemption idea. When the New Testament speaks of redemption, then, unless our linguistics are at fault, it means that Christ has paid the price of our redemption' (*The Apostolic Preaching of the Cross*, p. 58 [61]).
While this view of the extra-biblical evidence is correct (cf. Hill, op. cit., p. 52; E K. Simpson, *Words worth weighing in the Greek New Testament* [London, 1946], pp. 8f.), it is not quite true for the Old Testament. Although the meaning of *koper* (and λύτρον) is uniformly that of a payment which secures release, this is not always the case with the verbs *ga'al* and *padah*. Hill (op. cit., pp. 62f.) has rightly observed that they are sometimes rendered into Greek by words which simply indicate release and deliverance (e.g. ῥύομαι). This is particularly the case when Yahweh is the subject and the theme is the deliverance of his people. Here there is often reference to the mighty power which Yahweh displays in order to deliver his people, but this is in no sense a price.
We would suggest that the discussion has been befogged by a failure to define terms. Morris implies that 'price' and 'cost' are synonymous: 'there is reference to price in the insistence that Yahweh's redemption is at the cost of the exertion of His mighty power' (op. cit., p. 19 [26]). It would be more precise to use the term 'price' for those cases where some *payment* or exchange is *received* by the person from whom the captive is delivered, and to use the term 'cost' for whatever *expenditure* of money, life and effort is *demanded* on the part of the redeemer; obviously 'price, and 'cost' will often coincide, but it is possible to have 'cost' without payment of a 'price'.
One should perhaps also distinguish more clearly between the meanings of words and of concepts. Thus Isaiah 52.3 expressly states that Israel will be ransomed without money (cf.

Isa. 45.13). Here the word 'ransom' is used in a context which denies that Yahweh pays any kind of price for the deliverance of his people from their enemies; rather, he forcibly sets them free by the exercise of his power.

It may be failure to make this distinction clearly which leads to Morris's strange comment on Luke 24.21, where he admits in effect that there was a Jewish expectation of divine deliverance which did not lay any stress on the payment of a price; but, he goes on, 'the passage is not of first importance for our purposes; for clearly a redemption rendered impossible by the cross can tell us little about the redemption effected by the cross' (op. cit., p. 35 [38f.]). D. Hill rightly objects that the consideration adduced here is irrelevant to the meaning of the word as used here (op. cit., pp. 67f.). The passage may say nothing about the cross, but it does show that the word 'redeem' may be used without the idea of price being present. In fact, however, the passage does say something about the cross, for so far from the text showing that the expected redemption was 'rendered impossible by the cross' it indicates that it was rendered possible precisely by the suffering of the Messiah (Luke 24.26). The cross and resurrection are the means of redemption, although the ideas of 'price' and 'cost' do not appear to be present or to receive any stress.

⁵Cf. D. Daube, *The New Testament and Rabbinic Judaism* (London, 1956), pp. 268-84; J. D. M. Derrett, *Law in the New Testament* (London, 1970), pp. 389-460 (with bibliography).

⁶Morris, op. cit., p. 35 (38).

⁷Cf. H. Schürmann, *Das Lukasevangelium*, I (Freiburg, 1969), p. 135.

⁸Moses is so described in the Samaritan *Memar Marqah* 1.4 and in rabbinic sources from AD 300 onwards; parallelism between Moses and the Messiah is found earlier; cf. J. Jeremias, *TDNT*, IV, p. 860.

⁹In the Old Testament the redemption of Israel is always ascribed to Yahweh and not to any other figure.

¹⁰The aorist in Luke 1:58f. should he taken literally and not as equivalent to a prophetic perfect (Schürmann, op. cit., pp. 86f.)

¹¹Cf. F. Büchsel's comment on Luke's use of λύτρωσις: 'The reference is not to a ransom but to a redeemer' *(TDNT*, IV, p. 351).

¹²Note the use of the genitive absolute (H. Schürmann, *Der Paschamahlbericht* [Münster, 1953], p. 94); ἀνακύπτω is found elsewhere in the New Testament only in Luke 13.11 (narrative) and John 8.7, 10; ἐπαίρω occurs six times in Luke and five times in Acts; διότι occurs three times in Luke and five times in Acts, never in the other Gospels; ἐγγίζω occurs eighteen times in Luke, six times in Acts, seven times in Matthew and three times in Mark.

¹³The verse is regarded as belonging to a non-Marcan source by L. Gaston, 'Sondergut und Markusstoff in Lk. 21', *Th.Z*, 16, 1960, pp. 161-72; T. Schramm, *Der Markus-stoff bei Lukas* (Cambridge, 1971), pp. 180f. The linguistic considerations above, however, show that any source has been revised by Luke, and it must remain open whether the use of ἀπολύτρωσις is due to the source or to Luke himself.

¹⁴In Paul the use of ἀπολύτρωσις appears to be traditional; see below.

¹⁵Elsewhere in the New Testament, however, the same word is used for both aspects of redemption.

¹⁶F. F. Bruce, 'Galatian problems. 4: The Date of the Epistle', *BJRL*, 54, 1971-72, pp. 250-67. Even if this dating is questionable, Galatians should certainly be placed before Romans; it may be dated after 1 Corinthians, but this point does not greatly affect our argument.

¹⁷The first-born of men were redeemed (Exod. 13.13; 34.19f.) by the consecration of the Levites to God and the payment of a ransom price (Num. 3.44-51; cf. 8.16-19); a ransom was payable by all Israelites at a census (Exod. 30.11-16).

¹⁸It is improbable that the elements are the recipients of the ransom, since Paul's thought is basically related to the law rather than to the elements.

¹⁹At this point the terminology of redemption is linked to that of liberation and freedom: cf. Romans 8.21; 1 Corinthians 7.22f.; Galatians 5.1, 13; Romans 6.18, 22; 8.2; John 8.32, 36

(H. Schlier, *TDNT,* II, pp. 487-502).

[20]Cf. Diodorus Siculus 36.2.2: ἐξηγόρασεν αὐτήν . . . ταλάντων Ἀττικῶν ἑπτά.

[21]J. Bohatec has claimed that the four terms in v. 30 correspond to those in vs. 27f. ('Inhalt und Reihenfolge der "Schlagwörte der Erlösungsreligion" in 1 Kor. 1, 26-31', *Th.Z,* 4, 1948, pp. 252ff., as reported in H. Lietzmann and W. G. Kümmel, *An die Korinther I,* II [Tübingen, 1949], p. 169).

[22]It is curious that words associated with the third member of the set (ἁγιασμός) are entirely absent from Galatians.

[23]T. Holtz, *Die Christologie der Apokalypse des Johannes,* TU 85 (Berlin, 1962), p. 67.

[24]A. Deissmann, *Light from the Ancient East* (London, 1910), p. 329, notes how in sacral manumission it is expressly forbidden that the enfranchised may be re-enslaved.

[25]Although Paul is here speaking of two groups of people who have their status reversed when they become Christians, both groups are simultaneously free and slaves on a spiritual level, since the ἀπελεύθερος owes a certain duty to the κύριος (cf. C. K. Barrett, *The First Epistle to the Corinthians* [London, 1968], p. 171).

[26]Thus ἀγοράζω is used of simple purchase, ἐξαγοράζω of a purchase that leads to freedom.

[27]Isaiah 43.1; cf. Daube, op. cit., pp. 272-84.

[28]Deissmann, op. cit., pp. 322-34.

[29]Cf. H. Lietzmann, *Die Briefe des Paulus I* (Tübingen, 1910), p. 257.

[30]A number of further details form evidence that sacral manumission helps to provide the background to the New Testament statements. Deissmann (op.cit.) notes: 1. The association of a sacrifice with the act of manumission; 2. the phrase ἐπ' ἐλευθερία (Gal. 5.13, cf. 1) in the records of manumission; 3. the fact that slavery could be for debt shows the affinity between redemption and remission or forgiveness.

[31]W. Elert, 'Redemptio ab Hostibus', *Th.LZ,* 72, 1947, pp. 265-70.

[32]F. Lyall, 'Roman Law in the Writings of Paul—The Slave and the Freedman', *NTS,* 17, 1970-71, pp. 73-79 also notes the duties of a freed slave to his *patronus,* but states that the slave's former master was his *patronus.* But it seems unlikely that this Roman practice provides the background to Paul's thought, since the believer's duty is to the new *patronus* who has bought him, not to the old master from whom he has been released; Paul's point is that the old relationship has entirely ceased.

The term ἀπελεύθερος may be understood as equivalent to the Latin *libertus* (or *libertinus*), a 'freedman' owing service to his manumitter as his *patronus.* Lyall is thinking of a process in Roman law whereby a master might release his slaves. It is more likely that sacral manumission or *redemptio ab hostibus* is in Paul's mind.

[33]However, simple sale from one master to another is unlikely, because the new status is one of freedom and not simply of a change of master.

[34]The background of δεσπότης as a master of slaves is described clearly enough by K. H. Rengstorf *(TDNT,* II, pp. 44-9), but he fails to make use of it in explaining the present text, and hence finds the association of ἀγοράζω with δεσπότης surprising.

[35]The ἐκ is partitive, and does not indicate the owner from whom Christians have been delivered.

[36]In the Old Testament the first-fruits are specially dedicated to God for use in his service; hence the thought of dedication to his service is probably present here also.

[37]In a paper read at the meeting of the Catholic Biblical Association in Los Angeles in 1972, Miss E. Fiorenza defended the view that Revelation 1.5 represented a traditional formula and Revelation 5.9 the seer's reworking of it. If this view is correct, it shows that the use of λύω to express release from sin is early.

[38]λύω is also used with reference to sin in Job 42.9; Isaiah 40.2 and Sir. 28.2, but in these cases it is the sin which is 'released', i.e., pardoned, and not the person who is released from the sin; F. Büchel, *TDNT,* IV, p. 336, n. 8.

[39]It can be used non-sacrificially of murder or the slaughter of animals. In Revelation 6.9 the death of the martyrs is compared with the slaughter of sacrificial animals whose blood flows

frons the altar (O. Michel, *TDNT,* VII, pp. 934f.).

[40]Even if the annual Passover offering was not regarded as atoning in effect, the original Exodus Passover offering and the eschatological Passover were so regarded (J. Jeremias, *The Eucharistic Words of Jesus* [London, 1966], pp. 225f.; E. Lohse, *Märtyrer und Gottesknecht* [Göttingen, 1963], p. 142). However, it is possible that by New Testament times all sacrifices were regarded as having expiatory power to some extent (Morris, op. cit. [3rd edn.], pp. 131f.).

[41]J. Jeremias, *TDNT,* I, p. 340.

[42]Morris, op. cit., pp. 143-52 (161-70); cf. BDB s.v.; Hill, op. cit., p. 32. F. Büchsel *(TDNT,* IV, p. 341) shows that in rabbinic thought a ransom is an expiation for sin (see b.Bab.Kamm. 40a, cited in SB III, 644).

[43]Paul regards Jesus as the Passover (lamb) (1 Cor. 5.7) and 1 Peter 1.18 should be interpreted in the same way; the same allusion may also be meant in the Johannine tradition (John 1.29, 36), although Morris, op. cit. (3rd edn.), pp. 129-43, points out the weaknesses of this interpretation. Other ideas may well have been drawn into the concept in Revelation, but this one alone seems sufficient to explain the sacrificial imagery.

[44]Holtz, op. cit., pp. 55-7.

[45]Holtz, op. cit., p. 64; Morris, op. cit., p. 51 n. (55 n.).

[46]The description of the lamb as 'unblemished' (ἄμωμος) and 'spotless' (ἄσπιλος) is, however, not sufficient to identify it as the Passover lamb, since the former adjective is used freely of various offerings.

[47]See the references to the sprinkling of blood in 1.2 and to loins girt in 1.12. Paschal imagery has been found more widely by F. L. Cross, *1 Peter: a Paschal Liturgy* (London, 1954), but the picture has been overdrawn.

[48]Exodus 6.6; 15.13; Psalms 76 (77).15; 105 (106).10; Isaiah 63.9; Deuteronomy 7.8; 9.26 and frequently.

[49]Observe the same contrast between money and divine provision in Acts 3.6.

[50]The text is uncertain, Some MSS have 'the church of the Lord' (i.e., Christ), but this looks like an attempt to avoid the difficulty, There is in fact no difficulty about taking τοῦ ἰδίου to mean 'of his own One' (MH I, pp. 90f.); alternatively, one may supply ὁ Χριστός as the subject of περιεποιήσατο (Lohse, op. cit., p. 180 n.).

[51]περιποιέομαι most frequently translates *ḥayah* with the meaning 'to preserve alive' (ten times) and *ḥamal* 'to have compassion on'. It also translates 8 other roots, including the noun *segullah* 'property', 1 Chronicles 29.3.

[52]περιποίησις is found three times; it translates *segullah* at Mal. 3.17. This Hebrew word is more frequently rendered in the LXX by the adjective περιούσιος (Exod. 9.15; Deut. 7.6; 14.2; 26.18; Ps. 135.4; Eccles. 2.8).

[53]J. B. Bauer, *Encyclopaedia of Biblical Theology* (London, 1969), II, pp. 738-41. Note the link with the idea of the covenant in Hebrews 9.15, and the association of Moses with redemption in Acts 7.35.

[54]RSV; T. K. Abbott, *Ephesians and Colossians* (Edinburgh, 1922), pp. 23f.; M Dibelius and H. Greeven, *An die Kolosser, Epheser an Philemon* (Tübingen, 1953), pp. 62f.; H. Schlier, *Der Brief an die Epheser* (Düsseldorf, 1957), p. 39; cf. F. Büchsel, *TDNT,* IV, p. 353.

[55]NEB; Morris, op. cit., p. 57 (60); J. A. Robinson, *The Epistle to the Ephesians* (London, 1922), pp. 147-9; J. Gnilka, *Der Epheserbrief* (Freiburg, 1971), pp. 86 f.; cf. BAG, s.v. ἀπολύτρωσις. Gnilka observes that the former view requires that something be read into the text.

[56]O. Michel, *Der Brief an die Römer* (Göttingen, 1957), pp. 91f.

[57]Hill, op. cit., pp. 41-8.

[58]F. Hahn *(Der urchristliche Gottesdienst* [Stuttgart, 1970], p. 53, n. 29) has argued that the concept of sacrifice is applied to the death of Jesus only in Ephesians 5.2; 1 Peter 1.19 and Hebrews: 'the presentation as an atoning death ("for us") must not be equated with this, since it is based on a non-cultic atonement tradition'. Even, however, if the death of Jesus is understood in terms of the atoning effects of the martyr's death, the theology of martyrdom

had already applied the terminology of sacrifice to the death of the martyr. Hence Hahn's conclusion is erroneous.

[59]H. Lietzmann, *Die Briefe des Paulus,* I (Tübingen, 1910), p. 19, emphasizes that ἀπολύτρωσις should be taken here in its full sense to signify 'loskaufen', and should not be weakened to mean simply σωτηρία. K. Kertelge *('Rechtfertigung' bei Paulus,* Munster, 1971, pp. 48f.), claims that the passage is to be understood against the background of the covenant and the Old Testament usage of 'redemption' which signifies the eschatological deliverance wrought by God for his people in order that the covenant may be restored; Paul has taken over this concept from a traditional formulation and widened its meaning in order to indicate the free justification of all men by grace. It is unnecessary to bring in Hellenistic ideas of manumission in order to explain a biblical concept. Similarly, F. Büchsel *(TDNT,* IV, pp. 354f.) holds that no real idea of ransom is present here.

This view is to be rejected: 1. ἀπολύτρωσις is hardly a biblical term, since it occurs only in Daniel 4.34 LXX. 2. The biblical idea of redemption itself retains the metaphorical sense of deliverance *from slavery* in Egypt. 3. In the present context the notion of the cost of deliverance is present in the use of δωρεάν. 4. Whatever be the traditional formula which Paul is using (see next note), the present passage must be understood against the background of Galatians 3.13 and 2 Corinthians 5.14-21; in the former of these passages the idea of redemption at the cost of the death of the redeemer is clearly present, and it is quite impossible that this idea should be absent from the parallel passage in Romans (cf. Paul's use of αἷμα!). Kertelge has failed to take the significance of this earlier, parallel passage into account.

[60]See especially the discussion in Kertelge, op. cit., pp. 48-62, 71-84; also R. Bultmann, *Theology of the New Testament,* I (London, 1952), p. 46; E. Käsemann, 'Zum Verständnis von Römer 3, 24-26', *ZNW,* 43, 1950-51, pp. 150-4; K. Wegenast, *Das Verständnis der Tradition bei Paulus und in den Deuteropaulinen* (Neukirchen, 1962), pp. 76-80; P. Stuhlmacher, *Gerechtigkeit Gottes bei Paulus* (Göttingen, 1966), pp. 86-91; H. Thyen, *Studien zur Sünden vergebung* (Göttingen, 1970), pp. 163-72. There is general agreement that one may isolate a pre-Pauline formula more or less as follows: 'being justified by the redemption which is in Christ Jesus, whom God set forth as a propitiation by his blood to show his righteousness through the remission of past sins in the forbearance of God.' On this view the terms 'justified', 'redemption', 'propitiation' and 'blood' are from pre-Pauline tradition. 'Redemption' is then understood as in the previous note.

It seems doubtful to me whether we can delineate the content of the pre-Pauline formula so precisely, and whether we can indeed speak of a formula at all. For some proponents of this view, 'justified' is a pre-Pauline concept; thus Stuhlmacher (op. cit., p. 219) claims—without offering any evidence—that δικαιόω is pre-Pauline in Romans 3.24; 5.9; 6.7; 8.30 and 1 Corinthians 6.11. The indications are rather that 'to justify' in the sense of 'to forgive' was introduced into Christian theology by Paul (cf. Thyen, op. cit., p. 164). At most we can speak of a use of pre-Pauline phraseology in which some important concepts were beginning to be brought together.

It is noteworthy that 'blood' appears frequently in the context of redemption (Acts 20.28; Eph. 1.7; Heb. 9.12; 1 Pet. 1.18; Rev. 1.5; 5.9). It has been argued that the term 'blood' found its way into Christian theology through the influence of the Lord's Supper formulae; covenant associations are also present there. Hence it has been suggested (Käsemann, op. cit.) that the present formula is to be traced back to the Lord's Supper. The association of blood and covenant may well have led to a further link with the idea of redemption as part of an Exodus typology; see below.

[61]See n. 59.

[62]Here the verb ῥύομαι becomes associated with the concept of redemption, although the association is not very close. The verb is used in a very similar way to the words at present under consideration to express various forms of deliverance. There is no suggestion of cost or price in the usage; the accent falls on the dangers from which God delivers men in order

that they may enter into salvation. Cf. W. Kasch, *TDNT,* VI, pp. 998-1003.
⁶³The question arises as to why 'redemption' is glossed by 'forgiveness of sins'. J. B. Lightfoot
(*Colossians and Philemon* [London, 1886], p. 141) drew attention to later Gnostic perversions
of the concept so that it was equated with initiation into mystical secrets; he suggested that
some similar perversion at Colossae may have made it necessary for Paul to define the term
more closely. C. F. D. Moule *(Colossians and Philemon* [Cambridge, 1957], p. 58) suggests
that the Colossians may have held 'fancies about "escape" into immortality without a corresponding change of character'. This view might be supported by reference to the pregnostic
heresy reflected in 1 Corinthians, 1 John and 2 Peter, according to which the practice of sin
and immorality was thought to be compatible with claims to the possession of the Holy Spirit
and the experience of salvation.
⁶⁴Most reconstructions of the hymn assumed to underlie this section of Colossians start from
v. 15 and do not include v. 14 (see E. Lohmeyer and W. Schmauch, *Die Briefe an die Philipper,*
Kolosser und an Philemon [Göttingen, 1964], pp. 47-55; E. Lohse, *Colossians and Philemon*
[Philadelphia, 1971], pp. 41-6). If vs. 15-20 are based on such a hymn, then Paul's thought
of redemption in v. 14 and his addition to the hymn of the words 'by his blood' in v. 20 may
perhaps be linked more closely to each other. Further, the concepts of redemption and reconciliation arc brought together, being linked by the common idea of the means involved,
namely, the death of Christ viewed sacrificially.
⁶⁵Hill (op. cit., pp. 73f.) has objected that the phrase διὰ τοῦ αἵματος αὐτοῦ can hardly refer
to a price paid for redemption, since 'the shedding of blood is hardly to be regarded as the
price paid for the release from sins'. He is no doubt correct in asserting that the phrase
indicates 'means' rather than 'price', but the objection seems pedantic: the New Testament
evidence as a whole shows a close association between the ideas of redemption and sacrifice,
just as in the Old Testament atonement and 'ransom-price' are closely linked. We, therefore,
prefer the exegesis of F. F. Bruce (*The Epistle to the Ephesians* [London, 1962], p. 31) at this
point.
⁶⁶M. McNamara, *Targum and Testament* (Shannon, 1972), p. 139, draws attention to a parallel
to the phrase "eternal redemption" in Ps.Jon. (Gen. 49.18).
⁶⁷The genitive is one of separation.
⁶⁸The wording in Matthew 20.28 is identical, with ὥσπερ replacing καὶ γάρ.
⁶⁹J. Jeremias, 'Das Lösegeld für Viele (Mk. 10.45)', in *Abba* (Göttingen, 1966), pp. 216-29,
especially pp. 225f. Thyen (op. cit., p. 158) admits the Semitic colouring, but claims that it
does not establish the priority of Mark 10.45 over against 1 Timothy 2.6. On the contrary,
the secondary use of 'Son of man' and the use of ἦλθεν, which presupposes the Hellenistic
μεσίτης concept, indicate that Mark 10.45 is the later form. These arguments are to be
rejected. The first rests on a blanket rejection of the Son of man sayings (op. cit., p. 156) which
is totally unjustified; it is possible in any case to argue for the authenticity of Mark 10.45b
as a saying of Jesus as an independent logion separate from v. 45a. Nor does the use of ἦλθεν
speak against authenticity: cf. J. Jeremias, *New Testament Theology* I (London, 1971), p. 293,
n. 6; 'Die älteste Schicht der Menschensohn-Logien', *ZNW,* 58, 1967, pp. 159-72, especially
pp. 166f.
⁷⁰The verse should perhaps be taken as an expression of the divinity and humanity of Christ
(rather than as a two-member credal statement): 'There is one who is God, one who is also
(καί) the mediator between God and man, the man Christ Jesus.' Thus the mediatorial office
of Christ depends on his double qualification as God and man. In favour of this view is the
way in which in the parallel passage, Titus 2.13f., the writer can speak of 'the glory of our
great God and Saviour, Jesus Christ' (not 'the great God and our Saviour Jesus Christ').
⁷¹See especially Romans 5.9; Philippians 1.19; Hebrews 5.7; James 5.20; 1 Peter 4.18; Jude 5;
W. Foerster and G. Föhrer, *TDNT,* VII, pp. 965-1024.
⁷²F. Büchsel, *TDNT,* IV, p. 344. The arguments of Lohse (op. cit., p. 121, n. 3) to the contrary
fail to convince.

⁷³F. Büchsel *(TDNT,* IV, p. 343) stresses that the deliverance is from sin rather than merely from death.

⁷⁴The influence of Isaiah 53 is rejected by Thyen, op. cit., pp. 158-60, but he is unable to demonstrate that it is impossible. On the other side, see R. T. France, 'The Servant of the Lord in the Teaching of Jesus', *Tyndale Bulletin,* 19, 1968, pp. 26-52, summarized in *Jesus and the Old Testament* (London, 1971), pp. 116-21.

⁷⁵We have utilized Mark 8.37 to help elucidate the meaning of Mark 10.45 in its Marcan context. Some such background must be presupposed for the saying in its original setting.

⁷⁶Lohse, op. cit., Pt. 2.

⁷⁷In its present context Mark 10.45 appears in an ethical context unconnected with the Lord's Supper. But the parallel tradition in Luke 22.24-27 does appear in a Supper tradition, and hence it is possible that the tradition in Mark 10.42-45 was originally linked to the Supper. On the other hand, some scholars regard Mark 10.45b as an isolated saying, about whose origin it is difficult to be certain.

⁷⁸This warning also holds good for the attempt to see the element of 'price' in every, or almost every, use of the phraseology. We have been able to observe in the course of our study that this element is not universally present. In a number of cases the idea is that of 'cost' rather than 'price'. Nevertheless, when this *caveat* has been observed, it remains true that in about half of the texts the element of 'cost' or 'price' is fairly explicit. No less than seven times is redemption associated with the blood of Christ, and in a further four cases with his death.

⁷⁹See France, op. cit.

⁸⁰The other formative element in the redemption tradition, namely the cup-word at the Last Supper, is also of early date, as is seen in its attestation by Paul in 1 Corinthians 11.25.

⁸¹So also W. Mundle (with J. Schneider and L. Coenen), *TBNT,* I, pp. 258-72, especially p. 263.

⁸²Morris, op. cit., p. 59 (62). [1989] At the time of writing this essay I was unaware of E. Pax, 'ΕΠΙΦΑΝΕΙΑ Ein religionsgeschichtlicher Beitrag zur biblischen Theologie', *Antonianum,* 37, 1962, pp. 239-78, which disputes strongly the relevance of sacral manumission for understanding redemption in the New Testament and stresses the importance of the Old Testament and Jewish material. Pax appears to have made out his case that the terminological differences from sacral manumission are significant, but it still remains possible to use this concept as a useful illustration to explain the significance of Christian redemption. For a very detailed recent study of the whole topic, see W. Haubeck, *Loskauf durch Christus. Herkunft, Gestalt und Bedeutung des paulinischen Loskaufmotivs* (Giessen, 1985). The study by A. J. Hultgren, *Christ and His Benefits. Christology and Redemption in the New Testament* (Philadelphia, 1987), has a somewhat wider scope.

14
The Meaning of 'Reconciliation'

IT IS ONE OF THE MANY MERITS OF GEORGE E. LADD'S *A THEOLOGY of the New Testament* that he devotes a substantial section to a consideration of the Pauline use of the category of reconciliation as a means of expressing the significance of the action of God in Jesus.[1] Of all the concepts used to explain the effects of the cross, 'reconciliation' is the one that (along with 'forgiveness') belongs most clearly to the sphere of personal relationships, although it is also used in the language of diplomacy. Other categories express the significance of the cross more in terms of relations between legal parties (justification) or of commercial dealings (redemption) or of cultic ritual (sacrifice). 'Reconciliation', however, is a term used in interpersonal relationships. Unless, therefore, we regard the use of the term 'person' of God as metaphorical, we must claim that this is the least metaphorical and most concrete of the ways in which the new relationship of God to men is expressed.

In view of the aptness of its usage, it is mildly surprising that the word-group is used theologically only by Paul and is not taken up by any other writers,[2] although it is just possible that Paul inherited its use from earlier Christians. The terminology is not taken up by second-century writers,[3] and thus remains distinctive of Paul. Its origins remain unexplained: the word-group is not used in a theologically significant manner in the LXX, although it is found in the Apocrypha. One of the words used by Paul, ἀποκαταλλάσσω, appears in fact to be a new coinage. We may compare the way in which Paul also uses a largely non-Septuagintal vocabulary to express the concept of redemption, although he supplements this non-biblical element with material drawn from the LXX.

These considerations suggest that a brief examination of some features of this concept merits inclusion in a *Festschrift* honouring George Ladd that has as its theme unity and diversity in the New Testament. Here is a distinctively Pauline way of presenting the significance of the cross. At the same time the topic certainly demands further research. It is a remarkable fact that most discussions of the concept have explored the means of reconciliation, the effects of reconciliation, and the question whether men are reconciled to God or vice versa, but little has been said about the actual *meaning* of the words involved. Perhaps some light can be shed on this point and others regarding the significance and source of Paul's language.

I

The Greek verb διαλλάσσω is found once in the New Testament (Matt. 5.21).

1. It can be used in the active form to refer to the action of a mediator who persuades two quarrelling groups or persons to abandon their enmity toward one another (Xenophon, *Oeconomicus* 11.23; *Historia Graeca* 1.6.7; Plato, *Phaedo* 60c; *Symposium* 213d).

2. It can also be used in the active form to refer to the action of a person in persuading his enemy to abandon his enmity and treat him peaceably. Josephus relates how Machaeras killed some partisans of Herod, who retaliated by accusing him to Antony. Machaeras, realizing his errors, pursued the king, and by means of entreaties succeeded in pacifying the king (*Jewish War* 1.16.7 § 320).

3. In the passive form the verb can describe how an offended person gives up his enmity. In 1 Esdras 4:31 we are told of a concubine who could twist the king's little finger: 'When she laughed at him he laughed; when she was cross with him he coaxed her to make it up' (NEB), i.e., he coaxed her to stop being cross with him.[4] Josephus speaks of God in this way. He was angry with Israel over their treatment of the Gibeonites, and revealed through prophets that if the Gibeonites were allowed to exact satisfaction for the way in which Saul had massacred them, then he would be reconciled to Israel and would cease to express his anger by afflicting them (*Antiquities* 7.12.1 § 295). Similarly, when David confessed and wept over his sin in the matter of Uriah the Hittite, God took pity on him and was reconciled to him (*Ant.* 7.7.3 § 153). Josephus can describe God as one who is easily reconciled by the repentant (εὐδιάλλακτος, *J. W.* 5.9.4 § 415). The picture is of a God who is angry with men because of their sins, but whom they can persuade to put away his anger and cease afflicting them, i.e., to be reconciled to them.

4. Finally, we have the use in 1 Samuel 29.4 LXX. Here the leaders of the Philistines are unwilling that David, who has deserted Saul and attached himself to Achish, should accompany them to battle against Israel. They fear that David is still an Israelite at heart, and when he sees his former friends he will desert to them. But if he does so, David will need to ingratiate himself with Saul, who is angry with him. 'With what will this fellow reconcile himself to his master?' they ask; 'Will it not be with the heads of those men?' They recognize that only the heads of some dead Philistines will be an adequate appeasement for David to offer to Saul and thus to placate him. The significant point is that the verb is used in the passive (i.e., deponently) of David taking the initiative in reconciling Saul to himself. This gives the same meaning as in case 2. above. Here the verb does not refer to David giving up any hard feelings that he has against Saul, but rather to David's persuading Saul to give up his anger. The result will be the establishment of friendly mutual relations, but the verb refers specifically to the persuasion effected on Saul.[5]

It is this same deponent use which confronts us in the one New Testament example of the verb (Matt. 5.24). A man who is on his way to make an offering to God remembers that his brother has something against him; the brother is angry with him, although we are not told whether the brother's anger was justified or not. In such a situation the man must first go and 'be reconciled' to his brother. The passive form here is clearly in the same sense as the active, namely, of taking the action necessary to induce the brother to give up his anger and so to create friendly relations. There is no suggestion that the man himself was angry with his brother and needed to put away his own hard feelings. But where a state of enmity exists, he must go and take whatever action is needed to bring it to an end.[6]

II

By New Testament times the verb καταλλάσσω was becoming more common than διαλλάσσω,[7] but it has the same range of meanings:

1. It can be used in the active of a mediator persuading two warring sides to give up their enmity and hatred. Herodotus describes how 'Periander, son of Cypselus, reconciled the Mityleneans and Athenians, for they referred to him as arbitrator; and he reconciled them on these terms, that each should retain what they had' (Herodotus 5.95).[8] Josephus uses the noun καταλλάκτης of Moses in his role of interceding for the people with God and persuading God to spare them the continued punishment of wandering in the wilderness (*Ant.* 3.15.2 § 315).

2. The verb does not seem to be used in the active form of one person

persuading another to give up his anger against him.

3. In the passive, deponent form, the verb can refer to the action of one person in persuading another to give up his anger against him. This appears to be the meaning in a passage in Plato concerning a tyrant who 'is reconciled' to some of his enemies and destroys others of them, so that one way or the other peace results *(Republic* 8.566e).[9]

4. The passive can also be used of the offended person who is persuaded to give up his anger.[10] When God rejected Saul as king, Samuel entreated God to be reconciled to Saul and not be wroth with him. 'But God would grant no pardon to Saul at the prophet's request, accounting it not just to condone sins at the intercession of another; for nothing more favoured their growth than laxity on the part of the wronged, who in seeking a reputation for mildness and kindness are unwittingly the begetters of crime' *(Ant.* 6.7.4 § 144). To be reconciled to someone is to be willing to forgive or overlook their offence. In the same way Josephus records how David was petitioned to be reconciled to his son Absalom and let his anger toward him cease *(Ant.* 7.8.4 § 184).[11]

5. The verb can be used with a direct object (or perhaps an accusative of respect) to refer to the offences concerning which reconciliation needs to be made. Herodotus describes how the factious Greeks determined 'that, before all things, they should reconcile all existing enmities and wars with each other' (Hdt. 7.145).[12]

The corresponding noun καταλλαγή can refer to the act of being reconciled *(Ant.* 7.9.1 § 196) or the state of reconciliation (2 Macc. 5.20).[13]

A particularly important set of references is to be found in 2 Maccabees. The book opens with a mandate, or official letter, from the Jews in Jerusalem to their compatriots in Egypt. In the opening prayer or expression of good wishes the authors pray: 'May he open your hearts to his law and his precepts, and give you peace. May he hear your prayers and be reconciled with you, and not abandon you in time of evil' (2 Macc. 1.5 JB). The thought is that God will respond to the prayers of the Jews by overlooking their sins. But of particular interest is the story of the martyrdom of the seven brothers at the hands of Antiochus for their loyalty to their ancestral religion. The brothers interpreted their sufferings as being partly the divine punishment for their own sins (2 Macc. 7.18) but also as a means of inducing God to forgive the nation for its sin and apostasy. The seventh brother declares that he is 'calling on God to show his kindness to our nation and that soon, and by trials and afflictions to bring you to confess that he alone is God, so that with my brothers and myself there may be an end to the wrath of the Almighty, rightly let loose on our whole nation' (2 Macc. 7.37-8). It is against this background that we are to understand the earlier comment of the same young man: 'We are suffering for our own sins; and if, to punish and discipline us, our living Lord vents his wrath upon us, he will yet be reconciled with his own servants' (2 Macc. 7.32-3).

To complete the picture, two further passages should be considered. The first is in 2 Maccabees 5.11-20, where Antiochus is allowed by God to enter the temple and desecrate it without suffering any harm, in contrast to the face of Heliodorus, who experienced a supernatural punishment (2 Macc. 3.24-8). The writer explains that Antiochus 'did not realize that the Lord was angry for the moment at the sins of the inhabitants of the city, hence his unconcern for the Holy Place' (2 Macc. 5.17). Afterwards, 'the place itself, having shared the disasters that befell the people, in due course also shared their good fortune; forsaken by the Almighty in the time of his anger, it was reinstated in all its glory, once the great Sovereign had been reconciled' (2 Macc. 5.20). The other incident takes place after the defeat of Nicanor by Judas Maccabeus, when the victors 'joined in public supplication, imploring the merciful Lord to be fully reconciled with his servants' (2 Macc. 8.29).

The general picture that emerges is clear and consistent. The view of the writer of 2 Maccabees is that when the people fall into sin and apostasy they arouse the wrath of Yahweh. He proceeds to punish them, and on the completion of the punishment his anger is satisfied and he is reconciled to the people. But the experience of punishment may lead the people to pray to Yahweh to be reconciled to them and to give up his anger, and Yahweh may respond to such prayers. Even more powerful is the action of the martyrs who, while recognizing that their sufferings and death are primarily for their own sins, beseech God to accept their suffering as being on behalf of the nation and to be reconciled to the nation as a whole. In short, God is reconciled, that is, abandons his anger, as a result of the prayers of the people and their endurance (in themselves or their representatives) of the punishment which he inflicts upon them. Men act in such a way as to induce God to be favourable to them. These ideas are expressed with even greater clarity in 4 Maccabees 7.28-9; 17.22.[14]

III

The verb καταλλάσσω occurs six times in Paul (Rom. 5.10 [bis]; 1 Cor. 7.11; 2 Cor. 5.18, 19, 20).[15] The noun καταλλαγή is found four times (Rom. 5.11; 11.15; 2 Cor. 5.18, 19). Paul also uses the verb ἀποκαταλλάσσω three times (Eph. 2.16; Col. 1.20, 22). There is one secular example of the usage. This is in 1 Corinthians 7.11, which gives Paul's advice to a wife who has left her husband; she is either to remain unmarried or else be reconciled to her husband. Since the discussion is about a wife who takes the initiative in leaving her husband, it is to be presumed that she feels offended by him and in her indignation separates from him. She is now urged to take the initiative by laying aside her feeling of offence and seeking the restoration of friendly relations and the resumption of the marriage relationship. The passive form is used of the wife no longer being bitter against her husband. But the secondary thought of persuading the husband to lay aside any hard feelings he may have can also be present: 'you cannot run off and leave me, and then just come back when you choose,' may be his reaction. So the thoughts of the wife's putting aside her own wounded feelings and also of persuading her husband to abandon any such feelings on his part may both be present, and the action is complete only when friendly mutual relations are restored.[16]

It has long been noted that in the two main doctrinal passages in Romans 5 and 2 Corinthians 5 the passive form of the verb is not used with God as the subject, whether in the passive or the deponent sense. Nor is the active form used with God as the object. This in itself strongly suggests that it is God who takes the initiative in the act of reconciliation. Further, it is generally accepted that God's act of reconciliation takes place prior to, and independently of, any human action: it was while we were still sinners that we were reconciled to God. Paul speaks of 'the reconciliation' as something that we have received. All this suggests that the act of reconciliation is primarily something done by God. Nevertheless, the verb is also used in both passages in the passive form with men as the subject, and the question arises whether this is a real passive or a deponent usage.

If we start from the earlier passage chronologically, namely, 2 Corinthians 5, we observe that Paul arranges his material in a twofold pattern, with a repetition of the same twofold thought in the second part:

18. All this is from God,
    A^1 who through Christ reconciled us to himself
    B^1 and gave us the ministry of reconciliation
19. that is,
    A^2 God was in Christ reconciling the world to himself,
        not counting their trespasses against them,
    B^2 and entrusting to us the message of reconciliation.

These thoughts are then repeated a third time, in inverse order:

20. B^3 So we are ambassadors for Christ,
       God making his appeal through us.
       We beseech you on behalf of Christ, be reconciled to God.
21. A^3 For our sakes he made him to be sin who knew no sin,
       so that in him we might become the righteousness of God.

The effect of this structure is to show that for Paul the total act of reconciliation on God's side is in two parts. There is the act of reconciliation in Christ, and there is the ministry of reconciliation which consists in the proclamation of this prior act of God in Christ and the declaration of the message, which is then finally specified as an appeal to men to be reconciled to God on the basis of the prior act of God in Christ. Manifestly the act is completed only when there is a human response to the imperative demand to be reconciled.

We have, then, three statements of the divine act of reconciliation which took place prior to the appeal to men to be reconciled to God and which is proclaimed in the appeal to men. Two of the statements elucidate what this meant. The first declares that God does not count the trespasses of men against them, and the second that God made Christ to be sin for us in order that we might be made righteous. Against the background of thought which we have explored, particularly in 2 Maccabees, it follows irresistibly that the picture is of a God who is offended by the sins of men and acts in wrath and judgement against them. But now because of what Christ has done in identifying himself with their sin, God regards them as righteous and no longer holds their sins against them. When Paul says that God has reconciled us to himself, the meaning is thus that God has dealt with the sins which aroused his wrath and that there is no barrier on his side to the establishment of peace and friendly relations.[17] Three important points are made: first, the putting away of God's wrath against human transgressions was achieved by what Christ did; the earlier part of the passage speaks of his dying on behalf of men, and the final verse speaks of his becoming sin for us.[18] It is hard to understand this in any other way than that in dying Christ exhausted the effects of divine wrath against sin. Second, the action that took place 'in Christ' was the action of God himself who purposed that action (v. 21) and who himself acted in Christ.[19] Although Christ may be regarded as a 'third party' who intervenes between God and man, yet here in 2 Corinthians 5 it is clearly God who is the subject (vs. 18, 19). Third, the object of the action is described both as 'the world' and as 'us' (vs. 19, 18). The 'world' is understood in a personal sense as the totality of mankind; this is shown by the use of 'them' in verse 19b to refer back to 'world'. If 'world' can have a wider meaning in Paul, this is certainly not consciously in mind here.

'God reconciles the world to himself' thus means: God acts in Christ to overlook the sins of mankind, so that on his side there is no barrier to the restoration of friendly relations. The message of the Christian preacher is a declaration of this fact. It is first and foremost a gospel, a declaration of the good news of what God has done. Hence it can speak of 'reconciliation' as an accomplished fact. But at the same time the indicative forms the basis for an imperative. Now people are commanded: 'be reconciled to God'. In view of what God has already done, this cannot be understood to mean that they must render God amenable to them by appropriate action. Rather God and Christ appeal to them to accept the fact that reconciliation has been accomplished and to complete the action by taking down the barrier on their side— the barrier of pride and disobedience and hatred of God. Let them put away their feelings against God and enter into a new relationship with him. And this is possible because of the fact that God is willing to regard them as righteous despite their sin. The total action of reconciliation is thus incomplete until there has been acceptance of God's grace (2 Cor. 6.1) on the human side as men are reconciled to God. It is no doubt significant that the active sense of the verb is not used for this human action, because there is no need to reconcile a God who has reconciled the world to himself. The form 'be reconciled' could have a deponent sense, with reference to human putting away of enmity. Possibly, however, the verb is best understood as a passive: put yourself into the position of those whom God has reconciled. There is little to choose between these alternatives.

The second Pauline passage is Romans 5.10-11. The thrust of the section Romans 5.1-11 is to show that Christians who have been justified by faith can have sure and certain hope regarding their future acceptance by God at the day of judgement. Paul makes his point by arguing that if God showed such love to men while they were sinners as to send his Son to die for them, he will all the more save those who are now his friends at the day of judgement. Those who have been justified are now in a state of peace with God (v. 1). Consequently, having been justified by the blood of Christ while they were still sinners (v. 8), they will all the more be saved by Christ from the final wrath of God. This point is then repeated in different terminology. Those who were reconciled to God while they were still his enemies by the death of his Son will all the more be saved by his life. The parallelism between the two statements is very close:

	10. For if
8. while we were yet sinners	while we were enemies
Christ died for us.	we were reconciled to God
	by the death of his Son
9. Since, therefore,	
	much more,
we are now justified	now that we are reconciled,
by his blood,	
much more	

shall we be saved by him   shall we be saved by his life.
from the wrath of God.

It follows that Paul equates the states of sin and enmity, and also that he identifies the death of Jesus for sinners, by virtue of which they are justified, with the reconciliation of God's enemies by the death of his Son. The death of Christ is the basis for God's act of justification which takes place when men believe in Christ, and it is itself the act of reconciliation which becomes effective for men when it is preached to them and they accept it. The difference is that Paul does not speak of God justifying the world in the death of Jesus, but rather of God justifying individual men now on the basis of the redemption and propitiation which took place in the death of Jesus; but he does speak of God reconciling the world to himself in the death of Jesus, and thereby making it possible for individuals to accept the reconciliation. While he can say to men, 'Be reconciled', he cannot say, 'Be justified'. But these are unimportant differences, and they merely demonstrate that we are dealing with two very similar but not identical ideas. The important point is again that reconciliation is an act of God prior to and independent of any abandonment of enmity to God on our part, accomplished by the One who stands closest to him as his Son. It would seem that the verb is again used in two senses, first in verse 10a of God reconciling men to himself (passive, of men),[20] and second in verse 10b of men who have actually entered into the state of reconciliation. The contrast is the same as that between 'Christ died for us' and 'being now justified'. No doubt the slight shift in meaning is awkward, but it is by no means intolerable. It is supported by the use of 'we have received the reconciliation' in verse 11, which suggests an existing gift to be received by us. There is certainly nothing here to cause us to modify our understanding of the use of the term derived from 2 Corinthians 5.

Paul uses the noun 'reconciliation' once more in Romans (11.15). In Romans 11.11-16 he is discussing whether the Jews have fallen away from Christ permanently. This he denies fervently. It was the falling away of the Jews that led to the extension of salvation to the Gentiles, and the effect of the latter will be to make the Jews envious and so turn to Christ. Then Paul comments rhetorically that if the fall of the Jews had such a glorious result as to enrich the world, how much more will their full turning to Christ produce glorious results. Their rejection led to the reconciliation of the world, and their acceptance will lead to resurrection from the dead. Paul's reference is thus to the act of reconciliation wrought in Christ which is effective for the world of mankind as a whole. He uses the concept of reconciliation, as elsewhere, to indicate the world-wide scope of salvation,[21] and the term itself is used in conscious contrast to the thought of God's rejection of unbelieving Israel. It is God who accepts the sinful world, overlooks its sin, and offers peace to it.

In order to complete the picture we must examine the two further passages where the terminology of reconciliation is used. In both of these passages the verb used is ἀποκαταλλάσσω, an unusual form apparently used here for the first time. It is often argued that Paul is using an existing hymn in Colossians 1.15-20,[22] although it should be carefully observed that the fact that the hymn may be earlier in date than the composition of Colossians does not necessarily mean that it is earlier than the composition of Romans 5 or 2 Corinthians 5. The use of the unusual word may reflect incorporation of a non-Pauline hymn, but it still leaves unanswered the problem as to why the unknown author chose to introduce this unusual word when Greek already possessed an ample vocabulary of reconciliation. The answer may be that the new compound stresses more the thought of the restoration of a previously existing relationship, and that it is formed on the analogy of ἀποκαθίστημι (Mark 3.5; 9.12; Acts 1.6; *et al.*; cf. ἀποκατάστασις, Acts 3.21).

Paul uses the verb in the context of God's creation of all things by and for his Son. God intended that the Son should have first place in all things, because God in his fullness resolved 1. to dwell in him (hence he is worthy to receive the same honour as God), and 2. to reconcile all things to him through him. It is thus as the agent of reconciliation that Christ is worthy to be first in the universe, but the thought is rather loosely attached and the causal connection is not to be pressed here.

Reconciliation is made possible by the fact that God has made peace by means of the blood of his cross. This symbolical language expresses the sacrificial character of the death of Jesus, and thus indicates again that reconciliation is possible on the basis of the appeasing of God's wrath by means of the sacrifice which he himself has provided in Jesus. The participle may be expressive of action prior to or coincidental with the action of the infinitive, and it should probably be taken in the latter sense. A completed work of reconciliation is in mind, as in the earlier references.

Nothing is said at this point about the circumstances that have produced the need for reconciliation, although the fact of sin is implied by the references to peace and to the sacrificial blood of Jesus. But what was implicit becomes explicit in the following section in which Paul applies the general principle to his readers. They in particular were at one time estranged from God and hostile to him because of their evil deeds. But now they have been the object of an act of reconciliation in the body of Christ's flesh by means of his death. The tremendous emphasis upon the physical character of the death is probably anti-docetic, although it is possible that the reconciled are envisaged as being united with Christ in his death. The fact that they were once enemies indicates that now they are thought of as being in the state of reconciliation, so that 'reconcile' here has the sense of the actual restoration of good relations. In verse 20, however, the thought is simply of God's provision of reconciliation for the world. The difference between the two uses of the verb is demanded by the fact that in verse 23 Paul implicitly states the terms on which reconciliation becomes a reality: it depends upon faith and acceptance of the gospel preached by Paul. If the Colossians are urged to continue in faith and hope, the implication is clearly that their reconciliation began with their act of faith and hope.

This point has important consequences for understanding verse 20 with its reference to the reconciliation of 'all things'. It remains true, as in 2 Corinthians 5, that the realization of reconciliation is dependent on acceptance of the gospel and faith, and therefore it is most improbable that any kind of universal salvation of all creation is taught here. The thought is surely that no powers on earth or in heaven can reconcile men to God, since they all needed to be reconciled themselves because of their rebelliousness and sin.[23] Hence Paul's stress is not so much on the fact of their reconciliation as on their own need for reconciliation which renders them unfit to mediate between man and God; only Christ can act as reconciler, and nobody else. If this suggestion is accepted, we are saved from desperate attempts to give 'reconcile' a sense other than it usually bears,[24] and Paul's teaching receives a natural interpretation in the light of the errors or possible errors that menaced his readers. There is no question of the reconciliation of inanimate nature, but rather Paul's thought is of the rulers and powers in verse 16.

The thought in Ephesians 2.16 is basically similar. The cosmic dimension is absent here, and Paul's thoughts are concerned more with the fact that the one act of reconciliation is effective in breaking down the barriers between both Jews and Gentiles and God. The twin thoughts of their reconciliation to one another and of both to God run through the passage as a whole. Paul's concept is of the Church as a new Israel; formerly the Gentiles were outside Israel (i.e., the old Israel), but now they have been brought into the new Israel through their faith in Christ and so into unity with those of the old Israel who have likewise put their faith in Christ. In verse 16 the thought is primarily of reconciliation to God, and Paul's point is simply that one act of reconciliation—in the one body of Christ—has reconciled both to God. Thereby human enmity—whether towards God or towards other men—has been 'slain'. Here again, therefore, the thought is of what was achieved by the cross, and the overcoming of enmity is very much to the fore. Nevertheless, the general context with its though of the new possibility of access to God (v. 18) and of the sacrificial blood of Jesus (v. 13) strongly suggests that 'reconcile' here has its normal sense of God's overlooking the sins which otherwise he would have had to judge in view of the cross of Christ.

IV

In the light of this discussion we may now try to draw some conclusions.

1. Our study of the secular Greek usage of the two words meaning 'to reconcile' showed that they could be used in four possible ways:

A. X persuades Y and Z to give up their mutual anger (active).

B. X persuades Y to give up Y's anger against X (active).

C. X persuades Y to give up Y's anger against X (passive/deponent).

D. X gives up his own anger against Y (passive).

Sense D is found in 1 Corinthians 7.11, and sense C in Matthew 5.24. Paul's usage, however, does not fit into any of these categories. He uses the active form of the verb to describe how God initiates friendly relations between himself and men by putting away the sin which aroused his own anger against them. The meaning given by the passive in sense D is expressed by the use of the active voice. Paul's use thus forms a new category:

E. X removes the cause of his own anger against Y, namely, Y's sin (active).

This use of the verb seems to be unprecedented in Greek usage, although I cannot claim to have made anything like an exhaustive survey of the material. We are bound to ask what led Paul to use the verb in this highly unusual, and apparently unique, manner.

We saw also that Paul uses the passive form of the verb to refer to human acceptance of God's act. This is close to sense D above, but the thought is less of men putting away *their* anger against God at some cost to themselves and rather of their entering into the new relationship which God himself has made possible. God and men are not equal partners in reconciliation, but the initiative is on his side, and it is his attitude to human sin which has to be dealt with before reconciliation is possible.

2. The verb has a broader and a narrower meaning in Paul. The narrow sense is found when 'God reconciles men to himself' means that he puts away the wrath which he has towards men and women on account of their sins so that there is no longer any barrier on his side to fellowship with them. The broad sense is found when 'God reconciles men to himself' means that God enters into the fellowship with men which the death of Jesus has made possible. There are consequently *three* stages in the process of reconciliation. First, there is the reconciling act of God in the death of Jesus. Second, there is the proclamation of reconciliation by the 'servants' of reconciliation. As

Bultmann rightly emphasizes, this proclamation is every bit as much a saving act as the death of Christ.[25] The news of what God has done must be proclaimed, and the challenge to respond must be made. Third, there is the acceptance of God's message by men, when they accept his act of reconciliation by faith, putting away any feelings that they hold against God. The process is not complete until all three stages have taken place and people have entered into peace with God. The scope of reconciliation is potentially the world, and this can be 'unpacked' in terms of Jews and Gentiles or of men and spiritual powers. Paul uses the verb in the active form five times with God (or Christ)[26] as the subject, and three times in the passive of persons who are the objects of God's reconciling work; when the passive is used in the imperative form, it begins to approach a deponent use, but it refers to accepting God's completed work of reconciliation, not to trying to appease God.

3. Paul uses the concept (a) most fully and thematically in 2 Corinthians 5 where it occurs in an appeal to the members of the Corinthian church not to receive God's grace to no effect by refusing to accept him as God's ambassador of reconciliation; (b) as a means of underlining the fact of assurance of final salvation for those who have been justified by faith (Rom. 5); (c) in the context of a proclamation of the supreme place of Christ as the one agent of God in creation and the renewal of creation (Col. 1); and (d) in an argument designed to show the oneness of Jews and Gentiles in the Church of God (Eph. 2).

The use of the language is perhaps most surprising in 2 Corinthians. Here Paul is primarily urging the Church to receive him as its pastor and to abandon its hostile attitude to him personally. In effect he is making the point that to reject him is to reject the God whom he serves in the gospel. To accept the gospel of reconciliation involves acceptance of the designated servant of reconciliation. But the language that Paul is using sounds much more like a description of the gospel message proclaimed to the non-Christian. Paul is here making use of the language of evangelism in order to call members of the Church to welcome him back personally as their spiritual father. If so, the original use of the language of reconciliation is to be found in the proclamation of the kerygma, and what Paul is describing is the gospel of the cross which he preached. This is confirmed by the usage in Colossians and Ephesians which is also descriptive of Christian conversion. Paul is thus putting the language of the kerygma to a secondary use, and it seems likely that the specialized application in both Colossians and Ephesians is secondary and represents a development of the original use. If so, it would follow that the original source of the language is not the 'pre-Pauline' hymn in

Colossians 1, but rather this represents a development of the ideas already present in 2 Corinthians 5, which in turn spring from the preaching of Paul.

This raises considerable doubts regarding the thesis of E. Käsemann that the language is drawn from a hymnic tradition, reflected in the citations in 2 Corinthians 5, and that the language was originally cosmological, the application to the individual being secondary.[27] Rather, the language is that of a credal or kerygmatic formula, and the individual application is there from the beginning.

It is uncertain whether Paul is quoting Pre-Pauline kerygmatic tradition in 2 Corinthians 5 or is citing his own preaching. The virtual absence of the terminology elsewhere in the New Testament is an argument from silence that the language is Paul's own,[28] and this is confirmed by the way in which it has been so thoroughly assimilated into his argument and made to express the essential Pauline doctrine of justification by grace through faith.

4. In looking for a background to Paul's teaching, we are struck by the fact that Paul always makes God the subject of reconciliation and that he interprets the verb in terms of God's laying aside of his wrath and judgement against mankind. This stands in marked contrast to the teaching of 2 Maccabees where men urged God to be reconciled to them and made an offering for their own sins to him and for the sins of the nation. It is tempting to suppose that Paul's teaching was formulated in conscious contrast to this Jewish attitude.[29] The evidence for Paul's use of 2 Maccabees is admittedly very thin,[30] but there is a good case that Paul was familiar with the martyr tradition which is expressed in 2 and 4 Maccabees and that he made use of it in his interpretation of the death of Jesus as an atoning sacrifice.[31] It would be very like Paul to develop the thought that atonement rests not on the act of men but of God, that God does not need to be appeased by men because he himself has provided an atonement for sin and so reconciled them to himself, and that this action avails not merely for the Jewish race but for all mankind through the work of the second Adam. The point is beyond proof, but there is a high degree of probability that the Jewish martyr tradition, which surfaces in this particular form in 2 Maccabees, has provided the catalyst to the development of Paul's use of the category of reconciliation.[32]

5. The concept of reconciliation has assumed a far more central place in Christian theology than might have been expected from its limited use in the New Testament. Paul's use of the term was sufficiently creative to produce a concept which has come to the forefront in theological thinking. By his new use of the terminology he made it clear that reconciliation is a term for what God as subject has done in relation to the world as object. But whereas in popular usage 'to reconcile Y to oneself' means 'to remove Y's grounds

for being offended', Paul uses the phrase to mean 'to remove Y's offence'. The offence in question is the sin of mankind which arouses the wrath of God and prevents him from entering into friendly relations with them; when the sin is removed or cancelled the reconciliation is achieved.

We can now see how those theologians who speak of God *being* reconciled have some justification for their language. They rightly recognize that a change has taken place on God's side. Formerly the world was the object of his wrath because of its sin. Now it is the object of his love. It is not, however, that God has changed his feelings, as if he had somehow to swallow his wrath. Rather, in the love that he has always had for the world he has given his Son to bear the consequences of the world's sin and so to remove the barrier caused by sin. God has thus dealt with the sin of the world, and in so doing has rendered his wrath inoperative against those who accept his act of reconciliation. Since the act involved the removal of sin and hence of God's wrath against sinners, it is perhaps permissible to speak loosely of God being reconciled. Nevertheless, it must be clearly recognized that this is not the New Testament usage of the term, and therefore it must not be used without due care. For Paul 'to reconcile the world to himself' means 'to remove the barrier caused by human sin which prevents him from entering into friendly relations with the world'.[33]

We can, therefore, understand what Charles Wesley meant and with a good conscience join him in singing:

Arise, my soul arise,
   Shake off thy guilty fears;
The bleeding Sacrifice
   In my behalf appears:
Before the throne my Surety stands,
My name is written on His hands.

My God is reconciled,
   His pardoning voice I hear;
He owns me for His child,
   I can no longer fear;
With confidence I now draw nigh,
And Father, Abba, Father! cry.[34]

But the last word belongs to John Calvin:
   Incomprehensible and immutable is the love of God. For it was not after we were reconciled to him by the blood of his Son that he began to love

us, but he loved us before the foundation of the world. . . . Our being reconciled by the death of Christ must not be understood as if the Son reconciled us in order that the Father, thus hating, might begin to love us, but that we were reconciled to him, already loving, though at enmity toward us because of sin. Accordingly, in a manner wondrous and divine he loved us even when he hated us. For he hated us when we were such as he had not made us, and yet because our iniquity had not destroyed his work in every respect, he knew in regard to each one of us both to hate what we had made and love what he had made.[35]

Notes

[1]G. E. Ladd, *A Theology of the New Testament* (Grand Rapids, 1974), pp. 450-6. See further F. Büchsel, *TDNT,* I, 1964, pp. 251-9; R. Gyllenberg, *RGG,* VI, 1962, pp. 1371-3; A. Vögtle, *LTK,* X, 1965, pp. 734-6; R. Pesch, *EBT,* II, 1970, pp. 735-8; H.-G. Link and H. Vörlander, *NIDNTT,* III, 1978, s.v.; J. Denney, *The Christian Doctrine of Reconciliation* (London, 1917); V. Taylor, *Forgiveness and Reconciliation* (London, 1941); J. Dupont, *La Réconciliation dans la Théologie de Saint Paul* (Paris, 1953); G. W. H. Lampe, *Reconciliation in Christ* (London, 1956); L. Morris, *The Apostolic Preaching of the Cross* (London, 1955, repr. 1965); E. Käsemann, 'Some Thoughts on the Theme "The Doctrine of Reconciliation in the New Testament",' in *The Future of our Religious Past* (J. M. Robinson [ed.]; London, 1971), pp. 49-64; L. Goppelt, 'Versöhnung durch Christus', *Christologie und Ethik* (Göttingen, 1968), pp. 147-64.

[2]The Pauline authorship of Colossians has been contested on slender grounds, and that of Ephesians on rather more substantial grounds. Should either of them not be Pauline, they are written by close disciples of Paul, seeking to be true to his theological position. I am, however, strongly inclined to accept the authenticity of Colossians (so rightly R. P. Martin, *Colossians and Philemon* [New Century Bible; London, 1974], *contra* E. Lohse, *Colossians and Philemon* [Hermeneia; Philadelphia, 1971]), and regard the balance of probability as favouring the authenticity of Ephesians (A. van Roon, *The Authenticity of Ephesians* [*NovTSup,* 39; Leiden, 1974]).

[3]See G. W. H. Lampe, *A Patristic Greek Lexicon* (Oxford, 1960-68) s.v.

[4]For this use, see also *BGU,* III, p. 846[10]; *PGiss,* I, 17[13] (J. H. Moulton and G. Milligan, *The Vocabulary of the Greek New Testament* [London, 1930] s.v.); *Ant.* 16.4.4125.

[5]See further Thucydides 8.70.2; 71.3.

[6]In the associated parable Matthew 5.25-26 = Luke 12.58-59 the Lukan form has the phrase ἀπηλλάχθαι ἀπό to describe the action of a man with reference to his legal adversary. The verb means 'to free, release' (Heb. 2.15), (middle) 'to leave, depart' (Acts 19.12). Here it means 'to get rid of him' or 'to depart from him'. The implication is that the man comes to terms with his adversary and satisfies his claims. Hence the thought is of 'being reconciled' (NIV), a meaning which is associated occasionally with the verb. Cf. Matthew: 'make friends with your adversary'.

[7]Büchsel, *TDNT,* I, p. 253. The verb συναλλάσσω, which was common in classical Greek, especially in military and legal contexts, does not occur in the LXX, and appears in the New Testament only in Acts 7.26 of the action of Moses in reconciling two quarrelling Israelites.

[8]See further Herodotus 5.29; 6.108; Aristotle, *Oec.* 2.15; Thucydides 4.59.

[9]See further Sophocles, *Ajax,* 744; *Jos. Ant.* 5.2.8 §137.

[10]Xenophon, *Anabasis* 1.6.1.

[11]See also *Jos. Ant.* 11.6.2 §195; Philo, *Legum allegoriae* 3.134.

[12]See also *OGIS*, 218[105].

[13]See also Aeschylus, *Septem contral Thebas*, 767; Aristophanes, *Aves*, 1588; Demosthenes.

[14]See E. Lohse, *Märtyrer und Gottesknecht* (Göttingen, 1955). Dupont, *Réconciliation*, pp. 13-14, while rightly recognizing the element of mercy in God's action, overlooks the fact that his wrath has been appeased by the punishment of his people.

[15]It is also found in Acts 12.22 D with reference to Herod Agrippa I's reconciliation with the people of Tyre.

[16]Büchsel *(TDNT,* I, 255) argues that there is no reason to suppose that the wife left her husband in a spirit of ill-will. It is possible that she left him because he treated her harshly, but in any case she has to overcome any barriers that exist on her side to renewing the relationship with him.

[17]On 'peace' as the result of reconciliation, see especially Goppelt, 'Versöhnung,' pp. 160-64.

[18]Paul uses the abstract term 'sin' in order to avoid the dangerous implications of saying that Christ became a 'sinner'.

[19]On the meaning of verse 19, see especially M. J. Harris, 'Readers' Forum', *Theological Students' Fellowship Bulletin*, 61, 1971, pp. 27-8; J.-F. Collange, *Énigmes de la deuxieme Épitre de Paul aux Corinthiens* (Cambridge, 1972), pp. 270-2.

[20]So rightly Büchsel, *TDNT,* I, p. 256.

[21]There is of course no suggestion that the whole world will necessarily accept the reconciliation, any more than this is the case in 2 Corinthians 5.18-21.

[22]For details, see Martin, *Colossians,* pp. 61-6.

[23]See Goppelt, 'Versöhnung', p. 161, for an interpretation that tends in this direction.

[24]See the summary of such views in Büchsel, *TDNT,* 1, p. 259.

[25]R. Bultmann, *Exegetica* (Tübingen, 1967), p. 228, as translated by C. K. Barrett, *The Second Epistle to the Corinthians* (New York, 1973), pp. 178-9.

[26]For Christ as subject see Ephesians 2.16.

[27]Käsemann, 'Some Thoughts', pp. 53, 54. For discussion, see Collange, *Énigmes,* pp. 266-80, esp. pp. 268-9, 275-6, who claims that Paul is incorporating traditional language known to his readers, possibly his own earlier formulation.

[28]So Goppelt, 'Versöhnung', pp. 150-3.

[29]*Contra* Dupont, *Réconciliation,* pp. 14, 18.

[30]The alleged echo of 2 Maccabees 3.26 in 2 Corinthians 12.7 is quite unconvincing.

[31]D. Hill, *Greek Words and Hebrew Meanings* (Cambridge, 1967), pp. 41-8.

[32]For a similar view see Goppelt, 'Versöhnung', pp. 149-50, who also suggests that Paul took over the idea of 'peace' from the Roman imperial ideology of the Pax Romana; here he is following Käsemann, 'Some Thoughts', p. 54.

[33]Dupont, *Réconciliation,* pp. 14-15.

[34]*The Methodist Hymn Book* (London, 1933), (ed.) no. 368.

[35]J. Calvin, *Institutes of the Christian Religion* (Ed. 20, J. T. McNeill; Philadelphia, 1960), pp. 506-7 (II, xvi, 4). [1989] The discussion of the topic has been carried further in two important essays by O. Hofius: 'Erwägungen zur Gestalt und Herkunft des paulinischen Versöhnungsgedankens', *ZTK,* 77, 1980, pp. 186-99; ' "Gott hat unter uns aufgerichtet das Wort von der Versöhnung" (2 Kor 5.19)', *ZNW,* 71, 1980, pp. 3-20. R. P. Martin has found in reconciliation the *leitmotiv* of Pauline theology: *Reconciliation. A Study of Paul's Theology* (Atlanta, 1980) and the same theme has been pursued in numerous essays by P. Stuhlmacher *(Versöhnung,* Gesetz und Gerechtigkeit. *Aufsätze zur biblischen Theologie* [Göttingen, 1981]).

15
Some Observations on the Covenant in the New Testament

ΑS FAR BACK AS 1933, W. EICHRODT MADE THE CONCEPT OF the covenant the organizing principle of Volume I of his *Theology of the Old Testament*, although he did not attempt to structure the remainder of his work around this principle. According to his translator, J. P. Baker, the covenant is to be regarded simply as the most adequate 'way in' to the complex reality of God as revealed in the Old Testament.[1] In more recent years the discovery of a 'treaty pattern' current in the ancient Near East and often determinative of the way in which material is presented in the Old Testament has shown that covenantal thinking was much more widespread than had previously been thought and has led to much discussion.[2] The place of the covenant theme in the New Testament also continues to attract scholarly attention.[3]

In this brief discussion of the covenant in the New Testament we shall be concerned to determine what light may thereby be shed on our understanding of the Old Testament and we shall also comment on the relevance of the theme for Christian theology and worship.

The covenant in Christian worship and theology
To set our theme in this broader context we may briefly note the important place that the idea of the covenant has had in the Protestant churches. Within the Methodist tradition there is the custom of holding a 'covenant service', usually on the first Sunday in the new year, at which the members are reminded of the solemn covenant made between God and humankind in Christ, and are invited to renew their vows of loyalty and obedience to God.

The service contains elements of adoration and thanksgiving, in which the mighty acts of redemption are rehearsed, of confession of failure to maintain the stipulations, and of reaffirmation of covenant vows; and the whole act of worship culminates in the sacrament of the Lord's Supper which is the especial sign of the new covenant. The general atmosphere may be best sensed from the words of the opening homily, sadly omitted from the current form in *The Methodist Service Book:*

Dearly beloved, the Christian life, to which we are called, is a life in Christ, redeemed from sin by Him, and through Him, consecrated to God. Upon this life we have entered, having been admitted into that New Covenant of which our Lord Jesus Christ is mediator, and which He sealed with His own blood, that it might stand for ever.

On one side the Covenant is God's promise that He will fulfil in and through us all that He declared in Jesus Christ, who is the Author and Perfector of our faith. That His promise still stands we are sure, for we have known His goodness and proved His grace in our lives day by day. On the other side we stand pledged to live no more unto ourselves, but to Him who loved us and gave Himself for us and has called us so to serve Him that the purposes of His coming might be fulfilled.

From time to time we renew our vows of consecration, especially when we gather at the table of the Lord; but on this day we meet expressly, as generations of our fathers have met, that we may joyfully and solemnly renew the Covenant which bound them and binds us to God.

Let us, then, remembering the mercies of God, and the hope of His calling, examine ourselves by the light of His Spirit, that we may see wherein we have failed or fallen short in faith and practice, and, considering all that this Covenant means, may give ourselves anew to God.[4]

The concept of the covenant has also played a significant part in Reformed theology, so much so that one school of thought became known as 'covenant' or 'federal' theology. The Westminster Confession immediately follows its chapter on the Fall with a section that distinguishes two covenants. The first

was a covenant of works, wherein life was promised to Adam, and in him to his posterity, upon condition of perfect and personal obedience. Man by his fall having made himself incapable of life by that covenant, the Lord was pleased to make a second, commonly called the Covenant of Grace; whereby he freely offereth unto sinners life and salvation by Jesus Christ, requiring of them faith in him, that they may be saved.

Within this second covenant a distinction is made between two types of administration

in the time of the law, and in the time of the gospel: under the law it was administered by promises, prophecies, sacrifices, circumcision, the paschal lamb, and other types and ordinances delivered to the people of the Jews, all fore-signifying Christ to come, which were for that time sufficient and efficacious, through the operation of the Spirit, to instruct and build up the elect in faith in the promised Messiah, by whom they had full remission of sins, and eternal salvation . . . There are not therefore two covenants of grace differing in substance, but one and the same under various dispensations.[5]

A more complicated scheme is depicted by the Reformed theologian L. Berkhof, who distinguishes two aspects of the covenant of mercy. First, there is the covenant of redemption made between the Father and the Son by which the Father promised redemption to Christ as the representative and surety for the elect, on condition that Christ fulfilled the law perfectly on their behalf; this covenant with Christ was thus essentially a covenant of works, Christ fulfilling the requirements that Adam disobeyed. Second, there is the covenant of grace made between God and the offending but elect sinner in which God promises salvation through faith in Christ, and the sinner accepts this, promising a life of faith and obedience.

The scheme becomes even more elaborate when the various epochs in the covenant are distinguished—the proto-evangelium, the covenant with Noah, that with Abraham, the Sinaitic covenant and the new covenant.[6] If this sounds complicated, we should remember that dispensational theology, which is the main rival to Reformed theology in the more conservative branches of the Church, lists a total of eight covenants.[7]

The usage of the term 'covenant'

Certain basic facts seem assured about the Hebrew term *bᵉrit*, although some details remain uncertain. The etymology of the word is still disputed, the two principal theological dictionaries of the Old Testament adopting different etymologies.[8] Recent studies of semantics assure us that etymology does not determine meaning, so this difference of opinion does not matter very much. Nevertheless, etymology should not be dismissed as totally irrelevant to meaning. We also need to bear in mind that a word may have different meanings in different contexts, and we should beware of transferring associations from one context to another without good reason. The following ideas are present, to greater or less extent, in the various uses of the word:

1. It refers to the establishment of a relationship, usually a one-sided one, in which a superior party imposes his will on an inferior.

2. The relationship is usually based on advantages already bestowed by a superior, and these may be expressed in the historical preamble to a

covenant document. However, the stress may be on the promises of advantage to be bestowed in the future.

3. While a covenant is usually 'for ever' on the part of the superior, it normally includes stipulations to be observed by the inferior, the breaking of which releases the superior from his obligation to bestow advantages.

4. The covenant is initiated by a solemn ceremony which binds the partners to each other. There may be the thought of witnesses and observers of the pact, and the covenant is often preserved in a document or similar form to remind both parties of their obligations.[9]

These ideas are carried over into Greek usage by the adoption of the term *diathēkē* to translate *bᵉrit*, and it has been observed that the choice of this word rather than of the usual Greek words for a pact, *sunthēkē* or *spondē*, indicates that the translators were aware of some of the particular nuances of the Hebrew word, especially the fact that it signifies a unilateral initiative by one party rather than a mutual bond between equals.[10]

The noun *diathēkē* occurs thirty-three times in the New Testament. The corresponding verb *diatithēmi* occurs seven times, including five times with *diathēkē* as its object. Throughout (with one exception) the usage is related to that of the Old Testament, referring either to covenants made in the Old Testament or to the new covenant which is defined by contrast with the old covenant and whose name is indeed taken from the Old Testament (Jer. 31.31). We may observe, first of all, that Paul regarded the covenants (plural!) as part of the special privileges of the people of Israel, along with a filial relation to God, the presence of his glory, the giving of the law, the cult and the promises of future blessings (Rom. 9.4); from such blessing the Gentiles were excluded until the gospel was preached to them—they were strangers to the covenants of promise (Eph. 2.12). Paul uses the plural because he has at least two covenants in mind.[11]

The first is the covenant of promise made with Abraham, and it has a fundamental significance for Paul. It was earlier than the law and it contained a promise of blessing for all the families of the earth (Gal. 3.17). Paul regards this covenant as having been made not only with Abraham but also with Christ, who is regarded as his 'seed' or descendant. We gain the impression not only that the blessings were intended for Abraham and for his future descendants, but also that the promises were made both to Abraham and to Christ.[12] In any case, the fulfilment of the covenant blessings is seen to be in the Christian dispensation, as is further testified by Zechariah who saw that God was remembering his covenant with Abraham, that is, fulfilling the promises made in it, by raising up his son John the Baptist and the coming Messiah (Luke 1.72). The outward mark of this covenant with Abraham was circumcision, which was interpreted by Stephen as an indication that God would keep his promise (Acts 7.8), in the same way (we may add) as the rainbow was the sign that God would keep his covenant with Noah (Gen. 9.8-17).

Until the time of Christ the Gentiles stood outside the blessings of the covenant made with Abraham (Eph. 2.12), but now God's blessing is extended to them also. This appears to be the force of the divine promise quoted by Peter in Acts 3.25 from Genesis 22.18; 26.4. Curiously, the thrust of the passage is to assure the Jews that the promise made to Abraham and fulfilled in Christ is primarily for them; but, although it is not spelled out at this stage, the implication is undoubtedly that the same blessing is also for the Gentiles.

Perhaps the most difficult passage in Paul is that where he draws lessons from the births of two of Abraham's sons. In Galatians 3.24 he contrasts the birth of Ishmael by ordinary physical generation to the servant-girl Hagar and the birth of Isaac as a result of divine promise to the free woman Sarah. These are seen as typifying two covenants. The first is described as that which proceeded from Sinai, and it produces children destined for slavery; it can be seen as corresponding to contemporary earthly Jerusalem and its people, that is, to Judaism and the Jews. The other side of the typology is not stated expressly—we are not told what is the counterpart to Sinai, but perhaps we are to think of Calvary—but the birth of Isaac corresponds to the new heavenly Jerusalem and its children who are free.[13]

Although Paul does not expressly connect the birth of Isaac with the covenant with Abraham, it belongs with it in the sense that both the birth and the covenant involve the idea of promise. Over against it stands the second covenant to which Paul refers, that made at Sinai and associated with the giving of the law (Gal. 4.24). Paul's point in Galatians 3.15-17 is that this second covenant cannot annul the earlier one made with Abraham, so that the promises of future blessing made to him would no longer stand. By taking advantage of the broad, legal use of *diathēkē* Paul can affirm that, once an agreement has been made, it cannot be rendered invalid or have fresh conditions attached to it.[14] The purpose of the law, therefore, cannot be to provide the conditions by obedience to which the promises made to Abraham can be subsequently claimed, since these promises were promises, that is, offers of gifts. Rather, the purpose of the law was to bring people to Christ in order that they might gain salvation by faith in him; the law does this by demonstrating their sinfulness and inability to save themselves. Thus the law can be said to be beneficent, even if at first sight it appears to be contrary to the idea of divine promise.

It is the Sinai covenant that Paul has in mind when he speaks of the 'old covenant' in 2 Corinthians 3.14, a verse that should be taken to refer to the occasions when the passage about the institution of the old covenant is being read in the synagogue.[15] The Jews misunderstand that passage to refer to the works of the law as a means of salvation when in fact its purpose is to direct them to Christ. Over against this old covenant stands the 'new covenant', a phrase used by Paul earlier in the chapter (2 Cor. 3.6). The concept is drawn, as we have seen, from Jeremiah 31.31,[16] but Paul also found evidence for it in Isaiah 59.21, where God makes a covenant with those in Jacob who turn away from transgression, to give them his Spirit and his words (Rom. 11.26f.). For Paul the 'old covenant' has been superseded by the 'new covenant'.

In the Epistle to the Hebrews we have the fullest systematic use of the concept. Jesus is described as the mediator of a better covenant (Heb. 7.22; 8.6), which is also described as second, new and eternal (Heb. 8.8; 9.15; 12.24; 13.20). The contrast between this new covenant and the Sinai covenant is worked out in detail. The first covenant had its ritual appurtenances, especially the so-called ark of the covenant (Heb. 9.14; cf. Rev. 11.19[17]) and the tables of the law (Heb. 9.14). But its rites of sacrifice, being external, had no real power to secure forgiveness of sins, and the covenant itself has become obsolete, now that the new covenant promised by Jeremiah has been inaugurated (Heb. 8.8-13; 10.16f.). Forgiveness for sins committed under the first covenant is possible by means of the sacrifice offered by Christ (Heb. 9.15). A covenant can come into effect only by death. So the first covenant was ratified by the blood of the covenant sprinkled by Moses (Heb. 9.20), and in the same way the blood of Christ is the blood of the eternal covenant (Heb. 13.20) by which people are sanctified (Heb. 10.29) and brought into a new relationship with God.[18]

Behind this theological use of the concept in the New Testament there lies the important saying of Jesus at the Last Supper, in which he spoke of the cup as representing 'the new covenant in my blood' (Luke 22.20; cf. 1 Cor. 11.25) or, with the alternative wording, 'my blood of the covenant, which is poured out for many' (Mark 14.24; cf. Matt. 26.28). Whether or not the actual words go back to the Last Supper, and whatever be the original form of the wording,[19] there can be no doubt that this saying was current in the Church wherever the Pauline tradition of the institution of the Lord's Supper was recited, and we may safely assume that this text lies behind the theological development of the idea in Paul and Hebrews.

It is doubtful whether the covenant idea is present in the saying of Jesus in Luke 22.29 in which he assigns to his disciples a Kingdom, just as his

Father has assigned a Kingdom to him, so that they may share in his rule and sit at his table. The promise appears to be made solely to the Twelve, but, if it is correct to identify 1 Corinthians 6.2 and Revelation 3.20f. as echoes of it, it was later universalized. Perhaps the saying means that the blessing bestowed upon the disciples by the new covenant is the Kingdom of God, just as the Father first gave this to the Son, but the thought may be simply of a testamentary disposition and not related at all to the concept of the covenant.[20]

The significance of the covenant idea in the New Testament
1. Our discussion has shown that only one author, the writer to the Hebrews, has used the covenant concept as a structural principle in a discussion of any length. The contrast between Judaism and Christianity is expounded in terms of the old and new covenants. The Pauline use is more spasmodic. Paul uses it in discussing the relation of Judaism to Christianity, and the idea is also used by Paul and Luke to show how the Gentiles fit into God's plan of salvation. There is but one clear example of the concept in the teaching of Jesus. What is important is that the evidence of the saying in the Last Supper tradition and the sermonic material in Acts is sufficient to show that the idea was current in the early Church from a very primitive stage. Furthermore, the ideas found in Hebrews are seminally present in Paul, who obviously makes use of the same scheme of thought, although he nowhere develops it systematically. We thus have some evidence for the widespread knowledge of the concept in the New Testament period despite the apparent paucity of evidence. In this connection we note that associated themes from the Exodus and the wilderness wanderings of Israel are present throughout the New Testament and indicate that the attention of the early Church was often directed to the Old Testament context of the Mosaic covenant.[21]

2. The New Testament makes a selective use of the Old Testament evidence. Only 6 actual uses of the word in the Old Testament are explicitly cited out of a possible 287, although allusions to Old Testament covenantal texts are more common. But the attention of the New Testament writers is restricted to a small number of passages, and we hear nothing directly of the covenants with Noah or with David. The New Testament writers seize upon those passages which may fairly be regarded as looking forward to their own time, and they ignore the others. To this extent their use of the Old Testament is selective, and we should be warned against the possibility of ignoring the important teaching to be found elsewhere in the Old Testament.

3. The basic use of the covenant idea is to depict the relationship of Christianity to the religion of the Old Testament and Judaism, and this is

done in terms of continuity and contrast. The element of continuity is expressed in two ways, the first of which is in terms of the covenant made with Abraham. The essential feature in this covenant for the New Testament writers is the element of promise. The key Old Testament text (Gen. 22.18; 26.4) speaks of the way in which all nations will be blessed (future tense!), and this promise is seen to be fulfilled in the coming of Jesus and the establishment of the Church which incorporates men and women from all the nations of the earth. We have noted the possibility that Paul may think of the Abrahamic covenant as having been renewed to the seed of Abraham, rather than simply coming to the fulfilment in the Church.

The second way in which the element of continuity is expressed is in the use of Jeremiah 31: what has begun to take place in New Testament times was already prophesied by Jeremiah, so that the new covenant is part of an on-going divine plan. It is the fulfilment of what was promised in the Old Testament. But the use of Jeremiah brings us to the element of contrast in the New Testament idea of the covenant. If the relation to the Abrahamic covenant is one of continuity through the fulfilment of what was promised, the relation to the Mosaic covenant is one of continuity in that God still works in terms of a covenant rather than on any other principle, but at the same time the stress lies on contrast and the supersession of the old.[22] When the old covenant is mentioned, it is the Mosaic and not the Abrahamic covenant that is meant, and the former is regarded as having come to an end. For Jeremiah it came to an end because of the disobedience of Israel; it needed to be replaced by a new one involving a different kind of obedience.

4. How do the New Testament writers view the Mosaic covenant in relation to the Abrahamic covenant and the new covenant? So far as the Epistle to the Hebrews is concerned, the writer makes no use of the Abrahamic covenant as such, although Abraham occupies a significant place in his thought. The historical line runs from Melchizedek to Christ rather than from Abraham to Christ, and Abraham functions more as an example of faith in the promises of God than as the human partner in a covenant relationship (Heb. 6.13): the Abrahamic covenant is utilized as an example of an inviolable divine promise rather than on account of its specific content. Here we see an interesting difference from Paul.

The new covenant is chronologically later than the old, and thereby renders it obsolete. (One cannot add later conditions to an existing covenant, but a later covenant can cancel out an earlier one.) At the same time, it is in many ways better. It can effectually deal with sin, whereas the sacrificial system in the Old Testament had no real power of its own to do so and derived its virtue proleptically from the sacrifice of Christ, to which it functioned as a pointer. As a result of this 'prophetic' character, the old covenant could be said to contain the seeds of its own dissolution. There was, therefore, nothing basically 'wrong' with the old covenant in its own time. It served in its day by divine appointment, it functioned on the same principle of faith as the new covenant,[23] and it was meant to provide a pattern for the new covenant. We can say that the writer takes a thoroughly positive view of the old covenant so far as its own period of validity is concerned; like an early Ford car, it was good in its day, although not perfect, but now it has been rendered obsolete by the production of a new model.

There is insufficient evidence for us to see in detail how Jesus regarded the old covenant—or, indeed, whether he had an opinion on it at all. Certainly no word of condemnation of it by him has been preserved, and he upheld the validity of the written law of Moses in general terms. The saying at the Lord's Supper uses the Sinai imagery in a way that is typological and promissory: 'the implication is, as Hebrews 8.13 explicitly states, that the old covenant is now obsolete'.[24]

Paul's attitude is more tricky to assess. If the writer to the Hebrews sees the Mosaic covenant chiefly in terms of the establishment of a sacrificial system by which sins can be removed and people can in a limited way approach God, Paul sees it chiefly in terms of the establishment of the law. The law is something that, seen from one angle, came in 'sideways' and has disturbed the straight connection between Abraham and Christ (Rom. 5.20). The Abrahamic covenant has the character of promise and leads to righteousness, but the Mosaic covenant has the character of law, and the law cannot make righteous. Although Scripture says that the man who observes the law will live by it (Lev. 18.5, cited in Gal. 3.12; Rom. 10.5; cf. Rom. 7.10), Paul states that nobody can fulfil its demands and that the clear divine assertions of justification by faith in Christ rule the law out as a means of justification.[25] It is no wonder that Paul had to reiterate, despite all he said to the contrary, that the law was not opposed to the promises of God (Gal. 3.21), that it is not overthrown by the principle of faith (Rom. 3.31) and that it is in fact holy (Rom. 7.12).

Paul and the writer to the Hebrews are in effect fighting on different fronts. The latter is concerned with people who think that the Jewish sacrificial ritual is still valid as a means of forgiveness. The former is concerned with people who think that obedience to the law by means of the works of the law is the way of justification.[26] Paul's argument is *ad hominem,* and is directed against people who see obedience to the law as the means of justification. Such people had failed to appreciate the covenant pattern which is present in the crucial passages in Exodus where the law contains the stipulations that follow the covenant promises of God. Jeremias has illuminated the demands made by Jesus in the Sermon on the Mount by claiming that they are in effect preceded by the gospel, so that the desire to obey the demands flows from gratitude and faith and not from the need to win favour with God.[27] In the plan of God the law was to be understood in that kind of way; the decalogue itself begins with a declaration that Yahweh had brought the Israelites out of bondage in Egypt (Exod. 20.2; Deut. 5.6). The stipulations follow the declaration of God's salvation freely bestowed on his people. That this understanding of the law was alive in Paul's day has been vigorously asserted by E. P. Sanders.[28]

Paul's argument, however, does not rest on this type of consideration, unless we are allowed to see something like this argument in his reference backwards to the element of promise in the covenant with Abraham. He regards the present function of the law as being a means of demonstrating that man is a sinner; the law is meant to drive him to despair and so to lead him to see his need of Christ.[29] If somebody approached the law in the wrong spirit, seeing it as a means of obtaining life by means of works, then he needed to be shown that according to the law he was a sinner and could not save himself. Paul has little to say about what happened to a person who was convicted of sin by the law before the coming of Christ; how could such a person find justification? Clearly Paul thought of justification as taking place by faith in God, as was actually exemplified by Abraham (Rom. 4.6-8), but whether he regarded the sacrificial system as the means whereby people approached God in faith is not clear. The positive typological use that Paul makes of the sacrificial system suggests that he did so regard it. But, except in Romans 3.25f., Paul is basically not concerned with the question of what happened before Christ. He is more concerned with people who saw the works of the law as the way of salvation. His argument, therefore, is a criticism of the Jewish understanding of the law rather than of the law itself.

The covenant and the New Testament interpretation of the Old Testament

It remains to draw out some conclusions on the two areas mentioned at the outset. First of all, we have established that the basic use of the covenant concept in the New Testament is to show the continuity and contrast between God's earlier dealings with the Jews and his present action in Christ. A variety of relationships are thus seen to exist between the Old Testament and the New Testament, and thus the use of the covenant furnishes an excellent example of how the New Testament interprets the Old Testament.

1. The basic relationship between the various covenants is expressed in

terms of *Heilsgeschichte*. That is to say, the various covenants are thought of as real historical acts in which God made promises to historical people, Abraham, Moses and the Church. These followed on from one another in chronological order and were related historically to one another. They formed episodes in a series of divine actions, and hence the covenants in the Old Testament are depicted as historical stages in God's plan of salvation and not merely as patterns of literary interest.

2. The new covenant is regarded as the object of prophecy. Jeremiah received a revelation of what God would do in the future, and in due course events took place that the New Testament writers regarded as the concrete fulfilment of prophecy.

3. We should distinguish from prophecy the note of promise and fulfilment that is to be found in the covenants themselves. The covenant with Abraham was essentially a promise of future blessings which the New Testament writers believed to be fulfilled in Christ and the Church. The element of promise is also present in the Mosaic covenant, but it is much less significant for New Testament thought.

4. There is an element of typology. This means that the new covenant is seen as following the same pattern as the old. Paul develops this especially in 1 and 2 Corinthians, where the various events associated with the Exodus—the Passover, the crossing of the sea, the wilderness wanderings and the setting up of the tabernacle—are seen as types of corresponding features of the Christian dispensation.[30] The writer to the Hebrews builds his argument on an elaborate comparison of the sacrificial system with the sacrifice of Christ. For him the Old Testament legislation offers a shadow of the good things to come: it is like a shadow cast on the ground by which we can see the general shape of what has caused it without being able to appreciate the full splendour of a coloured, three-dimensional object (Heb. 10.1). But it functions in this way because it itself is a dim copy of the heavenly realities on which it was patterned by Moses (Heb. 8.5). In this way the Old Testament covenant can be seen as a pointer to the New Testament covenant. It is a pointer, however, for those whose eyes have been opened as a result of the revelation in Christ; we may presume that the original spectators of the sacrificial system would hardly have been able to grasp the point. Within the Old Testament there is a certain typology between the various covenant enactments which arises from their resting upon a common treaty pattern rather than upon a typological principle. What the New Testament writers have done is to take up two events between which a correspondence has been established and then to draw out the parallels.

5. In this way, the four main types of relation between the Old Testament

and the New Testament are brought together in the use of the covenant concept. Perhaps a fifth element should be added, which I would call 'explanation'. For an example of this I refer to the way in which the term 'mediator' is brought into the discussion of the covenant; primarily it is applied to Christ, but by implication it is applied to the priests or to Moses. The sense of the Old Testament narrative is expressed more fully by means of a feature not explicitly present in the narrative but which may legitimately be seen to be implicitly there.

In viewing the Old Testament in these ways, the New Testament writers at times do nothing more than recognize that various passages in the Old Testament are historical accounts of events that happened or are prophecies and promises of future events. This is to interpret the Old Testament according to its conscious sense. They move beyond strict exegesis of the text when they claim to recognize that certain specific events are the fulfilment of prophecy, that is to say, when they claim to be able to say 'what the prophet was foretelling was in fact such-and-such an event'. In the same way they may pick out certain events as being more significant than others because they are seen as leading up to a future dénouement, as when the New Testament writers take up the covenants with Abraham and Moses but ignore that with Noah. From their perspective the New Testament writers attach significance to a different series of events from that to which later Judaism might attach significance. Similarly, there is an element of interpretation when the sacrificial system is regarded as the type to which the sacrifice of Christ is the antitype. Typology is thus not simply a means of interpreting New Testament events (not, be it noted, of interpreting the New Testament) in the light of Old Testament patterns, but of interpreting Old Testament events as the divinely intended patterns pointing to New Testament events.

All this raises the question of the legitimacy of the New Testament interpretation of the Old Testament. If a New Testament writer expounding Exodus 24 says in effect that the sacrifice there points to the sacrifice of Christ, is this grammatico-historical exegesis of the original human author's text? Should he not rather say that, from the Christian point of view, God intended Exodus 24 to serve ultimately as the pattern for the sacrifice of Christ, although this would not have been evident to the original readers? If so, we can distinguish between interpretation on the grammatico-historical level and on the level of a *sensus plenior*, the validity of the latter depending on the validity of the New Testament faith.

We can thus see from this particular example how the New Testament interpretation of the Old Testament combines elements of grammatico-historical exegesis and of what we may call a *sensus plenior* approach. This then raises the question of how far Christian exegesis can follow this method, but that is a question which must remain beyond our present scope.[31]

The covenant in Christian theology

Finally, we should return briefly to the theological use of the covenant concept. First, in the light of our discussion it can be claimed that the Methodist Covenant Service is a good example of the positive use of an Old Testament concept in Christian worship, provided that it accentuates the biblical features of the covenant and does not degenerate into some sort of human bargain with God.

Second, our discussion has confirmed the basic tenet of Reformed theology that there is but one covenant of grace in the Old Testament and the New Testament alike. The general line of interpretation given by John Murray long before attention was directed to the treaty formulae has been completely vindicated by the new discoveries, and is an example of how on occasion theological instincts can be confirmed by archaeological research.

On the other hand, we have not found any support for the elaborate theological schemes of either developed covenant theology or of dispensationalist, both of which go well beyond the New Testament guidelines, and it seems clear that these schemes cannot take the central place as frameworks for biblical interpretation which have been assigned to them by their proponents. Here John Calvin proves (as often) to be a better guide than his *epigoni*.

In the New Testament the person of the Saviour has proved to be of far greater significance than the structure of the covenant. The new wine has burst the skins which tried to contain it. We cannot, therefore, regard the covenant as the supreme interest of the New Testament, although much of New Testament thought could be arranged around the principle. What we have found is that in the covenant we have a concept that illustrates all the various ways in which the Old Testament and the New Testament are related and in which the essential unity of the two Testaments is visible.

Notes

[1] W. Eichrodt, *Theology of the Old Testament,* vol. I (London, 1961); vol. II, 1967. The quotation is from vol. II, p. 10. The work was originally published as *Theologie des Alten Testaments* (Teil I, Leipzig, 1933); (Teil II, 1935); (Teil III, 1939).

[2] G. E. Mendenhall, *Law and Covenant in Israel and the Ancient Near East* (Pittsburgh, 1955); K. Baltzer, *The Covenant Formulary* (Oxford, 1971); D. J. McCarthy, *Old Testament Covenant* (Oxford, 1972); J. A. Thompson, *The Ancient Near Eastern Treaties and the Old Testament* (London, 1964); K. A. Kitchen, *Ancient Orient and Old Testament* (London, 1966). See also on the use of covenant in the Bible, W. C. Holladay, 'New covenant, the', *IDB Supp. vol.,* pp. 623-5; J. Guhrt, 'Covenant, Guarantee, Mediator', *NIDNTT,* I, pp. 365-72.

[3]For a brief survey, see W. G. Morrice, 'New Wine in Old Wine-Skins: XI. Covenant', *Exp.T,* 86, 1974-75, pp. 132-6. The major discussion of the covenant in the New Testament is E. Grässer, *Der Alte Bund im Neuen: Exegetische Studien zur Israelfrage im Neuen Testament* (Tübingen, 1985); pp. 1-134 contain an essay 'Der Alte Bund im Neuen: Eine exegetische Vorlesung', in which the material is considered in great detail. Grässer's concern is to underline the elements of difference and contrast between the old and new covenants, to indicate that the covenant concept is comparatively unimportant in the New Testament, and hence to show that a 'covenant-centred' theology of the Bible does not exist. New Testament theology is not concerned with a transformation of the covenant concept so much as with an eschatological new creation. See also C. H. Talbert, 'Paul on the Covenant', *Review and Expositor,* 84, 1987, pp. 299-313.

[4]Cited from the older form in *The Book of Offices* (London, 1936), p. 54. The history of the covenant service has been studied in detail by D. H. Tripp, *The Renewal of the Covenant in the Methodist Tradition* (London, 1969).

[5]*The Westminster Confession* (Edinburgh, 1948), ch. 7.

[6]L. Berkhof, *Systematic Theology* (Edinburgh, 1968), pp. 211-8, 262-301; cf. J. Calvin, *Institutes of the Christian Religion* (London, 1953), I, pp. 368-99; H. Heppe, *Reformed Dogmatics* (London, 1950), pp. 281-319, 371-409; J. Murray, *The Covenant of Grace* (London, 1954).

[7]*The Schofield Reference Bible* (Oxford, 1917), pp. 1297f. *et passim.*

[8]M. Meinfeld, *TWAT,* I, cols. 781, 808, especially 783-4; E. Kutsch, *THAT,* I, cols. 339-52, especially 339-41. On the word, see further G. Quell and J. Behm, *TDNT,* II, pp. 106-34; L. Morris, *The Apostolic Preaching of the Cross* (London, 1965³), pp. 65-111.

[9]For this summary, see the works cited in n. 2. It would be easy to produce exceptions and to make qualifications, but these do not affect the substance of the matter.

[10]Cf. J. Behm, *TDNT,* II, pp. 126-9; E. Kutsch, *THAT,* I, col. 352; Morris, op. cit., pp. 86f.

[11]C. K. Barrett, in *The Epistle to the Romans* (London, 1957), pp. 177f., thinks that Paul had the three covenants in the Exodus covenant narrative in mind—the covenants at Horeb, in the plains of Moab and at Mounts Gerizim and Ebal; this would then correspond with Jewish usage (SB, III, p. 362). F. F. Bruce (*Romans* [London, 1963], p. 185) prefers a wider meaning.

[12]Grammatically 'his seed' is the indirect object of 'were made' (literally 'were spoken').

[13]In addition to the commentaries, see A. F. Walls, 'Paul's "Allegory" in Galatians IV', *Theological Students' Fellowship Terminal Letter,* Spring 1956, pp. 5f.; E. E. Ellis, *Paul's Use of the Old Testament* (Edinburgh, 1957), pp. 52f.; C. K. Barrett, 'The Allegory of Abraham, Sarah and Hagar in the Argument of Galatians', in J. Friedrich *et al., Rechtfertigung: Festschrift für Ernst Käsemann* (Göttingen, 1976), pp. 1-16.

[14]The problem of whether Paul is thinking of a covenant or a 'last will and testament' in Galatians 3.15 is perhaps settled by the existence of the form of a 'covenant of grant'; the same factor enables us to retain the translation 'covenant' in Hebrews 9.16f. The evidence is collected by K. M. Campbell, 'Covenant or Testament? Heb. 9.16, 17 Reconsidered', *EQ,* 44, 1972, pp. 107-11.

[15]A. T. Hanson, *Studies in Paul's Technique and Theology* (London, 1974), pp. 139-42; cf. C. K. Barrett, *The Second Epistle to the Corinthians* (London, 1973), pp. 120f. On this chapter see especially R. S. Rayburn, 'The Contrast between the Old and New Covenants in the New Testament', unpublished Ph.D. dissertation (University of Aberdeen, 1978).

[16]Nothing in Jeremiah's language suggests that he thought of the new covenant as a renewal of the covenant made with Abraham.

[17]In Revelation 11.19 the reference is to a heavenly counterpart of the earthly tabernacle. Since the ark was normally hidden from view, the point of the verse is that the revelation of God is taking place, a theophany that spells judgement for sinful people who cannot see God and live. It is not clear whether the phrase 'of the covenant' is simply a stereotyped descriptive phrase with no special significance, or whether it serves to stress the faithfulness of God in

keeping his covenant promises.

[18]A special feature in Hebrews is the stress on Jesus as the mediator; no corresponding figure in the old covenant is mentioned here (but cf. Gal. 3.19), but the high priest (rather than Moses) appears to be the counterpart (Heb. 7.21-25; however, for a possible contrast with Moses, see A. Oepke, *TDNT*, IV, p. 620).

[19]For an assessment of the recent debate and a cautious acceptance of the Lucan-Pauline wording as closer to the original see I. H. Marshall, *Last Supper and Lord's Supper* (Exeter, 1980), ch. 2.

[20]Attempts have been made to find the idea of the covenant present elsewhere in the New Testament where the actual terminology is absent. For example, Baltzer (op. cit., p. 164f.) refers briefly to the formal structure in Revelation 3.1-6; Colossians 1.9-23 and 1 Peter 2.21-24, 25 as a covenantal structure, but he states his case rather than argues it, and it is far from convincing.

[21]R. E. Nixon, *The Exodus in the New Testament* (London, 1963).

[22]E. E. Ellis, *Paul's Use of the Old Testament* (Edinburgh, 1957), p. 130.

[23]This is not explicitly stated, but it is surely demanded by Hebrews 11 which indicates that the people with whom God was pleased in the Old Testament were those who had faith in him.

[24]R. T. France, *Jesus and the Old Testament* (London, 1971), p. 67.

[25]A problem is raised by Paul's statements in Romans 2 that appear to allow that doers of the law may be justified, but only a few verses later Paul makes it clear that, if there is a class of justified doers of the law, it is a null class (Rom. 3.9, 20).

[26]Historically, one might perhaps have expected the positions to have been the other way round, since Paul wrote before the cessation of the sacrificial system, while Hebrews is often thought to date from after the cessation when the sacrificial system was no longer such a live issue. But our argument suggests (what is probable on other grounds) that Hebrews belongs to the period before AD 70; Paul's environment, by contrast, is one in which the spiritualization of the cult, or the replacement of the cult by legalism, was already under way.

[27]J. Jeremias, *Die Bergpredigt* (Stuttgart, 1959).

[28]E. P. Sanders, *Paul and Palestinian Judaism* (London, 1977); *Paul, the Law and the Jewish People* (Philadelphia, 1983).

[29]That this is not the only function of the law for Paul is obvious. He sees it positively as the statement of the divine requirements which are summed up in the law of love and so are fulfilled by believers through the Spirit.

[30]Ellis, op. cit., p. 131.

[31]Cf. R. N. Longenecker, 'Can we reproduce the exegesis of the New Testament?', *Tyndale Bulletin*, 21, 1970, pp. 3-38. [1989] See also G. K. Beale, 'Did Jesus and his followers preach the right doctrine from the wrong texts? An examination of the presuppositions of Jesus' and the apostles' exegetical method', *Themelios* 16:3, April 1989, pp. 89-96.

16
Predestination in the New Testament

OUR FIRST TASK IN THIS ESSAY WILL BE TO SET OUT THE New Testament evidence relating to predestination (Part I). We shall then examine how this sort of language is used on a human level (Part II) as a prelude to observing the difficulties that arise when it is applied to God (Part III). This will lead to a consideration of the causes of these difficulties (Part IV), and then to a final statement of what predestination language is meant to do and what it cannot do (Part V).

I The New Testament evidence
The verb 'to predestinate' occurs in the KJV (AV) a total of four times as the translation of the Greek verb *proorizō* (Rom. 8.29, 30; Eph. 1.5, 11). The same Greek word also occurs in Acts 4.28 (translated 'to determine before') and 1 Corinthians 2.7 ('to ordain'). In accordance with its policy of always translating any Greek word by the same English word if possible, the ASV (RV) has 'to foreordain' in all six passages. Later translations adopt a variety of renderings. The RSV has 'to predestine' in Romans 8.29, 30; NIV uses the same translation in these two verses and in Ephesians 1.5, 11.

The Greek word is thus comparatively rare in the New Testament,[1] but of course the idea is much more widespread, and a larger word-field demands investigation. 'Pre-destination' in English, as in Greek, refers to an act of decision prior to a later action; one decides beforehand what one is later going to do. This means that all *pro*-verbs which refer to God purposing or choosing in advance must come into our field of interest. Such verbs can of course be used of human purposing. Thus Paul speaks of the Corinthians making their gifts each 'as he has made up his mind' *(proaireomai,* 2 Cor. 9.7), and of course there are many such verbs which simply indicate that one action preceded another. Prophets can *fore*-see what is going to happen, that is, see it before it happens, and *fore*-tell it or *'fore*-write' it (e.g., Acts 2.31; Gal. 3.8; Acts 1.16; Rom. 9.29; Heb. 4.7; 2 Pet. 3.2; Jude 4). In the same way God (who was of course the inspirer of the prophets) can have fore-knowledge of what is going to happen (Acts 2.23) or of particular people (Rom. 8.29; 11.2; 1 Pet. 1.2); a special case is where Jesus and 'his career are said to be foreknown by God (Acts 2.23; 1 Pet. 1.20).

But God also prepares things beforehand for his people (Heb. 11.40), and chooses people beforehand for various tasks (Acts 10.41; 22.14; 26.16; cf. 3.20 with reference to the Messiah). The verb *protithēmi* can be used in this way with the meaning 'to propose' or 'to plan beforehand'; in Romans 1.13 it refers to a purpose of Paul which had been thwarted, and in Ephesians 1.9 it is used of God's purpose of salvation.[2] The corresponding noun *prothesis* ('purpose, plan') is more frequent, and refers to God's purpose in Romans 8.28; 9.11; Ephesians 1.11; 3.11; 2 Timothy 1.9. Finally, we may note that the preposition *pro* ('before') can be used to refer to things that God planned, promised or did before the creation of the world (John 17.5; 1 Cor. 2.7; Eph. 1.4; 2 Tim. 1.9; Tit. 1.2; 1 Pet. 1.20; Jude 25).

In many of the above texts the use of *pro-* is strictly unnecessary, since it is obvious that willing and purposing must by their very nature precede the action willed and purposed. (We may perhaps compare the increasing use of 'pre-' in such phrases as 'pre-packaged vegetables'; pre-packaged vegetables are identical with packaged vegetables when they reach the shopper's table.[3]) But this means that all texts in which God is described as willing, planning and purposing must also come within our survey, since here too we are concerned with acts of *pre*-destination. So we must note the use of *thelō*, 'to will' and of *thelēma*, 'will'. This verb can be used to express what God desires (Matt. 9.13; 12.7; Heb. 10.5, 8) and what God actually *wills* to happen (1 Cor. 12.18; 15.38; Col. 1.27); sometimes the dividing line between these two is not absolutely clear (cf. John 5.21; Rom. 9.18, 22; 1 Tim. 2.4).

What God thus desires or purposes can stand in opposition to the desires of men and even of his Son (Mark 14.36; cf. Matt. 26.42 and Luke 22.42). What men purpose stands, therefore, under the condition 'if the Lord wills it' (Act 18.21; 21.14; 1 Cor. 4.19; Jas. 4.15; 1 Pet. 3.17). The noun can stand for what God wishes that men should do (Matt. 7.21; 12.50; cf. 21.31); so Jesus did the will of the Father and not his own will (John 4.34; 5.30; 6.38-40). God's plan of salvation can be spoken of as his 'will' (Acts 22.14; Eph. 1.5, 9; Col. 1.9), as can his plan in creation (Eph. 1.11; Rev. 4.11). The life

of the Church in detail—the choice of apostles and the actions they perform—follows the purpose of God (e.g., Rom. 1.10; 15.32; 1 Cor. 1.1); and
his purpose for men is that they should obey his will in ethical action and
holiness (e.g., Rom. 2.18; 12.2; 1 Thess. 4.3; 5.18).

A very similar picture is presented when we look at the synonymous verb
boulomai, 'to wish'; and the noun *boulē*, 'plan'. The former is used of God's
will that can stand over against man's (Luke 22.42), and of his plan of
salvation, whether only intended (2 Pet. 3.9) or actually carried out (Jas.
1.18; cf. Heb. 6.17); it is also used of the way in which the Son reveals the
Father to those whom he wishes (Matt. 11.27; cf. Luke 10.22). As for the
noun, it can be used in general terms of God's plan that he wants men to
follow for their lives (Luke 7.30), of his plan of salvation (Acts 20.27), and
of his purpose which is accomplished in the death of Jesus and the lives of
other men (Acts 2.23; 4.28; cf. 13.36). God is the one who accomplishes all
things according to the purpose of his will, says Paul, as he piles up the
expressions for rhetorical effect (Eph. 1.11).

Other words are also used for what God appoints to happen. Thus *horizō*
has a similar meaning to *proorizō*. The life of Jesus and his future activities
were appointed by God (Luke 22.22; Acts 2.23; 10.42; 17.31; cf. Rom. 1.4),
and God appoints the times at which things happen in the world (Acts
17.26), and the day of salvation (Heb. 4.7). Similarly, *proorizō* is used of
Herod and Pilate acting in accordance with God's plan in the condemnation
of Jesus (Acts 4.28). God made a plan before the ages for our glory (1 Cor.
2.7). He foreordained certain people to be like his Son (Rom. 8.29, 30), and
indeed to become his sons (Eph. 1.5) and his portion (Eph. 1.11). Again,
the verb *tassō*, 'to appoint,' can be used of rulers (Rom. 13.1), those appointed to eternal life (Acts 13.48), and the details of an apostle's career (Acts
22.10).

Finally in this catalogue, we have the verb *eudokeō*, 'to be pleased', and the
noun *eudokia*, 'pleasure, will', which often bring out the element of God's
pleasure in doing certain things or choosing certain people. He delights in
his Servant, Jesus (Matt. 3.17; 12.18; 17.5; cf. Col. 1.19). He delights to save
believers by the preaching of the word (1 Cor. 1.21), to reveal himself to
Paul (Gal. 1.15), and to bestow the Kingdom on the disciples (Luke 12.32).
It is his pleasure to reveal himself by the Son (Matt. 11.26; Luke 10.21);
salvation is for the men on whom his favour rests (Luke 2.14), and the
carrying out of his plan expresses his favour to them (Eph. 1.5, 9).[4]

II   The language of predestination—as applied to men

This summary of the terms used to express predestination in the New Testament may have been tedious, but it is necessary. It is not complete, for it has omitted words referring to calling and election. But it is comprehensive in that an attempt has been made to cover the whole vocabulary of predestination and to indicate in broad terms how it is used. The concept of God's plan as it affects his Son, the creation of the world, the redemption of mankind, and the individuals who compose the Church, is clearly present in the New Testament, and it is no part of our purpose to obscure this fact by hiding any of the evidence; our task is to be true to Scripture.

But it is one thing to state what Scripture says; it is another to understand it and to bring it into relation with the rest of what Scripture says. Here there are real difficulties, and we must now try to deal with them. A recent study of this problem was criticized for confining itself to exegesis and not tackling the problem theologically.[5] We hope that we shall not be criticized for turning to theology and philosophy in order to perform our exegesis better.

When we use the language of predestination and speak of God as willing and purposing, we are using human language to describe God in personal terms. If God is a person, we must use personal language to describe him— which is what the Scriptures do. That he wills and purposes is one aspect of the fact that he is a person. (We may recall that one argument for the personality of the Holy Spirit is that he wills certain things: 1 Cor. 12.11.) But the Scripture is using a human analogy when it describes God in this way, and we have to be very careful when using analogical language. We have to find out how the language is used when applied to men, and what similarities and differences must be noted when it is applied to God.

1. We observe first that willing and purposing is an essential attribute of persons. They can make plans, form intentions, and then act to carry them out; if they could not do so, they would fall short of being real persons.

2. We can distinguish between the elements of 'desire' and 'resolve'. The former is the wish to do something without necessarily being able to carry it out or even intending to carry it out (for example, because we prefer to follow some other wish). The latter is the actual decision to do something, and it entails at least attempting to put it into effect. For example, there is a difference between my present desire to read a novel instead of typing this essay, and my resolve to remain at my desk.

3. It is of the essence of both human desires and resolves that they may not be fulfilled. Paul wished to visit Rome in a particular way, but was not able to do so (Rom. 1.13). Circumstances prevent us doing all that we want to do, and these circumstances may include our own mental and physical limitations.

4. More important, there may be a clash between the wills of two or more

people, so that one of them does not achieve his desire or resolve. While I may not be tempted from my desk by the lure of my unfinished novel, I may he forced away by a persistent knocking at the door and the need to obey somebody else's command.

5. A particularly tricky situation arises when we ask whether it is possible for somebody to predict infallibly and in detail what I shall will and do. I am writing these words on the eve of a British election. It is possible for somebody who knows me well to make a good prediction of how I shall vote in the light of my general character, statements that I have made, and so on. He might even know the physical state of my brain and all the factors that will influence it over the next few hours, so that he can predict confidently what I will do. (The practical impossibility of anybody possessing such knowledge is of course overwhelming.) Does this mean that my behaviour is predetermined, so that I am not able to choose freely? There is one case at least where this is not so. If somebody says to me, 'I predict that you will vote for X', I know that I am free to falsify his prediction by voting for Y. For if he tells me what he predicts, this changes the situation on which the prediction is based and thereby makes it invalid.[6] It would seem to follow that I may be acting equally freely even when somebody makes such a prediction without telling me about it.

There are, of course, situations in which I am not free, and my behaviour is predetermined. The most obvious is that of a post-hypnotic suggestion. Here a person is hypnotized and told to perform a certain act at a given time. He is then released from hypnosis, and the experimenter can know confidently that he will perform the act (assuming that it is not physically impossible or morally repulsive). But the subject thinks that he is performing the act freely, although it is in fact in response to hypnosis. If a person thinks that he is free, is he 'really' free?

6. If an outside observer cannot predict my behaviour infallibly and inform me of his prediction, it follows that it is impossible for me to predict infallibly my own activity; for even if I can assemble all the information about myself, I can never dissociate my roles as observer and acting subject, and hence can always falsify my own predictions, if I want to do so. In principle I cannot predetermine my own future states of mind. The attempt is logically inconceivable, quite apart from its practical impossibility.

7. Even more difficult to imagine is the possibility of my predetermining a course of action involving myself and another subject. 'First I will say A to him, then he will say B to me, then I will reply with C, and he will respond with D. . . .' Naturally, this can be done to some extent: there have been games of chess in which one player has been able to force a predetermined

sequence of moves on his opponent, leading to checkmate, but this assumes that the opponent is playing according to the rules of the game (which lay down a finite set of possibilities) and that he will respond intelligently to each situation. But on the level of free agents it is impossible. For in the chess illustration, the moves of the opponent are not 'free' in fact or in his subjective consciousness. Moreover, we reach the situation that the 'moves' of the person doing the predetermination also cease to be free. Having decided what he is going to do at each particular state (if, for the sake of argument, this is possible), he is then bound to that course of action and cannot change it himself, for if he does, then he must replan the other subject's responses.

8. An interesting point arises if we consider the situation of the author of a play who invents his characters and has the actors perform their parts 'in character', but so that his ultimate goal for the action of the play is achieved.[7] We can then speak of the various characters acting 'freely,' but with the result that in their freedom they advance the action to the desired point, since the author has been able to foresee where their freedom would lead and to account for it in framing his plot. But when applied to real life this analogy breaks down at two points. One point is when the author himself walks on stage and becomes a participant. What happens then? D. M. Mackay admits that it lies beyond our conception. For then the drama becomes free and extempore, and the actors do not know what to say: the lines they learned do not take account of such untoward events, unless the appearance of the author as player is built into the original dialogue, in which case, as we have seen, the author has no freedom.

But the other point is perhaps more important. We have spoken in terms of the characters, but the characters are played by actors, and the actors are bound by the characters assigned to them and the lines that they have learned. There is no question of the 'character' saying 'I am free what to say'; this is an unreal question. He simply says what is in the script. But the actor too knows that he is bound by his lines, and his freedom lies simply in the way in which he says them; if he varies them, he ceases to be the character he is meant to be. A better possibility might be provided by a jazz band in which the various instrumentalists provide their own extempore harmony and counterpoint, yet in such a way that the piece does eventually come to a conclusion and has some sort of unity. But in this case the players collectively know roughly where they are going and their musical sense enables them to recognize where the music as a whole is going, and even to cope with changes in direction (if, say, the composer is playing the melody line and chooses to vary it). It is not so certain that sinful men are willing to cooperate with God in the same way.

The purpose of the above eight points has been to show something of what is involved in using the language of 'willing' in respect of free human agents, and it has brought out particularly the problems inherent in talking about predicting the free decisions of another person or of myself or of both of us interacting with each other. It emerges that it is doubtful whether I can predict the willing of another free person; that it is impossible for me in principle to predict my own willing; and that (consequently) it is impossible for me to predict the pattern of an interaction involving myself. (Note that 'predict' here means 'predict infallibly'.) Naturally, there are situations in which I can predict in broad terms what I am going to do, and what other people will do; a lover can reach the stage where he can determine that when he meets her tomorrow he will make a proposal of marriage and can predict with reasonable certainty that she will respond favourably; and similar things can happen in a host of other situations, but this is not the same thing as the strict determination that is at issue here.

III The language of predestination—as applied to God
1 *Factors in the situation*
So now the question arises of what happens when we use this kind of personal language in order to talk about God. Let us first ask what exactly the Bible is using this language to express. We may list the following ideas:

(a) God is personal. He can will and purpose what he wants to do, and has freedom to do so.

(b) God is sovereign. Ultimately his purpose for the universe will be achieved, so that 'God is all in all'.

(c) God is gracious. The salvation of sinful men depends entirely upon his gracious initiative; no man can come to Jesus unless the Father draws him.

It would not be too difficult for the theologian to construct a scheme in which these three elements are preserved. But the problem is sharpened by the existence of three other equally real factors which stand over against the three points we want to preserve.

(a) Men are personal and have wills of their own. We face the problem of possible opposition to the will of God, and the difficulty of balancing human freedom over against divine predetermination.

(b) Evil exists as a factor which is contrary to the will of God, and of which God is not the author. We have the difficulty of fitting it into God's plan.

(c) Some men are not saved. The implication is that grace was not shown to them, and we then have the difficulty that grace has been bestowed arbitrarily.

2 The Calvinist solution

The typical Calvinist approach in face of these factors admits the ultimate mystery of the problem with which we are dealing, but nevertheless attempts to come to terms with it. It plays down the fact of human freedom in two ways. On the one hand, it argues that divine predestination and prediction of human willing and acting and the subjective experience of human freedom are not incompatible, even if we find it impossible to explain how they can be compatible. (The important essay by D. M. Mackay is a major attempt to find a way of stating how they can be compatible.) On the other hand, so far as the limited area of faith in God is concerned, it asserts plainly that man has no freedom, not even to respond to the grace of God; he is dead in sins and must be given the capacity to believe by God (who gives this to the elect).

Second, the Calvinist allows that somehow even evil acts are included in the all-embracing purpose of God; he tolerates evil in his system so that good may come out of it. But while he allows men to commit evil, it is they who are responsible and bear the guilt for what they freely do, while God himself is not responsible and bears no blame.[8]

Third, the Calvinist insists that God is not under obligation to show grace to any guilty sinner, and therefore he does no injustice in merely showing grace to some, indeed (if many Calvinists are to be believed) to most sinners.[9] Moreover, no sinner need feel excluded from grace, because any person who looks for grace does so only because God has appointed him to do so; it is not possible that a person should seek for grace and yet find that he is not one of the elect.

In this way the Calvinist insists that he does justice to the antinomies which are found in Scripture. Moreover, he is able to do justice to the complete sovereignty of God and the apparent freedom of man. One difficulty that remains is that caused by statements that imply that God wishes all men to do what is right and to be saved. But this is solved by a distinction between the preceptive will of God and the decretive will of God. The former expresses what God wants men to do, while the latter (secret) will expresses what he in fact resolves will happen.

3 Difficulties in the Calvinist solution

This package solution, however, is exposed to considerable objections.

(a) In the previous section we have explored the difficulties that arise when we try to think of a person foreordaining the course of a relationship between himself and another person. This concept is logically self-contradictory, like the medieval concept of a God who can do anything, and therefore can create a stone so big that he himself cannot lift it. The difficulty arises, as we have seen, as soon as the creator of the universe is himself a participant in it. This produces a self-contradictory situation. It can be argued that God is above logic, and that the rules of logic do not apply, just as in mathematics the normal rules for finite quantities do not apply in the realm of trans-finite numbers.[10] But this objection misses the point. We are not concerned with what God can do, but whether we can use our language of predestination to describe him without the language breaking down, and the point is that when this language is applied to divine-human relationships it does break down.

It is worth reflecting that, by applying the scriptural language of human generation to the relation between Father and Son, the Arians (and others of their ilk) ran into difficulties and tried to solve them by the solution that Jesus had a beginning in time; Origen rightly saw that this false solution arose because language was being misused, and introduced the necessary qualification by speaking of the 'eternal generation' of the Son; here is a perpetual reminder that human language cannot be applied to God without qualification. It leads to results incompatible with other statements (as in the Arian controversy) or to self-contradiction. The Calvinist is using human language without observing that it breaks down when applied to God.

(b) The problem of evil also causes difficulties. The Calvinist view that God can cause evil and suffering through 'free' human agents without himself being responsible is untenable. I am responsible for what my agent does.[11] One may, therefore, seek refuge in a modified sense of the word 'cause', so that men are not the agents of God, following out his will when they commit evil. But this is another way of admitting that the model of thought we are using, in which God fore-ordains all things, is breaking down and will not bear the weight that we are putting on it.

(c) To say that God shows mercy to one sinner and not to the next, that is, to adopt a doctrine of double predestination (as is done in orthodox Calvinism), is to land in a moral difficulty. In this case, divine mercy is not being understood in terms of divine justice. I cannot see how it can be just arbitrarily to save one guilty sinner and not another; and there can be no doubt that any human judge (for it is the pattern of the judge which provides the model) who behaved in this way, and *a fortiori* any human father who treated his sons in this way, would be regarded as falling below the standards of Christian justice. To this the reply may be made that we cannot understand the secret working of the mind of God, that he has freedom to show mercy or to harden, as he chooses, and that we must be prepared to trust the inscrutable will of God as being ultimately just, even if we cannot see it from our limited point of view. But again this objection misses the point, which is that the use of the language has broken down; it does not explain, but leaves a mystery. Now there can of course be situations of this kind. There is the case of Job who does not know why he is suffering; the point of the suffering (from God and Satan's angle) would disappear if Job knew why it was happening. For God's aim is to show to Satan: here is a man whom I allow to suffer very grievously, and yet he will not curse me. The point of the experiment is lost if Job sees that he has no need to question the ultimate goodness of God. Similarly, Paul endured his 'thorn in the flesh' when it wasn't God's will to remove it, and then learned to experience the grace of God in a situation of human weakness. But it is one thing to attempt to reconcile experience with faith and another to have a faith that cannot reconcile an apparent contradiction in God himself.

(d) The contrast between the preceptive and decretive wills of God does not really help the situation. We should note that in these two phrases we are really talking about two different things, for the word 'will' is being used in two different senses. God's preceptive will is his desire that men should do certain things and that all men should be saved by responding to the gospel. It is God commanding men to do certain things, 'This do, and you shall live.' (For the Christian, 'this do' means of course 'believe in Jesus', John 6.28f.) But God's decretive will is the expression of his resolve that he will accomplish certain things by whatever form of causation leads men to act in accordance with it.

The problems that arise here are great. First, God's preceptive will is not always obeyed, and therefore his sovereignty not fully obeyed. What he desires is not accomplished. So, second, we have to fall back on his decretive will. But this means that his preceptive will and his decretive will stand in contradiction to each other on many occasions. In the Calvinist view he gives a man the precept 'believe in Jesus', and at the same time by his decretive will he resolves that this man is not one of the elect and therefore cannot obey his preceptive will. But such a self-contradiction is intolerable. The reason why the two wills do not coincide in their effects is of course because of human sin; but in the Calvinist view the decretive will of God embraces human sin, and the ultimate reason why some sinners are saved, and others not saved, rests in the secret will of God. If we say that it is God's will that not all will be saved, this stands in plain contradiction with his expressed desire that all men should repent and come to a knowledge of the truth. (The Calvinist way out of this difficulty is to deny that God does wish all men to be saved by reading an unlikely meaning into the verses and erecting a doctrine of limited atonement.)[12] So the sovereignty of God is not preserved by this distinction.

Worse still, perhaps, is the fact that it makes God out to be hypocritical, offering freely to all men a salvation that he does not intend them all to receive. Certainly, on the human level, all who wish to respond to the gospel can respond; nobody who wants to respond is excluded. But on the divine level, when we look 'behind the scenes' at what God is doing, he is doing one thing with his right hand and another with his left.

From these considerations it becomes clear that the Calvinist attempt to use the language of predestination with respect to God lands in great difficulties, both logical and moral.

IV   The causes of the difficulties

1. The basic difficulty is that of attempting to explain the nature of the relationship between an infinite God and finite creatures. Our temptation is to think of divine causation in much the same way as human causation, and this produces difficulties as soon as we try to relate divine causation and human freedom. It is beyond our ability to explain how God can cause us to do certain things (or to cause the universe to come into being and to behave as it does). Predestinarian language must not be pressed so as to become a doctrine of 'mechanical' causation.

2. A second difficulty is the fact of evil. The Bible is clear that God is not the author of evil. Its origin is and perhaps must be a mystery. Its evilness lies in its lack of good purpose, and thus in its irrationality and opposition to the purpose of God. How it can have come to exist in a universe created by God is unknowable. We must be content to leave the question unresolved. The Calvinist falls into error when he ascribes the reason why some people are not saved to the decretive will of God; in effect, he is trying to explain evil. It is wiser to locate the reason why some people are not saved in the sheer mystery of evil. Admittedly, this way of looking at things also has its dangers; the Calvinist suspects that it conceals an ultimate and intolerable dualism, which Christian theology has in general rejected as a false option; biblical faith, however, insists that in the sovereignty of God evil will be brought to an end.

3. A third difficulty is due to the existence of more than one type of language to describe God in the New Testament, or perhaps rather to the existence of different types of relationship between God and his creatures. The Calvinist approach regards all God's dealings with men as being expressed ultimately in terms of his decretive will, which means that his relationship to men is that of a dramatist to his characters; basically, what God does is to predetermine everything that men think, will and do. But this

approach has the effect of denying the validity of the other type of language used to describe God. Here God is regarded as standing over against the wills of men. He can give commands to them which they may obey or disobey (his preceptive will). He expresses desires. He speak of his love for them, demonstrates it in action and looks for answering love. He can place his will over against their wills, as when he threatens that those who disobey his will shall endure his wrath. This language is as real in the Bible as the predestinarian language, and it cannot be reduced to the latter or expressed completely in terms of it. This should be obvious from the analogy of the dramatist which, as we have already seen, breaks down when applied to God. A dramatist may indeed say that he has come to love his characters (Sir Arthur Conan Doyle, it is said, came to hate Sherlock Holmes!), but it is obvious that this is a special use of the term 'love'; it does not include the possibility of the characters loving the dramatist, and, even if he makes them say 'I love my creator' in his drama, this is not mutual love in the real sense. So too it makes nonsense of God's joy over the repentance of the sinner if the whole thing, joy and all, has been predestined by God. What the Calvinist approach does is to reduce all this language of interpersonal relationships to the expression of the decretive will of God; and to do this is to turn the story of creation and redemption into sheer farce.

The reason why the Calvinist does this is because he wants to insist that God is sovereign over all things and that his will is always done; he thinks that this can be done only by claiming that God predetermines all that happens. This solution does not work, because it creates a clash between what God desires (in his so-called prescriptive will) and what actually happens. It is not true that everything that happens is what God desires. But further this solution arises because the Calvinist cannot see any possibility of God's will being done other than by predetermination of all that happens. There is however, another way in which God's will can be sovereign, and that is by reason of its superior power, so that God can place his will over against ours, and say, 'You may want to do X, but you shall do Y.' And this is how the Bible portrays the ultimate victory of God; he will be all in all when all creatures bow down before his will and obey it, willingly or unwillingly (not because their wills have been predetermined to obey it, but because they have to bow to his superior power).

A solution to the problem of predestination must do justice to the way in which the Bible speaks of God as one who places his will over against ours and acts like another person, rather than as a being who does not enter into real relationships with his creatures but simply treats them as the unconscious objects of his secret will.

This does not mean, however, that we can do away with predestinarian language. We may illustrate this point by referring to prayer. The Bible commands us to pray that God's will may be done, as if this was dependent on our prayers. Prayer influences God. (We can, of course, say that we pray because God wills that he should be moved to act in response to the prayers which he himself has moved us to make. But this reply reduces God to the level of the dramatist.)

But prayer also influences men, in that (for example) the work of preaching the gospel effectively depends upon the intercession of the people of God. The wills of men can thus be affected by prayer—or else we would not pray for them. To believe in prayer is thus to believe in some kind of limitation of human freedom, and in some kind of incomprehensible influence upon the wills of men. (This raises a problem of a different kind: does A have a better chance of salvation than B because X prays for A and not for B? But this is part of the general problem of theodicy, e.g., that a person in Birmingham or Boston has a better chance of hearing the gospel than one in Borneo or Bangladesh.) We must freely admit that there is an element of mystery here, and not try to tone down either aspect of the language of the Bible.

V The purpose and limits of predestinarian language

1. The New Testament clearly teaches that God has desires and acts to put them into effect. He is God, and he is free to do what he likes, choosing one person for a particular task rather than another. He is sovereign in that he is supreme. But we do not yet see all things under the feet of Jesus or the Father. The language of predestination voices the assurance that in the end God's sovereignty will be entire and complete, all opposition having been quelled and his plan of salvation having been accomplished.

2. Predestinarian language safeguards the truth that in every case it is God who takes the initiative in salvation and calls men to him, and works in their hearts by his Spirit. Salvation is never the result of human merit, nor can anybody be saved without first being called by God. Men cannot in any sense save themselves. It must be declared quite emphatically that the non-Calvinist affirms this as heartily as the Calvinist and repudiates entirely the Pelagianism which is often (but wrongly) thought to be inherent in his position. When a person becomes a Christian, he cannot do anything else but own that it is all of grace—and even see that he has been affected by the prayers of other people. But whether we can go on to speak of an 'effectual' calling of those who are saved is dubious. The terminology is not scriptural, and is due to an attempt to find the explanation why some respond to the call

of God and others do not respond in the nature of the call itself. Rather, the effect of the call of God is to place man in a position where he can say 'Yes' or 'No' (which he could not do before God called him; till then he was in a continuous attitude of 'No').

3. Predestinarian language roots salvation in past eternity, 'before the creation of the world'. This leads to the temptation to think of God acting in terms of a blueprint prepared in eternity past. But this is to misinterpret the language and leads to illogical consequences. It destroys the freedom of God who can, for instance, be grieved that he has created sinful men, and then decide what he is going to do next. The Bible has the picture of a God deciding fresh measures in history and interacting with the wills of men alongside the picture of a God planning things in eternity past, and both pictures are equally valid. Neither is to be subordinated to the other. Our difficulties in appreciating this arise from our inability to cope with the concept of eternity and its relation to time. The predestinarian language is meant to affirm that God's plan has all along been one of salvation, and that he created the universe in order to have fellowship with man.

4. Predestinarian language expresses the fact that God can foretell what is going to happen, and can act to bring about his will. Somehow this truth has to be safeguarded despite the difficulties that attach to the idea of prediction. The answer may lie in the fact that in general individuals do not know about the existence of predictions relating to their willing and behaviour and hence do not have the possibility of refusing to obey them; nor is the language of God predicting what certain individuals will do confused with the language of God himself entering into personal relationships with them; nor, or course, is the language of prophecy entirely unconditional, but many prophecies are conditional on the obedience or disobedience of the people concerned; nor again is all prophecy concerned with the predetermining in detail of how certain people are going to act.

5. But now we must assert that predestinarian language must not be used to make God responsible for evil. Certainly he is able to make evil subserve his purposes, but this is not the same thing as being responsible for it. It follows that predestinarian language must not be used to assert that everything that happens is what God wants to happen. His preceptive will, that is, his desires, are not always fulfilled in this present world, although the New Testament promises that one day his complete sovereignty will be revealed. At the same time the Christian confesses that in all things God works for the good of those who love him (Rom. 8.28), and can rest in the goodness of God.

6. Predestinarian language must not be pressed to express *praedestinatio in*

malam partem, the reprobation of certain individuals by the will of God. God wants the wicked man to turn from his wickedness and live; he has no delight in the death of the sinner, and that is his last word on the matter. We have no right to go beyond Scripture and assert that he determines otherwise in the secret counsel of his heart. He is not willing that any should perish but that all should come to a knowledge of the truth and be saved (1 Tim. 2.4). 'Whoever wishes, let him take the free gift of the water of life' (Rev. 22.17). That is God's final word on the matter.[13]

VI Conclusion

It will be clear that the writer of this essay believes in predestination; he cannot do anything else and remain faithful to the testimony of Scripture. Our purpose, therefore, has been to explain the meaning of the phrase, to point out the logical difficulties and moral dangers involved in its use, to place alongside it other types of language which are equally valid and important in understanding the biblical doctrine of God, and so to see how the phrase may legitimately be used. In the end, however, we have seen that we are confronted by mysteries that cannot be solved by the theologian, and it is here that he must confess his faith that, although he cannot solve the problems rationally, what he knows of the power and goodness of God revealed in Christ means that there are answers.

Notes

[1]It is not found in the LXX.

[2]The meaning in Romans 3.25 is different: 'to display publicly'.

[3]The difference is presumably that 'pre-packaged' vegetables are packed *before* they reach the shelves in the retailer's shop, while others are packed (if at all) at the time of purchase.

[4]Most of these words are discussed in *TDNT,* I, pp. 629-37 (G. Schrenk); II, pp. 738-51 (G. Schrenk); III, pp. 44-62 (G. Schrenk); V, pp. 452-6 (K. L. Schmidt); VIII, pp. 164-7 (C. Maurer). See further the discussions of calling (III, pp. 487-96, K. L. Schmidt) and election (IV, pp. 144-82, G. Quell and G. Schrenk).

[6]R. T. Forster and V. F. Marston, *Strategy in Human History* (Wheaton, Ill., 1974). See the reply to this approach; S. Motyer 'Predestination in Biblical Thought,' *Theological Students' Fellowship Bulletin,* 70, autumn, 1974, pp. 10-15.

[6]See especially D. M. Mackay, 'The Sovereignty of God in the Natural World', *SJT,* 21, 1968, pp. 13-16; *The Clockwork Image: A Christian Perspective on Science* (London, 1974).

[7]D. M. Sayers, *The Mind of the Maker* (London, 1941), appears to be a major modern influence on the use of this analogy.

[8]The danger of this type of argument should be noted. A. G. N. Flew has argued (orally) that if God is omnipotent, and can create beings who while free will do what he intends and predicts (as in the analogy of post-hypnotic suggestion), then he could have created them so that they would freely choose good instead of evil, and thus would have avoided all the pointless suffering in the world; but since there is suffering, it follows that God is not omnipotent—or not good—or simply does not exist. Flew favours the last possibility.

[9]B. B. Warfield, *Biblical Foundations* (London, 1958), pp. 246-309, especially p. 304.

[10]A similar point has been made by C. Sampson (in a letter dated 19 November 1974) where he points out how a circle can be defined as a conic section which passes through two points on the line at infinity. These points are both 'real' and 'imaginary' (in the non-mathematical sense of these terms). The rules of logic do not apply in the normal way when we are dealing with the infinite, and hence we must recognize that logic has limitations when applied to the relations between man and God.

[11]Admittedly, the Jews argued that if a principal ordered an agent to do something illegal, it is the agent who carries the sin on his own shoulders; in this situation, there is no 'agency'. But this ruling was designed to prevent agents hiding behind their superior authority if they acted wrongfully (J. D. M. Derrett, *Law in the New Testament* [London, 1970], pp. 52f.).

[12]See V. C. Grounds, 'God's Universal Salvific Grace', in C. H. Pinnock (ed.), *Grace Unlimited* (Minneapolis, 1975), pp. 21-30.

[13]It should perhaps be added to avoid misunderstanding that Scripture does not teach that all people will inevitably be saved. The offer of the gospel is certainly for *all* people, but it does not necessarily follow that all will accept the offer.

17
The Problem of Apostasy
in New Testament Theology

I T MAY SEEM SLIGHTLY ODD THAT SOMEONE WHO KNOWS DALE Moody only through the printed word and who has had no particular associations with the Southern Baptist Theological Seminary should take part in a symposium in Dr. Moody's honour, when there are doubtless many others who have a better claim than I. The basis for my invitation to contribute to the *Festschrift* is that Dr. Moody and I share a common interest in the subject of apostasy and have both written on it. Thus, I have been asked to write on the topic of apostasy and to do so in the light of Dr. Moody's work. I am well aware that the topic can easily raise theological hackles, and I trust that what follows will be taken as an attempt to understand the word of God in the Scriptures, since they alone can constitute our supreme authority in faith and in practice.

Perhaps an autobiographical word may be helpful as an introduction to the subject. In 1969 I published a book entitled *Kept by the Power of God* with the subtitle *A Study of Perseverance and Falling Away.*[1] The book was a shortened and somewhat simplified version of a thesis I had completed for the University of Aberdeen six years earlier. I did not find it easy to interest a publisher, a fact which may indicate that, quite apart from the shortcomings of the book in itself, the topic was not one of general concern to the theological public. The publisher for his part may have regretted his rashness in undertaking the assignment; he did not print a lot of copies and not many of them were sold, with the result that the book was withdrawn from circulation after a comparatively short time. Yet it found one 'convert'. My friend, Professor Clark H. Pinnock, confessed that my book had exercised a decisive influence on his thinking in this area, and, as a result of his enthusiasm for exposing the North American evangelical constituency to its arguments, the book was republished with some slight revisions in 1975.[2]

The line of thought I developed was not, of course, original. Dr. Moody had come to similar conclusions at an earlier date. He in turn was dependent on the great Baptist scholar, A. T. Robertson. He has developed his position in one of the chapters of his comprehensive study of Christian doctrine, *The Word of Truth.*[3] Another scholar who has also defended the same general position is Robert Shank, in his books *Life in the Son*[4] and *Elect in the Son.*[5] A similar position was taken earlier by scholars of the Arminian persuasion, including John Wesley.

The reaction of scholars in the strict Calvinist tradition is to reject the position of writers like Moody and myself. They find the position indefensible on three grounds.

First, they regard the texts in the New Testament that appear to teach the final security of the believer as representing the clear and central teaching of Scripture. They say that other passages which may appear to teach differently, for example, by suggesting the possibility of apostasy, must be interpreted in line with the first texts on the grounds that scriptural teaching by definition is consistent.

Second, the systematic formulation of Christian dogmatics by Calvinist theologians leads to a set of basic and mutually related principles which include the final perseverance of the saints. If one grants that God determined from all eternity to save the elect, then the final perseverance of the elect follows logically. Similarly, if it is agreed that Christ offered an efficacious sacrifice and wrought a full salvation for the elect, then it is inconceivable that this salvation does not contain the element of perseverance.

There is a third reason that is also important, although it does not stand on the same level as the other two. This says that the thought is not congenial that I, a believer, may possibly fall away from my faith and my hope of ultimate salvation. Modern sociological study has shown us how much we need a sense of security if we are to cope with life and its problems, and the importance of a secure basis for early life in the caring love of parents has received the stress it deserves. If we need security on the human level, how much more do we need to be able to trust in God to keep us for time and eternity. How important it is that in our Christian life we have the security provided by God, and the knowledge that, whatever we do, nothing can separate us from his love or thwart his purpose for our lives.

Here, then, are three strong reasons for 1. criticizing a position that acknowledges the danger of falling away from the faith, and 2. for arguing that it rests on an unacceptable and false interpretation of Scripture. Some Calvinists will reject the position more or less out of hand. Others, however, recognize a genuine problem of biblical interpretation. Here, special mention must be made of two scholars. The one is Donald A. Carson, whose book, *Divine Sovereignty and Human Responsibility: Biblical Perspectives in Tension*, published in 1981, tackles the problem with particular reference to the Gospel of John and at a profound and scholarly level.[6] The other is Judy Gundry-Volf, whose dissertation on the problem of perseverance in the writings of Paul bids fair to be the most detailed and acute study of the topic thus far.[7]

What follows now is an attempt to look again at apostasy from an exegetical point of view using Moody's contribution as a starting-point. In the course of the discussion I shall, for sake of convenience, refer to theologians who believe in the final perseverance of the elect as 'Calvinists'. I shall refer to those who do not accept this doctrine in the way in which it was formulated at Dort[8] as 'non-Calvinists', since many of us who are unhappy with Dort are not happy to be lumped together as 'Arminians'.

While it is true that an important part of my own upbringing has been in the Methodist Church, I am by no means a 'dyed-in-the-wool' Methodist, and I owe a great deal to Christians in many other churches. My primary loyalty is to the word of God written in Scripture and not to any human denomination or theological group. My concern, therefore, is to establish what Scripture actually says, and I am grateful for the impulses from theologians of all camps who open my eyes to see things that otherwise any personal bias might prevent me from seeing. I hope that it is not inappropriate for me to regard it as part of my theological task to help other people to shed their blinkers.

Some moral and philosophical problems
First of all, however, let us mention briefly some of the theological and philosophical problems that the issue raises.

The upholders of the possibility of apostasy are not of course unaware of passages in Scripture that promise that God's people will persevere, but they make the point that these promises are for those who continue to abide in Christ and keep on following the Lord. But the Calvinist will ask whether that is an adequate form of assurance. It is some comfort to know that even if I turn away from the Lord, I can always turn back to him and find him willing to forgive. But knowing how fallible I am, I want the assurance that I can never turn away from the Lord to such an extent that I cannot turn back to him.

And here comes the problem. On the Calvinist view, the possibility of a return means that the Lord himself must so work in my life that I am preserved from the possibility of falling away by his overruling of my sinful will. Thus we find that perseverance depends on a divine determinism that overrules what I myself apparently do in freedom. And so, although the Lord may let me fall into sin, he never lets me sin to such a degree that I become totally deaf to his voice. He overrules my will so that I remain faithful. Indeed, he overruled my will in the first instance, so that I freely turned to him and became a believer.

To be sure, we all believe in the influence of the Holy Spirit in our hearts to transform our stubborn, sinful wills, and we insist that 'every thought of holiness, and every victory won are his alone', but this way of looking at things does raise some problems.

1. The Calvinist position cannot explain why it is that the converted sinner still sins sometimes and to some extent, and why God does not sanctify him entirely at conversion. In effect, God is left deciding to allow the convert to sin on some occasions (but never to the point of apostasy), and at other times to do good.

2. This means that in the end it is not the preaching or reading of God's word or any other external means of warning and persuasion that ultimately causes our salvation and holiness, but rather salvation all depends on the secret influence of the Spirit of God on our wills in accordance with a divine plan.

3. Consequently, the Calvinist view deprives the individual of real will power. When the person does wrong, it is because evil has control of him, rather than God. He is reduced to a mere automaton, apparently free to choose, but in reality at the mercy of the power of evil or the power of good. However, the believer does not know this, and perhaps it does not matter, because he acts as though he were free. The Calvinist can thus insist that divine determinism and human freedom are compatible. However, this view does seem to deny the reality of the personhood of God's creatures. Above all, it does not do justice to those passages in Scripture that clearly show that God treats people as free agents, able to decide for themselves.

4. The Calvinist position also has serious consequences for the doctrine of God, for it considers the individual's conversion purely an arbitrary act of God. The convert had been a sinner because sin had taken control of him—he had been dead in trespasses and sins from the time of his conception. But God acted to take control of his life and to deliver him from sin. However, no reason can be assigned as to why God chooses some individuals and rejects others (or, if you prefer, passes them by). Thus the problem is

that God appears to be capricious in granting his love. He may be steadfast in his love to the elect, but his choice of the elect is arbitrary. Of course, one may reply that God is free to show or to withhold mercy as he chooses, and so he is. But is it just to show mercy only to some? Shall not the judge of all the earth do right?

5. Finally, there is a philosophical problem in that this view presents God as the prisoner of his own predestining purpose. Were it merely a case of God's determining what other persons do, the problem would not be so great. In fact, however, predestination affects not only what God's creatures do but also what he himself does in relation to them. God decides whether or not he will act to save them. A solution to this problem may be to say that within God purposing and acting occur simultaneously since God is outside time, and therefore the idea that God first purposes and then acts is a mistaken one. But the determinist view does seem to me to make God the prisoner of his own will.[9]

The effect of these comments is to suggest that in the concept of predestination (whereby everything we do is predetermined) the basis of final perseverance contains moral and logical difficulties and leads to antinomies.

On the other hand, the non-determinist view also has problems. It does not explain how it is that God undoubtedly moves us at times by the working of his Spirit independently of our own wills. Also, it has to come to terms with those passages in Scripture that suggest that salvation from start to finish is the work of God who acts according to his own will. The non-determinist position also shares with the determinist view the problem of explaining the relation of God to evil.

Thus there are problems for both Calvinists and for non-Calvinists. I believe that these difficulties are inherent in any attempt to explain both the actions of God, who is not bound by time and space, and the way in which his actions impinge upon the world he created. Even though we cannot understand in principle how the eternal God functions to cause events in this world, I have the impression that the Calvinist has the greater set of problems. However, I am not philosopher enough to take the matter any further, and therefore I would not want overly to emphasize the fact that I find the greater difficulties in the Calvinist position.

Warnings against falling away

I therefore turn to the area where I feel more at home, namely asking what the New Testament says. A brief review of the textual material discussed by Moody affords a good starting-point for this investigation.

In regard to the Gospels, Moody is content to appeal to Luke 8.9-15. He is on strong ground in this passage. The interpretation of the parable of the sower indicates that there are people who receive the word but do not persevere or continue in faith. Commentators have seen two ways to apply the lesson of the parable. On the one hand, it may be seen as a warning to its hearers to beware of the temptations to give up believing and to stand firm against them. On the other hand, it may be seen as an explanation for the disciples of what will happen to different groups of people who respond to their mission. Either way, we have a clear warning against the danger, and therefore the possibility, of accepting the word and falling away.

There are various ways of avoiding this conclusion.

1. It can be argued that the presence of this and similar warnings in Scripture is part of the means by which God effectually keeps believers from falling away. The purpose of a warning such as this is not to describe actual cases of believers falling away but to describe the fate of hypothetical apostates in such terms that all believers who hear will be persuaded to remain in the faith. In other words, one of the means by which God enables his elect to persevere is through warning them in ways like this.

Now, if one holds that these warnings work in this way, one must also hold that God creates in the elect the correct response to these warnings and that his hidden action in the heart is what leads to perseverance at the end of the day.

But where is the evidence that this is the actual intent of Scriptures such as the present one? And is it not unreal to paint a picture of the fate of hypothetical apostates when such people do not and cannot exist?

2. It can be argued that the descriptions of people who fall away are in every case descriptions of people who had never in fact believed. They may have accepted the message with joy, but they did not believe. However, this explanation comes to grief on the wording in Luke. The presence of the word 'believe' in verse 13 and the contrast with verse 12 indicate that these are people who believe for a time. It is necessary, therefore, to claim that a distinction may be drawn between real and temporary or half-hearted belief. Or the distinction is between those who merely believe on a human level and those in whose hearts the Spirit kindles true belief. However it be expressed, this interpretation would be that such passages as the present one do not describe the elect but rather those whose faith was never of the saving variety.

Of these alternatives the second would appear to be the easier to defend. But let us note clearly what is happening. What this exegesis amounts to is that Luke teaches that a person will not be saved unless his faith is marked, positively, by holding fast the word, bearing fruit and demonstrating endurance, and, negatively, by not ceasing to believe in times of temptation or by not yielding to temptations. In other words, the parable is about the attitudes that believers must show: they are commanded to persevere, and they are told that, if they do not, they will be lost, just like those people who never believed at all. Thus, at the end of the day it will be seen that they did not have saving faith, since their faith did not last and was not strong enough to overcome temptation. It would appear, however, that up to that point they did believe.

The parable says that saving faith is persevering faith. But this surely carries the implication that at any given moment it is impossible to say of a person that he has saving faith; the only proof of saving faith is that the person persevered in the faith and died believing. (We can ignore the problem of people who died at a point when it was not possible for them any longer to demonstrate conscious faith. No one is going to deny salvation to such people.)

If we put the point in this way, we have stated precisely what the defender of the possibility of apostasy is stating. For the parable does not teach that people will infallibly persevere in faith; it simply describes the fact that there are people who do. Certainly I cannot look at my faith at this moment and say, 'Yes, so far my faith has lasted, withstood temptation and brought forth fruit, and therefore I can be confident of my future salvation', for I do not know what tomorrow will bring—at least so far as this parable is concerned.

The Calvinist interpreter, then, is saying: people who do not bring forth fruit and persevere show that they were not of the elect and that they never had saving faith. A typical presentation of the position is: 'Men must hold themselves responsible to persevere; but if they do so, it is God's grace upholding them; while if they fall away, *they demonstrate that they were not true disciples in the first place.*'[10] The non-Calvinist says: if people wish to attain to final salvation, they must persevere in faith, and only at the end will it be seen whether they persevered. For the Calvinist there is a quality in the initial faith that guarantees perseverance (or, God who inspired the faith will enable it to persevere), so that we can say that such a person was and is 'a true disciple'. The non-Calvinist, while not disputing that one can distinguish broadly between nominal and true believers, insists that perseverance is not so much a quality inherent in true faith at the point of conversion, as it is simply the lastingness of faith that is shown from moment to moment throughout the Christian life.

Thus one can read the parable from a Calvinist perspective. But one must insist: (a) that this perspective is not necessary for understanding the parable in itself; (b) that the parable (and similar teaching) does not *prove* the Calvinist interpretation.

Hence such a parable as this does not *teach* final perseverance. To the

Calvinist and the non-Calvinist believer alike it says: see that you persevere! Of itself it does not convey to the believer the assurance that he will persevere. We shall find that this is true for the 'warning' passages in general.

Moody briefly notes two passages in Acts that favour his position. One is the Ananias and Sapphira story (Acts 5.1-11). However, I do not think that any conclusions regarding the ultimate fate of the two sinners can be drawn from this passage. Acts 20.30 is a warning to the Church that fierce wolves will draw disciples away after them. Again, the Calvinist may claim that those who are drawn away were not 'true' disciples, but in order to do so it is necessary to demonstrate that Luke (or Paul) distinguishes between true and seeming disciples.

If the latter are meant, then (on Calvinist premises) the warning would appear to be futile because the seeming disciples do not belong to the elect. If it be argued that the purpose of the warning is to help any of these seeming disciples who are elect but not yet regenerate to come to true faith, then it must be remarked that this is a peculiar form of wording for the purpose. If the former group is meant, then the passage is being interpreted on the hypothesis that those who persevere to the end and do not become the prey of wolves are in fact the elect, and that they persevered because they were predestined to do so.

But does this really help? The fact is that no one can know for certain who are the true disciples and the false disciples. If a person is in the former group, he has still to heed the warning: only by so doing can he show that he is one of the elect. In other words, the Calvinist 'believer' cannot fall away from 'true' faith, but he can 'fall away' from what proves in the end to be only seeming faith. The possibility of falling away remains. But in neither case does the person know for certain whether he is a true or a seeming disciple. All that he knows is that Christ alone can save and that he must trust in Christ, and that he sees signs in his life which may give him some assurance that he is a true disciple. But these signs may be misleading.

It comes down to a question of assurance. Whoever said, 'The Calvinist knows that he cannot fall from salvation but does not know whether he has got it', had it summed up nicely. On this view, the ground of assurance is the evidence of a changed life. But this can be counterfeit and misleading. The non-Calvinist knows that he has salvation—because he trusts in the promises of God—but is aware that, left to himself, he could lose it. So he holds fast to Christ. It seems to me that the practical effect is the same.

Moody then turns to the epistles of Paul. Here he notes the encouragements and warnings to Christians and the fear that some would fall. The issues here are in principle the same as in the passages already discussed. And in a sense the exegetes are in agreement. For the Calvinist the warnings and the promises are the means by which God urges the elect to faithfulness on the empirical, human level, while he works in their hearts so that they respond positively. For the non-Calvinist the same passages are equally God's means of urging believers to persevere. In both cases it is recognized that the Spirit is the means of renewal without which believers would be unable to respond to God's word. The question is whether the Spirit always operates irresistibly and positively in the lives of some but not of others. Whether I am a Calvinist or not, I must heed the encouragements and warnings, in the former case to show that I am a real and not a seeming believer, and in the latter case for fear that I might fall away from the real faith that I have.

Most important are the passages in Hebrews to which Moody gives special attention. There are five of these: 2.1-4 (we must pay close attention to what we have heard, lest we drift from it); 3.7-4.13 (the danger of having an evil, unbelieving heart and thus falling away from the living God); 6.1-20 (the impossibility of restoring to repentance those who become partakers of the Holy Spirit and then commit apostasy); 10.19-39 (the punishment in store for those who sin wilfully after having been sanctified by the blood of the covenant); and 12.1-29 (the warning not to be like Esau who was given no opportunity to repent after he sold his birthright). The first and second passages can be understood by Calvinists like the cases of seeming believers above, but this is not the most natural interpretation of them. The third passage (Heb. 6.1-20) causes problems for the Calvinist because it is extremely implausible to interpret the passage as referring to people who were never genuine believers and then claim that the text describes a merely hypothetical danger. The same is true of the fourth passage, and (less clearly) of the fifth. That is to say, the view that the Hebrews passages speak of merely nominal believers is most unlikely. The Calvinist interpretation has to be that the dangers are purely hypothetical, since, it is claimed, God uses the passages effectively to warn all true believers against the danger of apostasy. But the passages in themselves do not require this interpretation, and it is safe to say that it would never have been offered except in the interests of a dogmatic theory that God will infallibly save a fixed group of the elect. However, even though the author of Hebrews emphasizes the faithfulness of God to his people, there is no suggestion in the text that the author shares this particular view of predestination.

Encouragements to persevere

We now have, on the one hand, a series of statements apparently addressed to believers, urging perseverance, warning against apostasy, and indicating the unpleasant consequences of apostasy. The believer must take these warnings seriously.

On the other hand, there are other strands of teaching that encourage the believer to persevere. These can be briefly summarized as follows:

1. The New Testament writers at least regard it as normal that believers will persevere and continue in their faith. Side by side with the warnings are statements that suggest that believers will travel safely to the end of their pilgrimage. The warnings are about behaviour that is regarded certainly as possible, but not as normal or inevitable.

2. The New Testament contains promises of heavenly glory to encourage believers to persevere in their faith. We have only to think of the promises to the overcomers in Revelation, and the fact that the author has visions of those who have overcome safely, reaching their final reward.

3. There are also promises that the powers arrayed against believers are not so strong that they must inevitably fall. In 1 Corinthians 10.13 Paul insists that there is no temptation so strong that believers must inevitably succumb to it, and insists that God will not let people be tempted beyond what they can bear. He will provide a way out so that they can stand up under it. To be sure, they still need to be warned against the danger in which they stand (1 Cor. 10.12!), but they are assured that, if they want to overcome temptation, they can do so. If people resist the devil, he will flee from them (Jas. 4.7).

4. It is also quite clear that if a believer does fall and then returns to the Lord in repentance, he will be accepted. This is very clear from the Lord's Prayer with its petition for forgiveness, and also from 2 Corinthians where the problem of sin within the Church is discussed at length. Despite the strong words in Hebrews 6 and 10, it seems unlikely that any repentant believer would find the Lord refusing pardon for past sins. The sin in Hebrews 10 is that of rejecting the means of forgiveness, the death of Christ, and Hebrews 6 is probably to be explained in the same way; it is clear that the person who seeks forgiveness on the grounds of Christ's death will not be rejected.

5. Believers have the promise of spiritual power to overcome temptation. The presence of the Holy Spirit in their lives enables them to overcome temptation and guides them in the path of God's will.

6. All these points relate to means by which believers can overcome. They are like soldiers sent out to battle with full armour and the knowledge that the enemy, though strong, is not impregnable. They can go out with full confidence. But is that enough, and is it all? After all, the strongest armies have been defeated by the secret weapons of the enemy or by fifth-columnists

within.

A vital element in perseverance is the assurance that God will certainly win in the end. This is an essential element in the faith of God's people; their faith is faith in the omnipotence of God, demonstrated in the death of Christ at which Satan and death were defeated (cf. Rom. 8.31-39).

Hence Christian faith is faith that one will persevere because God is almighty. Now if a person wonders whether he will persevere, he is doubting the content of his faith and is not believing. So the apostate is the person who has ceased to believe in the power and love of God. Hence by definition a believer is a person who believes that God will triumph—and that the triumph will include his share in it.

The person who falls away is thus one who prefers the pleasure of the moment—or the avoidance of the pain of the moment—to sharing the triumph of God, or who believes that God will not triumph. Falling away is giving up the faith that one will persevere by the power of God.

We must now consider whether the biblical teaching that speaks of God's election of his people and of his will to bring them to final salvation renders falling away impossible in principle.

In John we have some statements that indicate that believers will never perish. In his book, Moody draws attention to John 3.3-8 (those who have been born again cannot be 'unborn'); 5.24 (believers pass from death to life and do not come to judgement); 6.37 (all whom the Father gives to the Son will come to him); 6.39 (this is the will of God, that Christ should lose none of those given to him but raise them up at the last day); and especially 10.28 (my sheep shall never perish, and no one shall snatch them out of my hand).

Alongside these statements we have others that refer more specifically to believers as God's elect or chosen people. We find this thought in John 6.37, and also in such passages as Acts 13.48; 16.14 and 18.10. Above all, it surfaces in passages where God's people are specifically called 'the elect'. In one or two passages this phrase is conceivably used to refer to people who have not yet responded to the gospel, but who have been foreordained by God to do so (2 Tim. 2.10; Titus 1.1; Matt. 2.14; cf. Acts 9.15). We also read of God foreordaining people to be conformed to the image of Jesus and taking the necessary steps to bring them to that final goal (Rom. 8.28-30), and of his choosing people in Christ (Eph. 1.4f., 11). From these verses some would draw the conclusion that if God has a purpose for these people in electing them, then he will surely fulfil that purpose in their lives and bring them to final salvation.

Our problem is the relation between these statements and the former set. There can be only three solutions. The first is to give the election texts the primacy and to reinterpret the warnings to fit in with them by any of the means already discussed. This gives an unnatural rendering to the warnings. The second possibility is to recognize that there is a tension in the passages and not try to avoid it by twisting either set of statements. There is, of course, a third solution, which is to give primacy to the warnings and to twist the election statements to mean less than they apparently say. This is probably the least satisfactory solution. I am going to suggest that the election statements may be in danger of some misinterpretation, but I do want to take them seriously and to insist that they must stand alongside the warning statements.

So the question is what we make of the election and preservation sayings. I begin with a comment on the Johannine material. John 10.28 says that there is a group of people who are the sheep of the Good Shepherd. Whoever does not belong to this group does not believe. What leads to belief is not seeing signs that prove that Jesus is the Messiah, but hearing (that is, obeying) his voice and following him. Those who believe have eternal life and no one can take them out of the Shepherd's care—not even the evil one. The reason no one can do this is that the Father who gave the flock to Jesus is greater than any other power.

It is surely one thing for the devil to snatch the sheep away against the sheep's will—that cannot happen. It is another thing for the sheep to yield to temptation. How, then, is the activity of the devil seen? Does he merely tempt or does he cause people to fall? Is his appeal irresistible? It would be easy if we could say that he merely tempts and that it depends on us whether we fall.

Now on the level of exhortation and teaching, do we tell people that the devil is irresistible to Christians? Paradoxically, we do tell non-believers that they cannot avoid yielding to temptation, but since they are responsible they should not do so. The Christian schoolteacher does not tell his pupils that they cannot avoid doing what is wrong and that therefore he will not punish them if they commit wrong. Or do we tell people that the Spirit is irresistible, and that they can sit back and let the Spirit take control? Some may do so, but this attitude of 'quietism' would probably be rejected by serious theologians. What we actually do is to tell believers to resist the devil in the strength of God. They can win, but they will not win if they do not fight! Thus, whatever we believe about John 10.28, in practice we tell believers that they must resist the devil, or else they will fall. In other words, the force of a passage like John 10.28 is to encourage believers to resist the devil in the confidence that they can win because of the promises of God. Faith includes believing in the victory of God. Similarly, Jesus can look back in John 17.11f.

and state that up to this point he has safely kept his disciples, and then confidently pray that they will continue to be protected. Yet even in this context we hear of the one who was not kept, the one destined for perdition. Thus the teaching in John is meant to be a source of encouragement to believers to persist in faith in the omnipotence of God.

Next, we can consider the concept of election. The words 'election' and 'elect', like the concept, are used in a number of theologically relevant ways: 1. to refer to Jesus as the Chosen One of God; 2. in the plural ('elect') to refer to the Church and its members collectively. The second is the most characteristic use. 3. 'Election' also refers to the calling of individuals to special tasks such as apostleship (Acts 1.24; 9.15). 4. In the singular, the term 'elect' refers to an individual Christian. There seems to be only one possible case of the last usage, namely, in reference to Rufus in Romans 16.13. The fact that Rufus is singled out in this way suggests that the word is used here in an unusual manner, perhaps to mean 'outstanding' or something similar.

It is important to note that 'elect' is always used of those who actually belong to the Church, not of prospective believers. The two possible exceptions are in 2 Timothy 2.10 and Titus 1.1, but there the expression means that Paul labours for the sake of believers so that they will attain to final salvation, and that he works in accordance with, or to further, the faith of God's people.

Next, we note that the term is ordinarily used to describe those who belong to the Church in terms of outward profession, rather than to distinguish between those who really belong and those who are merely professors. Thus the term is not used of a group within the Church secretly known to God. There is a possible exception in Matthew 22.14, but this verse simply refers to those who are invited to the wedding, some of whom are found unworthy; many are called, but only some of them respond and become part of the 'elect'. So the 'elect' are those who are called by God and who become members of his people by exercising faith. The word is not used of a group of 'real' believers in the Church, as opposed to seeming, nominal believers.

Where, then, is the source of the idea of a secret group of elect individuals previously chosen by God to be saved and to persevere in salvation? This idea does not come from the use of the term 'elect', but from other passages that may suggest that God has chosen some and passed by others. It is of course true that God chooses specific individuals for particular tasks—there is an element of particularity here that cannot be avoided. But are there any real grounds for extrapolating from the principle of the calling of some individuals to service the conclusion that there is a predestination of those who are called to salvation? And does it in any case follow that those called to service will necessarily obey? Judas fell away from being one of the Twelve, and Paul gives the impression that he responded of his own choice (Acts 26.19). But it must be said that for a Calvinist the fact that somebody is said to respond to grace freely is no argument against effectual calling.

In John 6.64 Jesus states that there are some disciples who do not believe, for (says John) Jesus knew from the beginning who were the unbelievers and the betrayer. But there is nothing particularly problematic here: Jesus knows the hearts of people. Jesus goes on to say that people cannot come to him unless the Father enables them. He rejects the idea that people can 'control' him. Only if the Father calls can people come. But this does not necessarily mean that if a person is called he will respond with faith.

2 Timothy 2.19 has also been cited in this connection (the Lord knew those who were his people). But this text is only a recognition that the visible Church can contain plausible hypocrites who do not really belong to it, and no one denies that this can be the case.

More importance attaches to Romans 8.28-30. These verses say that the people who love God need not be afraid of tribulations (8.18), because the glory in store for them is greater than the tribulation; we can be confident that, no matter what painful experiences we have, all will be for the good of those whom God has called, because his final purpose for those whom he calls is their glorification. We know that because of two things. First, God's purpose for those whom he 'foreknew' was that they might share the image of Jesus, that is, share in his glory. Second, God has already started the process: God has called the people for whom he has this purpose. Calling was followed by justification, obviously of those who believed and thereby responded to the call. And justification is followed by a glorification that has already begun (2 Cor. 3.18). Thus this passage is meant to reassure God's people that his final purpose for them is glorification, a purpose that will be carried out despite their sufferings. The passage is not a statement about the effectual calling of those whom God foreknew. It is a guarantee that those who have responded to God's call with love (and faith) can be fully assured of his purpose of final glorification for them.

Finally, there is a group of texts in Acts that point to election. In Acts 13.48 we find that when Paul preached in Antioch of Pisidia the Gentiles who heard rejoiced, and all who were 'ordained' to eternal life believed. In 16.14 the Lord opened Lydia's heart to attend to what Paul said. And in 18.10 the Lord assured Paul that he had many people in Corinth, that is, many people who apparently were to be converted. These verses appear to suggest a divine plan to be carried out by Paul involving the salvation of individuals. With regard to Acts 16.14, however, no one would deny that people can hear and respond to the gospel only if the Lord takes the initiative. Acts 18.10 indicates the Lord's foreknowledge of the progress of the gospel in Corinth. But the text could also mean that, since there were now many Christians in Corinth, God's purpose for Paul was that he should continue there to teach them and ground them in the faith. Acts 13.48 could well mean that those Gentiles who had already begun to search for eternal life (like Cornelius in Acts 10) believed upon hearing the good news that salvation was now at last being offered to them through Jesus. Or it might mean that the Gentiles believed inasmuch as they had (collectively) been included in God's saving plan.

We have no desire to empty these verses of their meaning. It is beyond cavil that the Bible teaches that God takes the initiative in salvation, that he planned the creation of his people from eternity past, that it is he who calls to salvation, and that his Spirit leads people to faith in a way that we cannot understand. Calvinist and non-Calvinist alike believe that it makes sense to pray that the Spirit will lead unconverted people to respond. But whether we can conclude from this that a secret predestining will of God always operates when people are saved is doubtful.

Nor is there any question whatever that the Bible clearly teaches the loving purpose of God who keeps believers by his grace (1 Pet. 1.5). As Christians, we can and do rely completely on Christ, the Good Shepherd and we claim his promise that he will keep us and that he will not let us fall (Jude 24). We could not live the Christian life without these promises and their gracious realization in our lives.

What I am suggesting, then, is that the primary function of the election language in the Bible is to stress that God takes the initiative in salvation and that his purpose is to create a people who will attain to that salvation. But it is never said that this means either that there is a non-elect section of humanity who cannot attain to salvation or that there is a fixed group of previously chosen 'elect' who will be called, justified and glorified in some automatic fashion. We must not draw logical conclusions from the biblical material that go beyond its clear implications and which land us in logical contradiction with other biblical teaching.

It is this element of promise that needs to be emphasized to balance Moody's emphasis on the possibility of apostasy; Moody has deliberately offered a one-sided position in order to counterbalance a bias in the opposite direction that misinterprets important parts of Scripture.

Conclusion
What, then, are the theological and practical implications of our discussion?

We have seen that:

1. The New Testament contains both encouragements to believers to persevere and warnings against the dangers of apostasy. These warnings are best understood as calls to believers to persevere in the faith in view of genuine dangers rather than (a) as calls that 'true' believers will inevitably heed because God has predetermined that they shall do so, and which are therefore empty threats because in fact nobody will ever apostatize, or (b) as warnings that are addressed to people who are not true believers, and thus are again unreal warnings in that such people need to be told to repent and believe rather than not to turn away from a faith which in fact they do not have.

2. The New Testament also teaches that God takes the initiative in salvation and leads people to faith by the work of the Spirit. Those who respond to the gospel become God's people, his 'elect'. He gives his grace and power to his people to enable them to persevere, and with divine help there is no reason why they should ever fall away from him. Yet the possibility of falling away cannot be excluded. We do not know whether any will in fact fall away and be lost eternally, although there are some possible cases in the New Testament.

3. It is better not to think of a group of people who at their conversion become 'true' believers (because of God's election and call) and whose faith therefore will inevitably persevere. What the Bible offers is promises that believers can persevere and, therefore, encouragements to them to persist in faith and not to fall away. The warnings are meant quite seriously.

4. Can, then, a person claim that he will never fall away and have an assurance that will carry him through every situation of temptation and worry? Can he, for example, say, 'I am elect, and therefore I am safe; no matter how far I fall into temptation and yield to it, in the end God will bring me safely through?'

According to L. Berkhof,[11] there is some difference of opinion among Calvinists on whether faith includes assurance. Berkhof himself allows that true faith 'carries with it a sense of security, which may vary in degree' and that believers can attain to a subjective assurance from contemplating their own experience of the work of the Spirit. But, while many believers in the Calvinist tradition undoubtedly do have assurance of salvation, both present and final (for mercifully God's gifts are not bound by what our theological systems allow him to grant), it is difficult to avoid the impression that a strict Calvinist can never be fully certain that he is one of the elect. So soon as he believes that he is one of the elect, he knows that he cannot fall from grace; may he not begin to trifle with sin, and thus prove that he never was elect? Consequently, even if a person says, 'I know that I am one of the elect', the possibility remains that he may commit grievous sin and thus show that he was not elect.

The same thing is true if we try to work in terms of 'true believers' as opposed to nominal ones or those with an unreal faith. For the reality of faith is shown only by its continuance. And who can say that he has such persevering faith?

What, then, can the believer say that is neither presumptuous nor self-deceiving? He can say that he knows the One in whom he has put his trust, and that he believes in a God who is able to keep that which he has committed to him (2 Tim. 1.12; whether this is the correct exegesis is totally immaterial!). He can listen to the apostle who tells him that he belongs to those who are 'kept by the power of God ready for a salvation ready to be revealed in the last time' (1 Pet. 1.5). That is to say, his assurance is rooted not in the fact that he has faith, but in the character and promises of God. And that is surely the point of the language of God's election and choice. It is an affirmation of the commitment of God to those who are his people; it is a declaration of faith that God, having brought us thus far, intends to bring us to final glory. It stands alongside those passages that declare that there is a condition to all this—'provided that we also suffer with him'—and that warn us against unbelief.

And therefore the believer can and must affirm his faith and his assurance. If Paul can declare that he is sure that nothing in all the universe can separate him from the love of God, so too the believer can declare with full assurance in the words of Charles Wesley:

No condemnation now I dread,
Jesus and all in him is mine;
alive in him my living Head,
and clothed in righteousness divine,
bold I approach the eternal throne,
and claim the crown through Christ my own.

That note of solid assurance of final salvation comes from a so-called Arminian who believed what Paul said!

5. What, therefore, we have done is to insist that the warning statements are to be taken with full seriousness, and that the promises, expressed in election language and other ways, are also to be taken with full seriousness as affirmations of belief in the saving power of God. And faced by these we walk by faith, not by sight, for the essence of our faith is that it is faith in the final victory of the God who has shown his almighty power on Good Friday and Easter Day.

What the New Testament says to the believer is: 'You belong to the elect, therefore constantly seek to make your calling and election sure.' The New Testament calls on all who believe in Jesus Christ to persevere in belief, that is, to keep on believing. Those who know that they are God's children, who have the assurance that their sins are forgiven, must go on believing and committing themselves to the saving and keeping love of Jesus. Their assurance of final salvation does not rest primarily upon the evidences of election but rather on their Saviour, and, if they are non-Calvinists, they know that the grace which has been openly revealed in Christ is not cancelled by a secret plan of God which may have excluded them from salvation even though they have experienced some taste of it.

It emerges that in practice the Calvinist believer is in no better position than the non-Calvinist. The non-Calvinist may believe that there is a danger of his apostasy, but he also believes in the revealed grace of God, and he knows that there is no secret plan of God which may conflict with his revealed loving purpose; on the contrary, he knows that he is included in the will of God to 'bring many sons to glory', and consequently he knows that he can trust in God with complete confidence.

On both views the possibility of apostasy exists at the experiential level. The Calvinist view allows that people may be seeming believers and of course in the end they will not be saved; they will not persevere in faith because they never had the 'real' faith which contains the virtue of perseverance. The non-Calvinist view also allows that people may believe and yet fall away because they did not persevere. But whereas the former view attributes 'apostasy' to the fact that God did not elect these people to salvation, the latter view attributes it to the mystery of evil.

It can be protested that neither solution is wholly satisfying. The former has to allow that God does not show mercy to all, which suggests that he acts immorally. The latter has to allow that, although God acts morally, for some mysterious reason he cannot always conquer the evil in human hearts; but the reason for this lies not in the reprobating will of God but in the mystery of evil.

Perhaps, then, in the end it makes little practical difference whether we speak of the mystery of the divine will or of the mystery of evil. But on the theological level there is a serious difference. In both cases we face the problem of evil and admit that we cannot solve it. The former solution is problematic because it questions the goodness of God and has to read into much of the New Testament a 'hidden agenda' in the divine plan for salvation. The latter solution is also problematic because it appears to question the absolute power of God,[12] but exegetically it perhaps has fewer difficulties.

Thus we find that both Calvinists and non-Calvinists affirm the reality of God's preserving grace and both allow for the possibility of apostasy in the Church. But an exegetical study of the New Testament makes it quite clear that in view of the complexity of the evidence and the impossibility of denying the reality of the danger of apostasy, we are best to admit that there is a tension in Scripture on this subject. In the last analysis this is due to the impossibility of explaining both the mystery of divine causation and the mystery of evil. Therefore we should recognize that the strict Calvinist approach offers an oversimplification and systematization of the biblical material. It is to the credit of Dr. Moody that he has expressed his unease with over-systematization of biblical theology and is content to live with mystery.[13]

Notes

[1]I. H. Marshall, _Kept by the Power:A Study of Perseverance and Falling Away_ (London, 1969).

[2]Ibid. (Minneapolis, 1975).

[3]D. Moody, _The Word of Truth_ (Grand Rapids, 1981), pp. 348-65.

[4]R. Shank, _Life in the Son_ (Springfield, 1961).

[5]Ibid., _Elect in the Son_ (Springfield, 1970).

[6]D. A. Carson, _Divine Sovereignty and Human Responsibility: Biblical Perspectives on Tension_ (London, 1981).

[7]J. Gundry-Volf, 'Perseverance and Falling Away in Paul's Thought' (Inaugural-Dissertation zur Erlangung des Doktorwürde der Evangelisch-theologischen Fakultät an der Eberhard-Karls-Universität zu Tübingen, 1987).

[8]At the 1618-19 Church synod held at Dort in the Netherlands the doctrines of the Remonstrants (the followers of Jacob Arminius) were condemned in a statement which outlined five key doctrines of Calvinism: the total depravity of mankind; God's unconditional election of those whom he chooses to save; the limitation of the saving efficacy of the atonement to the elect; the irresistibility of God's grace in saving the elect; and the infallible preservation of the elect to final salvation. It is the last of these points that is under discussion in this essay, but upholders of Dort would insist that all five points stand or fall together. For a brief account of the Synod, see (for example) W. Elwell (ed.), _Evangelical Dictionary of Theology_ (Grand Rapids, 1984), pp. 331f.

[9]For a fuller discussion of some of these points, see C. H. Pinnock (ed.), _Grace Unlimited_ (Minneapolis, 1975).

[10]Carson, _Divine Sovereignty and Human Responsibility,_ p. 195; italics are mine.

[11]_Systematic Theology_ (London, 1969), pp. 507-9.

[12]For a helpful discussion of the philosophical problem, see J. L. Walls, 'Can God save anyone he wills?', _SJT,_ 38, 1985, pp. 155-72.

[13][1989] The issues treated in this and the preceding essay have now been carried further in C. H. Pinnock (ed.), _The Grace of God, The Will of Man_ (Grand Rapids, 1989).

Select Index of Biblical Texts

Genesis
3—*189f.*

Psalms
2.7—*121-33, 143, 145f., 158f.*
110—*204-8*

Isaiah
42.1—*121-33*
53—*160f.*

Daniel
7—*81, 96f., 103f., 115f., 119f.*

Matthew
8.20—*85f., 119*
11.19—*85*
11.27—*137-9, 155*
16.17—*140f.*
16.18—*229f.*
19.28—*83, 229*
24.42—*204*
24.44—*90*

Mark
1.11—*121-33*
2.10—*86f.*
2.20—*107*
2.28—*203f.*
8.31—*93f.*
8.37—*248*
8.38—*83, 110*
9.31—*93f.*
10.33f.—*93f.*
10.45—*248-50*
12.6—*142*
12.35-7—*204-6*
13.26—*109*
13.32—*139f.*
13.35-7—*204*
14.21—*93*
14.62—*83, 90f.*

Luke
7.34—*85*
8.9-15—*310-3*
9.58—*85*
10.22—*137-9, 155*

12.8f.—*83, 88-90*
12.40—*90*
18.8—*90*
19.10—*87f.*
21.28—*240*
22.29f.—*141f., 229*
22.48—*92f.*
24.21—*252*

John
1—*166-8*
1.34—*123, 125, 127*
10.28—*317f.*

Acts
2.36—*145*
3.20—*157f.*
13.33—*145f., 158*
13.48—*320*
18.10—*320*
20.28—*245*
20.30—*313*

Romans
1.3f.—*144f., 157f.*
3.24—*246f.*
5.10f.—*265f.*
8.3—*171f.*
8.28-30—*319*
11.15—*266*

1 Corinthians
1.30—*241f.*
6.20—*242*
7.23—*242*

2 Corinthians
3.14—*280*
5.18-21—*263-5*
8.9—*170f.*

Galatians
3.13—*241*
3.15-17—*279*
3.24—*279*
4.4—*171*
4.5—*241*

Ephesians
1.7—*247*
1.14—*245*
2.16—*268f.*

Philippians
2.6-11—*169f.*
2.6-8—*159-62*

Colossians
1.14—*247*
1.15-20—*267f.*
1.22—*172*
2.9—*172*

1 Thessalonians
1.10—*156f.*

1 Timothy
2.6—*248*
3.16—*173*

2 Timothy
2.10—*318*

Titus
1.1—*318*
2.14—*248*

Hebrews
1.1-3—*174*
2.1-4—*314*
3.7—4.13—*314*
6.1-20—*314*
9.11ff.—*247f.*
10.19-39—*314*
11.35—*247*
12.1-29—*314*

1 Peter
1.18—*244*
1 John—*168f.*
2 John—*168f.*

Revelation
1.5—*243f.*
5.9—*243f.*
14.3f.—*243f.*

Author Index

Aalen, S., *236*
Abbott, T. K., *254*
Arminius, J., *324*
Baillie, D. M., *179*
Baker, J. P., *275*
Baltzer, K., *287, 289*
Balz, H. R., *106, 114, 116*
Bammel, E., *77, 96, 236*
Barbour, R. A. S., *36*
Barr, J., *33, 149, 237*
Barrett, C. K., *33, 102, 109, 113-7, 253, 274, 288*
Barth, G., *132*
Barth, K., *18, 33*
Bauckham, R. J., *119*
Bauer, J. B., *254*
Beale, G. K., *289*
Beare, F. W., *141, 148*
Beasley-Murray, G. R., *69, 120, 210, 236*
Behm, J., *148, 288*
Beker, J. C., *39, 54f., 61, 68*
Berkhof, L., *277, 288, 321*
Best, E., *117, 131f.*
Betz, O., *33, 116, 147*
Beyschlag, W., *33*
Bieneck, J., *147, 149*
Bietenhard, H., *210*
Birdsall, J. N., *114*
Bittner, W., *120*
Black, M., *74, 79f., 95f., 103, 115, 117f., 210*
Bohatec, J., *253*
Boman, T., *114, 116*
Boobyer, G. H., *97*
Boers, H., *33*
Bornkamm, G., *62, 68, 77, 96, 101, 107, 114, 118, 132, 164*
Borsch, F. H., *102, 105, 110, 112, 114, 116f.*
Bousset, W., *17, 33, 74, 96, 121f., 130, 153-5, 163, 202, 210*
Bowman, J. W., *151, 163*
Bretscher, P. G., *133*

Brockington, L. H., *131*
Brown, C., *15, 32, 210*
Brown, D., *53*
Brown, R. E., *165, 178*
Bruce, F. F., *96, 114, 116f., 131, 145, 149, 163, 252, 256, 288*
Büchsel, F., *252-7, 273f.*
Bultmann, R., *18f., 21, 23-5, 27f., 33, 54, 58, 68, 74-7, 80, 83, 86f., 95-8, 101, 107, 114, 131, 148, 153, 163f., 255, 269, 274*
Burger, C., *237*
Cadman, W. H., *117*
Caird, G. B., *99*
Calvin, J., *272, 274, 287f.*
Campbell, J. Y., *74, 95*
Campbell, K. M., *288*
Caragounis, C. C., *120*
Carey, G., *195*
Carmignac, J., *166, 178*
Carson, D. A., *308, 324*
Casey, M., *65, 69, 119, 210*
Casey, R. P., *163*
Charlesworth, J. H., *120*
Chilton, B. D., *216-20, 236*
Coenen, L., *257*
Collange, J.-F., *274*
Colpe, C., *33, 102, 105-8, 112-8*
Conzelmann, H., *20, 21, 27f., 33, 77, 96, 114, 125, 132, 149, 236*
Cortes, J. B., *115*
Cranfield, C. E. B., *87, 95-9, 179, 203, 210, 237*
Cross, F. L., *96, 236, 254*
Cullmann, O., *33, 95, 99, 101, 114, 122, 130, 149, 164, 196*
Dalman, G., *121, 130, 137-9, 147f.*
Daube, D., *252f.*
Davey, F. N., *33*
Davies, W. D., *164*
Deissmann, A., *242, 253*
Denney, J., *273*

Derrett, J. D. M., *252, 305*
Dibelius, M., *254*
Dinkler, E., *149*
Dodd, C. H., *25, 54f., 99, 132, 219, 237, 251*
Downing, F. G., *118*
Dunn, J. D. G., *33f., 52, 56, 60-3, 65, 67-9, 119, 149, 165, 169-73, 176, 178-80, 195, 210, 237*
Dupont, J., *237, 273f.*
Ebeling, G., *68*
Eichrodt, W., *275, 287*
Elert, W., *242, 253*
Ellis, E. E., *288f.*
Ellison, H. L., *116*
Elwell, W., *324*
Ernst, J., *195*
Evans, O. E., *235*
Fairbairn, P., *53*
Fausset, A. R., *53*
Feine, P., *33*
Feuillet, A., *133, 164*
Fiorenza, E., *253*
Fitzmyer, J. A., *115, 210*
Flew, A. G. N., *304*
Foerster, W., *256*
Föhrer, G., *256*
Ford, J. M., *115, 118*
Formesyn, R. E. C., *115*
Forster, R. T., *304*
France, R. T., *131, 257, 289*
Fraser, J. W., *45, 54f.*
Freed, E. D., *117*
Friedrich, G., *15, 32, 163, 237*
Friedrich, J., *288*
Fuchs, E., *68*
Fuller, R. H., *95-7, 114, 117f., 130, 138, 146-9, 152, 154, 156-61, 163f.*
Funk, R. W., *68*
Gasque, W. W., *53, 179*
Gaston, L., *252*
Gatti, F. M., *115*
Gelston, A., *103*

Georgi, D., *149*
Gerleman, G., *120*
Getty, R. J., *53*
Glasson, T. F., *68, 116*
Gnilka, J., *254*
Goppelt, L., *17-9, 31f., 33f., 236, 273f.*
Goulder, M., *187f., 195*
Grässer, E., *219, 237, 288*
Grayston, K., *33*
Green, M., *195*
Greeven, H., *254*
Grounds, V. C., *305*
Grundmann, W., *147*
Guhrt, J., *287*
Gundry, R. H., *131, 133, 148, 164, 179*
Gundry-Volf, J., *308, 324*
Guthrie, D., *34, 54, 179*
Gyllenberg, R., *273*
Haenchen, E., *125, 132*
Hahn, F., *65, 69, 95-9, 114, 119, 130f., 135, 137, 140f., 146-9, 152, 154, 156f., 163f., 195, 202f., 210, 237, 254*
Hamerton-Kelly, R. G., *179*
Hanson, A. T., *288*
Hare, D. R. A., *132*
Harris, M. J., *274*
Haubeck, W., *257*
Haufe, G., *114*
Heitmüller, W., *153, 163*
Held, H. J., *132*
Hemer, C. J., *53*
Hengel, M., *54, 179*
Hennecke, E., *131*
Henry, C. F. H., *163*
Heppe, H., *288*
Hick, J., *178, 195*
Hiers, R. H., *236*
Higgins, A. J. B., *78-81, 85, 88, 90, 92f., 95-9, 100f., 107, 114, 116, 118f.*
Hill, D., *239, 246, 251f, 254, 256, 274*
Hindley, J. C., *115*
Hirsch, E., *33*
Hodgson, P. C., *80, 95f.*
Hofius, O., *274*
Hofmann, J. C. K., von, *33*
Holladay, W. C., *287*
Holtz, T., *253f.*
Hooker, M. D., *102, 106, 109-12, 113-8, 131f., 163f.*
Horbury, W., *120*
Hoskyns, E. C., *33*
Hultgren, A. J., *257*
Hunter, A. M., *15, 25, 32f., 36, 56, 95, 98, 148, 224, 228, 237*
Huntress, E., *149*
Jamieson, R., *53*
Jeremias, J., *29-33, 90, 92, 96-9, 102f., 107, 112-5, 118, 122, 124-6, 130-3, 135, 137-42,*

146-9, 160, 163f., 236f., 243, 252, 254, 256, 289
Jonge, M. de, *132*
Kähler, M., *21, 33*
Kasch, W., *256*
Käsemann, E., *33, 57-69, 89, 98, 114, 117, 179, 255, 270, 273f.*
Keck, L. E., *33, 164, 195*
Kertelge, K., *255*
Kilpatrick, G. D., *131*
Kim, S., *119, 170, 179, 237*
Kinniburgh, E. M., *117*
Kitchen, K. A., *287*
Kittel, G., *15, 32f.*
Klappert, B., *235*
Klein, G., *235*
Knox, J., *74, 80, 96*
Kramer, W., *144, 149, 156, 159f., 163*
Kümmel, W. G., *28f., 32f., 54, 89, 97-9, 116-9, 142, 147f., 235f., 253*
Kutsch, E., *288*
Ladd, G. E., *30f., 33, 147, 235f., 258f., 273*
Lampe, G. W. H., *273*
Le Déaut, R., *115*
Leivestad, R., *114, 116, 118*
Levertoff, P. P., *164*
Leitzmann, H., *74, 253, 255*
Lightfoot, J. B., *256*
Lindars, B., *99, 119, 125, 130-3, 163, 210*
Lindeskog, G., *118*
Link, H.-G., *273*
Lohfink, G., *69*
Lohmeyer, E., *117f., 132, 148f., 160, 237, 256*
Lohse, E., *30, 33, 64, 69, 132, 249, 254, 256, 273*
Longenecker, R. N., *289*
Lövestam, E., *114, 131-3*
Lyall, F., *253*
McCarthy, D. J., *287*
Machen, J. G., *180*
McHugh, J., *180*
Mackay, D. M., *295, 297, 304*
Mackey, J. P., *34*
McNamara, M., *132, 256*
McNeill, J. T., *274*
Maddox, R., *114, 116-8*
Manson, T. W., *24, 33, 74, 79, 81, 95-7, 100, 147, 164, 224, 228, 237*
Marlow, R., *114*
Marston, V. P., *304*
Martin, R. P., *132, 164, 179, 273f.*
Martyn, J. L., *164*
Mascall, E. L., *163*
Mason, W. J., *53*
Maurer, C., *126, 130-2, 304*
Meinfeld, M., *288*
Mendenhall, G. E., *287*

Merklein, H., *236*
Meyer, B. F., *228f., 237*
Michel, O., *147, 164, 254*
Milligan, G., *36, 273*
Milligan, W., *36*
Mitton, C. L., *164*
Montefiore, H., *147*
Moody, D., *306-8, 310, 313f., 316, 320, 324*
Moore, A. L., *67, 69*
Morgan, R., *33*
Morrice, W. G., *288*
Morris, L., *34, 239, 244, 251f., 254, 257, 273, 288*
Motyer, S., *304*
Moule, C. F. D., *115, 178, 180, 256*
Moulton, J. H., *36, 273*
Müller, M., *119*
Mundle, W., *257*
Murray, I., *233, 238*
Murray, J., *287f.*
Neander, A., *33*
Neill, S., *32, 34*
Nicole, R., *239, 251*
Nineham, D. E., *147, 237*
Nixon, R. E., *289*
Ogletree, T., *163*
Oepke, A., *289*
O'Neill, J. C., *114f.*
Pannenberg, W., *114, 180*
Pax, E., *257*
Percy, E., *89, 98*
Perrin, N., *82, 97, 101f., 106, 109, 112, 114, 116f., 119, 215-7, 220, 235f.*
Pesch, R., *118f., 210, 273*
Pinnock, C. H., *305, 306, 324*
Plooij, D., *132*
Plummer, A., *237*
Procksch, O., *132*
Quell, G., *288, 304*
Rad, G. von, *33, 116*
Ramsay, W. M., *35*
Rayburn, R. S., *288*
Rehkopf, F., *93, 99*
Rengstorf, K. H., *133, 148, 253*
Richardson, A., *25f., 33*
Riches, J., *221f., 237*
Ridderbos, H., *15, 32, 55, 237*
Robertson, A. T., *307*
Robinson, J. A., *254*
Robinson, J. A. T., *68, 98, 163*
Robinson, J. M., *273*
Roloff, J., *34*
Rollins, W. G., *68*
Rowland, C., *62, 67-9*
Rylaarsdam, J. C., *114*
Ryrie, C. C., *26, 33*
Sampson, C., *304*
Sanders, E. P., *54, 284, 289*
Sayers, D. M., *304*
Schelkle, K. H., *34*
Schlatter, A., *18, 33*

Schlier, H., *253f.*
Schmauch, W., *256*
Schmidt, K. L., *304*
Schmithals, W., *66, 69*
Schnackenburg, R., *33, 55, 117f., 130f., 140, 148, 235f., 238*
Schneemelcher, W., *69, 96, 131*
Schneider, G., *118*
Schneider, J., *257*
Schniewind, J., *33*
Schofield, C., *288*
Schramm, T., *252*
Schrenk, G., *131, 147, 304*
Schürmann, H., *55, 99, 118, 141, 148, 225, 236f., 252*
Schulz, S., *117*
Schweizer, E., *79f, 83, 85, 87f., 95-8, 114, 118, 131-3, 149, 163f.*
Shank, R., *307, 324*
Sharman, H. B., *96*
Shogren, G. S., *238*
Simpson, E. K., *251*
Skehan, P. W., *131*
Smalley, S. S., *111, 117, 210*
Souter, A., *35, 53, 132*

Sparks, H. F. D., *147*
Stählin, G., *194, 196*
Stauffer, E., *19, 22, 26, 30, 33, 77, 96, 106, 116*
Stendahl, K., *33, 132*
Strecker, G., *16, 33, 54, 164, 210*
Stuhlmacher, P., *54, 99, 255, 274*
Styler, G. M., *152, 163*
Talbert, C. H., *288*
Taylor, V., *95, 97, 99, 114, 121, 130, 142f., 149, 150f., 163, 234f., 238, 273*
Teeple, H. M., *77, 96, 99, 114, 118*
Thompson, J. A., *287*
Thyen, H., *255-7*
Tödt, H. E., *75, 77-80, 82, 84-6, 88, 90-9, 101, 107, 114f., 118f.*
Tripp, D. H., *288*
Turner, C. H., *132*
Turner, H. E. W., *95*
Van Iersel, B. M. F., *131, 133, 140, 146-8, 163*
Van Roon, A., *273*
Van Unnik, W. C., *149*

Vermes, G., *95, 103f., 115, 119, 131*
Vielhauer, P., *74-7, 79, 81-3, 85f., 88-91, 95-9, 101, 114f., 146, 149, 163, 210*
Vögtle, A., *140, 148, 273*
Vorländer, H., *273*
Walls, A. F., *288*
Walls, J. L., *324*
Warfield, B. B., *251, 304*
Wegenast, K., *255*
Weinel, H., *147*
Weiss, B., *33*
Wellhausen, J., *87, 97*
Wengst, K., *179*
Wesley, C., *272, 322*
Wesley, J., *307*
Wilckens, U., *131f.*
Wiles, M., *178*
Winter, P., *147*
Wood, H. G., *132*
Wrede, W., *17f., 33*
Wright, N. T., *179*
Young, E. J., *116*
Young, F., *187*
Zahn, T., *33, 132*
Zimmerli, W., *96, 99, 130f., 164*